History's Place

After the Empire:
The Francophone World and Postcolonial France

Series Editor
Valérie Orlando, University of Maryland

Advisory Board
Robert Bernasconi, Memphis University; Alec Hargreaves, Florida State University; Chima Korieh, Rowan University; Françoise Lionnet, UCLA; Obioma Nnaemeka, Indiana University; Kamal Salhi, University of Leeds; Tracy D. Sharpley-Whiting, Vanderbilt University; Nwachukwu Frank Ukadike, Tulane University

See www.lexingtonbooks.com/series for the series description and a complete list of published titles.

Recent and Forthcoming Titles

French Civilization and Its Discontents: Nationalism, Colonialism, Race, edited by Tyler Stovall and Georges Van Den Abbeele

After the Deluge: New Perspectives on Postwar French Intellectual and Cultural History, edited by Julian Bourg, afterword by François Dosse

Remnants of Empire in Algeria and Vietnam: Women, Words, and War, by Pamela A. Pears

Packaging Post/Coloniality: The Manufacture of Literary Identity in the Francophone World, by Richard Watts

The Production of the Muslim Woman: Negotiating Text, History, and Ideology, by Lamia Ben Youssef Zayzafoon

France and "Indochina": Cultural Representations, edited by Kathryn Robson and Jennifer Yee

Against the Postcolonial: "Francophone" Writers at the Ends of French Empire, by Richard Serrano

Youth Mobilization in Vichy Indochina and Its Legacies, 1940 to 1970, by Anne Raffin

Afrique sur Seine: A New Generation of African Writers in Paris, by Odile Cazenave

Memory, Empire, and Postcolonialism: Legacies of French Colonialism, edited by Alec G. Hargreaves

Ouregano: A Novel, by Paule Constant, translated and annotated by Margot Miller, introduced by Claudine Fisher

The Transparent Girl and Other Stories, by Corinna Bille, selected and translated by Monika Giacoppe and Christiane Makward

Time Signatures: Contextualizing Contemporary Francophone Autobiographical Writing from Maghreb, by Alison Rice

Breadfruit or Chestnut?: Gender Construction in the French Caribbean Novel, by Bonnie Thomas

History's Place: Nostalgia and the City in French Algerian Literature, by Seth Graebner

Collective Memory: Transmission of Memory in France of the Algenan War (1954–1962), by J. McCormack (forthcoming)

History's Place

Nostalgia and the City in French Algerian Literature

Seth Graebner

LEXINGTON BOOKS

A division of
ROWMAN & LITTLEFIELD PUBLISHERS, INC.
Lanham • Boulder • New York • Toronto • Plymouth, UK

LEXINGTON BOOKS

A division of Rowman & Littlefield Publishers, Inc.
A wholly owned subsidary of The Rowman & Littlefield Publishing Group, Inc.
4501 Forbes Boulevard, Suite 200
Lanham, MD 20706

Estover Road
Plymouth PL6 7PY
United Kingdom

British Library Cataloguing in Publication Information Available

Library of Congress Cataloging-in-Publication Data

Graebner, Seth, 1970–
  History's place : nostalgia and the city in French Algerian literature /
Seth Graebner.
     p. cm. — (After the empire)
  Includes bibliographical references and index.
  ISBN-13: 978-0-7391-1581-7 (cloth : alk. paper)
  ISBN-10: 0-7391-1581-2 (cloth : alk. paper)
  ISBN-13: 978-0-7391-1582-4 (pbk. : alk. paper)
  ISBN-10: 0-7391-1582-0 (pbk. : alk. paper)
  1. Algerian Literature (French)—History and criticism. I. Title.
  PQ3988.5.A5G72 2007
  840.9'965—dc22   2007001383

Printed in the United States of America

∞™ The paper used in this publication meets the minimum requirements of
American National Standard for Information Sciences—Permanence of Paper for
Printed Library Materials, ANSI/NISO Z39.48–1992.

Contents

Table of Figures

Acknowledgments

This book began life as a thesis directed by Susan Suleiman, with Tom Conley and Jann Matlock. I am grateful to all of them for their incisive readings and advice, and must acknowledge my great intellectual debt especially to Jann Matlock, without whom I would not have begun the research I do. At Harvard University, Susan Miller gave me my initial primer in Maghribi historiography, and Bill Granara, Arabic assistance beyond what one hopes for in several years of courses. Tassadit Yacine of the École de Hautes Études en Sciences Sociales was especially helpful with chapter three in Paris, and with a timely apartment in Agadir. Anonymous readers at *Research in African Literatures* (*RAL*) and *PMLA* helped with two of the chapters here, and Paul Silverstein, Joshua Cole, and Patricia Lorcin gave advice on several of them. Valérie Orlando, Mireille Rosello, and David Prochaska kindly undertook to read the manuscript in its final stages, and readers might share my gratitude to Professor Rosello for making the suggestions that shortened it. I would also like to thank the reference staff at the Archives d'Outre-Mer in Aix-en-Provence and in the services now distributed between the departments of *Recherche bibliographique* (Salle X) and *Documentation sur le livre* (Salle T) at the Bibliothèque Nationale in Paris.

A version of the chapter on Boudjedra appeared in *RAL*, and a much earlier one of part of chapter three in *Continental North-South and Diaspora Connections and Linkages: Annual Selected Papers of the ALA (New Series)*.

Editors of all three kindly allowed their reprinting here. A version of chapter six appeared in *Sub-Space*. The black-and-white illustrations appear by permission from the Fonds documentaire Editions J. Gandini in Nice, at www.photos-algérie.com.

A number of organizations funded parts of this work, including the Krupps Foundation, the American Council of Learned Societies (with a Fellowship in International Studies at the Library of Congress), and most recently, Washington University in Saint Louis. My Saint Louis colleagues have been most generous in their support in the final phases of seeing this work off to the publisher. Harriet Stone and Elyane Dezon-Jones at Washington University, and Kathryn Funk and Kelly Rogers at Lexington Books helped with certain publication issues about which I was initially clueless. Finally, few books come to fruition without the support of family, in which I include the acuity and generosity of Madia Thomson.

Introduction

Out of Time and Out of Place

Tartarin de Tarascon, the hero of Alphonse Daudet's 1872 travel-book satire, steps off the boat in Algiers determined to find exotic thrills. Primed by the experiences of previous travel writers and armed to the teeth, he sets out to hunt big game in the suburbs and to seduce a Moorish lover in the Casbah. His lion proves to be an aged mule, and his Arab princess, a cabaret dancer from Marseille. He laments his disappointment in a jeremiad that had become de rigueur in travel writing about North Africa: the exotic simply was not what it used to be; and local color, the particularities of place which had attracted readers of previous travelers' accounts, was disappearing, replaced by the debased products of Europe. Nineteenth-century travelers sensed that they were out of place in Algeria, and not only in the traditional sense conveyed in French by the term *dépaysé*, or even in the sense exemplified by Tartarin, hunting lions in a vegetable garden. In addition to betraying their suspicion that they did not belong, their prose suggests that they had run out of place, since the place they had hoped to find no longer existed. They were "out of place" in the way one is "out of time" or "out of pocket"; the resources they had counted on for inspiration were already exhausted. On discovering that the exotic city of their dreams had mostly vanished (if it had ever existed), nineteenth-century travelers found that they had run out of places in which they could feel out of place; they became nostalgic for a past place in which *dépaysement* would have been possible, had they reached it in time.

This book explores the manifestations of nostalgia for vanished cultures and places as one of the defining tropes of the relationship between

1

France and North Africa from the moment about 1900 when the colony began to distinguish itself culturally from the metropole, to the decades following independence in 1962. It considers literary and nonliterary texts from both the colonial and the postindependence periods. Nostalgia quickly became a dominant trope for representing history in the French-language literature of Algeria and remained so almost to the present day. The place which most often triggered travelers' nostalgia, the North African city, became the focus of historical discourses about Algeria and its relation to France. This study historicizes the development of new modes of writing about the city in North Africa and shows how Algerian writers have continued to use the city to focus perceptions of their history. *History's Place* stresses the importance of architecture, urban form, and physical details of place as markers of historical development and the passage of time. Urban form became the sign of cultural and historical difference between the metropole and the colony, and the terrain on which arguments about history and identity took place. Changes in the urban texture of nineteenth-century Algiers were endlessly commented upon and at times hotly debated (both in literature and in historical and topographical texts) as signs and stakes of an argument not only about the identity and development of the colony, or the colony's relation to France, but also about the nature of the modern city in France itself. I argue that the Algerian city became a privileged place for writers to talk about the relationship between literary and historical discourses in the colony. As Algeria developed a consciousness of its past together with an identity of its own (with, or at times against, the metropole), the changing Algerian city remained the locus and focus of debate, a debate colored by various sorts of nostalgia.

The study not of an abstract notion of "Place," but rather of particular places, provides a basis for a new consideration of the dialogue between literature "high" and "low," and history popular and academic. The category of "place" has commanded much attention in literary and cultural studies over the last fifteen years, at various levels of abstraction. This book insists on the particularities of and differences among specified places, rather than on some hypostatized "Difference," supposedly constitutive of an archetypal colonial "Space." Such a concept of difference does not help us understand the particular local contexts in which colonial cultural exchanges occurred. Furthermore, colonial space as a generalized notion also empties particular places of their explanatory or evidentiary potential. If, however, we take "places" as specific and plural, it seems that long after events have "taken place," the places themselves remain to bear witness to them, among the few signs of past events left behind when most of the rest have disappeared. Given a willingness to do the necessary investigation (in the library and elsewhere), we can in fact get a very precise notion of what particular places of historical significance looked and "felt" like at any given moment, thus grounding in verifiable fact our attempts to understand what they meant to the people who inhabited them. Places have a certain persistence, for want of a better word, that makes them particularly appealing as objects of study, especially in cultural studies, in which some of the objects under consideration (images, prejudices, and popular discourses) may seem rather diffuse. Nonetheless, this very specificity raises the question of the ultimate goals and accomplishments of a study taking individual places as its touchstones or focal points. After all, what would one really accomplish in an exhaustive prosopography of any heavily invested place: the Palais Royal in Paris, for example, or the Al-Shuhadā' square in Algiers? If we charted the life of every shop in the arcades and dated every statue erected and removed on the site, what would we have discovered? Any answer compelling enough to tempt us to undertake even a far more modest picture must lie beyond the space itself. Without claiming emblematic status for every place discussed in this book, I will argue that attention to them, while never a replacement for theoretical self-awareness or textually grounded literary interpretation, can indeed provide clues to the significance of cultural discourses in their own times, and, in the best cases, make it harder to impose our own biases on the past.

Speaking of biases, the terms I use in this study may seem to betray several. I refer consistently to Algeria between 1830 and 1962 as a colony, despite the variety of labels the French used for their government of Algeria, including that of three *départements* (Oran, Algiers, and Constantine) supposedly fully integrated with the *départements* of mainland France. Some of these changes had administrative consequences, but from the point of view of the colonized, most remained merely semantic. They may actually obscure Algeria's true status during the period as a dependent territory consistently ruled in ways radically different from France itself, so the choice of "colony," though officially inaccurate, seems best. Things get more difficult when speaking of people. By 1900, colonial usage, with transparent motives, reserved the term *Algérien* for those of European descent born or adopted into the colony, while labelling Arabs and Imazighen as *indigènes*.[1] Other labels are no less complicated. Strictly speaking, *colons* were landowning farmers, but the term could refer to any lifelong European resident in the colony. The origins of *pied-noir* confuses matters further, since it may first have designated Algerian *indigènes* before coming to mean people of European descent. In any case, it did not see widespread use until the Algerian war of 1954–1962. In keeping with the usage of contemporary historians of several ethnicities, and to avoid confusion with the language of my sources, I have occasionally used the term *indigènes*, when historically appropriate, to refer to people we would

now simply call "Algerians." The term "Muslim" has the obvious problem of imparity when used to mean the opposite of "European Algerian"
(furthermore, using "European" and "Muslim" as antonyms seems extremely shortsighted these days). In the colony, however, that is what they
were, and I have used "Muslims" as a descriptor of what most authors
during the colonial period saw as the most salient difference between colonized and colonizer. In later chapters of this study, dealing with the period of the Algerian struggle for independence and the following decades,
I have frequently used "Algerian" to mean the Arabs and Imazighen native to the country.

Up to now, most work on the cultural history of the relationship between France and North Africa have focused either on the colonial or the
postindependence period, leaving aside the vitally important connections between them.[2] My investigation spans a large portion of the colonial and post-colonial periods in North Africa (roughly the twentieth
century) and considers fictional and nonfictional narratives by writers of
many of the ethnicities present in Algeria at the time. It demonstrates
that the experience of being out of place and out of time was common to
writers of several periods and ethnic origins in Algeria. In his study of
early colonial novels, Alain Calmes characterizes the colonial condition
as "une précarité qui s'éternise" [a precarity that lasts].[3] I argue that this
experience and the manifestations of nostalgia stemming from it were
symptoms of a historical anxiety generated by conditions in the colony,
but with literary consequences for mainland France as well. Using elements of literary studies, cultural history, and architectural history, I explore essays, journalism, and novels in order to revise our understanding
of how France's most important colony developed a historical consciousness through literature. While works traditionally called "literature" (in this study, novels, short stories, and literary travel writing) offer distinctive richness for interpretation, they enter into dialogue with
other works of "topographic literature," writings about "place" in genres
as diverse as guidebooks, city descriptions, histories, sociological observations, and government documents.[4] Consideration of nonliterary
genres allows me to historicize debates over the identity of the colony,
debates argued in terms of urban history.

This introduction examines the prehistory of the period the study addresses. It outlines connections between Algerian travel literature and
Parisian topographic literature in the mid- to late nineteenth century, in
works that defined the codes of urban description and history-writing.
Chapters one and two concentrate on the first major European writers to
originate in Algeria in the early twentieth century, Louis Bertrand and
Robert Randau, and show how their literature countered the idea of being
out of place by constructing a historical discourse justifying European

presence in Algeria. Chapters 3 and 4 focus on literary, ethnic, and historical discourses on the colonial city, leading up to the centenary of French Algeria in 1930. Chapter 5 considers the Algerian writings of Gabriel Audisio, Albert Camus, and Emmanuel Roblès, examining the resurgence of sensations of loss of place among Franco-Algerians sensitive to the breakdown of colonial views of Algerian history at the approach of independence. The last chapters interpret canonical novels of Francophone literature by Kateb Yacine and Rachid Boudjedra, tracing their uses and revisions of previous historical discourses in order to reinvent places with significance for Algerian national history.

By tracing such debates over more than a century, I do not mean to suggest that Algeria's colonial past determines its present, or that colonialism has a globally or historically transcendent effect on all societies it touches. The historical discourses established in Algerian literature around and after independence revised a set of commonplaces inherited from previous literary treatments of Algerian history. The canonical works of Algerian Francophone literature transformed these modes of expression without abandoning their privileged locale, the North African city. We cannot understand discourses that are post-colonial in the chronological sense, and especially not those about history, without studying the local practices and negotiations of colonial power: in short, without dealing with the particularities of specific colonies and their successor states. Formerly colonized countries share few cultural or historical characteristics, and local differences often appear more compelling than global similarities. Algeria is hardly "post-colonial" in the same way as Brazil, Cameroon, or Hong Kong, to say nothing of cases like Martinique or Guadeloupe, where the "post-" represents a factual error. Several critics have challenged the notion of "postcolonial" critique and pointed out the contradictions and difficulties inherent in the term.[5] Designating certain countries, or even a period of world history, as "post-colonial" (with or without the hyphen) implies that the brief time during which those countries were ruled from Europe constituted the defining moment of their past.[6] It allows interpretation of their present state to be overshadowed by the colonial elements of their history. Postcolonial critiques have also suggested a binary opposition between the colonizing and noncolonizing worlds and, in practice if not in theory, implied that colonialism is a form of domination both unique in itself and uniquely European. Finally, the postcolonial label is not very helpful regarding the practices sometimes called neocolonialism: it offers few ways of dealing constructively with the effects of the phenomena so labelled, and signals no end to the "post" condition.

I have tried to address these concerns in several ways. First, this book focuses on a single colonial relationship, that of France and Algeria; second, it considers the two-way operation of the cultural relations between

them, in order to avoid treating Algerian cultural productions as predetermined by discourses emanating from Paris, or as inevitably "responding" to them. As the historian David Prochaska points out, postcolonial
studies, in which literary critics have taken the lead, have only recently
looked carefully at the historical evidence of the concrete practices of colonialism.[7] In the case of Algeria, such a careful examination requires parallel and mutually informing analysis of texts both literary and nonliterary,
colonial and post-colonial, in order to understand the history of the urban
culture elaborated between France and North Africa since 1830. Finally, I
try to lay a course between two competing ideas of order that operate in
any study of a particular colonial context. On the one hand, French colonizers attempted to maintain a remarkably complete grasp on Algerian
society, via land expropriations that reduced peasants to subproletariat,
censorship laws that prevented effective expression of dissent, and an educational system that underserved the vast majority of the colonized
while claiming to offer the possibility of assimilation to a very small minority. Viewing it in this way leads us to think of the colonial regime as an
all-powerful, totalizing enterprise. On the other hand, the colonial administration regularly failed in its aims and ultimately had to go. Viewing
it in this way leads us, with hindsight and a desire to find "resistance,"
ambiguity, and fluid signifiers in the works we study, to make the colonial
project seem an incoherent affair of shifting signs: largely a semantic or
discursive phenomenon. Both these points of view have their roots in the
notion that discursive orders accurately mirror the political orders of
those who stand behind them. This often does prove true, but without
precautions it can lead us to confuse writing about political and other concrete phenomena with the phenomena themselves. Furthermore, these
two viewpoints also tend either to depict, over and over, a monolithic
power structure opposed in a small number of highly predictable ways,
or to minimize the crude facts of daily domination in a celebration of hypostatized "Difference." Both points of view risk transforming the concrete problems of the everyday world into diffuse issues of subjectivity
and epistemology.[8]

Most critics studying the place of the colonies in European literature
have focused on the major works of exoticist fiction or travel writing by
European authors. They have shown how these works reflected or undermined both official conceptions of the colonial project and popular
stereotypes regarding colonized people. These studies have often had
limited ability to make interpretive sense of the larger colonial context:
studies focused essentially on Parisians reading about Algeria, for example, reproduce the dynamic of center and periphery they analyze. In addition, they remain unable to theorize the ways in which colonial literature did more than simply construct images and popularize them. Up to

now, few scholars have analyzed the practical consequences of interactions among literary, anthropological, historical, and political discourses in the colonies. Only in the 1990s did critics begin to evaluate fiction produced in the French colonies by local authors, for audiences both local and foreign.[9] Attention to the colony as both producer and consumer of fictional images of itself serves as a useful corrective to the focus of earlier scholarship on Europe as the site of both production and consumption of literature about the colonies.[10] Colonial literature had concrete consequences for the histories and identities of people in the colonies, consequences simply not apparent when we focus on major works of exoticist fiction and their reception in Europe.

NOSTALGIA AND ITS CITIES: PARIS AND ALGIERS, 1830–1890

Paris has not always been the capital of a colonial empire, and Algiers was not always its colony. Since 1830, however, the two cities have been bound up in troubled relations of which settler colonization was only one facet, albeit the dominant one for 132 years. From the beginning of the colonial period, the relationship between the countries Paris and Algiers represented and governed came to be embodied in the urban fabric of the two cities. In Algeria, authors wishing to write about the modern history of the colony or its successor state turned to the city to focus and situate their discussions. In France, arguments about history and identity have not always focused on the city as a colonial expression, but during a period roughly coincident with French rule in Algeria, discussions of "Frenchness" involved talk of the city and the colony in ways impossible to ignore. Scholarship like the essays collected in Alec Hargreaves and Mark McKinney's *Post-Colonial Culture in France* (1997), Charles Forsdick and David Murphy's *Francophone Postcolonial Studies* (2003), and Alec Hargreaves's *Memory, Empire, and Postcolonialism* (2005) demonstrate the necessity of considering the position and impact of the colonies in the cultural struggles over defining French identity in the twentieth century.[11] Studies have also emphasized the centrality of urban forms and re-created places in reading the architectural and cultural projects of the Third Republic, for example, in the exposition halls and pavilions of the 1931 *Exposition Coloniale*.[12] As a modern capital, Paris was a quintessential metropolis, attracting colonized people and reflecting what procolonial writers liked to call its *vocation coloniale*. The very term used in the colonies to designate mainland France, *la métropole*, metonymically invokes the city. Beginning around the turn of the century, *la métropole*, the metropolitan pole of attraction, became the logical opposite of the *colonie*. This conception of the French mainland defined by its urbanism descended from a nineteenth-century Parisian idea that French history and identity was summed up in the urban fabric of the capital. While the century of Michelet and Taine certainly had other means of imagining the evolution of the nation, an extremely widespread literature of popular histories and urban descriptions promoted the idea that the history of France as a whole could be understood via the history of the streets and monuments of Paris.[13] Historical arguments thus framed in the nineteenth century found in the city a symbol of both change and stasis, a useful shorthand for evoking the conflict between tradition and modernity. Observers could easily see the passage of time registered on the face of the city in changes to monuments, architectural styles, and urban layout. The resulting changes affected the very texture of physical experience one could have in places which evoked the history of the city. While French historiography developed other preoccupations, especially following World War II, the historians producing works like *Les Lieux de mémoire* have returned to the notion of places at once physical and metaphorical as focal points for historiography.[14]

No such return was necessary in Algiers. Beginning with the French conquest, Algerian historiography kept its attention fixed on place; it has invested especially in a specific set of urban places. The major histories of the colony, whether in the initial flurry of publications between 1850 and 1870, or around the centenary of 1930, focused both on colonial "progress" as manifest in the modernizing cities of Algiers, Oran, and Bône (Annaba) and on cultural difference figured in the remaining Arab neighborhoods. Authorities in the contemporary historiography, Jacques Berque, Benjamin Stora, Charles-Robert Ageron, and David Prochaska, have laid great stress on the imagination of physical and cultural spaces to be colonized or decolonized and on their creation on the ground.[15] Today, Algerian fiction writers continue to deal with their country's history in the context of constantly evolving discussion about the value, significance, and potential of place.

The importance of place in Franco-Algerian history and literature stems in large part from one of the major activities of French colonialism, the constant reconstruction of colonized cities. The ideological motivations and political consequences of these rebuilding programs were not unique to the colonies. Architecture and urban design generally reproduce ideologies approved by their builders, but they also reflect amendments or subversions of them: individual users of the spaces accept, reject, or modify the habits of movement that designers attempt to them.[16] Attempts at imposing order through physical structures become even more evident in the colonies, where the colonizers' cities clearly express their cultural and political projects, and where contestation from below was all the more marked.[17] The colony thus provides an ideal place to study architecture, urban design, and the local articulations of power. It also demonstrates their modifications and subversions, since relations between dominator and dominated are never uniform or unidirectional.[18] In their colonies, French builders reconfigured the cities to suit the colonizers' needs, to mark their presence, and to encourage social progress as they saw it. Considerable scholarly literature describes the history of French urbanism in the colonial period, from the original *comptoirs* in Gorée and Saint-Louis-du-Sénégal to Saigon in the 1890s and Rabat in the 1920s. Historians and anthropologists have given accounts of France's urban interventions in its colonies around the world, stressing the ideological purposes these reconstructions served for the colonial empire.[19] French administrators aimed first to create spaces that would lend themselves to commerce, traffic, crowd control, and speculation based on French models, reflecting the needs of modern urban and industrial capitalism. Secondarily, administrators often attempted to preserve or create anew what the French believed were the most typical or picturesque elements of local design.[20] Colonial urban interventions rarely represented a seamless application of urban design from metropolitan France, and despite the use of several colonial cites as testing laboratories for ideas later applied in France, urbanism in the colonies remained quite different from urbanism at home. The availability of new fields of action for planning in the colonies, especially in Madagascar, Indochina, and Morocco coincided with the transformation in France of the various *métiers* involved in urban planning into formal academic and professional disciplines, roughly between 1890 and 1914.[21] Even early in the development of colonial urbanism (in North Africa, the period from 1830 to 1860), when architects often simply transferred mainland French forms or styles to the colonies, new ideas emerged and new techniques evolved there, independently or in advance of France. Among these "firsts," streets in Algiers received macadam paving before the *grands boulevards* of Paris, and in 1840, the Algiers harbor saw concrete used underwater for the first time in modern history.[22] In addition, French colonial authorities quickly convinced themselves that colonial cities required solutions adapted to colonial problems. New forms developed, reflecting colonial administrators' ideas of what constituted constructions appropriate to the ethnic and cultural milieu. In North Africa, these ideas reflected a tension in colonialist discourses between the desire to assimilate the population to French cultural norms and the admission of radical and irreducible cultural difference between Europeans and *indigènes*. This tension led to projects as diverse as the construction of a Qur'anic school in imitated Arab style in Algiers and a failed attempt at ethnic separation in Rabat.[23] Administrative practice contradicted the official rhetoric about assimilation of colonies to metropole on many levels, including those of urban design and cultural policy.

In general, scholars have yet to consider the ways in which literary and historical discourses interacted with architectural projects, supporting, redefining, or occasionally undermining the cultural programs those projects expressed.

In Algeria, the French colonial presence began with demolition. Algiers had suffered several episodes of shelling by European powers before 1830, but the real destruction began after the French conquered the city in a three-week campaign in June of that year. A few months after the Turkish ruler, the Dey Hussein, had been shipped into exile and the legendary millions of his treasury carted off to France, military authorities began to demolish buildings near the waterfront to clear space for the place d'Armes, which, under various names, would remain a focal point for the city for more than a century. They designed it as military men, basing its dimensions on the space required to maneuver a batallion. Military objectives also influenced further modifications to the lower city; the rue Bab-Azoun and the rue Bab-el-Oued, its principal streets, were laid out wide enough to accommodate troops, and in dogleg fashion to prevent an enemy from firing down their entire length from one end. Furthermore, military imperatives initially determined the French not to let the city expand outside a succession of fortifications, a policy which required them to demolish and reconstruct the old inside the walls, rather than build new construction outside. These projects cut into old Algiers, demolishing many private houses, mosques, and buildings owned by the former government.

France had no clear colonial objective in dispatching its army to Algiers in 1830. Charles X and his minister Polignac aimed to enhance French prestige by punishing a rogue state and to make the Restoration government more popular at home with a lucrative conquest. The project of colonizing Algeria emerged soon thereafter, but was vehemently criticized even after it became official policy in the mid-1830s. As occupation became colonization, houses with European-style windows and balconies began to replace the blank facades of Arab architecture. The major axes of traffic (the Rue de la Marine and the Rue de la Lyre, as well as the main thoroughfare from Bab Azoun to Bab-el-Oued) received uniform, arcaded constructions reminiscent of the Rue de Rivoli or the Rue Castiglione in Paris. Despite the promises made in the surrender agreement of 5 July 1830, the majority of real property in the city passed into French hands, and a great many religious buildings were destroyed or confiscated in the first twenty years of the colony's existence. By 1847, the year the Emir Abd-el-Kader's defeat ended the first phase of armed struggle over the territory that had become known as *l'Algérie*, Algiers looked quite different from the city of 1830. The Second Empire brought further alterations as the city finally began to move outside the walls; most of the styles then current in French architectural decoration appeared in the construction of new neighborhoods in Isly, the future commercial district, as well as Agha, Bab-el-Oued, and Mustapha, suburbs successively incorporated into a capital which grew almost without interruption through the second half of the nineteenth century. In the following chapters, I will return to this history to sketch out subsequent episodes of demolition and reconstruction in several Algerian cities.

The domain in which French and colonial intellectuals thought with the greatest concentration about Algeria's past and future was literature. There, historical debates privileged a place, the colonial city, but also an affect, nostalgia. Nostalgia has proven sufficiently difficult to define to interest many critics and psychologists in attempting to do so. We have thus both an etymology (Greek *nostos*, return [home] and *algia*, pain) and a well-studied genealogy of the term, created in 1688 in a medical thesis by Johannes Hofer, who used it to describe an illness suffered by soldiers far from home. In 1803, it again appeared in a medical thesis, the first to use the word in French rather than Latin, and still referred to a potentially fatal illness, this time observed by Denis Guerbois (1775–1838) among the conscripts of 1793 and 1799. The concept had nonetheless shifted somewhat in meaning in the intervening years, in brief passages by no less than Jean-Jacques Rousseau and Immanuel Kant, both of whom had touched on the subject toward the ends of their respective careers. Rousseau in the *Dictionnaire de Musique* reasoned that the trigger for nostalgia works not on the subject's imagination, as Hofer had believed, but rather on memory. In the words of the psychologist André Bolzinger, nostalgia "prend désormais les couleurs de la modernité en s'inscrivant dans les rapports que l'homme entretient avec son passé et les lieux de son histoire" [from then on acquires a modern character, attached to the relations people maintain between their past and the places of their history].[24] In remarking that a tune he was discussing no longer seemed to have the same dramatic effect on listeners, Rousseau also became the first person in French literature to complain that nostalgia was not what it used to be.[25] Thirty years later, at the very end of the eighteenth century and of his own life, Kant extended Rousseau's argument by suggesting that the nostalgic did not want only to return to his village, as Hofer had argued, but rather to his childhood: for him, regret for past time rather than place became the critical ingredient of nostalgia.[26] By the time the word appeared in the dictionary of the Académie française in 1835, it referred to a sensation rather than a sickness: in some measure, the nineteenth century normalized nostalgia, and twentieth-century psychologists have generally pointed out that today's widely accepted definition of the term, "the desire to come back to an idealized past," refers to a sentiment that need not reach pathological proportions requiring professional intervention.[27] Many have stressed the positive functions of nostalgia, "a self-relevant emotion that involves reliving one's past, and in particular events involving one's important but bygone relationships. . . . [Nostalgia,] a stock of positive feelings, can ward off external threat or distressing thoughts. Nostalgia serves three core existential functions: self-enhancement, alignment with the cultural worldview, and fostering of close relationships. Successful fulfillment of one or more of these functions contributes to positive affectivity and a state of reassurance, warmth, and security."[28] Like many psychologists' definitions of nostalgia, those cited here make no reference to place, which was nonetheless fundamental in earlier elaborations of the concept. Given the interests of this study, it seems important to retain in our thinking about nostalgia the idea that it often becomes a subject's predominant affect when particular places coincide with or trigger specific memories. This seems true for both individual and collective memories.

One of the most helpful recent theories of nostalgia comes from the comparative literature scholar Svetlana Boym, whose definition reflects the connection between the sentiment and the places, real or imagined, associated with it: for her, nostalgia "is a longing for a home that no longer exists or never existed."[29] We will see in the course of this study a great deal of longing for places or states that probably never existed. Boym also distinguishes two contrasting modes of nostalgic discourse: "restorative nostalgia puts emphasis on *nostos* and proposes to rebuild the lost home and patch up the memory gaps. Reflective nostalgia dwells in *algia*, in longing and loss, the imperfect process of remembrance."[30] This study will examine instances of both, among authors with divergent politics. If all nostalgia does not ultimately deserve the conservative label it often gets, restorative nostalgia probably does. This is the kind of dubious ideological project favored by nation builders and political "reformers" claiming to recreate a status quo ante, which sometimes needs no more justification in the eyes of its proponents than that it indeed have been *ante*, or at least imagined to have been. Those in favor of the colonial regimes in North Africa always found a past to suit them, even if they had to construct it: in Algeria, they usually chose to privilege first the period of Roman rule, and second, the heroic days of the early French occupation. Authors who deployed such nostalgia routinely proclaimed that the French regime legitimately "reestablished" Latin rule. With them, nostalgia did indeed characterize a highly conservative position.

Yet their restorative nostalgia did not prevail unopposed throughout the development of twentieth-century literature in Algeria. Boym's other variety, reflective nostalgia, had practitioners as well. Reflective nostalgic discourse does not lend itself automatically to conservative uses; in fact it seems hard to capture for any concrete political project at all. Kateb Yacine muses on the past in ways that undoubtedly valorize Amazigh heroism, but not in any way that could easily serve the leaders of a revolution. Similarly, Emmanuel Roblès combines his nostalgia for his childhood in Oran with a clear vision of the ethnic discrimination prevalent at the time, and his work hardly serves to justify the French regime in the way many of his predecessors did. No ethnic group or political formation had a monopoly on either restorative or reflective nostalgia. Rachid Boudjedra's novels portray (without necessarily indulging in) the restorative nostalgia of former independence fighters, and Albert Camus's writings on Algeria are tinged with enough nostalgia of both varieties to justify characterizing him both as a proponent of continued French rule and as a destabilizer of the Franco-Algerian vision of the past. Similar combinations of nostalgic discourses lie beneath a significant number of the works discussed in this study.

The discussion of nostalgia in a book focused on the portrayal of urban spaces evokes the question of a potential link between the two, in either lived experience or literary affect. First, is there a particular urban form of nostalgia? Second, are descriptions of cities in literature inevitably nostalgic? Although observers of urban space can and do sometimes reject nostalgia altogether in their discourse on what the city is or should become, cities are par excellence the space for the emergence of nostalgia. In answering the first question, it might seem as if a sizable portion of urban dwellers feel nostalgia for a lifestyle they associate with country or small-town living. Here, however, I will concentrate on a slightly different variety, the longing for an imagined previous state of the city itself, for an experience of urban space somehow more comprehensible, less standardized, and less dehumanizing. I mean here something like Victor Hugo's famous desire in *Notre-Dame de Paris* (1830) for the beauty, meaning, and fulfillment he imagined possible in the medieval city, and his protest against the widening and standardizing of streets that he felt made the city less attractive, but just as important for me here, less legible. Authors writing about Paris and other cities since Hugo have very often expressed their regrets that as old buildings and street patterns give way to new, the city's territory becomes less readable on its face. We will see examples in this book of narrators who express nostalgia for a time when their city's history was more readily legible in the very texture of the urban fabric. Urban nostalgia of this sort can adopt either the restorative or the reflective mode. I will argue that whereas the first tends to run into dead ends by attempting to fix its city in some previous moment of physical and historical development, the second has the potential, though not the guarantee, of producing new visions of what urban space could be, and how one could see one's relationship to it.

The affect of nostalgia may also prove gendered, or at least to have gender-inflected consequences: could nostalgia be a male malady? Psychoanalysis has long considered nostalgia to reflect, ultimately, the desire to return to the mother characterized either as pre-Oedipal or as the "all-good mother of symbiosis."[31] In replacing one with the other, and thereby focusing on the premature withdrawal, by whatever cause, of the mother's attention, the psychoanalyst Salman Akhtar makes more plausible his implication that men and women experience nostalgia similarly. Other investigators and practicing analysts assert that nostalgia is a universal and archetypal experience. Empirical evidence allows us for once to leave aside our doubts regarding the stability in the face of gender variation of anything described as archetypal: at least within a given culture, women appear to feel nostalgia substantially as do men. In a statistically rigorous investigation of over 600 subjects, the psychologist Krystine Batcho found that gender had no effect on responses to an extensive questionnaire on nostalgia, nor any documentable interaction with the variable of age.[32] The assertions contained in several studies, however, suggest that we should distinguish between nostalgia as actually experienced among living people and nostalgia as a literary affect projected in fiction or nonfiction prose. "Nostalgia may only be felt for things actually experienced," claims the psychologist Melinda Milligan; we shall see nonetheless that not having experienced the objects of longing rarely stopped a novelist or colonial historian from writing nostalgically about them.[33] Treating nostalgic discourse, rather than the nostalgic emotion felt in everyday human relations, allows us to see some ways in which its results may be more gendered than studies of its daily experience may demonstrate. If nostalgia in practice is not actually an exclusively or even largely male malady, nostalgia in ideology has seemed to many critics to have affiliations with patriarchy. Longing for the good old days may imply longing for a "return" to tendentiously constructed "family values" which may never have existed, or at least to a conservative view of women's proper roles.[34] Some feminist critics have seen mostly the restorative variety of nostalgia, and therefore stressed its dangers for women.[35] Others have pointed out that nostalgia for what might have been, for "the unrealized dreams of the past and visions of the future that became obsolete" may not in fact lead to political stasis or social reactionism.[36] The sample of works studied in this book suggest that some forms of nostalgia, especially those not bent on reconstructing an idealized moment of the past, may serve progressive purposes.

A look at the table of contents of this book suggests that the connections among nostalgia, urban description, and gender remain under-studied. Put bluntly, where are the women writers? Some (Malika Mokaddem and Nina Bouraoui, for example) do not appear here because the work of these canonical women writers of Maghribi origin has often had preoccupations not immediately related to the construction of a collective historical consciousness in colonial and post-colonial Algeria. Often, but not always, one might object: surely Assia Djebar's *Quatour Algérien* addresses this question directly, and perhaps we could say the same for any of the various works by these authors attempting to recover or preserve women's collective memories. I decided not to discuss Djebar's *Quatour* simply because it is so difficult to say anything new about these novels and their treatment of history, a privileged subject in the substantial critical bibliography devoted to them.[37] The several women grouped among the "beur" writers represent the most compelling cohort of women writers associated (in the French imagination) with the Maghrib to comment on the city and the ways in which women move in it. Recent criticism has examined the ways in which Tassadit Imache and Farida Belghoul have developed *lieux de mémoire* in the Paris of Maghribi immigrants and their descendants.[38]

We might also reflect on the gendering of the terms of this book's investigation. The city, as exterior space, appears at least stereotypically coded as male, especially in the Maghrib, where women's access to exterior spaces has traditionally varied in inverse proportion to the degree of urbanization of those spaces. Endorsing generalities about supposedly global restrictions on the occupation of urban space in the Arabo-Muslim world, however, would essentially abandon this book's aim to speak of particular places, rather than of an archetypal notion of Place. We would need investigations of the various spots in Algiers or Oran that appear in this study, for instance, to say anything reliable regarding the way women moved through them. Turning to the ideological or mytho-historical significance of cities evoked by these authors, we find the example of Kateb Yacine, who calls the predecessor towns to Constantine and Bône *villes-mères*, suggesting at least the possibility of feminizing certain urban spaces. Although gender is not its principle category of analysis, this book attempts to account for gendered effects where they arise.

Chapter one of this study concentrates on the first generation of European writers actually born or adopted into the colony, a group beginning to form in the first decade of the twentieth century. Louis Bertrand and other writers active in Algeria during the first third of the century rejected the "outsider's" perspective of earlier authors, who had produced what these subsequent writers and critics disparaged as *littérature d'escale* [stopover literature]. They adopted instead an energetic valorization of European efforts and cultural productions in the colony at the expense of the Arab features sought by earlier visitors. Bertrand radically changed the literary landscape of the colony with the invention of the doctrine of

"Latin Africa," an attempt to create a historical and cultural identity for the new race he imagined forming in Algeria, in a fusion of Mediterranean immigrants building a new country under French political and cultural leadership. These people were the "true" *Algériens*, as opposed to the Arabs and Imazighen excluded from the hoped-for racial fusion. Bertrand aimed to provide a historical justification for the dispossession of the colonized (whose extermination he occasionally imagined, if not recommended) by discovering in French Algeria the reincarnation of Roman colonization, the renewal of the Latins who had rightfully ruled the Mediterranean's southern shore in the ancient world. Contemporary *colons* were thus the descendants of the legitimate possessors of the land, temporarily usurped by an Arab invasion Bertrand considered culturally insignificant.

Novels like Bertrand's *Le Sang des races* (1899) and *Pépète le bien-aimé* (1904) were thus the first significant works of Algerian literature in French to focus on the heroicized European farmers and laborers rebuilding the empire which France had inherited from Rome. The novels of Latin Africa invested the Algerian city in ways entirely different from previous French writing about the colony, preferring the sites of contemporary colonial engagement to those of perceived Arab decadence. In addition, they privileged ruins of a different sort from those admired by earlier visitors: with a tone varying between piety and nostalgia, Bertrand's texts constantly sought to excavate Roman ruins for the author's ideological purposes in defining the new Latin Africa. Bertrand's nostalgia stemmed in part from a sense that the French nation had lost essential values and traditions at home, which it would recover in the colony. His sense of loss, and the ideology he constructed in response, meshed with the ideas of right-wing regionalist writers in France, especially Maurice Barrès, whom Bertrand succeeded in the Académie Française. Having lost his place in the conquered Lorraine, the home province he shared with Barrès, Bertrand aimed to construct a history to justify France's place in Algeria. The doctrine of Latin Africa, meant to reenergize France, helped reorient French literary regionalism away from "local color" in the provinces, and toward a concentration on youthful vigor in national reconstruction. The discourses of cultural reconstruction in Algeria and France demonstrate how developments in the colony influenced those in the metropole as much as those in mainland France impinged on Algeria.

The North-African born Robert Randau's Algerianist movement, analyzed in chapter two, represented in some respects a broadening of Bertrand's search for the authentically Algerian, an effort to write "out of" a particular place, in prose marked by that place's specificity. Its appearance between 1910 and 1914 coincided with a notable change in large-scale architecture in the colonies, as colonial designers and administrators sought forms adapted to local climates, cultures, and artistic traditions. In North Africa, the *style du vainqueur* [victor's style] in public buildings gave way to a *style du protecteur* [protector's style], at least according to observers of the day. In a mix of nostalgia and innovation, French architects attempted to imitate or adapt what they considered "traditional" forms (stylized minarets, crenellated walls, Moorish arches, etc.) in their designs. In literature, the Algerianist desire to valorize all aspects of Algerian specificity (from the European point of view) led Randau and the writers around him to return to the sites that rendered Arab history visible, such as the Casbah of Algiers, as well as to continue to privilege the constructions of ancient Rome and modern France. Through the establishment of critical reviews, a writers' association, and a literary prize, they tried to promote a specifically Algerian identity in literature either within or alongside the French. A large share of their polemic revolved around what this identity would include, and to what extent it involved difference from the French metropole. Urban constructions continued to serve as the signs and stakes circulating in these arguments. Randau's characters' promenades in the Casbah complemented his plots set on colonists' farms. His descriptions of both asserted that despite Bertrand's disapproval, Arab and Amazigh culture, as expressed in architectural form, was the heritage of all Algerians. Randau thus laid foundations for later elaborations of ethnic identity based on interpretation of the urban fabric.

Despite Randau's vigorous optimism, and the participation of several Muslim members in the *Association des Ecrivains Algériens*, the Algerianists continued to have difficulty determining how to deal with non-Europeans in the colonial identity. Their movement, after all, depended on the premise of French Algeria, and they often preferred to skirt the issue of representing the colonized as fully formed characters. Chapter three of this study investigates the perception of Muslims in literature by European Algerians, in dialog with the very earliest literary productions of Muslims themselves writing in French. Colonial literature included an under-studied genre, the *roman indigène*, novels by Europeans or their Algerian descendants, featuring exclusively Arab or Amazigh characters and presenting events deemed likely to occur in the Muslim milieus imagined by the authors. The "anthropological" novels of Ferdinand Duchêne exemplify the category; the author set his characters and plots in Kabylia, the heart of Amazigh Algeria relatively unsettled by Europeans. His writings demonstrate many of the most common stereotypes about the two principal ethnic groups of Algerian Muslims, the Arabs and the Imazighen. His books enter an already established discourse of cultural difference which French administrators used to keep the groups separate. As Duchêne was writing in the early 1920s, several social reform

movements got under way, tepidly encouraged by the colonial administration, to improve the status of Kabyle women and children. Duchêne's
vision remained quite conservative: it constituted a project of reconstructive nostalgia tending to foreclose new developments in Kabyle society by
fixing it according to nineteenth-century French observations. Major
French actors in the debate on reform received Duchêne's fiction as anthropological documentation; rather than merely reflecting cultural
trends, colonial literature had an unexpected impact on the way administrators imagined local practices and power relations. These relations received further elaboration in the first novels by Muslim writers in French,
the relatively unknown predecessors of the now canonical Algerian authors who emerged in the 1950s, such as Mohammed Dib, Mouloud
Feraoun, and Kateb Yacine. This chapter complements study of the *roman
indigène* with a reading of three novels by Muslims from the 1920s and
1930s, vital for understanding the historical dynamics of identity politics
and assimilation in Algeria. The writings of A. Ben Cherif, Khodja Chukri,
and Mohammed Ould Cheikh illustrate the stakes of the struggle over political and cultural assimilation between the world wars. At the time, most
of the leaders of the nascent Muslim opposition demanded an effective
application of the assimilationist policies reiterated but not implemented
by colonial officials. While a very few began to formulate demands for independence, many more agitated instead for the rights of French citizens.
While such positions seem conciliatory or even compromised from a postindependence viewpoint, they nonetheless constituted a tenuous counterdiscourse to the position of the *colons* who dominated the political scene.
These works stand even today as examples of how oppositional identities
can be negotiated in the face of censure.

Chapter four takes up the hidden complexities of the discourses and
counterdiscourses of commemoration, tracing the genesis of another moment of collective nostalgia, the official commemoration of the centenary
of French Algeria in 1930. The years 1928–1932 saw an outpouring of popular novels set in Algeria, illustrating the ideological investment of commemorating a century of occupation figured in the continued evolutions
of the colonial city. By the 1930s, French urbanism and architecture in
North Africa were moving beyond the kind of "Arabisant" decor used
twenty years earlier, to more progressive designs reflecting international-
ist and modernist trends.[39] Planners at the time routinely cited these constructions as state of the art, and Algiers, Rabat, and other North African
cities provided the locales in which to illustrate or criticize French ideas
on urban design. Arguing over the shape and state of the city was also a
way of arguing over its history; and describing it, in both novels and
guidebooks, a way of commenting on the official version of that history.
This chapter demonstrates how writers around 1930 participated in these

debates, and argues that they developed a discourse on the history of colonization that would become central to the self-definition of European Algerians for the next thirty years. Ironically, this idea of Algerian identity based on the pioneer *colons'* struggles against the climate, the land, and its former possessors became codified at the last moment in history in which the Europeans in Algeria could easily reassure themselves about their political future. In addition to the Centenary, 1930 also saw the failure in the National Assembly of a serious proposal for substantive reform of the status of the colonized, by granting some of them citizenship. In retrospect, it appears as a watershed date, the final real opportunity for structural change to assimilate the Muslims as French citizens. Taken together, the legislative battles and the commemorative ceremonies demonstrated once and for all that assimilation would never work, not least because the dominant ethnic group refused to consider it seriously. At the time, however, a very few European Algerian writers inadvertently produced an unexpected counterdiscourse to the reigning triumphalism, hinting almost in spite of themselves that the colonial peace was based on unstable or fictitious grounds. The discursive relations between such positions emerging in the margins and the dominant tone of colonial triumph suggest the difficulty of preventing doubts from infiltrating a dominant discourse, even one flexible enough to incorporate and subvert opposition.

While the Centenary represented the last moment for the colony to extricate itself from the political impasse caused by a majority demanding civil and cultural rights and a minority refusing them, the 1930s nonetheless saw a renewal of the Algerian literary scene, marked by the appearance of the young Albert Camus, one of the subjects of chapter five. Camus and other intellectuals such as Gabriel Audisio and Emmanuel Roblès became known around World War II as the "École d'Alger," and came to dominate the cultural production of the colony just as its political scene was steadily worsening, as evidenced by the massacres of Muslims following demonstrations on 8 May 1945, and by the massive fraud in the postwar elections in which Arabs and Imazighen were allowed to vote.[40] Beginning with a concept first developed by the Franco-Algerian writer Gabriel Audisio, Camus attempted to rethink the colony's collective identity and historical narratives, using the Mediterranean and its cities as a source of interethnic imagery and ideals. He soon discovered that the official version of Algerian history as expressed in the centenary celebrations was inadequate for imagining a tenable future for the colony, but also that his own Mediterranean humanism would fare little better. He and the writers around him began to express a feeling analogous to the "belatedness" in the discourse of nineteenth-century visitors. Despite these twentieth-century writers' efforts to develop a basis for cultural *entente* between the various ethnic groups in confrontation, they expressed their justified fears of having run out of time to make the decisive changes necessary. Camus understood that the problem was essentially historical, figured in his own perceptions of colonial history in Algiers and Oran. *La Peste* [*The Plague*] and the unfinished novel *Le Premier homme* [*The First Man*] record his intellectual grappling with the problems of Algerian identity in cities he saw either as lacking significant history, or as forgetting or ignoring any history they did have. This forgetfulness, explored in an unfinished novel, demonstrated for Camus the impossibility of a national history for Algeria based on the premises admitted by colonial historiography. Camus explores tentatively the possibilities of a nostalgia far more reflective than reconstructive. His novel suggests the impossibility of the continued historical existence of the *Français d'Algérie* who had engaged in urban reconstructions since 1830, and who would soon be "out of place" in every sense of the phrase.

The final two chapters of this study concern two of the authors most important to the construction of new modes of thinking about Algerian history in the independence era and later, writers who recreated places they had been written out of by colonial literature. In the last years of the French colony, Kateb Yacine, subject of chapter six, wrote *Nedjma* (1956), the novel many consider the founding text of contemporary Francophone Algerian literature. In a plot set in motion by the historical trauma of riots and repression of May 1945, the disoriented heroes of *Nedjma* wander in the cityscapes of Constantine and Bône, attempting to find their way through baroque configurations of ruins. Kateb revises the nostalgic appreciation of ruins inherited from previous Algerian writers, in order to rethink the choice and importance of physical remnants of the past for contemporary historical discourses. His complex plot structure draws on the conception of cyclical historical progression invented by the fourteenth-century Maghribi historian Ibn Khaldūn, through which the novelist reappropriates ruins either discounted by the French, like those of the ancient Amazigh city of Cirta, or actually produced by them, like the remains of buildings destroyed by French shells in Constantine. This reappropriation avoids linking ruins with essentialized notions of national identity. For Kateb, the importance of the ruin lies less in the ancient building, imagined to represent past grandeur, than in the very fact that the building presently lies ruined, resisting contemporary interpretation. Kateb's project contains a reflective nostalgia that values past stategies and postures rather than states that may not have existed. He embraces the impermanence symbolized by his ruins in order to reterritorialize Algerian history in them; his characters learn to move among them in ways which will have historical consequences, at a time when participation in History was dangerous or impossible for Algerians.

Movement in the city remains the focus in chapter seven, which examines the work of Rachid Boudjedra, one of the most significant novelists of the generation that succeeded Kateb's. By situating two of his most important novels in Paris, Boudjedra reopens negotiations over urban history and topography between France and Algeria. *Topographie idéale pour une aggression caractérisée* (1975) traces the movements of a newly arrived immigrant lost in the Métro, decidedly out of place, and soon out of time as well; racist hooligans murder him just before he reaches his destination. *Le Vainqueur de coupe* (1981) tells the story of a real (and much more effectual) immigrant in Paris, the terrorist Mohammed Ben Sadok, the historical figure who assassinated a pro-French Arab official attending the final match of the Coupe de France in 1957. Both works focus on characters learning what Michel de Certeau calls tactics of movement in hostile territory; the novels connect such tactics (or their failure, in *Topographie idéale*) with the understanding and transmission of a collective memory.[41] Boudjedra represents Algerians failing or succeeding in reading the Parisian landscape and in sensing its historical implications for their own struggles. Furthermore, his work seems to demand a reconsideration of historian Pierre Nora's notion of *lieux de mémoire*: he shows how the function of such *lieux* for minority groups, whose mode of historical transmission has been a mix of written documents and oral traditions, might be quite different from that imagined by Nora.

This study does not address directly the events that have marked Algeria since 1988, nor the suddenly renewed self-consciousness in Muslim societies, including Algeria, since the emergence of contemporary international terrorism. Were one to undertake an anlysis of the latter phenomenon, the terms of this study might still prove useful. The declared desire of several terrorist organizations to recreate the califate is transparently a project of restorative nostalgia of a pernicious kind, and understanding its origins would prove helpful. Nonetheless, the rapid evolution and persistent complexities of the Algerian situation defy generalization in the context of a literary and cultural-historical study.[42] While no one would argue that the civil war has been anything but horrific, it has fomented a political debate much healthier than the one pursued with knives and bombs around the city. This development in the debate about the past, present, and future of Algeria would have been unthinkable before 1989, under the sclerotic institutions of the ruling party, the FLN. No work of North African cultural history, by an author without a personal stake in Algerian affairs, can afford to pronounce on the costs of that debate without risking conventional piety, irrelevance, or worse, callousness. Nonetheless, this book does suggest some of the stakes and bases of Algerian political and cultural struggles. Investigating the concrete, the local, and the particular in the continuum of colonial and post-colonial history lays the groundwork for understanding the cultural dynamics of the Maghrib, and, with due care, perhaps of some other places labelled "postcolonial."

NOTES

1. The people we and the French know as Berbers call themselves *Imazighen* (sing. *Amazigh*) in their own language. (The sound represented by *gh* resembles more a Parisian *r* than a *g*.) The term frequently covers all of the indigenous peoples of North Africa: in Algeria, these include those of Kabylia and the Aurès and M'zab regions, as well as the Touaregs of the Sahara.

2. Peter Dunwoodie's excellent studies, *Writing French Algeria* (Oxford: Clarendon Press, 1998) and *Francophone Writing in Transition: Algeria 1900–1945* (Bern: Peter Lang, 2005), are among the very few in English to treat the colonial literature of Algeria; they concentrate on Franco-Algerian and Muslim writers, respectively. Though more limited in historical scope, Ahmed Lanasri's *La littérature algérienne de l'entre-deux-guerres: génèse et fonctionnement* (Paris: Publisud, 1995) provides a model for the investigation of literature by Arabs, Imazighen, and Europeans in a single and well-integrated study.

3. Alain Calmes, *Le roman colonial en Algérie avant 1914* (Paris: L'Harmattan, 1984), 13.

4. I adopt the term from Jann Matlock's Harvard seminars in 1994 and 1995.

5. Ania Loomba, "Overworlding the 'Third World'," in *Colonial Discourse and Post-Colonial Theory: A Reader*, ed. Patrick Williams and Laura Chrisman (Hemel Hempstead, UK: Harvester Wheatsheaf, 1993), 305–23; Arif Dirlik, "The Postcolonial Aura: Third World Criticism in the Age of Global Capitalism," in *Contemporary Postcolonial Theory: A Reader*, ed. Padmini Mongia (London: Arnold, 1996), 294–320; Richard Serrano, *Against the Postcolonial: 'Francophone' Writers at the Ends of French Empire* (Lanham, MD: Lexington Books, 2005).

6. Some critics have attempted to maintain a distinction between post-colonial, referring to the period chronologically following independence, and postcolonial, referring to the entire set of cultures, power relationships, theories, and practices that stemmed from the colonial encounter, at any historical moment. Both spellings nonetheless continue to suggest that colonization is the primary disjuncture in the culture histories of the countries concerned.

7. David Prochaska, "History as Literature, Literature as History: Cagayous of Algiers," *American Historical Review* 101, no. 3 (Fall 1996): 670–71.

8. Dirlik, "The Postcolonial Aura: Third World Criticism in the Age of Global Capitalism," 315.

9. For example, in Prochaska's study just cited.

10. Examples of this model of study include Martine Astier Lotfi, *Littérature et colonialisme: l'expansion coloniale vue dans la littérature romanesque française, 1871–1914* (Paris: Mouton, 1971); and Denys Lombard, ed., *Rêver l'Asie: exotisme et littérature coloniale aux Indes, en Indochine et en Insulinde* (Paris: Editions de l'EHESS, 1993); see also the following collections: Alain Buisine, Norbert Dodille, and

Claude Duchet, eds., *L'Exotisme* (Saint-Denis-de-la-Réunion: Université de la Réunion, 1988); and Dominique de Courcelles, ed., *Littérature et exotisme: XVI-XVIIIe siècle* (Paris: École des chartes, 1997).

11. Alec G. Hargreaves and Mark McKinney, "Introduction: The Post-Colonial Problematic in Contemporary France," in *Post-Colonial Cultures in France*, ed. Alec G. Hargreaves and Mark McKinney (London: Routledge, 1997), 3–25; Charles Forsdick and David Murphy, "Introduction: The Case for Francophone Postcolonial Studies," in *Francophone Postcolonial Studies: A Critical Introduction*, ed. Charles Forsdick and David Murphy (London: Arnold, 2003), 1–14; Alec G. Hargreaves, ed., *Memory, Empire, and Postcolonialism: Legacies of French Colonialism* (Lanham, MD: Lexington Books, 2005). Debra Kelly provides a critical overview of the the-oretical implications of our choice of terms in the introduction to her *Autobiography and Independence: Selfhood and Creativity in North African Postcolonial Writing in French* (Liverpool: Liverpool University Press, 2005).

12. Catherine Hodeir, *L'Exposition coloniale: 1931* (Paris: Ed. Complexe, 1991); Patricia A. Morton, *Hybrid Modernities: Architecture and Representation at the 1931 Colonial Exposition, Paris* (Cambridge, MA: MIT Press, 2003).

13. Among the many examples, the indefatigable magazine-writer Édouard Fournier's *Paris démoli: mosaique de ruines*, 1853, preface by Théophile Gautier (Paris: E. Dentu, 1855), and the 400-page collaborative volume *Les Rues de Paris, ou Paris chez soi, Paris ancien et nouveau . . . avec tous les changements exécutés ou projetés récemment. . . . Terminé par une Revue générale du nouveau Paris* (Paris: P. Boizard, 1859).

14. Pierre Nora, ed., *Les Lieux de mémoire* (Paris: Gallimard, 1984).

15. See for example Jacques Berque, *Le Maghreb entre deux guerres* (Paris: Seuil, 1962); Benjamin Stora, *Histoire de l'Algérie coloniale (1830–1954)* (Paris: La Découverte, 1991), as well as the Prochaska and Ageron works in the bibliography.

16. Lawrence Vale's *Architecture, Power, and National Identity* (New Haven: Yale University Press, 1992) is one of the basic references here.

17. Nezar Al-Sayyad, "Colonialism and National Identity," in *Forms of Dominance: On the Architecture and Urbanism of the Colonial Experience*, ed. Nezar Al-Sayyad (Avebury, UK: Brookfield, 1992), 5.

18. In addition to the articles in AlSayyad's edited volume, a number of book-length studies have appeared on colonial urbanism, architecture, and urban social history, including Anthony D. King, *Colonial Urban Development: Culture, Social Power, and Environment* (London: Routledge, 1976); Robert Grant Irving, *Indian Summer—Lutyens, Baker, and Imperial Delhi* (New Haven: Yale University Press, 1981); and Frederick Cooper, *On the African Waterfront: Urban Disorder and the Transformation of Work in Colonial Mombasa* (New Haven: Yale University Press, 1987). While these works focus on the effects of restructuring preexisting cities, other studies have emphasized that the cities that predated the colonial transfor-mations were themselves the sites of articulations of power, in some cases com-parable to those of a colonizing venture. On the Arab city, see Hichem Djiait, *Al-Kufa, naissance de la ville islamique* (Paris: Maisonneuve et Larose, 1986), and AlSayyad's "The Islamic City as a Colonial Enterprise," in *Forms of Dominance: On the Architecture and Urbanism of the Colonial Experience*, ed. Nezar AlSayyad (Avebury, UK: Brookfield, 1992), 27–43. More recently, Nnamdi Elleh writes about

pharaonic projects in post-colonial Africa in *Architecture and Power in Africa* (Westport, CT: Praeger, 2002).

19. The extensive bibliography here includes Janet Abu-Lughod, *Rabat: Urban Apartheid in Morocco* (Princeton: Princeton University Press, 1980); François Béguin, *Arabisances: décor architectural et tracé urbain en Afrique du Nord 1830–1950* (Paris: Dunod/Bordas, 1983); Jean-Jacques Deluz, *L'Urbanisme et l'architecture d'Alger: Aperçu critique* (Alger: Pierre Mardaga/Office des Publications Universitaires, 1988); Paul Rabinow, *French Modern: Norms and Forms of the Social Environment* (Cambridge, MA: MIT Press, 1989); Gwendolyn Wright, *The Politics of Design in French Colonial Urbanism* (Chicago: University of Chicago Press, 1991); and Zeynep Çelik, *Urban Forms and Colonial Confrontations: Algiers under French Rule* (Berkeley: University of California Press, 1997). The other essential reference in English on Algerian urban history is David Prochaska's *Making Algeria French: Colonialism in Bône, 1870–1920* (Cambridge, UK: Cambridge University Press, 1990).

20. In addition to François Béguin's work, see Shirine Hamadeh, "Creating the Traditional City: A French Project," in *Forms of Dominance: On the Architecture and Urbanism of the Colonial Experience*, ed. Nezar Al-Sayyad (Avebury, UK: Brookfield, 1992), 241–59.

21. See the last chapter of Paul Rabinow's *French Modern* and Gwendolyn Wright's introduction to *The Politics of Design in French Colonial Urbanism*.

22. Léopold-Victor Poirel, *Mémoire sur les travaux à la mer, comprenant l'historique des ouvrages exécutés au port d'Alger, et l'exposé complet et détaillé d'un système de fondation à la mer au moyen de blocs de béton* (Paris: Carilian-Goeury et V. Dalmont, 1841).

23. See Abu-Lughod's *Rabat: Urban Apartheid in Morocco*.

24. André Bolzinger, "Jalons pour une histoire de la nostalgie," *Bulletin de psychologie* 42, no. 389 (January-avril 1989): 311. All translations in this book are mine, unless otherwise indicated on first reference to the work.

25. Jean-Jacques Rousseau, *Dictionnaire de musique*, 1768 (Genève: Éditions Minkoff, 1998), 317.

26. Bolzinger, "Jalons pour une histoire de la nostalgie," 313. The relevant passage in Kant comes from his *Anthropologie in pragmatischer Hinsicht* (1798) part I, §32.

27. J. Kleiner, "On nostalgia," *Bulletin of the Philadelphia Association for Psychoanalysis* 20 (1970): 11.

28. Constantine Sedikides, Tim Wildschut, and Denise Baden, "Nostalgia: Conceptual Issues and Existential Functions," in *Handbook of Experimental Existential Psychology*, ed. Jeff Greenberg, Sander L. Koole, and Tom Pyszczynski (New York: Guilford Press, 2004), 200.

29. Svetlana Boym, *The Future of Nostalgia* (New York: Basic Books, 2001), xiii.

30. Ibid., 41.

31. Salman Akhtar, "'Someday' and 'If Only' Fantasies," in *The Subject and the Self: Lacan and American Psychoanalysis*, ed. Judith Feher Gurewich and Michel Tort (Northvale, NJ: Jason Aronson Inc., 1996), 212.

32. Krystine Irene Batcho, "Nostalgia: A Psychological Perspective," *Perceptual and Motor Skills* 80 (1995): 135.

33. Melinda J. Milligan, "Displacement and Identity Discontinuity: The Role of Nostalgia in Establishing New Identity Categories," *Symbolic Interaction* 26, no. 3 (Summer 2003): 398.

34. Sinead McDermott, "Future-Perfect: Gender, Nostalgia, and the Not Yet Presented in Marilynne Robinson's *Housekeeping*," *Journal of Gender Studies* 13, no. 3 (November 2004): 261.

35. J. Doane and D. Hodges, *Nostalgia and Sexual Difference: The Resistance to Contemporary Feminism* (New York: Methuen, 1987); G. Greene, "Feminist Fiction and the Uses of Memory," *Signs: Journal of Women in Culture and Society* 16, no. 2 (1991): 290–321.

36. Boym, *The Future of Nostalgia*, xvi. See also McDermott, "Future-Perfect," 261.

37. In the extensive literature on Djebar, one might begin with H. Adlai Murdoch, "Rewriting Writing: Identity, Exile and Renewal in Assia Djebar's *L'Amour, la fantasia*," *Yale French Studies*, no. 83 (1993): 71–92; Clarisse Zimra, "Disorienting the Subject in Djebar's *L'Amour, la fantasia*," *Yale French Studies* (1995): 149–70; Patricia Geesey, "Collective Autobiography: Algerian Women and History in Assia Djebar's *L'amour, la fantasia*," *Dalhousie French Studies* 35 (Summer 1996): 153–67; Anne Donadey, "Rekindling the Vividness of the Past: Assia Djebar's Films and Fiction," *World Literature Today* 70, no. 4 (Autumn 1996): 885–92; and Mildred Mortimer, "Assia Djebar's Algerian Quartet: A Study in Fragmented Autobiography," *Research in African Literatures* 28, no. 2 (Summer 1997): 102–17.

38. Susan Ireland, "Rewriting the Story in Tassadit Imache's *Une Fille sans histoire*," *Women in French Studies*, no. 3 (Fall 1995): 112–22; Daphne McConnell, "Family, History, and Cultural Identity in the Beur Novel," in *Maghrebian Mosaic: A Literature in Transition*, ed. Mildred Mortimer (Boulder, CO: Lynn Reinner, 2000), 253–68; Karima Laachir, "The Interplay between History/Memory/Space in Tassadit Imache's *Presque un frère* and *Le Dromedaire de Bonaparte*," *Modern and Contemporary France* 13, no. 4 (November 2005): 449–64.

39. See the second chapter of Çelik's *Urban Forms and Colonial Confrontations*, as well as Deluz's *L'Urbanisme et l'architecture d'Alger*.

40. The purely theoretical accordance of citizenship rights to Arabs and Imazighen in 1947 did not give them any political power, since the government systematically tampered with election results (Charles-Robert Ageron, *Histoire de l'Algérie contemporaine: de l'insurrection de 1871 au déclenchement de la guerre de libération (1954)* [Paris: PUF, 1979], 410ff).

41. This analysis is indebted to Michel de Certeau's work in *L'Invention du quotidien. 1. Arts de faire*, 1980, ed. Luce Girard (Paris: Gallimard, 1990), and notably part one, chapter three, "Faire avec: usages et tactiques," published in English as *The Practice of Everyday Life*, trans. Steve F. Rendall (Berkeley: University of California Press, 1984).

42. Hugh Roberts provides cogent discussions of contemporary Algerian politics in *The Battlefield of Algeria 1988–2002: Studies in a Broken Polity* (London: Verso, 2003).

1

✦

Louis Bertrand and the Building of *l'Afrique latine*

Louis Bertrand arrived in Algiers in 1891, on his way to becoming the first major twentieth-century French writer to make a career of Algeria. His observations there, architectural and anthropological, soon led him to develop his signature concept, the notion of a Latin Africa, an idea that would suffice for an oeuvre of nearly a dozen books about France's North African territories. This chapter will examine how he arrived at this notion and what it meant for him and his contemporaries, as the first literary and cultural theory specifically evolved by the French to explain the cultural past, present, and future of their Algerian colony. Gabriel Audisio, a Franco-Algerian critic who would take Bertrand to task forty years later, claims that the first major literary school in Algeria owed its birth to a mistake in interpreting the architecture of Algiers: "du pont du bateau [Bertrand] aperçoit le Pavillon de la Santé maritime. C'est un petit édifice à colonnes: il y voit comme un temple antique. Naissance de l'Afrique latine: pendant trente ans, des littérateurs de tout poil vont se persuader que chaque Arabe et chaque Berbère est un Latin qui s'ignore." [From the deck of his ship, Louis Bertrand caught sight of the pavilion of the *Santé maritime*, a little building with columns, in which he saw an ancient temple. Thus was born Latin Africa: for thirty years, writers of every stripe would persuade themselves that every Arab and Berber was a Latin who didn't know it.][1] (See figure 1.1.) Bertrand attributed to this alleged temple the ability to dominate the city's indigenous architectural forms

Figure 1.1.   Algiers, Santé maritime building. Fonds documentaire Editions J. Gandini.

and to express a vital part of its past. For Audisio, however, nothing in Algeria's past made buildings with classical columns seem inevitable; the Santé maritime was simply a neoclassical amusement in the urban fabric.

The elevation of a "Latin"-dominated North Africa, where French *colons* inherited directly from Roman ancestors, and where Arabs and Imazighen were interesting only to the extent that they showed they had acquired "Latin" traits from previous or current colonizers, might well have seemed ridiculous to Audisio in 1935. To readers today, it seems evidently self-serving. Audisio's characterization of the misprision under which proponents of Latin Africa were laboring, however, suggests another way of looking at Bertrand's interested pronouncements. Misinterpreting the construction of Algiers seems to have been tantamount to misconstruing the identity of the colony. Instead of simply condemning Bertrand's vision, this chapter asks what ideological purposes it might have served. At the turn of the century, Franco-Algerian intellectuals felt a need to assert the identity of Algeria within (and sometimes in opposition to) the French *patrie*. The literary evolution of this identity, in its early phases, both followed and informed the development of regionalism in metropolitan France.

In its first incarnation in the final decades of the nineteenth century, regionalism generally meant nostalgically celebrating the traditional in
France's provinces and mourning its passing. It was a valorization of
provincial diversity within the context of national unity, illustrating the
depth of French roots and the richness of French traditions. It sold rather
well. To capitalize on public taste for the picturesque, French novelists of
the 1890s produced so many regional works, so many "romans de
province," that at least one critic assisted the public in its choice by providing lists organized by province, giving literary travelers an itinerary of
authentic local color from Picardie to Provence.[2] The thirst for local color
did not stop at the Mediterranean, however. The nineteenth century's
well-known taste for exoticism had long ago made local color the standard by which critics judged both novelists and travel writers working in
France's North African possessions. The fin-de-siècle in both places
would radically refocus regionalism, however, leading it to abandon celebrations of traditional headdresses, local wines, and village steeples (or
veiled women, couscous, and minarets) and turning it toward the political task of rejuvenating France.

France's leading conservative novelist of the period, Maurice Barrès
(1865–1923) became the country's major proponent of literary regionalism.
To Barrès and his fellow *antidreyfusards,* the fin-de-siècle represented the end
not only of a period of revolutions for France, but also of any real chance to
bring to fruition their conservative and nationalist vision of the country's
self-image and position in the world. Dreyfus was tried and convicted for a
second time in September of 1899, but a pardon tacitly acknowledged his innocence; for Barrès, this was only the last in a series of defeats for the cause
of nationalist regeneration, beginning with the failed adventure of
boulangisme. The "Founder of French Nationalism" became convinced that,
like the ending century, "tous les peuples ont leurs jours comptés" [the days
of every people are numbered] and that the French nation was headed for
oblivion, "à moins d'un considérable apport d'énergies" [without a considerable infusion of energy].[3] In his extended commentary on Barrès's nationalism, Zeev Sternhell provides convincing analysis of his subject's perception of the origins of France's decadence.[4] More recently, Eric Roussel has
emphasized that this idea of France's declining position in world affairs was
"véritablement le point de départ du nationalisme français" [truly the point
of departure for French nationalism].[5] Barrès himself made his position extremely clear in perhaps his best-known *roman à thèse, Les Déracinés* [The
Rootless] (1897), the first part of his trilogy, *Le Roman de l'énergie nationale.*
Decadence, he believed, stemmed from detaching young people from their
hereditary milieus; this made them susceptible to pernicious influences emanating from Paris and abroad. In tracing the development of seven young

lycéens from Nancy, the novel lays the blame for their *déracinement*, their "uprooting," on an educational system which denied any regional specificity, instead promoting what Barrès considered empty and abstract humanist ideals. In giving the seven their philosophical background, the *lycée* professor and Kantian universalist Bouteiller leads them far astray from any regional or national consciousness:

> ne devrait-il pas prendre souci du caractère général lorrain? Il risque de leur présenter une nourriture peu assimilable. [. . .] En ménageant ces tendances naturelles [du Lorrain], comme on ajouterait à la spontanéité, et à la variété de l'énergie nationale! . . . C'est ce que nie M. Bouteiller. [. . .] Déraciner ces enfants, les détacher du sol et du groupe social où tout les relie, pour les placer hors de leurs préjugés dans la raison abstraite, comment cela le gênerait-il, lui qui n'a pas de sol, ni de société, ni, pense-t-il, de préjugés?

> [should he not concern himself with the general character of the *Lorrain*? He risks presenting them with indigestible nourishment [. . .] By treating the natural tendencies of the *Lorrain* with consideration, how much one could add to the spontaneity and variety of national energy! . . . That is what M. Bouteiller denies [. . .] Uprooting these children, detaching them from the soil and the social group to which everything tied them, in order to place them in abstract reason, outside their prejudices: how would that bother Bouteiller, the man who had neither soil nor society, nor, he thought, prejudices?][6]

The antipathetic Bouteiller prides himself on exactly what Barrès reviles, his lack of rootedness, and on his devotion to the Third Republic's abstract civic ideal. He soon wins a seat in the Assemblée, thanks to payoffs from the Compagnie du Panama, about to go scandalously bankrupt. Full of his misleading teachings, his seven students follow him to Paris. In her work on the *roman à thèse* or ideological novel, Susan Suleiman analyzes how the trajectory of each of Barrès's characters, always clearly approved or condemned by the narrator, illustrates his thesis about uprooting as the cause of national decadence.[7]

In addition to recounting the downfall of the worst two of Bouteiller's problematic protegés, the murderers Racadot and Mouchefrin, *Les Déracinés* also begins to tell the story of the most enigmatic of the seven: François Sturel, dreamer, lady's man, and Boulangist man of action. Suleiman has pointed out what difficulties Sturel's character will present for a reading of the *Roman de l'énergie rationale* trilogy as a classic *roman à these*: he is both rooted and drifting, active and passive, the embodiment of positive nationalist ambitions, but finally a political failure.[8] In *Les Déracinés*, we discover how Sturel's promising potential is forever contaminated, and not only by the deleterious influence of Bouteiller and the Third Republic's education system. Sturel, like the Lorraine itself, is the victim of an invasion from the east. In his Paris *pension*, he meets his first and fatal infatuation: Mme. Astiné Aravian, an exotic Levantine with whom he immediately falls in love. The narrator, who never hesitates to dictate the interpretation of events, tells us that in his initial ecstasy, "Sturel, qui subit l'invasion énervante de l'Asie, en croit d'abord sa clairvoyance plus étendue. Quelle erreur! Ce n'est pas une plus-value que lui laisseront ces grands mouvements: les vagues sentiments qui l'envahissent ou qui, déjà présents en lui, s'y développent, ne valent que pour le détourner de toutes réalités ou du moins des intérets de la vie française." [Sturel, prey to the enervating invasion of Asia, initially believed that his perceptions had thereby increased. What a mistake! These great upheavals left him no benefit: the vague feelings invading him, or which, already present in him, were developing, served only to turn him away from the realities, or at least the interests, of French life.][9] As a cosmopolitan migrant from the East, Mme. Aravian cannot be integrated into Barrès's determinist vision of the French *patrie*; she constitutes a dangerous element, especially to subjects as weak as Sturel, enfeebled by an education which gave him no sense of attachment to what Barrès calls his "national domain."[10] Even after Barrès gets rid of Mme. Aravian by having her murdered, her influence will arise at dramatic moments throughout the trilogy to explain Sturel's inability to act as a heroic agent of national energy. The Nancy *lycée* did nothing to protect him from this invasion by a foreign mentality and everything to encourage him to succumb; Mme. Aravian plays a role in the realm of affects similar to that of Jews, Germans, and Anglo-Saxons in the realm of politics. Sturel's poetic sensitivity predisposed him to be spoiled by Mme. Aravian's foreign influence in a way French society cannot remedy: "Quand même la moralité sociale française repousserait justement Mme. Aravian, Sturel à jamais porte sa marque: quelle atmosphère pourrait contenter celui qui respira une fleur d'Asie portée par le vent des orages!" [Even if French social morality might justly reject Mme. Aravian, Sturel had been marked by her forever: what atmosphere could satisfy someone who had breathed the scent of an Asian flower carried on stormy winds!][11] The "erotic and exotic East" had already become the theme of a genre of French literature coalescing notably around Pierre Loti in the last twenty years of the nineteenth century; in exotic literature, the East often "spoiled" characters for prosaic life in France. For Barrès, however, the danger was not so much the loss of an individual, as that of a collective energy: the foreign generally, and the East particularly, were in his mind fatal for the "national energy."

BERTRAND'S ALGERIA AND THE ENERGY OF THE LATINS

Shortly after Maurice Barrès's death in 1924, the Académie Française gathered to choose his successor. With whom could they replace France's leading conservative writer and the major exponent of regionalism in French literature? When the *Immortels* announced their decision, many observers thought they had voted on "regionalist" lines: Louis Bertrand (1866–1941), successor to Barrès's seat, came from his predecessor's home province of Lorraine. Could that have been the only reason for his election? At first glance, their respective oeuvres could not seem more different. Bertrand had inspired the *Algérianistes*, a school of naturalist, often picaresque novelists devoted to promoting Algerian interests, often apparently against those of metropolitan France, and well-known for their opposition to romantic exoticism. What besides his provincial origins made Bertrand a suitable successor to Barrès? The British critic Peter Dunwoodie's *Writing French Algeria* briefly indicates several points at which Bertrand's ideology overlaps with his predecessor's at the Académie.[12] The connections run deeper than Dunwoodie suggests: Algerianism was neither an isolated development, nor a simple offshoot of regionalism, but a twin movement, playing a vitally important part in regionalism's transformation from literary curiosity to political force.

Bertrand attended *lycée* in the Lorraine several years after Sturel and his classmates; he too would become fascinated with the Orient in a way initially similar to Sturel's, but finally quite different. Sent to teach at the Algiers *lycée* in 1891, he stayed for six years, doing exactly what the fictional professor Bouteiller refused: studying what gave the new province the particular kind of youthful energy he found there. Where Bertrand found that Parisian literary travelers such as Gautier, Fromentin, and Loti had seen only the decadent exoticism of an Islamic civilization crumbling from inertia and the regrettable (if necessary) excesses of the French conquest, he saw a young, vibrant, and energetic European race forming itself out of the efforts and the collective consciousness of immigrants from Spain, France, Italy, and (not least) Alsace-Lorraine. He quickly baptized his vision *l'Afrique latine* and restated his claim to its discovery in the prefaces of each of his Algerian works: "je crois avoir introduit dans la littérature romanesque l'idée d'une Afrique latine toute contemporaine, que personne, auparavant, ne daignait voir. J'ai écarté le décor islamique et pseudo-arabe qui fascinait des regards superficiels, et j'ai montré, derrière cette vaine figuration, une Afrique vivante qui se différencie à peine des autres pays latins de la Méditerranée. Le reste n'est que mort et que décrépitude, et c'est dans les cadres de cette Afrique neuve que devront entrer tous les Africains,—quels qu'ils soient,—qui veulent vivre de la vie moderne." [I believe I introduced into novelistic literature the idea of a

wholly contemporary Latin Africa which no one had deigned to see before. I pushed aside the Islamic and pseudo-Arab decor which fascinated
superficial viewers, and showed, behind these sham appearances, a living
Africa barely distinguishable from the other Latin countries of the
Mediterranean. The rest is only death and decrepitude, and all Africans
who wish to live modern life—whoever they are—will have to enter into
the framework of this new Africa.][13] Rather than being invaded by a Mme.
Aravian, Bertrand treats all such imaginations as "vaine figuration," decadent and outmoded literary affectations, which he banishes with a Latin
counterinvasion of his own. He appreciated the new "race" of settlers he
saw forming itself in Algeria and reoriented colonial literature to celebrate
them as the "genuine" Algerians. His work would not valorize palm trees,
camels, or other exotic backdrops (and certainly not Arabs) but instead,
the new farms, cities, roads, ports, and the Europeans building them.
These alone were genuine and worthy of literary treatment. To justify his
claims, and to give the *colons* their *titres de noblesse*, Bertrand turned to ancient history. The flourishing discipline of North African archaeology
gave him ammunition for the argument that would make his literary career: the race of "Latins" then forming in Algeria were the modern representatives of that which had reigned there for over a thousand years, before the Muslim conquest. As builders, legislators, and bearers of Greek
and Roman civilization, these ancient predecessors of the French colonists
had been the legitimate possessors of the land; the Arabs, far from con-
tributing anything, wrecked the provinces and usurped the natural authority of the Latins.

This style of historiography has many parallels; most immediately, perhaps, in treatments of the annexed territories in the East, by Barrès and
those around him. *L'Appel au soldat*, Barrès's 1901 sequel to *Les Déracinés*,
attempts to justify *boulangisme* (which included calls for revenge for the
defeat of 1870) by "proving" historically the eternal Frenchness of Alsace
and Lorraine.[14] Lorraine had thus always been French, at least to anyone educated in the Third Republic's schools, who legendarily began by
reciting "Nos ancêtres les Gaulois," and ended by reading Fustel de
Coulanges.[15] Such a position easily justifies military reconquest of lost
provinces, whether in Alsace or in Algeria, "provinces perdues de la latinité" [lost provinces of *latinité*].[16] For the proponents of (re)conquest, the
very unchangeability of the provinces, their eternal stability, constituted a
basic article of faith. In the current of regionalism that the historian Anne-
Marie Thiesse has documented, the unchanging local identities expressed
in the provinces became part of the national patrimony, a valuable and
fertile resource for a nation losing its ideological coherence and reproduc-
tive capacity.[17] For Barrès, once a Celt, always a Celt; for Bertrand, once a
Latin, always a Latin. "L'Afrique française d'aujourd'hui, c'est l'Afrique

romaine, qui continue à vivre, qui n'a jamais cessé de vivre, même aux époques les plus troubles et les plus barbares" [French Africa of today is Roman Africa, which continues to live, which has never ceased to live, even in the most troubled and barbaric periods], asserts Bertrand, declaring his pride in having conceived of "les Africains de tous les temps comme une seule et même âme collective, dont la vie se perpétue à travers les siècles" [Africans of all times as a single collective soul, whose life perpetuates itself through the centuries].[18] Bertrand makes very explicit his conviction that while the Latin provinces in Africa had a venerable history, it was essentially a history of stasis, without historical development. That this could figure as a positive trait may seem paradoxical when we recall that colonial historiography generally ascribed stasis to the denigrated precolonial period. Here, the construct of Latin eternity provided yet another way of justifying reconquest, but also an uncontaminated source of energy for French national rebuilding. The inherent conservatism of the provinces, properly interpreted, would furnish the energy needed to counter the nation's political and moral decline, a common idea among proponents of radical nationalism in France. Sternhell has noted how Barrès's nationalism comes down to "l'idéal d'une société fermée, d'un monde cloisonné et statique, voué à la défense de ce qui est, et vivant dans la crainte de l'évolution" [the ideal of a closed society and a static, partitioned world, devoted to defending that which is already, and living in fear of evolution].[19] Barrès's famous lecture, "La Terre et les Morts" [The Land and the Dead], published in 1899 by the Ligue de la Patrie Française, explains how the combined forces of territory and ancestry, products of this provincial conservatism, are alone capable of regenerating France. These concrete realities provide far more solid bases for rebuilding the French consciousness than any abstract ideal espoused by Bouteiller; in order to work, however, they must be rooted in "[l]e terroir [qui] nous parle et collabore à notre conscience, aussi bien que les morts. C'est même lui qui donne à leur action sa pleine efficacité. Les ancêtres ne nous transmettent intégralement l'héritage accumulé de leurs âmes que par la permanence de l'action terrienne" [the soil which speaks to us and collaborates in the development of our consciousness, just as do the dead. It is indeed the soil which gives their activity its full effect. Only through the constant action of the soil do the ancestors transmit the entire cumulative heritage of their souls].[20] Since he had to admit himself beaten on the front of *antidreyfusard* nationalism, a strategic retreat into contemplation of an inalienable heritage transmitted from generation to generation represented Barrès's best hope for regaining the vigorous "national energy" his trilogy wishfully evokes in its title.[21]

By citing at length in "La Terre et les morts" from the chapter of his then-unpublished *L'Appel au soldat* describing Sturel's voyage of initiation in the Lorraine, Barrès illustrates his conviction that the pull of territory and ancestry are particularly strong on France's eastern fringe, painfully conscious of the proximity of the eternal German enemy. Bertrand corroborates this in his autobiography, where he lays considerable stress on his Lorrain ancestry, alluding to the "sens de l'ennemi" so well developed among his fellow easterners. He found this sense salutary in Algeria, where it constantly reminded him that the Arab Algerian was "l'Ennemi, —un ennemi qui n'a rien oublié, rien pardonné, et qui ne désarme pas" [the Enemy—an enemy who has forgotten nothing, pardoned, nothing, and who is not giving up his arms].[22] In his inaugural speech at the Académie Française, he would claim to have reacted in Algeria in "exactement la même façon que Barrès en Lorraine" [exactly the same way as Barrès in the Lorraine]: his instincts as a Lorrain told him instantly whom to regard as the enemy.[23] However, Bertrand's novels show that while regionalism on the French periphery stemmed from shared ideological roots and followed a common development, its flavor and impact would depend very much on which part of the periphery it took as its field of action: his reactions in Algeria differed in fact notably from those of Barrès in Lorraine. In travelogues and in prefaces to his novels (prefaces mostly written for postwar reeditions) Bertrand would constantly return to the theme of conserving the ancient Latin Africa; the African novels themselves (written much closer to the composition of Barrès's trilogy) have a different thrust. In them, he demonstrates his own conviction of the vitality present in the new French departments (or old Latin provinces) in Algeria, but in a way quite different from Barrès.

Despite his extreme conservatism, Bertrand's Algerian works follow two contestatory, not to say radical, traditions: naturalism and the picaresque. Two points need to be made about Bretrand's artistic choices. First, although as several critics have argued, later writers in the colony would adhere to naturalist norms long after these had become passé in mainstream French literature, Bertrand in 1895 chose a genre that still appeared to have life in it. Second, in saying that Bertrand worked in a picaresque vein of the naturalist novel, I do not mean that he had either the talent of Cervantes or the moral compass of Zola: even if he chose the latter's style, his texts never betray the slightest temptation to ally themselves politically with France's prototypical public intellectual. Bertrand recuperated a genre associated with progressivism for his conservative project.

Le Sang des races [The Blood of the Races] (1895), his first novel, recounts the adventures of Rafael, son of Spanish immigrants to Algeria. Rafael works in the profession Bertrand would idolize throughout his Algerian cycle, that of carter and caravan driver in the South; his roadside adventures constitute a long series of street fights won, lost, and avenged and women loved, seduced, and abandoned. With Rafael, the carter's vocation takes on central importance for a conquest of the land figured in sexual terms. Even his lyrical evocations of the countryside, in which he shows himself as sensitive to natural beauty as Barrès's heroes in Lorraine, carry the sexual charge which Rafael's overflowing machismo imposes on all he surveys: "Aux flancs des roches arides, les violets et les mauves s'adoucissaient, les verts et les roses devenaient plus pâles. Les sommets s'arrondissaient comme des seins. . . . Sous les voiles légers du matin, la terre prenait une couleur vermeille. Elle luisait ardemment à travers les vapeurs languissantes. Elle vibrait déjà au choc du soleil. . . . Rafael, en entrant dans ce Sud depuis si longtemps désiré, éprouvait comme la joie d'une conquête. Sous les ondes de la chaleur, son énergie s'exaltait. Il triomphait de sentir ses veines plus ardentes que le soleil." [On the dry rock faces, the violets and mauves were lightening, and the greens and pinks were becoming paler. The hill tops rounded off like breasts. . . . Under the morning's light veiling, the earth took on a crimson tone, shining brightly through the languishing mists. Already it was vibrating from the impact of the sun. . . . Rafael, entering the South he had desired for so long, felt something like the joy of a conquest. Under the ripples of heat, his energy rose. He felt triumphant, his veins more ardent than the sun.][24] The unchanging countryside becomes for Bertrand's hero a feminized object of desire and conquest, the *Latine* welcoming back her rightful master. Explicitly eroticized unions between man and countryside will rebuild Latin Africa; unions between Rafael and his half-dozen roadside conquests of various national origin will repopulate it with members of the new Latin race.

We have yet to see, however, how they will rebuild France. Bertrand must propose a mechanism to forge the unruly crowd of Piedmontese, Genovese, Valencians, Maltese, Provençaux, and Alsatians into a union recognizable as French and capable of regenerating French ideals, French politics, and the French international image. When Barrès speaks of his archetypal provincial city, Metz, he adopts his most reverent tone when describing the city's cemetery and his most revolted when reviling the cloddish Germans defiling it.[25] When Bertrand evokes his archetypal colonial city, Algiers, he adopts Zola's manner both to portray the crowd on the boulevards, and then later to describe the "degenerate" Arabs contaminating it:

Il y avait là des hommes de toutes les nations, des terrassiers piémontais, les plus bruyants de tous, avec leurs faces roses de Gaulois aux longues moustaches blondes et leurs yeux bleus. Ils étalaient de grandes bottes et des pantalons de velours aussi larges que des jupes, à côté des cottes de toile bleue des charpentiers marseillais. Par-ci par-là éclataient les tailloles multicolores des petits charretiers de la Camargue et de la vallée du Rhône, qui gesticulaient entre les larges épaules des Piémontais. Une blouse de Montélimar, déteinte par les lessives et dont les broderies noires s'effaçaient sous la poussière, se démenait avec des gestes amplifiés par les plis. Tous se comprenaient, s'excitaient, s'enivraient de leurs propos, que les Piémontais martelaient de rudes accents toniques. Le vin coulait dans les verres, incendiait les visages et dilatait les yeux.

Plus pacifiques, les hommes du Nord se tenaient à l'écart: c'étaient presque tous des Alsaciens immigrants, des Badois de la Forêt-Noire. . . . Pour se distinguer, tous affectaient à l'auberge de ne parler que le français, ce qui faisait rire ceux de Marseille. Il y en avait qu'on interpellait des autres tables, en singeant leur mauvais allemand. . . . Près des Espagnols, il y avait des tables entiers de Maltais, de Napolitains, de Mahonnais, tous charretiers ou maçons, très à l'aise et parlant haut comme des gens qui sont chez eux. Les Maltais au teint mat et au visage gras caressaient de grosses moustaches à la Victor-Emmanuel. Plusieurs avaient des anneaux d'or dans leurs oreilles. Mais, au fond, les autres les méprisaient à cause de leur sang mélangé et de leur ressemblance avec les Maures et les Juifs.

[There were men present from every nation. The Piedmontese laborers, the noisiest of all, had rosy Gallic faces, long blond mustaches, and blue eyes. They showed off their large boots and velour pants as wide as skirts, next to the blue canvas overalls of the Marseillais carpenters. Here and there the multicolored cummerbunds of the little cart-drivers from the Camargue and the Rhône valley stood out, as their owners gesticulated between the broad shoulders of the Piedmontese. A Montelimar shirt, faded from washing, with black embroidery disappearing under the dust, gestured with movements amplified by the folds. Everyone understood one another as they became excited, drunk on their own words, which the Piedmontese hammered out with heavy stresses. The wine ran in the cups, lighting up faces and dilating eyes.

The more peaceful Northerners kept themselves apart: they were almost all Alsatian immigrants or Badois from the Black Forest. . . . To set themselves apart, all of them affected to speak only French in the inn, which made the Marseillais laugh. There were some whom the others hailed from other tables, imitating their bad German. . . . Near the Spaniards, there were whole tables of Maltese, Neapolitans, and Majorcans, all cart-drivers or masons, very much at ease and speaking loudly like people who feel at home. The Maltese, with chubby, matte-complected faces, stroked their heavy Victor-Emmanuel mustaches. Many had gold earrings. At bottom, however, the others despised them because of their mixed blood and their resemblance to the Moors and the Jews.][26]

Bertrand, though inclusive in his enumerations of the so-called Latin races, nonetheless gives pride of place to those who might be considered already French, or at least those on the margins of the nation, whom France could claim: those from Montélimar and Marseille merge with

Piedmontese and Alsatians. The rest, though for Bertrand rightfully at home in Algeria, are distinctly un-French, and despite their importance in the novel, they receive a great deal less space in this initial description of the Algiers crowd. Some, like the Maltese with gold earrings, even come in for the sort of exoticizing treatment Bertrand affected to banish from his writing. Those at the top of this scale of Latins look down on those at the bottom because of their mixed blood and their resemblance to the two outcast groups of Latin Africa, Jews and Arabs. Despite its diversity, the rest of the crowd is promiscuous, but not "mixed": each group retains its individual characteristics. Clearly, the crowd as a whole can neither claim nor create Frenchness by blood; the "*sang des races*," while strong, does not have the uniformity for which Barrès seemed to wish. Nor will language suffice to bring them into the French fold, as Algiers dialect (spottily reproduced in the novel in epithets and vulgarities) presents more a conglomeration of pidgins than the Lorraine's provincial patois with its roots in the Middle Ages. Bertrand must look elsewhere for the material that will unite this crowd lacking both a hereditary *terre* and a commons set of *morts*. He has yet to discover how the force represented by these people will transform the colony into a regenerator of France.

Predictably, he will find the common ground for this crowd in hatred of the enemy. Obviously the Arabs represent the primary enemy, and Bertrand will later insist that his readers never forget this; however, most commentators on his novels agree that his vengeance for the Arabs' alleged usurpation—both of Latin Africa and of a place in exotic literature rightly belonging to the *colons*—consists in simply banishing them altogether from his pages. Critics like Peter Dunwoodie and Alain Calmes have repeatedly noted the exclusion of Arabs from Bertrand's conception of Algeria and insisted on the anti-Arab racism both implicit and explicit in his vision. Arabs are indeed conspicuously absent, and the primal scene of group solidarity in this crowd opposes not Latins and Arabs, but Latins and Jews: the crowd tenses at the sight of two Jews crossing a neighborhood where they are not welcome, and the violence lurking just beneath the surface of Bertrand's Mediterranean men bursts out without warning. Under a hail of rocks and cries of "*A mort!*" [Kill them!] the Jews flee, but "Comme ils étaient travestis à l'européenne, les huées redoublèrent" [Since they were disguised as Europeans, the catcalls increased].[27] "Disguised," yet instantly recognizable as unassimilable outsiders, the Jews excite the hatred of Rafael and his friends as much by their attempt to disguise their identity as by their presence in a space whose inhabitants suddenly discover must be restricted to Europeans. Bertrand leaves his two Jews undescribed, except by their illegitimate European dress; by letting us know that they are those whom European Algerians called "juifs indigènes," he further racializes them and distances them from any group that might have ambitions to join his conception of *Latinité*.

Not that he is particularly interested in distinguishing Ashkenaz and Sepharad; doing so would not have moderated his tone since for him, all Jews share in the same race. While Barrès faulted the Jews for being cosmopolitan, non-French, and vaguely identified with Germany, Bertrand faulted them for being non-European altogether, and specifically identified as Asiatic. In later writings, Bertrand would equate not only the Jews but also Germany with the Asian menace he believed threatened France, thus Orientalizing everyone east of Strasbourg.[28] Though cloaked in appreciation for the un-French promiscuity and rowdiness of an apparently diverse crowd of Latins, Bertrand's anti-Semitism appears at least as strong as Barrès's, and used for similar ends, even more crudely stated.

Having defined the in-group he admires against one of France's perennial out-groups, and thus established its right to participation in defining French identity, Bertrand still confronts the problem of harnessing the Latins' youthful energy for the purpose of rejuvenating France from the periphery inwards. He will do so by canalizing the energy of his picaresque heroes into their work, their families, and ultimately, their new country. For all their irascibility, sexual predation, and attitude of carefree slovenliness, Bertrand's Latins are nonetheless quite conservative. "Sous ce prétendu barbare" [under this alleged barbarian], he says,

> je découvris peu à peu l'éternel Méditerranéen, avec son goût inéluctible pour les odyssées de la Route et de la Mer,—pour la vie en parade et en beauté, pour le labeur harmonieux qui ne brise pas les corps et qui n'avilit pas les âmes, son respect de la famille, du père, de l'enfant, de l'épouse féconde, des rites immémoriaux de la naissance, du mariage, de la mort et de la sépulture,—son sens très vif et très jaloux de l'indépendance et de la valeur individuelle. C'était encore le moment où les textes antiques étaient journellement entre mes mains, où, par métier comme par goût, je les lisais assidument et les commentais. Dans le voisinage de mes héros, Homère, Pindare, Théocrite vivaient pour moi d'une vie nouvelle, plus profonde, plus splendide, et en même temps plus humaine!
>
> [I discovered little by little the eternal Mediterranean, with his inescapable taste for odysseys on the road and the sea, for showy, beautiful living, for harmonious labor which does not break bodies or demean souls, and with his respect for the family, the father, the child, the fertile wife, the immemorial rites of birth, marriage, death, and burial, and with his very sharp and jealous sense of independence and individual value. At that time, I had the ancient texts in my hands daily, and both by taste and by profession, I read them assiduously and wrote about them. Next to my heroes, for me, Homer, Pindar, and Theocritus lived a new, deeper, more splendid, and at the same time more human life!][29]

Ultimately, Bertrand sums up the interests and ideology of Rafael and his friends as a sort of perennial Mediterranean "Travail, Famille, Patrie," dignified with Homeric roots.[30] As befits a group so closely linked to the mythical, Bertrand's heroes share an almost unchanging trajectory: after an extended youth spent in brawling and brothels, they settle down as steady workers and respectful husbands, fathering the large families France so desperately needed. They have little time and less patience for political agitation apart from chasing Jews and disdain the boredom and restrictive discipline of socialist or trade-unionist meetings. Of another of his heroes, Bertrand says "Il faut être . . . déplorablement de son Landernau littéraire et parisien pour ne pas sentir combien un Algérien comme Pépète est supérieur en tant que valeur social, au prolétariat métropolitain d'aujourd'hui, miné par l'alcool et la tuberculose, ahuri par une presse imbécile ou criminelle, réduit à l'état de bête de troupeau par la tyrannie syndicaliste" [One must be . . . deplorably provincial and Parisian not to sense how much Pépète is superior in social worth to today's metropolitan proletariat, undermined by alcohol and tuberculosis, bewildered by an imbecile or criminal press, and reduced to the state of herd animal by trade-unionist tyranny].[31] In her study of Third-Republic regionalism, Thiesse points out how the regionalist discourse ignored or decried the proletariat in favor of the peasantry. Barrès for his part could never acknowledge that national salvation could come from any class based in the city; this position would soon make the regionalist discourse seem anachronistic in an already well-urbanized Third Republic. Bertrand escapes this difficulty by glorifying an urban proletariat whose members prove devoted sons of the soil, and at the same time immune to leftist propaganda. They act as a counterbalance to the dangerous classes of France, too easily swayed by a press purportedly in the hands of an evil syndicate of foreigners, Jews, businessmen, and politicians to do anything to renew France's sense of itself.

For his heroes to do more than set a good example, however, Bertrand would have to give regionalism a decisive push away from its addiction to the past. Bertrand read Barrès almost exclusively as a traditionalist, despite many passages which show that Barrès was very aware that regional strength lay as much in adaptation as in stasis. Bertrand alludes to his fellow Lorrain as if he had read only "La Terre et les Morts" and ignored the rest of Barrès's complex ideological apparatus, as laid out in the debates in *L'Appel au soldat* between Sturel, the historian Roemerspacher, and the traditionalist Saint-Phlin.[32] In a preface from 1901, Bertrand made explicit his dissatisfaction with the limitations of the formulation of "La Terre et les Morts": "Si sévèrement qu'on juge les mœurs nouvelles des milieux coloniaux, il n'en est pas moins vrai que c'est là surtout que s'affirme la vitalité de la France. Cette patrie française dont on parle tant aujourd'hui, elle n'est pas là où dorment les morts, comme on voudrait nous le faire croire, elle est sur tous les chemins du monde, où passent nos armées et nos flottes, dans tous les pays où nos industriels et nos colons font fructifier les réserves d'or et d'énergie lentement amassées sur le vieux sol natal." [However severely one judges the new manners of colonial environments, it is nonetheless especially there that the vitality of France is affirmed. That French fatherland about which so many people are talking today does not lie where the dead sleep, as some would have us believe. Rather, it may be found around the world on all the paths taken by our armies and fleets, in all the countries where our industrialists and *colons* are turning a profit from the reserves of gold and of energy slowly amassed on the old native soil.][33] This is how Algeria will revive the decadent metropole: "Contre ces agités ou ces dégénéres, c'est le Barbare qui a raison! Voilà pourquoi j'ai écrit maintes fois et je répète encore . . . qu'*il faut nous rebarbariser*. . . . [N]ous rebarbariser, c'est nous rendre capables de lutter victorieusement contre le Barbare, c'est lui prendre toutes les qualités qui font sa force, si nous ne voulons pas etre écrasés par lui." [Against these degenerates and overexcited people, the Barbarian is right! That is why I have written so many times, and why I repeat again . . . that *we must rebarbarize ourselves*. . . . Rebarbarizing ourselves means rendering ourselves capable of waging the struggle against the Barbarian, and taking from him all the qualities that make up his strength, if we do not wish to be crushed by him.][34] The tone of this article seems to owe much to the war, though other articles in the collection that predate hostilities are just as violent. Nothing could be further from Barrès's cultured contemplations or from his revulsion for the barbarous Germans. France must harden itself and resolve to imitate the barbarism of the world around it. By inspiring the *patrie* as a whole to become like its colony, Algeria would save the metropole.

REMEMBERING UNITY: BERTRAND LOOKS BACK

Bertrand's publication of his Algerian trilogy, beginning with *Le Sang des races*, coincided exactly with the first intimations of political devolution for Algeria: the three departments of Algiers, Oran, and Constantine got an elected assembly in 1898 and a special budget in 1900.[35] Bertrand begins the first of these three novels by placing himself in rigid opposition with the purveyors of colonialist nostalgia: "on bâtissait l'Alger moderne" [they were building modern Algiers], declares the narrator, sweeping aside any regrets for the old, the picturesque, or, specifically, the Arab or Islamic. According to the literary critic Majid El Houssi, Bertrand will instead construct "la légende des colons, bâtisseurs, conquérants et civilisateurs" [the legend of the *colons*, the builders, conquerors, and civilizers].[36]

In literature and in architecture, the time had come to celebrate the present, an enterprise which always involves restructuring the past.

Despite Audisio's ironic critique of Bertrand's architectural misperception, to which I alluded at the beginning of this chapter, no one could really have mistaken the neoclassical Santé maritime building for an actual Greek temple expropriated, like so many other precolonial buildings, for administrative use. The real sense and impact of Bertrand's alleged misprision lies elsewhere. Bertrand believed passionately that the Roman occupation had fundamentally Latinized North Africa; the Roman precedent of sending "Latins" (as we have seen, anyone from the northern shores of the Mediterranean) to colonize foreshadowed the French colonial project. In declaring that "la véritable Afrique, c'est nous, nous les Latins, nous les civilisés" [we are the true Africa, we the Latins, we the civilized], Bertrand was at least realistically inclusive of the groups which made up the majority of the European population of Algeria: Spaniards, Provençaux, Languedociens, Corsicans, Balearic Islanders, Maltese, Sicilians, and mainland Italians. However, he explicitly excluded ethnic groups he considered undesirable or moribund: the Jews, and "l'ennemi commun, le musulman, qu'on a eu la sottise de laisser vivre alors qu'il fallait l'exterminer sans pitié" [the common enemy, the Muslims, whom we were stupid enough to let live, when we should have exterminated them pitilessly].[37] Critics who commonsensically cited the persistent fact of an Arabo-Berber population soon discredited Bertrand's rather difficult-to-defend theories about Algeria's fundamentally "Latin" cultural character. His idea, however, retained considerable political currency. Around 1930, a political party called the *Union latine* appeared to revive the anti-Semitic rhetoric of the turn of the century. Although they especially targeted Jews, they had no particular love for other Semitic groups either; the very name of their movement demonstrates that the idea of a coalition of Europeans to beat back (or indeed exterminate) non-Europeans persisted in Algerian politics.

Bertrand too would persist, undaunted in his vision of Algiers, as he proves in his account of his first arrival there in *Nuits d'Alger* [Nights of Algiers], a collection of essays published in 1929. There he returns to a literary ancestor that, with Apulius and Saint Augustine, he felt supported his claims for a Latin Algeria: none other than Flaubert's *Salammbô*. Apparently unworried that he is looking at Algiers and not Carthage (or even modern Tunis), he identifies several landmarks visible from the harbor with the monuments of Flaubert's novel. The Amirauté tower recalls the high priest's observatory; the Darse (the inner harbor) stands in for the naval port of Carthage; the Santé maritime, with its "airs de faux temple grec ou de mausolée carthaginoise" [look of a faux Greek temple or Carthaginian mausoleum] becomes the Suffète's palace, complete with Salammbô herself.[38] Flaubert's heroine provides a useful link between the

Latinized version of North Africa's roots and the French literary canon. Furthermore, Flaubert's mass expedition of mercenaries from every corner of the Mediterranean world into the interior of the continent foreshadows Bertrand's portrayals of expeditions of hard-living and heavily armed travelers of diverse Latin origins in *Le Sang des races* and *Sur les routes du Sud* (1930).

Evocations of a Latin or Punic past (almost exclusively mediated by Flaubert) continue to appear throughout Bertrand's rather contradictory musings about the distant past of North African history as visible in the city of Algiers and about the more recent past of North African literature as exemplified by his own career. *Nuits d'Alger* began a series of three books written toward the end of his life, in which he reminisces about the city and works through its history in order to assert once more the centrality of "Latin" conceptions in Algerian literature.[39] Here, he describes wandering about at night in the upper part of the Casbah:

Personne! J'étais seul. Je pouvais croire que ce décor était planté pour moi seul, et que j'étais le maître de la ville et de la nuit.

Et puis la griserie physique me reprenait, le besoin d'errer, de courir. . . . Et, sur les seuils, des femmes accroupies, des couples qui chuchotaient ou s'injuriaient bruyamment. Pas d'éclats de rire, pas de plaisanteries joviales, mais des dents serrées, des figures contractées, des yeux hagards. Ce qui se traitait là était une affaire sérieuse: la tragique luxure africaine. Mais, si rude que fut ce milieu, si brutale cette humanité, nulle bassesse, nulle vulgarité, ne s'y mêlait pour moi. Tout cela se rattachait au souvenir de rites perdus, de civilisations lointaines. Par ces nuits brûlantes, l'ardeur de mes veines exaspérait encore l'ivresse de mon imagination. Je revivais tout un passé hallucinant. Ce n'était pas un vain déguisement, une figuration créée par ma fantaisie: ces femmes voilées jusqu'aux yeux, ces hommes longs drapés, dont les pieds nus s'étalaient sur les dalles, ces cothurnes de cuir jaune, ces paquets de cierges bariolés, ces pains qui reproduisaient l'image mystique de Tanit, tout ce qui se montrait aux devantures des petites echoppes encore ouvertes,—tout cela m'introduisait dans des moeurs plusieurs fois millénaires.

[No one! I was alone. I could believe that this decor had been put up for me alone, and that I was master of the city and the night.

I felt a physical exhilaration, the need to wander or run . . . Women and couples crouched on the thresholds, whispering or insulting each other loudly. No bursts of laughter, no jovial joking, but instead clenched teeth, tense faces, and haggard looks. The dealings there were serious business: the tragic lust of Africa. Yet however crude the environment, however brutal the humanity in it, for me no vulgarity or baseness contaminated it. The whole scene was connected to the memory of lost rites and distant civilizations. On these burning nights, the heat of my blood stimulated still more the intoxication of my imagination; I relived an entire haunting past. It was not a vain

disguise, a representation created by my fantasies. The women veiled up to
their eyes, the men draped in long cloths, with bare feet on the flagstones, the
yellow leather buskins, the packages of multicolored candles, and the loaves
of bread reproducing the mystic image of Tanit, everything visible in the displays of the little shops still open: all of this placed me among customs many
thousand years old.][40]

The rhetoric echoes Flaubert's, describing Salammbô's sacrifices to Tanit;
flagstones and *cothurnes* evoke the ruins and artifacts of ancient Africa,
destroyed by its own inherent "tragic lust," and which Bertrand would
assimilate as "Latin." For Bertrand to find Algeria's ancient roots he had
first to clear away the contemporary Arabs and Imazighen who pose obstacles to his theories. Although the European population had indeed
dominated Algiers numerically for many years, with 112,000 Europeans
to 33,000 *indigènes* in 1906, and still about 150,000 Europeans to 100,000 *indigènes* around 1930, this domination was slipping, and in any case never
applied in the Casbah, always the Arab neighborhood par excellence.[41]
Clearly Bertrand invented the emptiness of the Casbah to serve his purposes: fantasmatically alone there at night, he can have the sense of mastery he needs. In declaring himself "alone," however, he immediately
records the presence of others; discounting the presence of the
colonized, he adopts one of the common habits of colonialist discourse.
Instead of meaning "no people at all," "personne" here means "no competing Europeans," admitting the existence of faceless *indigènes*. These
"figures" are just that: evocative theatrical extras devoid of any cultural
background or significance other than that assigned to them by Bertrand.
He knows many readers will regard his musings as pure literary rambling
and quickly counters this interpretation by asserting that far from "vain
disguise," his fantasy did indeed "introduce" him—in the penetrative
sense *introduire* carries—into the ancient world.

Bertrand's self-declaration of sole mastery enables him to cast the prostitutes and their clients as he sees fit, as priests and servants of Salammbô's
deity. Of the ten chapters of *Nuits d'Alger*, five explicitly describe places
well known for prostitution. These were also the parts of the city most
visibly falling into ruin under the influence of European penetration: the
area between the boulevards and sidewalk-staircases forming the perime-
ter of the old city. Bertrand's nocturnal promenades though these neighborhoods have ambiguous goals, and it remains difficult to determine what
persona he adopts to narrate them: is he the well-known Academician looking for remnants of a Latin atmosphere, or is he the young high school
teacher looking for a prostitute? How, in this context, should we understand European "penetration"? Just as the Roman or Punic past gives justification to France's imperial project, the ancient overlay, the connection

with *Salammbô*, gives prostitution (and specifically relations with North African prostitutes) an ancient and honorable coloring: "au milieu de ma confusion je vis se dresser devant moi la grandeur quasi sacrée de la prostitution orientale . . . [Les prostituées] me ramenaient au plus lointain des âges africains, aux prostitutions rituelles dans les temples, lorsque le geste sexuel était une chose profondément sérieuse, un geste religieux, et l'amour un mal terrible; lorsque les hommes croyaient que l'acte de la génération aidait à la fécondité de la terre, à l'éclosion des germes" [in the midst of my confusion I saw rising before me the quasi-sacred grandeur of Oriental prostitution. . . . [The prostitutes] took me back to the most distant age of Africa, to the ritual prostitution of the temples, when the sexual act was a deeply serious thing, a religious act, when love was a terrible ill, and when men thought that the act of reproduction helped the fertility of the earth and the germination of seeds].[42] The connection to the ancient world allows Bertrand to follow his trilogy of Algerian novels with a trilogy of his own Algiers reminiscences, giving his escapades in the red-light district of the upper Casbah all the significance of the gestures of the founders of empire. Frequenting prostitutes, he is as linked to the ancient Roman conquests as the wagon-driver Rafael. By using *Salammbô* to justify France's military conquests, Bertrand can turn hints of his own licencious behavior into archetypal and foundational acts.

In the trilogy of descriptions of Algiers, it is difficult to situate the exact historical moment of Bertrand's wanderings in the Casbah. This confusion of timing adds to the uncertainty about the probable goals of these excursions, although the narrator seems amply to demonstrate that an architectural walk can turn into an excursion to the brothel (or vice versa), regardless of one's age or position in historical time. As the monuments visited give way immediately to disparaging remarks on the remaining Islamic architecture in the neighborhood, some ambiguity creeps in: is Bertrand speaking of his first trip to Algiers, or of his latest? The Casbah's appearance would have deteriorated considerably in the years between those visits. The uncertainty persists when he attempts to specify what moment of the history of Algiers he will try to describe. To do so, he cites approvingly a long passage from the beginning of Eugène Fromentin's *Une année dans le Sahel*, to say that it described the city correctly "au lendemain de la conquête" [in the days following the conquest]: "Ce charme, je l'ai senti toujours vivante, quarante ans plus tard, en 1891, lorsque pour la première fois j'ai débarqué à Alger. Certes, à cette époque-là, la ville barbaresque était déjà à moitié détruite. Mais il en subsistait encore des fragments assez intacts, pour permettre une imagination avertie de la reconstituer tout entier. C'est cette ville à peu près disparue que je voudrais essayer d'évoquer." [I sensed this charm still alive forty years later in 1891, when for the first time I landed in Algiers. Granted, the Barbary city was already half-destroyed at that time. However, fragments of it sub-sisted intact enough to allow an experienced imagination to reconstitute it whole. It is this city which has almost disappeared that I would like to try to evoke.][43] Again, the text leaves some confusion about which city "à peu près disparue" he means. It could be that of 1891, which he assures his readers was very different from the contemporary capital of 1938, or that of Fromentin in 1852, very different from either of the others; or again it could be the precolonial city mourned by Fromentin, but that Bertrand seems to think he can approach via his predecessor's descriptions. This last assumption should give pause; Fromentin constantly regretted that when he arrived on what Bertrand calls the "le lendemain de la con-quête," twenty years had already passed between the time of his arrival and the year (1831) the Army engineers began clearing the Place du Gou-vernement. Which version of old Algiers should the partisans of *l'Afrique latine* admire?

The answer may well be none of the above; though Bertrand would probably have appreciated the question, he would surely have found our historical scruples misplaced. In fact, historical precision matters little to Bertrand when he speaks of the Casbah, since its slowly disintegrating ur-ban fabric represented neither classical Latin remnants nor neo-Latin prowess.[44] For him, the precolonial architecture of Algiers and its ruins ex-isted unchanged through time; his constant switching of verb tenses, from imperfect to present and back again, seems to indicate that whatever vis-itors had seen forty (or eighty) years before, they could still see in the 1930s. The worthwhile remnants subsisted, because for Bertrand's Latin Africa, the architectural productions of colonial Algeria simply deserved far more recognition than anything the Army had knocked down.

Bertrand and writers who followed him used these two points of archi-tectural appreciation to distinguish their literature and the view of Alger-ian history it espoused from those of the nineteenth-century travel writ-ers they pejoratively called "exotes." According to the preface of a 1937 anthology of French North African writing, "les écrivains de l'Afrique du Nord ont cessé d'être des passants, des touristes, des visiteurs pressés. . . . [Ils] ont longuement habité le pays, jusqu'à se sentir plus Africains qu'Européens. Beaucoup y sont nés et voient en lui leur vraie patrie" [the writers of North Africa have ceased to be passersby, tourists, and hurried visitors. . . . They have lived in the country for a long time, long enough to feel more African than European. Many were born there, and see in it their true country].[45] With this stronger personal identification with the country came a reordering of priorities. For Bertrand and his contempo-raries, the nineteen-century exoticists had wrongly concentrated their at-tention on the Arabs and Berbers, at the expense of those who really de-served remark: the *colons*. Anti-exoticist fulminations, along with those of the subsequent writers inspired by him who gathered under the label of Algerianists, at times even seem to constitute the defining feature of the movement. The Algerian-born Robert Randau, himself author of twenty novels set in colonial Algeria and West Africa, criticized exoticist literature as written by and for tourists: "L'exotisme à l'ancienne mode, tel que l'entendent les littérateurs d'escale, n'est qu'un décor" [exoticism in the old style, as the stop-over writers understood it, is just a decor].[46] Bertrand himself would say that "il faut bien commencer par l'avouer: ce que nous aimons dans le vieil Alger est quelque chose de passablement factice, 'littéraire', au sens défavorable du mot. Pour nous, ces vieux logis mauresques et le peuple aux costumes bariolés qui les habite, c'est du décor et de la figuration" [we had better begin by admitting that what we like in old Algiers is something fairly artificial and "literary," in the pejorative sense of the word. For us, these old Moorish dwellings and the people with multicolored costumes who inhabit them, are scenery and extras].[47] Working against this decor, Bertrand had made his name with the dramas of Algeria he found truly interesting, those of the farmers, wagon drivers, hunters, soldiers, and shopkeepers who were (re)building the *Afrique latine* he so admired. "Ce qui est indigène est souvent absolument quelconque" [that which is *indigène* is often entirely unremarkable], he declared, speaking specifically about architecture, but also attacking broadly the purveyors and consumers of exoticism.[48]

Bertrand's novels, many have noted, bear out this aesthetic: as "entirely unremarkable," the Arabs and Imazighen are simply banished from their pages. Speaking as both tour guide and literary critic, he informs us that "Ce qui m'intéresse avant tout dans ce pays, c'est ce que nous en avons fait. Le colon d'abord, l'indigène ensuite . . . je veux que la première pensée du Français qui débarque devant les quais monumentaux de cette belle et grande ville soit une pensée de gratitude et de piété envers ceux qui ont donné leurs forces, leur argent et leur sang pour mettre debout cela!" [What interests me above all in this country is what we have made of it. The *colon* first, and the *indigène* second . . . I want the first thought of a French person landing at the monumental docks of this large and beautiful city to be one of gratitude and piety toward those who gave their strength, their money, and their blood in order to build this!][49] This remark serves as a guide to both Bertrand's novels and his vision of Algiers: he was not only the first to concentrate on the European population of the colony, but also one of the first (and very few) authors to admire the architecture of "Orleanist Algiers," the constructions of the July Monarchy almost universally reviled by observers before and after him, as the very opposite of the exotic appeal many expected to find in Algiers.[50] Exoticism and its regrets, Bertrand believed, must be banished in favor of nationalist and imperialist pride in accomplishment. Roland Lebel, theorist of colonial literature and Bertrand's contemporary, dismissed exoticism as "plus romantique que coloniale. Exotisme s'oppose à colonialisme comme romantisme s'oppose à naturalisme" [more romantic than colonial. Exoticism is opposed to colonialism as romanticism is opposed to naturalism].[51] If in this pronouncement Lebel seems to have created a new literary school called *colonialisme*, he is perhaps only extrapolating, for the sake of inclusiveness, from Bertrand and Randau's *Algérianisme*. His critiques generalize the ideologies of Algerian literature for use in every portion of the globe then occupied by France. Lebel also suggests at least an analogy between colonialism and literary naturalism, both phenomena that, according to a rhetoric of progress, superseded their predecessors.

Despite the proclaimed opposition to exoticism of the new colonial(ist) literature, Bertrand had not yet finished either with it or romanticism. His ideas on the persistence of the cult of Tanit and the purity of ritual prostitution had already betrayed his views. His tone in describing the monuments and ruins of early colonial Algiers clearly echoed that of writers like Fromentin, speaking of the visible remnants of the Moorish city: "Dans ce plus vieil Alger, il y a un Alger orléaniste, qui, certes, n'a pas la grandeur ou le style des choses anciennes, mais qui touche et qui plait, par une sorte de charme suranné, un air provincial et créole,—un Alger romantique et bourgeois, qui rappelle à la fois *Les Orientales* et le roi citoyen." [In this oldest Algiers, there is an Orleanist Algiers which admittedly does not have the grandeur or style of the ancient city, but which touches and pleases the viewer with a sort of superannuated charm and a provincial and Creole look: a romantic, bourgeois Algiers which recalls at the same time *Les Orientales* and the citizen-king.][52] This sort of nostalgia, alluding to Hugo's famous poems of 1830, would have revolted Bertrand if applied to the upper Casbah by a tourist. Algiers, for him, recalls nothing truly "Oriental," but rather the people for whose nostalgia *Les Orientales* so eloquently spoke. Nostalgia remains the affective mode of colonial history. Bertrand admires the *charme suranné* of what he calls *"ce plus vieil Alger"*; what could inspire more nostalgia than buildings and people long outdated? Nonetheless, he also continues his rewriting of urban and colonial history in a well-trodden direction, effacing the record of precolonial periods: his "oldest" Algiers is the Marine neighborhood, the lower Casbah completely gutted and rebuilt between 1830 and 1850, rather than the upper Casbah, much less affected, and with an indisputably longer historical pedigree. Bertrand has simply changed the object of nostalgia, moving it forward about twenty years, from the unhistoricized and amorphous precolonial period to the historically situated past of the 1840s.

The precolonial period remains not only fuzzily defined but also culturally unproductive for Bertrand, as he had already suggested in the preface to *Le Sang des races.* For him, there exists nothing at all genuinely Arab; all attempts at capturing this chimera, he believes, result in insipid "local color." Instead, Bertrand will tell the story of the brave young men risking their lives on the wagon tracks of the Hauts Plateaux and the desert, men of action building and serving the infrastructure of a new country. Nothing could appear more virile, or more inexorably bound for Progress. *Le Sang des races,* however, was not Bertrand's last word on colonial life in the Algerian south, the endlessly inspiring setting for heroism. He would return there at least metaphorically on his last literary excursion in North Africa, a circuitous trip from Algiers to Fez. With deepening nostalgia, he views his former haunts: "A Boghar même, je ne reconnais plus l'antique auberge des rouliers, où je m'arrêtais lors de mes voyages à Laghouat et qui s'appelait déjà pompeusement: Hôtel Baptistin. A présent, c'est l'Hôtel des Hespérides. La littérature s'y met. Tout y a été bouleversé pour satisfaire les goûts d'une clientèle nouvelle: chauffeurs, mécaniciens, employés de chemin de fer." [In Boghar itself, I no longer recognized the old wagoneers' hotel where I stopped on my trips to Laghouat, and which was already pompously called the Hôtel Baptistin. Now it's the Hôtel des Hespérides. Literature has gotten involved. Everything has been turned upside down to satisfy the tastes of a new clientele: drivers, mechanics, and railway employees.][53] These modern-day wagoneers cannot approach the glory of the Algerian pioneers on the southern roads. Worse, literary exoticism has penetrated the public taste, to the degree that hotel owners name their establishments after mythical gardens, with the overall effect of spoiling part of the country.

On the same road, Bertrand does not so much discover Roman ruins as build them; on the already fading memories of heroic French Algeria, he fabricates vestiges worthy of Empire. Whereas the ruins Fromentin had admired and regretted in Laghouat were created by the conquest itself, Bertrand's ruins date from a moment of colonial history he found at least as inspiring as Fromentin's precolonial desert town: "A Bougzoul, il ne reste plus que le portail d'un de ces vieux caravansérails; de loin, on dirait une ruine romaine. C'était peut-être le plus ancien de toute la route. Autant qu'il me souvienne, il datait de 1853. Je vois encore le millésime au-dessus de la porte. On avait dû en commencer la construction presque immédiatement après la prise de Laghouat. . . . A l'époque de mes premiers voyages, la sécurité était parfaite, de sorte que ce caravansérail fortifié était déjà un anachronisme." [All that remains in Bougzoul is the gate of one of these old caravanserais; from a distance, one would say it was a Roman ruin. It was perhaps the oldest of the entire route. As far as I recall, it dated from 1853. I can still see the date above the door. They must have started building it almost immediately after the taking of Laghouat. . . . At the time of my first trips, there was complete security, so this fortified caravanserai was already an anachronism.][54] North Africa was visibly covered with genuine Roman ruins; though the best-preserved of these appear in Tunisia, French Algerians could go into transports over the impressive remains at Cherchell and Tipasa. North African antiquarianism began early in the colonial period with Louis Adrien Berbrugger's publication of *Algérie historique, pittoresque et monumentale* [Historic, Picturesque, and Monumental Algeria] (1843), and continued into Bertrand's time with a large body of work published in the first decades of the twentieth century in the *Revue d'Alger* by historians like Stéphane Gsell.[55] Bertrand has found the caravanserai he naively set out to Algeria to find at the age of twenty, with visions of the *1001 Nights* in his head, as he had explained in the preface of *Le Sang des races*. On this last trip, however, his site turns out to be a remnant of a French building already anachronistic when he had first seen it. Despite, or perhaps because of, this anachronism, the ruin concretizes and consecrates France's colonial inheritance as a Latin empire.

LATIN AFRICA AND ITS CRITICS

To circle back to Algiers with Bertrand, we see that after forty years of visits, he was well placed to give that modern city, disdained by his predecessors, the history he claimed it deserved. The first two essay collections of his Algiers trilogy coincide both with the centenary of the French conquest and with the publication of René Lespès's enormous thesis on the city's history.[56] Bertrand may have invented spurious "Roman" ruins for his own ideological purposes, but he also perceived some newer elements of Algiers as worthy of historical regard, not to say nostalgia. Many Algerian towns, he says, "ont déjà pris de l'âge, et avec l'âge, un certain caractère: ils datent déjà, ils ont une couleur et une physionomie archaïques, quelque chose qui annonce l'entrée prochaine dans le passé et dans l'histoire. Bientôt il en sera de ces villes d'Algérie comme des villes de l'Amérique du Sud, où l'historien et l'archéologue peuvent étudier les époques du style colonial espagnol" [have already aged, and with age, have acquired a certain character. They are already dated, and have an archaic color and physiognomy, something predicting their entry, soon, into the past and history. Soon theses cities of Algeria will be like those of South America, where the historian and archaeologist can study the periods of Spanish colonial style].[57] Bertrand accurately predicted the future interests of historians of North Africa, though he could scarcely have foreseen their concentration on the way early French urban design in the colony pushed aside the needs (or even the existence) of the preexisting population. Despite the undeniable merit in giving a history to previously ignored or despised urban changes, Bertrand's enormous blind spot for everything having to do with the Muslims' existence made him unable to account for large portions of the colony's history.

Amazigh and Arab writers understood very well the implications and subtext of Latin Africa, and criticisms of Bertrand appeared repeatedly in their press. A polemical article by Bertrand in the *Figaro* in 1926 gave Ferhat Abbas, the pharmacist turned proto-nationalist political leader, occasion to respond with an indictment of French historical pretensions in general and Bertrand's conception of North Africa in particular: "Lorsque l'Occidental, déjà d'une mentalité si différente de la nôtre, est un Louis Bertrand qui n'a jamais rien compris à l'Islam, sa prétention de vouloir enseigner aux peuples leur propre histoire et à dicter à l'humanité son code et sa loi devient d'un comique violent." [When the Westerner, who already has a mentality very different from ours, is someone like Louis Bertrand who has never understood a thing about Islam, his pretension to want to teach a people its own history and to dictate his code and law to humanity become wrenchingly comical.][58] Abbas bases his opposition to the claims of Latin Africa on a glorification of the Islamic conquest, an effective place, in the twenties, from which to contest Bertrand's characterization of Algerian history.[59] Abbas had never minced words about Latin Africa; a few years earlier he had declared that "Évidemment les collaborateurs de M. Louis Bertrand sont des gens fort habiles. Il semble donc malaisé de contredire en eux cette vieille culture Greco-Latine. Cependant je le fais. La vérité n'a pas de patrie et n'a jamais eu besoin, en effet, de tant de littérature pour s'imposer, car le beau langage n'abuse que les imbéciles et les niais" [Obviously M. Louis Bertrand's collaborators are very clever people. It would thus seem difficult to contradict them about this old Greco-Latin culture. Nonetheless, I do. The truth has no country, and has indeed never needed so much literature in order to establish itself, since fancy language deceives only imbeciles and dolts].[60] Abbas's critiques of Bertrand appeared first in a vigorous political editorial on an incident of drunken rowdiness at Jemmapes, blamed on *indigène* students, and later in a tract demanding parity of military obligations for all residents of Algeria regardless of ethnicity. In both their formulations and their publishing contexts, Abbas's arguments demonstrate his recognition of the political nature of Bertrand's project, and his realization that it demanded above all political and historical refutation.

Algerians of ostensibly Latin origins did not necessarily speak more kindly, especially if they saw where Bertrand's politics placed him. Of Bertrand's 1930 novel, *Le Roman de la conquête*, which glorifies the right-wing opportunist General de Bourmont, leader of the 1830 expeditionary force, a reviewer in the centrist *Annales africaines* wrote: "Pour M. Louis Bertrand, Bourmont avait une haute conception de l'honneur. . . . Opinion

que l'on peut discuter, comme d'autres du même romancier aventuré parfois et assez fâcheusement, dans l'Histoire. Ainsi, M. Louis Bertrand affirme que, depuis les Romains, l'Afrique du Nord a toujours été latine. Il
fait simplement abstraction des invasions arabes et de l'occupation
turque! Aujourd'hui, il malaxe de nouveau une science qui, sous sa plume
deviendrait certainement conjecturale tant elle semble convenir à
l'extrême droite." [For M. Louis Bertrand, Bourmont had an elevated conception of honor. . . . This is a debatable opinion, like others ventured,
sometimes rather unfortunately, by the same novelist regarding history.
Thus M. Louis Bertrand insists that since the Romans, North Africa has always been Latin. He simply discounts the Arab invasions and the Turkish
occupation. Today he is once more working over a science that in his
hands will probably become entirely conjectural, since it suits the far
Right so well.][61] Though *Annales africaines* routinely attacked Communists
with even greater vigor, its reviewer commented ironically on Bertrand's
"unexpected good luck" in succeeding Barrès in the Académie Française.
Bertrand would supplement this good fortune through his own political
writings. Despite his adamantly anti-German *Le Sens de l'ennemi*, his 1936
polemic entitled *Hitler* helped cast some doubt even in the mind of his
postwar hagiographer Maurice Ricord about possible collaboration during the Occupation, though Bertrand's death in 1941 precluded any official accusations.[62]

During Bertrand's lifetime, other critics retained the objection to his
blindness to the Muslims, while avoiding commentary on his rightist politics. The great majority of the Algerianist literature which followed
Bertrand's novels in the 1920s and 1930s would be procolonial virtually
by definition and, to varying degrees, right-wing. The Algerianists' stated
goals, however, did not include furthering fascism in France. Rather, they
aimed to promote all aspects of the colony, including portrayals of the colonized, the people who continued to interest French readers most. In this
regard, Algerian colonial authors following Bertrand moved in the same
direction as the growing colonial schools of literature elsewhere in the
empire. Colonial writers, most newspaper critics at the time agreed,
should contribute to an understanding and informed view of the colony
they represented: the pair of colonial novelists who wrote under the pseudonym of Marius-Ary Leblond subtitled their 1929 *Anthologie coloniale*
"Pour faire aimer nos colonies" [To make our colonies loved].[63] In his preface to the critic Eugène Pujarniscle's 1931 study of colonial literature,
Pierre Mille attacks the writers he blames for having discredited the
colonies around the turn of the century; more recent authors, he says
approvingly, have acquitted themselves better of their political and promotional responsibilities. In case a reader missed which school his pref-
acer had meant, Pujarniscle insisted repeatedly that the guilty were the

exoticists.[64] Bertrand's followers could disagree with his premises regarding Latin Africa while still approving his fight against literary exoticism.

Bertrand's denunciations of exoticism reached an impressive height in his own perceptive preface to one of the very first anthologies of North African writing, *Notre Afrique* [Our Africa] (1925).[65] Here Bertrand pursues an analysis that ironically, no one would phrase so forcefully again until the work of Edward Said in the 1980s, albeit from a political perspective diametrically opposed:

> Le romantique ou l'exotique semble dire à l'étranger, "Je ne sais rien de vous, ni de votre pays, ni de votre histoire, mais cela m'est égal. Et même je ne veux rien savoir. . . . Je professe même que, moins je saurai de vous, mieux cela vaudra pour ce que j'entends faire de vous. Vous n'êtes pour moi que de la couleur et des lignes, des silhouettes pittoresques et émouvantes, que je vais essayer de fixer par le pinceau ou par la plume. Que vous le vouliez ou non, vous allez poser devant moi. Et surtout gardez-vous bien de déranger ou de démentir l'image que je me suis faite de vous. Je vous vois d'une certaine façon. Vous serez tels que je vous vois, ou vous ne serez point.

> [The romanticist or exoticist seems to say to the foreigner, "I know nothing about you, your country, or your history, and I do not care. In fact, I do not want to know anything. . . . I even profess that the less I know of you, the better, for what I plan to make of you. For me, you are only color and lines, picturesque moving silhouettes that I will try to pin down with the brush or the pen. Whether or not you wish, you will pose for me. And above all do not disturb or deny the image I created of you for myself. I see you in a certain way; you will be as I see you, or you will not be at all.][66]

Bertrand's exoticist operates in complete disregard for the point of view—and necessarily for the history and national reality—of the people he portrays, much the way the "Orientalist," in Said's view, ignores anything that does not coincide with his project to fix, diminish, and "orientalize" his subject (or rather, his object). The exoticist authors or painters skewered here might in many cases be the same people as Said's artistic Orientalists. Of course, one detail suffices to make Said's and Bertrand's uncannily similar indictments diverge radically: the putative interlocutor of those they criticize. Rather than accusing the exoticists of addressing the Arabs or Imazighen of Algeria in this way, Bertrand accuses them of addressing their intolerable remarks to the country's European inhabitants. The colonizers, not the colonized, suffer misrepresentation of "their" country by exoticism. Ultimately, as we have seen, Bertrand does not care how writers represent the colonized, as long as they show them to be inferior to the Latins; this same preface contains a virulent attack on those who, in their exoticist delusions, seem to him to do the opposite. Despite the inclusion of the novelist and short-story writer Abdelkader Hadj

Hamou, the anthology does little to conceal the strength of anti-*indigène*
feeling among many of its authors. The collection even includes a story
entitled "Le Bicot" [The Wog] portraying a young Arab raised in France
who reveals himself an insensitive brute under his suave exterior.[67] The
antiexoticism of this portrayal of Algeria has no intention of redressing
the grievances of misrepresented Arabs and Berbers, since the new writers did not conceive of them as exoticism's injured party but instead as its
undeserving beneficiaries. In this view, exoticism's victims were in fact
the *colons*; only they merited a history and an agency of their own.

The most visible colonial *littérateurs* of the first twenty years of the century seem to have at least paid lip service to the ideal expressed in the
Leblond anthology subtitle, "faire aimer nos colonies." This ideal was
subject to a wide variety of personal interpretations. Although Bertrand
maintained his devotion to *l'Afrique latine* until his death in 1941 (and as
we have seen, continued to write vigorous prose in its favor throughout
the thirties), other writers tended to de-emphasize the *latine* in favor of
l'Afrique. The colony's image of itself might appear to have become
slightly more inclusive of the colonized, at least on paper, and apparently
in stone as well. As nearly always happened, architecture and urban design conveyed the intimations of change in the colony's self-image and
also provided the site for arguing about those changes. While Bertrand
looked on with scarcely veiled disapproval, the twenty-five years leading
up to the centenary of 1930 saw the emergence and flourishing of *arabisance*, the most distinctive and creative architectural style to emerge in the
North African colonies. At that point it had been twenty years since he
had produced a major work of fiction, and he was fully engrossed in
mythologizing his own career in his fictionalized memoirs and reminiscences on Algiers.[68] When officials in Paris and Algiers drew up the guest
list for the commemorative visit of President Doumergue to the colony,
they did not invite Louis Bertrand.[69] Algeria's self-image had moved on,
as demonstrated by its architectural productions, in a direction of which
Bertrand openly disapproved.

BUILDING A RETURN TO ROOTS

In its origins in turn-of-the-century Tunisia, the *arabisance* style of decor
essentially consisted of attaching "Arab" architectural elements and decorations to virtually any public building. The Hôtel de Ville and Palais de
Justice in Sousse displayed rows of horseshoe-arched windows with intervening columns, fluted domes, and crenelated roof lines, giving these
buildings decidedly Turkish-looking exteriors, while coffered ceilings
with carved and painted geometric designs and incised plaster panels on

the walls completed the surprisingly rich decor inside. Other constructions in Tunisia in the same period went further to appropriate the minaret, the defining feature of the mosque (and, for some, of all Islamic architecture). Ministries, post offices, train stations, and even casinos suddenly sprouted highly decorated (and of course purely ornamental) minarets in a variety of forms; the Belvédère Casino of Tunis had a campanile surmounted by a finial with a regulation crescent ornament, as if to emphasize the provenance of the design.

As for Algiers, two factors distinguished the city of 1930 from the young Bertrand's city of 1891: its radical population growth and its architecture. Visitors noted the first in the suburbs, just beginning to spread, with the first shantytowns appearing around the centenary year itself. The second type of change occurred most evidently in the very center of town. The city of Algiers had perhaps 60,000 inhabitants before the conquest, and at various moments during the subsequent century, the Arab and Amazigh population may have fallen as low as 20,000. The conquest had razed or deconsecrated some thirty mosques in the old city of Algiers, and the subsequent draining and replacement of the Muslim population by the Christian had hardly encouraged building more.[70] Citizens might thus reasonably have been surprised, around 1910, at the sight of minarets reappearing in their city. They could have been all the more nonplussed to see these nonfunctional copies of mosque architecture, together with their domes and keyhole-arch portals and windows, proliferating not in the Casbah but in the middle of the most active French-built commercial areas, on the Boulevard de la République and the Rue d'Isly, and around the Rue Michelet and the Boulevard Lafferière. The Nouvelle Poste, completed by the architect Jules Voinot in 1910, had two small domes crowning its facade, and a row of keyhole-arches and short columns across the upper story. (See figure 1.2.) The new Préfecture, facing the harbor, looked remarkably similar, capped with *koubbas*, as did the *Galeries françaises*, the department store on the rue d'Isly: more short columns, domes, and carved portals. A bit further south on the boulevard Laferrière, at the headquarters of the daily *Dépêche algérienne* (see figure 1.3), there could be no doubt. The square corner tower had several sets of arched windows and a campanile and finial on top, ornamented with spheres: neither more nor less than a Maghribi minaret.[71] Some residential construction in the suburbs followed suit, in a vogue which, according to the architectural historian of Algiers Jean-Jacques Deluz, seems to have crested before 1930.[72] Despite some incongruities, this *arabisance* style produced some of the most striking architectural decoration in the colony. Several decades after the fashion had passed, a newspaper columnist in Algiers identified the period of *arabisance* as the *belle époque* of his city, crediting it with exactly the right mix of innovative design and respect for the local pictur-

Figure 1.2. Algiers, la Grande Poste. Voinot, architect, 1911. Fonds documentaire Editions J. Gandini.

Figure 1.3. Algiers, headquarters of the daily *Dépêche algérienne, at left.* Fonds documentaire Editions J. Gandini.

esque.[73] What was causing the return of traditional Arab architecture, or at least of details inspired by it, to the modern colonial city?

A variety of cultural exigencies caused this marked change in public architecture. In tracing it to the Arab countries' pavilions at Expositions Universelles as far back as 1867, Zeynep Çelik accounts for its forms; even at the time, writers noticed the similarity between the new public buildings and the overwrought kitsch of exposition halls, and some even voiced complaints about it. However, as Çelik herself suggests, the social ideologies behind changing architectural styles were a good deal more complicated than a desire to make striking public buildings, even though the *arabisance* style did produce some of the most remarkable structures in colonial North Africa.[74] As Tunisian architects led by Robert Guy, designer of the Sousse buildings, pursued their study and practice of local details, a group of Algiers intellectuals led by Henri Klein were forming the *Comité du Vieil Alger* [Old Algiers Committee], explicitly adding historic preservation to the *arabisance* program.[75] Klein's first article in the *Dépêche algérienne*, "Pour la survivance d'El-Djezair," appeared in December 1903 (before the paper had moved into its minareted headquarters) and set the tone for the committee's later activities. The committee, actually formed two years later, responded to the longstanding sentiment among artists and writers that too much of Arab Algiers (Al-Jazā'ir) had disappeared in demolitions and neglect. If only they had started their work fifty years earlier, lamented Klein, "Que de choses charmantes auraient été en effet conservées en cette ville pittoresque, que notre civilisation eut tant de hâte, jadis, de réduire en poussière . . . ! Légendaire Jenina! jolies Djama au minaret pittoresque, des rues disparues, des quartiers oubliés! patriciennes demeures mauresques dont il ne reste plus que des images en nos musées, que n'a-t-on laissé votre orientalisme sourire dans la féerie de notre gai soleil!" [How many charming things would indeed have been conserved in this picturesque city, which our civilization was in such a hurry to reduce to dust, in the past . . . ! Legendary Jenina! Pretty Djamas with picturesque minarets; streets disappeared, neighborhoods forgotten! patrician Moorish homes of which all that remain are pictures in our museums, why did we not let your Orientalism smile forth in the magic of our gay sunshine!][76] Such regrets for the Djenina palace, razed in 1856, and for the mosques (jam'a) and villas occupied or destroyed since 1830, exemplified perfectly the kind of exoticist nostalgia Bertrand found deleterious. The committee's rhetoric appears as a throwback to the ideas of romantic travelers like Eugène Fromentin and Théophile Gautier, the continuation of a discourse that Bertrand and his friends had never been able to bury completely.

In reality, the committee's discourse included much more than orientalist nostalgia. First, their program included the preservation of French monuments and sites, such as the 1830 expedition's first camp at Sidi Ferruch. Some members saw the committee essentially as a means of perpetuating memories of precolonial European interventions and influence in the Regency; a number of them were mostly interested in projects to find physical evidence of the precedents for the French invasion. For a certain lieutenant-colonel de Grammont, writing to the *Dépêche* in 1905, the time had come for the committee to commemorate Charles V's failed expedition against Algiers in the sixteenth century: "ce sera l'heure d'une solennelle réparation" [it will be the time for a solemn reparation], presumably for earlier forgetfulness.[77]

Second and more importantly, the committee conceived of old Algiers only in its relation with the new. To preservationists today, this might not seem a bad idea, and could in fact represent a sophisticated view of the connections of older elements of the urban fabric to their new surroundings. For the committee, however, this conception contributed instead to a binary view of the built environment: "les termes employés pour caracteriser l'héritage mauresque la définissait comme un ensemble de 'choses indigènes', ou comme des échantillons d''art mauresque'. Cette approche restreignait la notion d'héritage à des fragments isolés, et attribuait au Comité du Vieil-Alger un rôle de promoteur du nouvel Alger." [the terms used to describe the Moorish heritage defined it as a set of 'indigenous objects' or as samples of 'Moorish art.' This approach restricted the notion of heritage to isolated fragments, and attributed to the Old Algiers Committee the role of promoter of the new Algiers.][78] Even Bertrand did not disapprove of keeping some small section of the Casbah artificially preserved for tourists, with the craft shops which should "naturally" congregate there. Thirty years after the *Comité du Vieil Alger* called for the grouping of artisans in a sort of open-air exhibit in the heart of the Casbah, Bertrand suggested the same idea, though on the "periphery" of the Casbah, as if to emphasize yet again how insignificant the Muslims really were. It cost him little to suggest; his phrasing makes clear that in any case he thought it too late to save anything of the Muslims' "civilisation en voie de disparaître" [disappearing civilization].[79]

Rather than content itself with simple preservation, however, the *Comité du Vieil-Alger* took a proactive stance to combat what it saw as the growing banality of public buildings in the capital. This goal, set forth in their "platform" text probably dating from 1905, complemented Gouverneur Général Célestin Jonnart's directives for a new architecture for Algiers. The committee gave itself two missions: to protect what could still be saved and to lay down the historical guidelines for the *arabisance* style, now quasi official (as the architectural historian François Béguin has pointed out, perhaps the only example of an official style in French architecture in the twentieth century).[80] This they did in the course of architectural walks and visits to houses owned by rich French residents and Arab notables; they especially liked the "djenanes" or Turkish-style country houses on the hills of Mustapha Supérieur, south of the city. They reported on their expeditions in *Feuillets d'El-Djezair* from 1905 to about 1910, the period in which the *djenane* would become the source of inspiration for public architecture in the colony for the next twenty years. The space Klein and his friends accorded in their accounts to the uniformly gracious receptions they received from rich Muslim owners on penetrating their private spaces made it clear that the field research from which Algerian *arabisance* emerged participated in the colonial appropriation of space by extending it into private homes.[81]

In the city, Jonnart succeeded in imposing the *arabisance* model on most major monuments built during his terms in office. Three appointments as Gouverneur Général, the revolving-door post considered one of the richest preferments the French government could give a civil servant, allowed him ample opportunity to regulate taste, from 1898 to 1900, 1903 to 1911, and for a brief period beginning in 1919. According to the historian Charles Robert Ageron, Jonnart's *indigénophilie* sufficed to make him suspect to the *colons*; he asserted they must consider "les indigènes comme des collaborateurs . . . nous ne sommes pas de ceux qui marchent sur les vaincus . . . nous voulons marcher à coté d'eux, fraternellement" [the *indigènes* as collaborators . . . we are not the sort of people who walk over the vanquished . . . we want to walk alongside them, fraternally].[82] In fact, Jonnart changed very little in the administration's treatment of the colonized, and his terms in office coincided with the origins of two institutions solidifying *colon* control in the colony and blocking reform from even the most determined and liberal governors: the *Délégations financières* (an assembly created in 1898 and elected by the colony's French citizens) and the special budget for the colony, instituted in 1903. To many observers, Jonnart's *indigénophilie* came down to his taste for *arabisance* as the regional architecture most appropriate to the colony and most conciliatory to the Muslims.[83]

Whatever their views of the new architecture, travel writers and novelists alike agreed that the image it projected was of critical importance. Most brief visitors admired the new monuments; Voinot's palatially decorated Grande Poste attracted special attention in Antoine Chollier's guide of 1929, with its "style mauresque extremement bien équilibré et qui mérite de retenir l'attention du touriste" [extremely well-balanced Moorish style, which deserves the tourist's attention]; in this case, the attention of a traveling novelist who had nonetheless previously characterized the Mediterranean as "plus latine qu'orientale" [more Latin than Oriental].[84] The colony, for some, became the place of magnificence in modern public architecture "à quoi nous ne sommes guères habitués . . . en France" [which we are scarcely used to . . . in France].[85] Other writers thought more abstractly about what tourists wanted in coming to Algeria, to conclude that while neither Louis-Philippard architecture nor aggressive modernization did anything for the colony's image, *arabisance* served Algeria's public relations needs admirably well. In the monthly *Terre d'Afrique illustrée*, Gabriel Audisio warned in 1929 that "ce que les touristes viennent chercher à Alger, ce ne sont pas les puissances du port, mais la Kasbah, qui sent la chèvre et le jasmin, comme dit Jean Cocteau,— ce n'est pas la race néolatine chère à Louis Bertrand (et d'autres que je sais), mais les Arabes" [what tourists come looking for in Algiers is not the capacity of the port, but the Casbah, which smells of goats and jasmine, as Jean Cocteau says; it is not the neo-Latin race dear to Louis Bertrand (and to others I know), but the Arabs].[86] In a single article, Audisio rates both architecture and literature according to how well they do the job of attracting tourists; though elsewhere he made clear his condemnation of *littérature d'escale*, here he articulates his reservations about the colony Bertrand worked so hard to promote. More than that, however, he confirms the view of critics like Lebel and the Leblonds: colonial literature, like colonial architecture, must take part in the public relations business.

A great deal of the criticism Jonnart's architecture received from Bertrand and writers around him seems at least partly fueled by this sense that it gave ground unduly to the Muslims, and worse, furthered debased exoticist misperceptions of the colony among visitors. The colonial intellectuals' unremitting press campaigns to improve Algeria's image in France probably arose as much from their struggles with a suspicious metropolitan press and parliament, as from any colonial bad conscience. In any case, they held Algerian architecture to the same standard for public relations as Algerian literature. As we might expect, Bertrand agreed with the premises of this evaluation, only to disagree with its conclusions. In his view, buildings like the Grande Poste did not merit unmitigated condemnation, but they definitely remained suspect. They did promote a colony in North Africa; for Bertrand, however, it was the wrong colony. Predictably, he expressed his reservations for a government policy emphasizing the Muslim heritage of an exotic colony at the expense of the Latin roots of three *départements* of France. He phrased his literary and ideological objections in terms of an architectural critique that was nonetheless far from negligible. He first faulted the designs of a "préfecture qui ressemble à un Eden-théâtre, un bureau central des postes qui à l'air d'un Alhambra de Montmartre ou des Batignolles" [prefecture which resembles an Eden-théâtre, and a central post office which looks like an Alhambra of Montmartre or Batignolles], pointing to what many saw as the ridicule of *arabisance*'s roots in the Expositions universelles and in café-concert kitsch.[87] More bitingly, he also pointed out that Petit's neo-Islamic *madrasa* (religious school; see figure 1.4) visually crushed the Sidi Abderrahman mosque, one of Algeria's best-known genuine Islamic monuments; Petit's building represented the cultural and spatial appropriation of *arabisance* in its most cumbrous expression.

Most important, however, came the public relations question inevitably raised by writers concerned with the colony's reputation: "Et puis enfin il fallait cela [le style arabisant] pour le touriste, qui autrefois pouvait se plaindre qu'Alger manquait de couleur locale. Aujourd'hui, on lui sert, au débarquer, un Orient de la place Clichy, qui est exactement à sa portée et qui satisfait tout son idéal d'exotisme." [They needed the *arabisance* style for the tourist, who could in the past complain that Algiers lacked local color. Today, when he lands, they serve him up an Orient from the Place Clichy, which is exactly within his graps and which satisfies all his exoticist ideas.][88]

We have already heard what Bertrand thought tourists should admire in Algiers; *arabisance*, for him, constituted playing to the masses' bad taste, informed by decades of exoticist literary and architectural kitsch at home. That this taste supposedly developed in France rather than Algeria is important; for many European Algerians, the colony played the role of perpetual victim of misperceptions born and nurtured in France before their

Figure 1.4.   Algiers, the Madrasa, dwarfing the Sidi Abderrahman mosque to the left. Fonds documentaire Editions J. Gandini.

application on the other side of the Mediterranean. The views of arriving French visitors, perceived by colonials as "soft" on the Muslims, constituted only the most widely remarked of these attitudes which residents of the colony found unacceptable. Most colonial novels portraying the newly arrived emphasize their extreme naiveté; they expected dazzling exotic architecture, as Bertrand admitted he himself had in 1891. Worse, these newcomers were perceived as permissive and oversensitive cultural relativists in their dealings with Muslims: in cases where colonial Algerian novels show characters suggesting timid reforms to the most spectacular abuses of the colonized, they always turn out to be new arrivals and soon either change their views or leave the colony. In Bertrand's 1901 novel *La Cina*, for example, the only character to question harsh treatment of farm workers is the sentimental *Académicien* Baptistin Girgois, for whom the narrator has only contempt, and who in any case is only visiting.[89] Charles Géniaux's *Le Choc des races* expresses the changes of view of those who stay: the newly arrived architect Henri hopes to encourage cooperation among workers of all ethnic origins on his projects in Tunisia. He thus treats educated Muslims as equals, to the point of allowing one to court his sister Jeanne.[90] At the novel's climax, Henri inaugurates the *arabisance* palace he designed for the Bey of Tunis at Sidi Bou Said on the very day a jealous Italian murders Jeanne's suitor Chadli as they are visiting the ruins of Carthage. Though the palace marries Arab and European styles very successfully, no such marriage will take place in the flesh on the site of the ruins of Latin Africa. In fact, before his death, Chadli had made it clear to Jeanne that his "Muslim" character remained unchanged despite contact with Europeans; if they married, he would expect her to veil. However much the French "veiled" their architecture with Arab decorations, Géniaux seems to say, they would still fail to penetrate the veil separating them from the Arabs themselves. Despite Jonnart's hopes at least to project an attitude of inclusiveness, architecture would engender no cultural rapprochement.

Pessimism from the likes of Géniaux did not stop highly influential architects and urban planners from trying. *Arabisance* soon fell under the leadership of Henri Prost in Morocco and M. J. Cotereau in Algeria, who would do a great deal to move it beyond the state represented by the Galeries françaises (essentially a department store with a minaret) in the Rue d'Isly. In Lyautey's Morocco, Henri Prost famously reigned over urban planning and architecture for more than a decade during and after World War I and supervised the separation of Moroccan cities into traditional and modern centers separated by walls and wide *non edificandi* zones.[91] He intended to preserve the *medinas*, the old cities, from French incursions, exactly as had not been done in Algeria, but also to provent unwanted mixing of ethnic groups. With Lyautey's blessing, he laid down guidelines for his collaborators that successfully purged *arabisance* of the features that had drawn so much negative comment in Algeria. Prost and Lyautey saw Algiers as an example of how not to build a colonial city, and, perhaps responding to such critiques, the architect M. J. Cotereau began to move *arabisance* beyond the specifically neo-Islamic, to a more generalized Mediterranean style. Cotereau designed no neo-Islamic buildings, but his work in the architectural review *Chantiers nord-africains* classes him among the regionalists, more akin to Prost in his desire to subject form to local requirements, than to Le Corbusier, whose famous "Obus" plans for Algiers demanded that form follow an abstractly conceived function.[92] Like the proponents of *arabisance*, Cotereau wished to preserve the local. His conception of the local, however, diverged from theirs on several points.

Cotereau proposed conserving all the diverse styles he grouped under the rubric of "Mediterranean architecture." In fact, his review of them in a series of articles in *Chantiers* in 1930 works equally well as a review of the literary and historical visions applied to the colony. He indicted the French destruction of Arab houses, calling for their preservation, and in some cases imitation, but he also spent considerable time discussing forms dear to those with other agendas: the Greek temple (without mentioning its pastiche in buildings like the Algiers Santé maritime) and the Roman villa, with its supposed Spanish, Provençal, and Arab derivatives. Cotereau makes the Turkish house derive from Roman architecture, just as the eminent anthropologist Émile Masqueray had attempted to prove (at much greater length, though with little more success) that the Kabyle house inherited its form from a Roman precursor.[93] Bertrand himself had declared that the ideal ancestral form of North African domestic construction lay in the Roman villa; at one point he actually proposed to build a new residential district around the ruins of Carthage, composed of such villas in strict conformity with Roman designs.[94] With Cotereau, the new hybrid *arabisance* no longer rigidly opposed *latinité*. The two styles rather came to constitute complementary projects to sensitize architecture to regional requirements and to occupy more effectively the built space of North Africa.

Startlingly, however, Cotereau's call for the establishment of a Mediterranean architecture, "sous l'égide des races latines" [under the leadership of the Latin races], turns into a call for what he terms "pure form," an "Aryan architecture" opposed to the merely decorative "Semitic architecture."[95] In one sense, Cotereau is even more of a racial purist than Bertrand, since he does not conflate the grandeur of Carthage with that of Rome; for him, Carthage lay irretrievably on the wrong shore of the Mediterranean, and he lumps it with the "Asiatic Semitism" which Aryan designers must always keep in check.[96] Cotereau never advocates complete substitution of "Aryan" forms for "Semitic" decor, and he does value "borrowing from others": the adaptive and regionalist principles behind *arabisance* meet with his approval. Phrases recalling Charlemagne's defeat of the "Semites" at Poitiers, however, and declarations like "soyons Aryens" [let us be Aryans] underline the similarities of Cotereau's position to Bertrand's. Two years after Bertrand's 1936 book on Hitler, in which, referring to the Nuremberg rallies, he regretfully asks "pourquoi ne voit-on rien de pareil chez nous" [why do we see nothing like this at home], Bertrand would praise Mussolini's "Roman" architecture in present-day Libya, a monumental style of which Cotereau would surely have approved.[97] The Italians "ne commettent pas la faute absurde, ils ne se donnent pas l'attitude piteuse de copier humblement l'indigène. Ils cherchent à créer une style impérial qui soit bien à eux, tout en restant bien africaine, et qui, en même temps se rattache à un passé glorieux" [do not make the absurd mistake of taking the pitiable position of humbly copying the *indigène*. They seek to create an imperial style very much of their own, all the while remaining African, and at the same time, linking it to a glorious past].[98] Mediterranean mixing was just a step away from fascist imperial (and racial) purity. Louis Bertrand was one of the most prominent (in the eyes of his contemporaries) of those willing to take that step, and to attach Algerianism to a fascist vision of history. Most other writers of the Algerianist tendency did not, preferring to see Algeria independently of political movements from outside, and situated (both in architecture and in literature) between Franco-Moroccan "indigénophilie" and Italo-Libyan "Latin" imperialism. Nonetheless, many would continue to flirt with the ideas of the French right. While Bertrand helped separate regionalism from its focus on the past, French regionalism helped link colonial Algerianist literature to a conflicted right-wing nationalism, on the level of both the colony and the empire.

NOTES

1. Gabriel Audisio, *Jeunesse de la Méditerranée* (Paris: Gallimard, 1935), 122.

2. Jean Charles-Brun provides such a list in *Les Littératures provinciales, avec une esquisse de géographie littéraire de la France, par M. P. de Beaurepaire-Froment* (Paris: Bloud, 1907).

3. Maurice Barrès, *Scènes et doctrines du nationalisme*, 1902 (Paris: Editions du Trident, 1987), 73, 80. See also Zeev Sternhell, *Maurice Barrès et le nationalisme français* (Paris: Presses de la Fondation Nationale Scientifique, 1972), 283. The characterization of Barrès as "Fondateur du Nationalisme Français" has been repeated often, though not by Sternhell; see, for example, the back cover of the 1987 edition of *Scènes et doctrines du nationalisme*.

4. Sternhell, *Maurice Barrès et le nationalisme français*, 282ff.

5. Eric Roussel, "Préface," in *Maurice Barrès: Romans et voyages*, ed. Vital Rambaud (Paris: Robert Laffont, 1994), lxx.

6. Maurice Barrès, *Les Déracinés*, 1897 (Paris: Robert Laffont, 1994), 502–3; unbracketed ellipsis in the original.

7. Susan Rubin Suleiman, *Authoritarian Fictions: The Ideological Novel as a Literary Genre* (New York: Columbia University Press, 1983), 121–3.

8. Ibid., 123–4.

9. Barrès, *Les Déracinés*, 553.

10. Ibid., 554.

11. Ibid., 555.

12. Peter Dunwoodie, *Writing French Algeria* (Oxford: Clarendon Press, 1998), 106–7.

13. Louis Bertrand, *Les Villes d'or. Algérie et Tunisie romaines* (Paris: Arthème Fayard, 1921), 5.

14. Maurice Barrès, *L'Appel au soldat*, 1900 (Paris: Robert Laffont, 1994), 910.

15. In 1875, Numa Fustel de Coulanges published the first volume of his *Histoire des institutions politiques de l'ancienne France*, which he did not live to complete. Nonetheless, it became, with Hippolyte Taine's *Les Origines de la France contemporaine* (1876), a milestone in the Third Republic's historiographic consciousness.

16. Bertrand, *Les Villes d'or*, 5.

17. Anne-Marie Thiesse, *Ils apprenaient la France: l'exaltation des régions dans le discours patriotique* (Paris: Editions de la Maison des sciences de l'homme, 1997), 1, 4. See also her chapter on responses to the declining birthrate and rural exodus experienced in France in the second half of the nineteenth century.

18. Bertrand, *Les Villes d'or*, 6.

19. Sternhell, *Maurice Barrès et le nationalisme français*, 269.

20. Maurice Barrès, *La Terre et les morts (sur quelles réalités fonder la conscience française)* (Paris: Ligue de la Patrie Française, 1899), 24.

21. As Suleiman puts it, "the last refuge of political losers is self-contemplation"; in the case of Sturel, that self-contemplation aims to make him "de plus en plus Lorrain." See Suleiman, *Authoritarian Fictions*, 132, and Maurice Barrès, *Leurs figures*, 1902 (Paris: Robert Laffont, 1994), 1211.

22. Louis Bertrand, *Un destin: sur les routes du Sud* (Paris: Arthème Fayard, 1936), 71.

23. Louis Bertrand, *Discours prononcés dans la séance publique tenue par l'Académie française pour la réception de M. Louis Bertrand, le jeudi 25 novembre 1926* (Paris: Firmin-Didot, 1926), 23.

24. Louis Bertrand, *Le Sang des races* (Paris: Ollendorff, 1899), 70–71.

25. Barrès, *L'Appel au soldat*, 928–30.

26. Bertrand, *Le Sang des races*, 23–24.

27. Ibid., 28.

28. See the articles entitled "Le sens de l'ennemi" and "La monstrueuse Asie," dated September 1910 and July 1913 respectively, in *Le Sens de l'ennemi* (Paris: A. Fayard, 1917).

29. Bertrand, *Les Villes d'or*, 10.

30. "Work, Family, Fatherland" was Pétain's slogan for Vichy France.

31. Louis Bertrand, *Pépète le bien-aimé* (Paris: Ollendorff, 1904), 3–4.

32. See for example *L'Appel au soldat*, 964, where Roemerspacher responds to Saint-Phlin's traditionalism, which he finds outdated.

33. Louis Bertrand, *La Cina* (Paris: Ollendorff, 1901), x-xi.

34. Bertrand, *Le Sens de l'ennemi*, 22.

35. The other two novels of the trilogy were *La Cina* and *Pépète le bien-aimé*. The latter novel reappeared in 1920, as *Pépète et Balthazar*.

36. Majid El Houssi, "Louis Bertrand et le mythe de la colonisation," *Awal: Cahiers d'études berbères*, no. 16 (1997): 55.

37. Bertrand, cited in Maurice Ricord, *Louis Bertrand l'Africain* (Paris: Fayard, 1947), 89.

38. Louis Bertrand, *Les Nuits d'Alger* (Paris: Flammarion, 1929), 11–12.

39. Following *Nuits d'Alger*, Bertrand published *D'Alger la romantique à Fès la mysterieuse* (Paris: Editions des Portiques, 1930), and *Alger* (Paris: Sorlot, 1938).

40. Bertrand, *Alger*, 59–60.

41. Figures from Farouk Benaita, *Alger: agrégat ou cité: l'intégration citadine de 1919 à 1979* (Algiers: SNED, 1980), 37.

42. Bertrand, *Les Nuits d'Alger*, 46–7.

43. Bertrand, *Alger*, 18.

44. The members of the *Comité du Vieil Alger*, the Algiers historic preservation society, could find discouragingly few physical remnants of Icosium, the city's Roman precursor. See their articles collected in Henri Klein, *Feuillets d'El-Djezair* (Algiers: L. Chaix, 1937).

45. Georges Hardy, "Préface," in *Méditerranée nouvelle: Extraits des pricipaux écrivains contemporains de Tunisie, Algérie, Maroc*, ed. Camille Bégue (Tunis: La Kahena, 1937), 6. Hardy served as Lyautey's director of public education in Morocco.

46. Robert Randau, "La littérature coloniale, hier et aujourd'hui," *Revue des deux mondes*, 15 July 1929, 420.

47. Bertrand, *Alger*, 21.

48. Bertrand, *D'Alger la romantique*, 23.

49. Ibid., 25.

50. Bertrand, *Alger*, 31.

51. Roland Lebel, *Histoire de la littérature coloniale en France* (Paris: Larose, 1931), 86.

52. Bertrand, *Alger*, 31.

53. Bertrand, *D'Alger la romantique*, 85.

54. Ibid., 87.

55. Louis Adrien Berbrugger, *Algérie historique, pittoresque et monumentale. Recueil de vues, monuments, cérémonies, costumes . . . des habitants de l'Algérie*, 3 vols. (Paris: J. Delahaye, 1843). Stéphane Gsell published nearly fifty works on Algeria in antiquity. His *Histoire ancienne de l'Afrique du Nord* (Paris: Hachette, 1913) became the standard work in the field.

56. Lespès provided the first truly comprehensive work on the subject in his thesis, published as *Alger: étude de géographie et d'histoire urbaine* (Paris: Felix Alcan, 1930).

57. Bertrand, *D'Alger la romantique*, 24.

58. Ferhat Abbas, "Les incidents de Jemmapes: Notre infériorité intellectuelle," in *Le Jeune Algérien: de la colonie vers la province* (Algiers-Paris: La Jeune Parque, 1931), 55. Most of the articles collected in this volume appeared originally in the opposition journals *Trait d'Union* and *Attakkadoum* (*Le Progrès*) during the mid-twenties. The title of the collection illustrates one reason why I call the Abbas of 1931 at most a proto-nationalist; here he seems to advocate Algeria's integration into the French nation.

59. Following independence, a new generation of activists and writers, especially Imazighen, would begin to contest a national identity based solely on the Arab conquest. Up to independence, however, the Arab nationalist arguments proved very effective in theorizing the Algerian opposition.

60. "Le service militaire des indigènes algériens," in *Le Jeune Algérien: de la colonie vers la province*, 13, an article written in Constantine in December of 1922 and published in the Communist newspaper *Trait d'Union*.

61. "Une opinion discutable sur un Général factieux et déserteur," *Annales africaines* 42:, no. 2 (15 January 1930): 17.

62. See Maurice Ricord, *Louis Bertrand l'Africain*, appendix, 391. For the critic Daniel-Henri Pageaux, there can be no doubt about Bertrand's Nazi leanings, any more than about his avowed liking of Mussolini ("Le Mirage latin de Louis Bertrand," in *Espagne et Algérie au XXe siècle: Contacts culturels et création littéraire*, ed. Jean Déjeux [Paris: L'Harmattan, 1985], 107).

63. Marius-Ary Leblond was the pseudonym of Georges Athenas and Aimé Merlo; hence the confusing references to them in reviews as both "Leblond" and "les Leblond." The cited phrase appears on the title page of their *Anthologie coloniale, morceaux choisis d'écrivains français* (Paris: Peyronnet, 1929).

64. Pierre Mille, "Préface," in *Philoxène ou de la littérature coloniale*, Eugène Pujarniscle (Paris: Firmin-Didot, 1931), 6.

65. *Notre Afrique, anthologie des conteurs algériens*, preface by Louis Bertrand (Paris: Editions du Monde Moderne, 1925). Some fifty years later, an association of former *Français d'Algérie* in Montpellier would call itself Africa Nostra and publish works of unabashed colonialist nostalgia and historical revisionism.

66. *Notre Afrique*, 4.

67. American English does not have a one-word pejorative for Arabs of anywhere near the venom of the French "bicot": the British "wog," for nearly any Asian, carries a similar nastiness. The story appearing under this title is by the otherwise unknown Marthe Cleuzière.

68. "De fait, 1925 sonne bien pour lui le glas de l'inspiration," says Pageaux in "Le Mirage latin de Louis Bertrand," 107. Pageaux counts Bertrand's substantial later texts on Algiers for rather little.

69. The Algiers *Presse libre* noted and deplored this oversight in an article appearing on 7 May 1930. The archives relating to the commemoration festivities of 1930, conserved at the Archives d'Outre-Mer in Aix-en-Provence, offer no explanation.

70. Klein, *Feuillets d'El-Djezair*, 16ff. Many of the texts assembled in the 1910 collection of the committee's publication (*Feuillets d'El-Djezair*) appear to have been published between 1903 and 1910 either separately or in the daily *Dépêche algérienne*. Klein published another book under the same title (Algiers: L. Chaix,

1937), with texts apparently unpublished elsewhere. Citations without issue numbers refer to the 1937 volume.

71. See the photos for illustrations of several of these buildings. Minarets show great geographical variation in form. Unlike the tall, slim cylinders of the Arabian Peninsula and Persian Gulf, or the pointed-roofed polygons of the eastern Mediterranean, minarets in Algeria, Morocco, and Andalusia are generally stockier, square towers, sparingly fenestrated with small arched windows, with flat tops often ornamented with square campaniles.

72. Jean Jaques: Apergin critique Deluz, *L'Urbanisme et l'architecture d'Alger* (Alger: Pierce Mardaga/Office des Publications Universitaires, 1988), 32.

73. Henri Murat, "Cent années d'urbanisme et de construction," *La Presse libre*, 7 January 1930.

74. See for example the chapters on housing developments in *Urban Forms and Colonial Confrontations* (Berkeley: University of California Press). Chapter 5 and the epilogue of her earlier study, *Displaying the Orient: Architecture of Islam at Nineteenth-Century World's Fairs* (Berkeley: University of California Press, 1992) consider the effects of world's fair pavillions on architecture in Turkey and Algeria.

75. Robert Guy's *L'Architecture moderne de style arabe* (Paris: Librairie de la construction moderne, n.d.) reproduces photographs and plans documenting for the first time (around 1910) a large array of architectural details and decorations in the North African idiom.

76. Henri Klein, *Feuillets d'El-Djezair* (Algiers: Fontana, 1910), no. 1.

77. E. de Grammont, letter in the *Dépêche Algérienne*, 16 January 1905, cited by Nabila Oulebsir in "Discours patrimonial et création architecturalé: le Comité du Vieil-Alger," in *Alger: Une ville et ses discours*, eds. Najet Khadda and Paul Siblot (Montpellier: Praxiling, 1996), 143. The author of the letter was the brother of the historian of Algiers Henri de Grammont.

78. Oulebsir, "Discours patrimonial et création architecturalé," 145.

79. For this miniature "historic district," the committee suggested the Rue Kléber and the Rue d'Anfreville, in the heart of the Casbah; Bertrand suggested those adjacent to the Boulevard de la Victoire on its uppermost edge (Bertrand, *Alger*, 26; and *D'Alger la romantique*, 50). The Comité's project appeared in Klein, *Feuillets d'El-Djezair*, no. 1, 10.

80. François Béguin, *Arabisances*, 34. On the committee's mission, see Oulebsir, "Discours patrimonial et création architecturale."

81. Oulebsir, "Discours patrimonial et création architecturale," 148.

82. Deluz, *L'Urbanisme et l'architecture d'Alger*, 31, citing Charles Ageron, *Les Algériens musulmans et la France*.

83. Victor Trenga's brilliant futurist satire of Algerian politics, *Berberopolis* (1922), has citizens of the "Berber Republic" he imagines for 1962 revering a distant hero, Celestinus Io-nart, proconsul and benefactor to the Berbers; this Io-nart they connect by mythical association with Louis Napoléon, patron saint of government-decreed building projects (*Berberopolis, tableaux de la vie nord-africaine en l'an quarante de la République berbère. Préface posthume d'Eugène Fromentin* [Algiers: Impr. de Rives-Lemoine-Romeu, 1922], 83).

84. Antoine Chollier, *Alger et sa région* (Grenoble: B. Arthaud, 1929), 41.

85. Ibid.

86. Gabriel Audisio, "A Propos d'une concurrence touristique," *Terre d'Afrique illustrée* 139 (January 1930): 12.

87. Bertrand, *Alger*, 140.

88. Bertrand, *Alger*, 140.

89. Bertrand, *La Cina*, 173ff.

90. Charles Géniaux, *Le Choc des races* (Paris: Arthème Fayard, 1923).

91. Prost's influence in Morocco extended far beyond his actual service there, from 1913 to 1923; Lyautey governed the Protectorate from May 1912 to October 1925.

92. Cotereau's name does not figure in François Béguin's founding study of *arabisance*. For a discussion of Le Corbusier's Obus plans in their Algerian context, see Çelik's *Urban Forms and Colonial Confrontations*, 73–78. Several studies in architecture and urban planning treat Le Corbusier's designs for Algiers as idealized abstractions; for example, Michele Lamprakos, "Le Corbusier and Algiers: The Plan Obus as Colonial Urbanism," in *Forms of Dominance: On the Architecture and Urbanism of the Colonial Experience*, ed. Nezar Al-Sayyad (Avebury, UK: Brookfield, 1992), 183–210.

93. Emile Masqueray, *Formation des cités chez les populations sédentaires de l'Algérie*, 1886, introd. by Fanny Colonna (Aix-en-Provence: Edisud, 1983); M. J. Cotereau, "La Maison mauresque," *Chantiers Nord-Africains*, June 1930, 536.

94. Bertrand, *Les Villes d'or*, 105.

95. M. J. Cotereau, "Les Architectures méditerranéennes du passé," *Chantiers nord-africains*, February-May 1930, 117.

96. Ibid., 119.

97. Louis Bertrand, *Hitler* (Paris: Fayard, 1936), 61. Though Bertrand has a few reservations about Nazi street violence, he regrets the lack of unified nationalist spririt in France and justifies Nazi hatred for Jews with the usual argument that the Jews were Communists. Pageaux notes also that Bertrand admired Mussolini, "latinité oblige" ("Le Mirage latin de Louis Bertrand," 107).

98. Bertrand, *Alger*, 143. Bertrand takes the Italian rhetoric on their architecture at face value, while in fact, as the historian Krystyna von Henneberg has shown, the Italians were having trouble achieving the ambitious goals they had set for imperial architecture ("Imperial Uncertainties: Architectural Syncretism and Improvisation in Fascist Colonial Libya," *Journal of Contemporary History* 31, no. 2 [April 1996]: 373–95).

2

✝

Robert Randau and the
Algérianistes' Algeria

Under the pseudonym "Robert Randau," the Algerian-born colonial administrator Robert Arnaud (1873–1950) wrote twenty novels, a topographic "Album" of images and text on Algiers, and several book-length political essays in a career spanning the first forty years of this century. The majority concern the adventures of colonial officials in Afrique Occidentale Française (AOF), where Randau spent a large part of his career in the Haute Volta. He nonetheless devoted a number of novels to Algeria, beginning very early in his career with *Les Colons* [The Colonists] (1907, reissued in 1926), and continuing with *Celui qui s'endurcit* [The One Who Gets Tough] (1913), *Cassard le Berber* [Cassard the Berber] (1926), and *Le Professeur Martin, petit bourgeois d'Alger* (1936).[1] Though he would never actually endorse separatism, he unabashedly defined the *Algérianistes*, a literary school devoted to promoting an Algerian specificity in literature, as those who "désirent que l'Algérie ait son autonomie administrative et financière complète, et préconisent la fusion des races et estiment que l'union des intérêts est avant courrière de celle des coeurs" [want Algeria to have complete administrative and financial autonomy, who advocate racial fusion, and who believe that the union of interests is the precursor to the union of hearts].[2] The Algerianists often paid homage to Bertrand as their inspirer, but broadened considerably his search for the authentically Algerian. As the colony's architecture moved from neo-Islamic *arabisance* to "Mediterranean," its literature moved from an ideology of *latinité* to one of Mediterranean racial fusion. While these intersecting moves would eventually lead to a softening of racial categories in North

African fiction, they would do little to counter ethnic stereotypes. Perceptions of the colony's history and ethnic relations in Algerianist novels would include variations on Bertrand's themes, even as they valorized elements of an Algerian identity significantly different from the one contained in his version of North African history.

A brief sketch of the life-story given by Randau to Jean Cassard, protagonist of *Les Colons* and *Cassard le Berbère*, will help us clarify the colonial history the author advocated. The orphan Cassard descends from a long line of *colons* (just how long will become clear later), and owns, with his sister Romaine, a handsome farm on the coast, complete with its own *bordj* or fort. During his adolescence and studies at the Lycée d'Alger and the École coloniale in Paris (the school which formed administrators for the AOF and other colonies), a lazy relative let the estate run down. Soon after his return to Algeria, Jean and Romaine come into their own and set about rebuilding a plantation, with slow but steady success. Jean meets Hélène Lavieux, a young widow connected to several important *colon* families; he marries her in the same ceremony in which Romaine marries her brother-in-law. The four join Jos Lavieux, Hélène's hard-drinking, patois-speaking, *indigène*-cheating ex-father-in-law, in maneuvers to avert the threat of political assimilation with France. Of the many consequences of assimilation to which they object, they fear two in particular: the loss of Algeria's autonomous budget control and the oversight of uncomprehending French legislators with misplaced humanitarian concerns. With these threats safely averted, the death of the elder Lavieux at the end of the novel positions Jean as a natural political leader of the *colons*.

In *Cassard le Berbère*, Jean Cassard's story takes up again just after World War I, in which he fought bravely and brilliantly at the head of a unit of Berber troops recruited from his estate. Cassard's command in Europe crowned a long series of armed expeditions; the Ministère des Colonies had repeatedly called him away from his farm (where administrative detail bored the man of action) for delicate missions throughout the Sahara and the AOF. In his spare time, moreover, he has written "quelques romans sur la vie réelle en Afrique" [a few novels about real life in Africa].[3] This novel opens as Cassard returns to Algiers as a war hero and retires to his estate. However, an unscrupulous *marabout* inspired by an unlikely mix of Communism and revivalist Islam stirs up violent revolt, and Cassard must turn his farm into an armed camp and lead a campaign to defeat the rebels. This he does with considerable bloodshed among the *indigènes*, amid frequent comments by Jean and other *colon* characters on the administration's ineptitude. In the end, the hero returns to his family, his *bordj*, his books, and his explorer's paraphernalia, to muse on his own "barbarian roots" until, readers understand, his inevitable thirst for adventure strikes again.

We can note a number of striking departures from Bertrand's novels about the early adventurers to whom he attributed the founding of French Algeria. First, although Randau presents few *indigène* characters, he does not write as if Arabs and Imazighen had never existed in or influenced North Africa. His characters identify themselves as "sons of *latinité*," but that in itself does not represent a historical *telos*: they are also "les précurseurs de la grande race méditerranéenne de demain" [the precursors of tomorrow's grand Mediterranean race].[4] Randau provides the beginnings of a discourse on ethnic union, albeit one full of racial slurs, and kept within limits set by the Europeans. Cassard's friendly anarchist neighbor has this to say about the Berber, for example: "Malgré qu'un cochon c'est plus propre qu'eux, ils sont pas refractaires au progrès. Sûr, avec quatre millions qu'ils sont et un million des Algériens français, ça fera un peuple! Et ça sera fini des coyonnades qu'on nous impose de Paris. Les enfants de nous ils verront de belles choses! Merde!" [Even if they's filthier'n pigs, they don't fight progress. Sure, four million of them and one million French Algerians, that'll make a country! And we'll be through with the bullshit they send us from Paris. Damn, our kids'll see great things!][5] Randau's Algerianism, redefined as cultural and financial, if not political, separatism, takes precedence over (some of) the old ethnic prejudices. The text presents Cassard's neighbor as a plain-spoken anarchist, an egalitarian sort with little concern about people's antecedents as long as they are not Communist. His speech demonstrates that stereotypes still underpin even a discourse supposedly more open to the colonized than that of Latin Africa. Prejudice, for these characters, will not go away; self-interest will simply prove stronger. Cassard's earlier phrase about the "union of interests" preceding the "union of hearts" implies receptivity on the part of the *colons* as well as the Muslims.

At this point, we should consider the people Randau's spokesman for unity is evoking: the Imazighen, "les types de montagne" [mountain types] as opposed to the supposedly shiftless Arabs of the plains, figured here as the rabble-rouser Moussi's murdering horde, marching under banners displaying both the crescent and the hammer and sickle, a combination readers are already expected to find nightmarish.[6] The critic Peter Dunwoodie remarks on the graphic violence of Randau's Arab rabble, who readily commit atrocities the moment no French authority prevents it. This effectively justifies the continuing violence of occupation, construing it as punishment, and also "allowed a widespread repressed fear to surface, namely fear of what the settler sees as the deep-seated hostility and hypocrisy of even the most overtly subservient Arab."[7] European Algerians tended to divide the Muslims quite rigidly into two distinct ethnic groups, Berbers and Arabs, and to valorize the first as assimilable and amenable to French rule, while dismissing the second as hopelessly atavistic and immune to evolution. Randau seems to take a cue from Bertrand in seeming to fantasize the erasure of a highly visible cultural group (the Arabs) from Algeria's future, and very nearly from its past as well; however, both the reasons and consequences of this erasure were quite different from Bertrand's. The Arabs represent only an overlay for Randau, one of many invading groups temporarily overshadowing the Berbers, the true Algerians, and, equally important, the true Mediterraneans.

Randau pushes the Mediterranean identification of the Berbers as far as anyone could; the title of his second work makes Cassard himself a Berber. Randau's fantasy hero, the *nec plus ultra* Algerian, represents much more than an "honorary" Berber; he is Berber, in the literal, hereditary sense. A Rabelaisian genealogical chronicle offered to the reader in the prologue details the "faits et discours cassardiques" [deeds and speeches Cassardish] of the family's past eight centuries, revealing that Cassard descends from a Provençal pirate with Kabyle origins. Randau thus traces his dream *colon* family in a circle back to eleventh-century North Africa. The present Cassard therefore merely reclaims the heritage of a seventeenth-century pirate ancestor in returning to the ancestral *bordj* on Kabylia's Mediterranean shore. While this family history may seem to us no more than the author's far-fetched fantasy (one that substitutes an Amazigh Pantagruel for a Latin Salammbô) it has dramatic consequences for the Algerian identity imagined in the text. Randau's move may not diverge fundamentally from Bertrand's, though their respective tones are entirely different. Both authors identify ancient (or at least venerable) precedents for colonization. The Cassard family only recolonized the Kabylia they had previously left in order to settle in southern France; their move is as much a putative return home as that of Bertrand's Latins.[8] In addition, however, Randau provides a historical connection through which he can personify the "African" qualities of Europeans born in the colony. The Leblond preface to *Les Colons* notes that Cassard's story might carry the subtitle "how a race is made."[9] In Randau's view, the process involves Africanizing the Europeans as much as Europeanizing (or eliminating) the Africans. For Bertrand, "tout indigène est un latin qui s'ignore"[every native is a Latin who doesn't know it]; we might say that for Randau "tout colon est un Africain qui s'affirme" [every colonist is an African who confirms it]. If so, we might ask of what their Africanness consists, apart from a fantasized genealogy.

Most visibly, it consists of language. Exoticist writers of both fiction and topographic texts had almost always included a few "local" words derived from the French idea of Algerian Arabic to mark Algeria's difference from France; some (*moukère, kahoua, casbah*) became generic properties marking the colony's topographic literature and fiction, both exotic and locally produced.[10] The theorists of the "new" colonial literature of the first third of the century knew this, but did not always condemn the practice: "l'emploi discrète des mots exotiques est peut-être autorisé et même recommandé. De tels mots localisent un récit, une description" [the discreet usage of exotic words is perhaps admissible, and even recommended. Such words localize a story or a description].[11] Randau does not use exotic speech merely to situate his characters in Algeria; instead, he uses it to ascribe to them a cultural identity and set of political beliefs. Undaunted by the critics' directives to the writer to "s'arranger pour que le mot exotique soit compris" [manage it so that the exotic word is understood], Randau's characters deliver sporadic patois tirades that depend on context to make them (marginally) comprehensible to readers outside the colony.[12] At an Algerianist dinner, for example, Jos Lavieux refuses to serve French wine, but

> du champagne d'Algérie que je fabrique dans mon chai et qui est mousseux numéro ouahad. Et au kahoua, on se coulera entre les gencives la grande fine de plateau de Sersou! Nous sommes entre frères, quoi!
> —Que notre pays s'attache de plus en plus à se suffir à lui-même! Avant tout, soyons des Africains.
> —Hommes de l'Algérie nous n'obéirons qu'aux lois bonnes pour l'Algérie et que nous aurons par avance discutés. Mais la France est une garce chbabe, quand on l'engueule beaucoup on obtient d'elle ce que l'on veut![13]

Patois words like Jos's give Randau a way for virile colonial literature to bawl out the mother country, here figured as a self-centered bitch (*garce*), without going so far as to demand independence from "her." In this passage, the non-Arabic-speaking reader has little trouble determining from the context the meaning of "chbabe" and "ouahad"; the same may not be true for this exclamation: "Il a du culot, le béni kelb! . . . Remémore-toi la froideur avec laquelle ce cahouete et sa smala nous accueillirent à ta prise de fonctions. A cette époque-là notre çof n'était pas au pouvoir." [He's got nerve, the sonofabitch! . . . Remember how coldly that low-life and his rabble welcomed us when you took up your position. Our crew wasn't in power back then.][14] Though "*smala*" ("family," with pejorative overtones) entered the French lexicon with the capture of Abdelkader's *smala* in 1845, several of the other words would have remained opaque for many readers in France. Such passages occur, as if by chance, at moments when characters make their most vigorous political pronouncements; unglossed patois constituted a language of political independence from Paris, in addition to amusing readers in the know and marking difference for readers who are not.

Although patois is the most heavily used linguistic marker of difference in Randau's work, and the one most explicitly represented in the text,

Randau frequently implies that Algerian Arabic, with its heavy admixture of Tamazight, French, and Spanish, lies just under the surface. All his sympathetic characters speak it; and by making the self-proclaimed pro-*indigène* French troublemakers unable to do so, Randau alleges their ignorance of Algerian reality and forces them to abandon the field of knowledge of the Arabs and Amazigh to the *colons*. The archetypal old-time *colon* of the generation which built Algeria's fortune for the French in the 1880s, Jos Lavieux, received the Arabic name Kaddour for his extreme "Arabophilie."[15] Love them he may. Nonetheless, his love for the Muslims follows an essentially feudalist model: an exchange of deference from below for protection from above, predicated on an immutable social hierarchy and a rejection of outside "interference" aimed at introducing more egalitarian arrangements. As the Leblond preface notes, Randau has "l'idée la plus intégrale de l'unité algérienne" [the most solid idea of Algerian unity]; his novels promote this unity through an explicit endorsement of feudalism.[16]

Randau has a curious (though, in his day, not entirely inaccurate) notion of the workings of cooperation between *indigènes* and *colons* when the relationship between them is more equal than that of serf and lord. Both Jos Laveiux and Cheikh Ahmed, a local notable, deal shadily with one another, but they profit most when cooperating to exploit others. In the sequence narrating Jos's death, the old *colon* is travelling companionably with Ahmed to inspect land they have extorted from the peasants who will be unable to prove legally that they own the fields they have worked for centuries: the two are involved in the underhanded dealing which constituted one of the principle tactics in the great Algerian landgrab of the late nineteenth century.[17] Jos falls ill on the trip and dies, after declaring to Ahmed (as if he or the reader needed confirmation) "je suis un Africain; je crée moi-même ma justice; je ne suis ni un fainéant d'Arabe, ni un chien de Maltais, je suis un colon" [I'm an African and I make my own law. I'm neither a lazy Arab nor a Maltese dog, I'm a colonist].[18] Both his Spanish mistress Claudia and his friend Cheikh Ahmed are present at his death and proceed to divide the contents of his wallet between them: "en grande sympathie, pleins d'égards l'un pour l'autre, ils veillent Jos, boivent du café et fument des cigarettes" [with great friendliness, full of consideration for one another, they kept vigil over Jos, drinking coffee and smoking cigarettes].[19] Cooperation between *indigène* and *colon*, or *indigène* and Latin, succeeds beautifully when it involves cheating or petty thievery. These events occur under the benevolent eye of the narrator, who almost encourages the reader to believe that this dubious sort of cooperation built the colony. As the narrator says elsewhere of a young and idealistic administrator in the sub-Saharan colonies who ends up taking a concubine, beating his house boy, and dispensing feudal justice to "his" natives, "il ne s'en porta que mieux" [he was all the healthier for it].[20]

Building the Algeria Randau wishes to see in the future will obviously require more than emptying the wallets of rich old *colons*, though the author, as the Leblond preface notes, never recoils from even the most unsavory aspects of Algeria's foundation. For Randau, say the Leblonds, Algeria is "la terre du Moloch Carthaginoise, de la furie arabe, de Pélissier l'enfumeur des indigènes, des politiciens antijuifs" [the land of the Carthaginian Moloch, the land of Arab fury, of Pélissier the asphyxiator of *indigènes*, and of anti-Jewish politicians].[21] Neither the notorious atrocity of Colonel Pélissier asphyxiating an entire clan hiding in a cave, nor Max Régis's anti-Jewish campaigns in 1898, actually figure in Randau's novel, but to his prefacers, they seem to symbolize the sort of country they saw the Algerianists valorizing. For Randau the country's future nonetheless demands both more benign physical efforts and a certain intellectual attitude from the *colons*, an attitude personified by Cassard: "[il] rumine la composition d'un roman épique sur la grande Berberie, la création d'une revue algérianiste, le groupement en faisceau des activités intellectuelles de son pays; il ne ressemble en rien à un homme de lettres, n'a de jalousie ni de dépit contre personne, gouverne ses fermes et parle d'abondance le français énergique mais d'une souveraine incorrection des Africains. . . . Dans un coin de son bibliothèque est disposé, sur des étagères et des tréteaux, l'arsenal de l'homme du bled; selles, bries, sacoches, fontes, nécessaires, cantines, bidons, gourdes, manteaux, revolvers, trousses d'outils, bottes, chaussures de chasse" [he pondered the composition of a an epic novel about Greater Barbary, the creation of an Algerianist review, and the grouping of his country's intellectual activity in a united front. In no way did he resemble a man of letters, and he had neither jealously nor disdain for anyone. He ran his farms and spoke volubly the energetic French of the Africans, with its haughty disregard for grammar. . . . In a corner of his library, shelves and trestle tables held the arsenal of a man of the bush: saddles, satchels, rucksacks, holsters, canteens, jugs, overcoats, revolvers, toolkits, boots, and hunting shoes].[22] All this manly clutter evokes, as the narrator insists, the active life of his fantasy *colon*, who governs from his fort like Montaigne from his tower, writing, in his spare time, rousing adventure tales set in exotic places. In a French that Cassard twists to assert his Africanness, he plans a truly worthwhile literary project, away from the vain literary squabbles of Paris: a historical novel on "Greater Barbary." By this ambiguous politico-ethnic label, Cassard manages to designate not only the whole of North Africa, from Libya to Morocco, through its original inhabitants (minus its decadent Arab invaders), but also the whole sweep of its history from the ancient Amazigh to the modern-day heroes, namely himself, Cassard le Berbère.

While still retaining the importance of Latin heritage, Cassard's North Africa is "Berber" and "Mediterranean" in a (somewhat abusively) broad sense. An architectural metaphor expresses this historical vision, and as so often happens in Randau, fantasy liberally supplements established historical connections. Cassard's ancestral home, a Berber fortress, occupies the site of a Byzantine (not Ottoman) citadel, which replaced a Roman villa, which replaced a Punic construction, which, finally rests on a site of Neolithic sacrifices. Randau does nothing by half measures. He seems to need a superabundance of architectural coincidences in order to situate Cassard's Hemingway-like mix of fighting, philandering, and philosophizing in a historical context wide enough for it to achieve ideological force. Such a degree of overkill makes readers wonder to what extent he would succeed.

As we know by now, all historical roads in the colony lead to Algiers (a true Rome for others besides Bertrand), and our arrival there as readers of the Cassard's story will let us follow the concrete manifestations of Randau's thoughts on the colony's past and future. Nothing in Randau's city descriptions themselves makes him radically different from his predecessors, and what follows reads like an earthier version of Bertrand's anti-Semitism:

Des boulevards maritimes ils montent vers les rues enjuivées, où déjà tremblotent aux carrefours les jambes frêles des ancêtres d'Israel, sordides guenillards qui clignent de leurs yeux éteints, frappés d'amaurose symptomatique, courbent l'échine, perdent et rattrapent leurs babouches dépenaillées, remuent les babines sur leurs masseters édentés, relèvent leurs bas bleus ou leur turban noir. La racaille pénarde des ghettos grouille sur le trottoir qui pue la friture. Les filles au voluptueux regard se bousculent, mal juponnées, sur les marches gluantes d'escaliers en colimaçon, à la clarté fumeuse d'une lampe kabyle; elles déboulent en piaillant dans les allées qu'encaquent, alignés contre le mur, les petits enfants, contiennent à deux mains leurs seins sans retenue, nouent un foulard ou une fouta autour de leurs hanches molles dont une chemise crasseuse ne dissimule pas l'exubérance; les persiennes claquent ou se rabattent; des lessives louches flottent déjà sur des cordes tendues de fenêtre à fenêtre en travers de la rue.

[From the waterfront boulevards they climbed toward the Jewified streets where the frail legs of the ancestors of Israel already trembled: sordid, ragged old men blinking their amaurotic eyes, bending their spines, losing their tattered slippers and finding them again, working their lips over toothless mandibles, and pushing up their blue stockings or black turbans. The idle scum of the ghetto swarmed on the sidewalk, which stank of frying. Badly pinned-up girls with voluptuous gazes jostled one another on the sticky steps of spiral staircases, in the smoky light of a Kabyle lamp. They piled out squawking into the alleys clogged with little children leaning up against the walls; the girls supported in both hands their overflowing breasts, and knotted a scarf or a towel around their soft hips whose exuberance a filthy shirt did nothing to hide. The

Venetian blinds clattered open and shut, and already dubious laundry flapped on the lines strung from window to window across the street.][23]

The rabid adjective *"enjuivé"* sets the tone for this anti-Semitic outburst, an unusual occurrence in the eroticized Casbah descriptions common in Algerian topographic literature. Bertrand's anti-Semitic passages generally involved other neighborhoods; moreover, most Casbah descriptions stressed the presence of Arabs, not Jews. Here, the description at dawn of the neighborhood (probably just above and behind the Jewish-inhabited Rue de la Lyre) becomes a heavily stereotyped portrait of its inhabitants. Randau sends the Cassards on a classic tourist route, from the French-built Boulevard de la République on the waterfront, up through the Casbah to the fortress at its summit, pausing in his narration to pass lascivious and racist comment on the animalized bodies and low standards of modesty of the women along the way. Even when it has other preoccupations, however, a walk through the Casbah cannot help but constitute a reflection on Algerian history. Here, that history passes through the in-between space of the Jewish quarter, physically marked by sidewalks, spiral stairs, and Venetian blinds added to converted Arab houses inhabited by the poorer classes of *juifs indigènes*, who could nonetheless claim French citizenship since 1870. If the Jews have been made citizens, and their houses somewhat Frenchified, Randau's narrator insists that the bodies of those inside (the ill-clad and overflowing women, the spineless men) remain distinctly un-French. Even the familiar parts of the lower Casbah are French only in the most superficial way; scratching the surface, or arriving at dawn, the observers find themselves in a most Algerian space. Although nothing can lessen the impact of Randau's anti-Semitism, other effects also operate in this passage. Cassard, who later declares his wish "qu'on lave son linge sale en famille" [that we wash our dirty laundry in private], finds nothing repulsive in the already-dirtied clothes hanging across the street; for a proponent of the unity of the Algerian "family," a Casbah street is still domestic space.[24] This dirty, promiscuous domesticity remains part of what makes Algiers Algerian; Randau imagines a surprising reversal of values in which the entire Casbah, figured in all its filth, and with all its stereotyped and maligned inhabitants, will come to constitute the "true" Algeria.

Via their anti-Semitic detour in the Rue de la Lyre, the Cassards arrive at the summit of the Casbah with something other than either the usual regrets at French architectural intervention, or the traditional celebration of French military triumph:

Il est grand jour quand ils escaladent dans la Casbah les tortueses ruelles du quartier réservé; les hautes façades sont barbouillées d'ocre rouge ou d'indigo; le pavage en petits cubes de pierre a la couleur bleuâtre des cottes de maille en acier. Des maisons à gros numéro, fermées, suintent des relents de sentine, de musc et de peau d'Espagne; de chaque bouche d'égout s'env-olent les exhalaisons fadasse d'eaux de savon, de sueur d'aisselles, de petits bains fangeux; l'enduit des murailles est creuse de graffiti, d'inscriptions turpides, d'offres homosexuelles, de mentules genates [sic]. Aux meurtrières grillées des bouges apparaissent des faces bouffies de matrones.

Parvenus au terme de leur ascension, les deux Cassard dominent Alger; le panorama de la mer se déploie; les maisons fuient à leurs pieds. Le soleil jette sur leurs épaules son voile de pourpre; des détachements de zouaves les croisent, clairons sonnants; derrière eux est la vieille forteresse arabe d'El Djezair; à leur gauche s'élève la prison Barberousse.

[It was broad daylight when they climbed the little twisting streets of the red-light district in the Casbah. The high facades were daubed reddish brown or indigo, and the small cubes of the paving stones had the bluish color of links of steel chain mail. Closed houses leeched stale odors of musk and vice, and from every sewer grate wafted cloying smells of soapy water, underarm sweat, and little muddy baths. The paint on the walls was scratched out with graffiti, turpid inscriptions, and homosexual offers. The madams' bloated faces peered out of the grilled peepholes of the dives.

Having reached the end of their ascent, the two Cassards overlooked Al-giers, the spreading panorama of the sea, and the houses receding at their feet. The sun threw its purple veil over their shoulders; detachments of zouaves passed and trumpets sounded. Behind them was the old Arab fortress of El Djezair; on their left rose the walls of the Barberousse prison.][25]

For the Algerianist calling the Casbah fortress by its Arab name, this heap constitutes the mass of humanity accumulated on the site since the begin-ning of civilization, a heap out of which will come the new Algerian race of the Mediterranean. These passages strikingly evoke and sexualize the ethnic promiscuity of the city. In contrast to a similar walk described in Randau's later novel *Le Professeur Martin* as taking place in 1888, in which the city's multiethnic crowds do not mix, here they rub more than shoulders. If Bertrand found ritual prostitution the necessary sexual prelude to reconsti-tution of Latin Africa, Randau credits generalized promiscuity as the vital re-productive mechanism for creating Algerianness. The dinner party which Jean and Hélène leave for their lovers' promenade in Algiers was a Roman bacchanale drunk in Algerian vintages: "[u]ne belle *mokotte* célèbre, avec des amies, des rites de maison close. . . . Les autres, à grands fracas d'érudition, exposent à tue-tête les principes qui, selon eux, gouverneront une intellectu-alité proprement africaine . . . une Algérienne à peau dorée, modèle à l'im-peccable plastique et au visage de madone, danse nue des danses d'almées" [with some girlfriends, a beautiful mokotte celebrated brothel rites. . . . With great bursts of erudition, the others expounded at the top of their lungs on the principles which, according to them, will govern a truly African intellectual life . . . a bronzed Algerian woman of impeccable forms and the face of a madonna, danced, nude, the dances of Oriental courtesans].[26] The "Algérienne" (a European, of course, imitating the Arabs) could as easily have been Hélène herself, as by this time Randau has accustomed the reader to admiring her curves outlined under a light *gandoura*. As the Leblonds noted, in Randau's Algeria, "se modèlent, dans la lumière en fusion, les Algériens énergiques et sensuels mais pour qui le plaisir sexuel n'est ni but, ni exclusive fonction, une simple traverse dans le grand champ de travail qui requiert toute la force de la race" [energetic and sensual Algerians are shaped in the vivid light, people for whom sexual pleasure is neither a goal nor a mere function, but a simple task in the great field of action which requires all the strength of the race].[27] Nothing could be further from the languid and nostalgic sexuality which pervades Nerval's and Flaubert's Orientalist works.[28] Sex is still bound up with military conquest, but its fantasized object had changed in the decades since Salammbô: Randau dreams not of submissive Moorish courtesans, but of vigorous Franco-Algerian lovers. Though a party guest expresses his wish to see the "*imperium* of the Latin races," Randau purposefully chooses the decadent Roman empire, rather than the nascent republic, as the colony's Latin precursor; its atmosphere is somehow vital to hashing out the ideas on which he bases Algeria's cultural autonomy. At the end of *Les Colons*, once the Cassards have won their political fight and overturned the self-serving pro-Arab administrator standing between them and power, Jean returns home to write amid the paraphernalia of his virility, and to have sex, the other act necessary for the colony's advancement: "Aimons-nous" [Let's make love], Hélène proposes. "Comme des bêtes, ma chère!" [Like animals, my dear!], says Jean. "Posons les termes de notre idylle. Nous sommes des gens d'action mal déguisés en poètes par un vernis d'éducation et de lectures sentimentales! Labourons notre terre d'Afrique!" [Let's lay down the terms of our idyll. We are people of action, badly disguised as poets with a veneer of education and sentimental readings. Let's work our African soil!]][29] As "gens d'action," they will work both the ground and their bodies, fighting, farming, fornicating, and writing the Algerianist ideal.

So far in treating Randau's Algerian novels, I have mentioned a number of peculiar ideological phenomena only half-explained by the politics to which I have so far alluded: the disgusted fascination with Jewish women, the positive valorization of a trash-strewn Algiers full of perversions, and the degree to which male libido underlies the entire construct. In addition to these three manifestations of racial and sexual tension in the Algerianist novel, Cassard's repeated insistence on his barbarism adds a fourth issue: "Tu es le barbare" [You are the Barbarian], he declares to himself at the end of *Cassard le Berbère*, "Tu engloutis et digères la civilisation comme les bêtes liminivores engloutissent et digèrent la vase au fond des abîmes . . . Pareil aux hommes de couleur, tu profites de la culture européenne sans l'aimer. Tu n'es quand tu parles à un civilisé, que mensonges et faux-semblants. Au fond de ton coeur grouille le sauvage." [You devour and digest civilization like the sea-worms which devour and digest the mud in the depths of the ocean. Like men of color, you profit from European culture without liking it. When you speak to a civilized person, you are nothing but lies and false appearances. At the bottom of your heart lurks the savage.][30] Each of these points has much to do with Randau's vision of the colony's history and future. An adequate analysis of them, however, requires consideration of the literary polemic between proponents of colonial literature and Parisian high modernism.

Most colonial writers, including the Algerianists, regretfully admitted that literary approval came from Paris. As the critic of colonial literature Eugène Pujarniscle notes in his compendium of pronouncements on the genre, "C'est le public métropolitain qui confère la notoriété et tous les avantages qu'elle comporte. Le public colonial est disseminé, peu stable, peu écouté, il montre souvent à l'égard des choses coloniales une indifférence complète, il emboîte docilement le pas au public métropolitain." [Fame and the advantages that come with it are conferred by the mainland audience. The colonial audience is scattered, unstable, and little listened to; it often shows complete indifference for colonial matters and docilely follows in the footsteps of the mainland public.][31] Even cultural militants like Randau would have had to agree; perhaps Cassard reflected Randau's dream of remedying this situation by assembling Algerian intellectuals into a bonded group, a *"faisceau,"* he says, to enlighten their fellow inhabitants. (The link between *faisceau* and *fasces* seems allusive at most, though a project to form a tightly disciplined group of intellectuals forging their own national identity might be read as having fascist overtones.) In any case, colonial literature found itself forced into an uneasy relationship with more mainstream currents of literary production in France. Pujarniscle drew the obvious conclusion from the literary market: "C'est donc aux Français de France que s'efforcera de plaire l'écrivain français d'Afrique ou d'Asie" [The French writer from Africa or Asia will therefore strive to please the French in France], if only for commercial reasons.[32] A great deal of rhetoric among colonial critics and authors, however, demonstrates that they did not always accept these terms of literary exchange without a struggle.

Colonial critics wishing to praise works by Algerianist writers tended to do so by extolling the vigorous, masculine quality of their prose; they seemed unable to avoid drawing invidious comparison to mainstream metropolitan writers whom they generally left unnamed. According to

Jean Pomier, Secretary of the *Association des Ecrivains Algériens* and editor of the review *Afrique*, "Notre littérature, depuis quelque trente ans, est dans l'ensemble, une littérature de bars, d'"ouverts-la-nuit', de bordels, de sanatoria, de sleepings, une littérature d'"allongés', d'horizontaux. Randau, lui, son oeuvre est verticale, athlétiquement." [For the last thirty years or so, our literature has overall been a literature of bars, of nightime establishments, of brothels, sanatoriums, and doss-houses, a literature for those "lying down," for horizontal people. As for Randau, his works are athletically vertical.][33] Randau could only have been pleased; the attitude of his heroes shows "verticality" in more ways than one. In fetishizing "energy" rather than aesthetics, colonial literature joined colonialism itself, according to many of its proponents, in supposedly rejuvenating French culture: "L'esprit colonial est une affirmation d'énergie morale. La littérature coloniale, fille de cette résolution saine, s'affirme en réaction contre le décadentisme. Elle nous assainit en s'opposant aux déliquescences de l'esthétisme et du pessimisme. Elle est une doctrine d'action; elle est, comme la colonie elle-même, un acte de foi. . . . Contre les subtilités malsaines ou les recherches corrompues d'une civilisation trop raffinée où s'épuise la vitalité de la race, elle indique le remède dans la vertu primitive de l'effort, où l'énergie se retrempe aux sources des instincts ancestraux." [The colonial spirit is an affirmation of moral energy. Colonial literature, the product of this healthy revolution, asserts itself in reaction to decadence. It cleanses us by opposing deliquescent aestheticism and pessimism. It is a doctrine of action; like the colony itself, it is an act of faith. . . . To counter the unhealthy subtleties or corrupt searchings of an over-refined civilization in which the vitality of the race is exhausted, it proposes a remedy in the original virtue of effort, in which energy is reinvigorated at the font of ancestral instincts.][34] This rhetoric provides us some clues to the aesthetic and ideological significance of Randau's hero's "barbarism." Cassard opposes precisely those "unhealthy" tendencies of an overrefined civilization. Calling his protagonist a barbarian at the gate of Parisian culture lets Randau take the high ground of criticism from outside the system. Absence from the excessively rarefied literary world of Paris thus became a virtue, rather than a sign of poor quality, or a defect in itself. This stance particularly attracted writers like Randau who proclaimed themselves all but political separatists. Algerianist literature for the most part wished to construct at the very least a differentiated cultural order outside mainland France, and, in more extreme cases, a quasi-independent, self-sufficient unit of the French empire. We can see elements of this in works by nearly all the authors of the movement, and most particularly in Randau himself, universally acclaimed the movement's leader and prime exemplar. When Cassard discovers his barbaric tendency to devour and digest, profiting from European culture without liking it, a whole politico-cultural project subtends his words. First, his self-identification (however factitious) with a portion of the Berber population marks his radical difference both from the earlier exoticists, who kept a careful distance between themselves and the people they described, and from Bertrand, whose suggestion that France "rebarbarize" itself did not imply any moral rapprochement between Muslims and Europeans. Second, the malaise Cassard feels when forced by the presence of a "civilized person" into hypocrisy and false pretences emerges as a symptom of the salutary alienation Algerianists should feel in relation to metropolitan France, the alienation which motivated them to construct a new cultural identity for the colony.

A poem which Jean Pomier says he wrote as a preface to a Randau novel typifies the confrontational stance of Algerianism toward Paris and the Parisian *littérateurs*, a position at once joyfully belligerent and jealously embittered:

> Vous, les pisseurs d'eau claire et les encotonnés
> vous, les blancs allongés des cliniques proustiennes
> les fadés, les rancis, les ressasseurs d'antiennes,
> les demi-morts geignant des "Pace, Domine",
>
> Vous, brancardiers de l'Acte ou voyeurs mitonnés,
> les castrats, les voués aux morphines urbaines,
> mitrés à casque-à-mèche et frileux à mitaines,
> vous tous, les implorants, vous tous, les prosternés,
>
> Ah, laissez-nous crever de rire, faces pâles,
> Nous, les Rouliers du Bled au blair emboucanné,
> nous les vivants, nous les durcis, nous les tannés,
>
> Nous les Aventureux, les Maîtres et les Mâles
> qui, chaque coup de tête ou de verge donné,
> faisons jaillir d'Hier des Demains couronnés.[35]

Pomier's critical rhetoric outruns his poetic ability, but the condensation of his sonnet presents a complex polemic in handily encapsulated and highly suggestive form. For Pomier, the opposition between "us" colonials and "you" metropolitans could not be clearer; they oppose one another physically, sexually, and aesthetically. Rhetorically, of course, the poem assumes that the reader joins the narrator, on the side of "us," the colony. The poem's title, "Agir," draws the demarcation line between the two camps: the passive "half-dead," "prone," and "faded" will never move to take "action," the key concept of the Algerianist novel. Elsewhere Pomier remarked that Algeria had more men of action than poets, and declared "C'est dans l'ordre: Primum vivere" [that is as it should be: *Primum vivere*].[36] Cassard's insistence on his status as man of action rather than of letters begins to resonate more clearly. For the Algerianists, aware of their marginal status vis-à-vis a Parisian literary scene dominated by conflicts between the *NRF* and the historical avant-gardes, self-definition as men of action provided a way of casting their difference as a virtue. The *NRF* writers, including Gide, largely ignored the aspects of colonial Algeria the Algerianists celebrated. As for the various Parisian avant-garde movements, they would prove considerably more hospitable to foreigners than to colonials, and some of their members would in fact become the first literary figures actually to oppose colonialism (famously, for example, in the Surrealist tracts against the Exposition Coloniale of 1931) and therefore to reject the very premise of Algerianist literature. By describing Cassard as a nonparticipant in the world of "hommes de lettres," Randau suggests that Algerianist literature would go beyond the petty jealousies which supposedly characterized Parisian literary life.

This constituted only the first step in the Algerianists' declaration of literary autonomy. The real difference between "active" Algerianists and "passive" Parisians turns out to be sexual. The writers insulted in Pomier's poem are only grammatically masculine; in all other respects they exude effeminacy. "We" hardly needed the reference to Proust for the audience to understand that these "castrated" writers are capable only of voyeurism (or at the very most, masturbation); we can hardly doubt that their "passive" role extends to homosexual sex as imagined by the straight Algerianists. The Parisians' manly opponents (both "Maîtres" and "Mâles") construct the colony's future with aggressively sexualized metaphors: the "coup de verge" refers not only to the weapon of choice of Bertrand's wagon-drivers, but also to his (and others') sexual escapades. Condemning the entire *Nouvelle Revue Française* as moribund homosexuals would seem only puerile if it were not also so telling about the self-image of the Algerianists.

Randau's sexualization of the scenes in which he stages debates over history and literary aesthetics thus begins to come into focus; he seems to see Algerianism providing a salutary dose of libidinal energy to counter the effeminate and decadent tendencies of the literature that he imagined being produced in Paris salons. The orgy-like scenes of his dinners paradoxically oppose their own productive "decadence" (figured rather as a healthy absence of sexual hypocrisy) to the sterility of "real" decadence of a homosexual kind. The "perversions" of these scenes are all heterosexual; even the implicit lesbian play of the "belle mokotte" in *Les Colons* takes place at a party for the amusement of straight men busy debating questions of colonial culture and economy. As for the "homosexual offers" of Casbah graffiti, they seem to offer the bodies of male prostitutes for penetration by their clients. In this way, even a Franco-Algerian man with a penchant for boys would keep, unquestioned, his "active" nature. The apparent perversion and decadence of Randau's Algerianist parties actually represent, for the author, a willingness to look beyond sexual hypocrisy, to write in a Rabelaisian tone without censoring any portion of colonial reality. He will not clean up his descriptions of the goings-on at soirées of rich *colons* any more than he will prettify the streets of the Casbah, as Bertrand had accused the nineteenth-century exoticists of doing.

Readers today may wonder how far Randau's rhetoric succeeds in portraying the very real problems of establishing an Algerian identity which would truly allow the participation it claimed to grant to at least some of the *indigènes*. To take first the case of the Jews, the colonial context allows Randau to transform France's archetypal minority from social-climbing *littérateurs* to licentious potential prostitutes. This transformation is not tangential to the construction of Algerianist identity; issues of the relationship of Algerian culture to French, and of Europeans to Arab and Amazigh Algerians, coalesce around it. Randau stresses sexual difference in the Jews: the weak male figures among them quickly disappear, leaving the highly sexualized women. The Algerianists denigrate a certain sort of French cultural production by insisting on sexual difference, replacing reviled unmanly aesthetes (e.g., Proust and Gide) with available heterosexual teases (the eroticized but disgusting Jewish women of the Casbah). They replace high culture with sexual availability, throwing a vulgar insult at mainstream literary culture, and figuring, in crude terms, the relationship between the "horizontal literature" of mainland France, and the "vertical literature" of the colony.

In Algiers if not elsewhere, Randau has made the Jews (and especially the Jewish women) stand in for the entire non-European population. At the time he was writing, the Jews of Algiers were in fact steadily moving out of the Casbah streets around the rue de la Lyre, leaving only the very poor behind in their flight to neighborhoods like Koubba and El Biar. During this time the Casbah would truly become overwhelmingly Muslim and impoverished. In writing as if this has not happened, Randau creates an anachronism, or at the very least, a significant exaggeration. He had much to gain by doing so. By replacing the Muslim population of the Casbah with *juifs indigènes*, Randau provides a population imagined as docile, assimilable (if not already partially assimilated), and above all visible, available to be viewed by outsiders. The rarity of veiling among Jewish women had already made them the favorite models of Orientalists painters since Delacroix, who were often not above labelling their subjects generically as "Algériennes," "Mauresques," or "Fatmas," and thereby implying that they had somehow penetrated a Muslim harem. A precedent thus existed for substituting Jews (and especially Jewish women) for

Muslims. Randau follows this precedent, but also portrays the Jewish women as already more "Mediterranean" than Semitic or Berber. Once again, the Algerianists' Algeria shows itself Mediterranean rather than Arab, even though Randau will not pretend, as Bertrand did, that the colony (and all the population that counted) was really Latin and European. These Jewish bodies remain quite foreign, despite their perceived sexual availability, their most useful feature. It figures the fantasy of easy penetration into the colonized population, open to advances from the Franco-Algerians, as docile subjects of a conquest accepted as a fait accompli.

Several problems arise here for today's reader, however. The "élaboration d'une race" [elaboration of a race] so dear to the Algerianists never included any actual biological mixing outside the "Latin" communities. They never seem to have imagined children produced by mixed couples as useful proponents of their doctrines, or as steps on the way to racial union. This should perhaps not surprise us; mixed marriages remained quite rare, and the majority of such children were probably conceived during visits to the red-light districts of the colony. However, it does represent a hole in the Algerianist argument, which preached racial union without postulating any means to reach it. Under the circumstances, this oversight functioned as a barrier to participation in that union by anyone not already a European. Since most European Algerians could not imagine mixed marriages favorably, it is not surprising that Randau did not see the Jewish women as fit mothers of future Latins. The real significance of the Cassards' inclusion of only Jewish women in their Casbah description seems to be that the presence of Jews led conveniently to an almost explicit erasure of the Muslims from citizenship in the Algerianists' colony. Despite the Algerianists' apparent relative inclusiveness, the conditions for citizenship for the Muslims they unofficially advanced ultimately paralleled those "offered" by the French government in the colony: citizenship granted regularly, *en masse*, to successive waves of European immigrants; citizenship foisted on as much as given to Jews, in order to add elements imagined as more "assimilable" than the Muslims to the French majority, shrinking among other arriving Europeans; and citizenship systematically refused, via a variety of subterfuges, to Muslims.[37] Despite Randau's vehement opposition to most central government policies in Algeria, his ideas on whom to include when handing out citizenship rights in the new colony do not greatly differ from those proposed by the government in Paris.

Similarly, Randau's unflinching portrayal of the seamy side of the city, and his positive view of the contestatory possibilities for cultural liberation through decadence and perversion may have provided few new tools for reaching ethnic unity. Hindsight, knowledge of the colony's end, foreshadowed by anticolonial agitation as early as World War I, makes it difficult for an observer today to see past the decadence. The constant references to Rome in Bertrand and the subsequent Algerianists make it hard not to take scenes of orgies (even congenial ones) as ominous signs in a city full of moral and physical degradation. By World War II, Casbah descriptions, ever central to Algerian literature, and always symptomatic of wider cultural conditions in the colony, would take a much gloomier turn, reflecting both the physical state of the old city and the social tensions becoming harder to ignore. The transplanted French novelist Lucienne Favre produced three quite different editions of her book-length Casbah description, *Tout l'inconnu de la Casbah d'Alger*, which moved from lighthearted and picturesque in 1933, to gloomy and foreboding of social unrest in 1949.[38] Randau's decadence may seem more than metaphoric, that is, the sign of a city actually beginning to crack, even if he used it to suggest an atmosphere of productive cultural ferment in the colony.

FROM COLONIAL NOVEL TO LITERARY *FAISCEAU*

Cassard's wish to see the *"regroupement en faisceau"* of Algerian writers might seem to foreshadow the foundation of the *Association des Écrivains Algériens* in 1919. The Association soon began to publish its own review, *Afrique*, a sixteen- to twenty-page monthly in small format, costing six francs per year. Jean Pomier, a colonial transplant from Toulouse, edited it from its inception to its folding thirty years later, within a year of the outbreak of the *événements* [events]: the Algerian War. Most of the major Algerianists participated, notably Charles Hagel, Louis Lecoq, Charles Courtin, and Robert Randau himself. Pomier very soon found himself elected president of the Association, in addition to being editor of the review, in which he seems sometimes to have written half the articles. In spite of the apparent limitations of a tiny review closely held by a small group of friends, *Afrique* constituted a vital stepping-stone on the way from Bertrand's ideas on Algeria to the productions of the so-called "École d'Alger": Edmond Brua, Gabriel Audisio, and nominally at least, the young Albert Camus. Pomier did this largely by adopting a particularist position in favor of cultural autonomy *à la* Randau and sticking to it, but also by publishing the liveliest literary criticism in Algeria.

Declaring the need to work *"algériennement"* [Algerianly], the opening article of the first issue in April 1924 established Pomier's mantra in the early years of the movement.[39] His formula *"oeuvrer algériennement"* constituted a declaration of separation, if not independence, from Parisian literary schools, and an affirmation of the local, both as a foundation for literature and as an ideal audience.[40] But what in fact did the slogan mean to its coiner? The introductory article attempted to clarify:

À la différence des penseurs de la métropole qui, pour la plupart, s'enfer-
ment dans l'altier dédain de leur temps, nous pensons que la meilleure et la
plus riche manière d'oeuvrer, c'est de ne rien négliger des décors, des aspects, et des forces de la vie. Les écoles littéraires, les modes et les modalités
de l'expression ne nous préoccuperont pas outre mesure: il y a là un certain
mandarinat qui ne saurait convenir à une pensée jeune, émerveillée de
croître, et pour qui nulle beauté ne saurait dépasser la Beauté de l'Action:
Philosophie de Force et de Mouvement, que nous n'avons pas l'outrecuid-
ance d'avoir découverte, mais qu'il nous a paru nécessaire et opportun de
dresser aux frontons de l'art français d'Algérie.

Par application de ces principes, nous considérerons comme nôtre tout le
mouvant domaine algérien: Politique Générale, économie politique, rapports
ethniques, mêlées d'âmes, la rue, la ville et le bled, l'Homme, la Terre et la
Mer, l'Algérie d'Icosium et celle d'El-Djezair.

[Unlike the thinkers of mainland France who, for the most part, close themselves off in haughty disdain for their times, we believe that the best and
richest way to work is to neglect none of the decor, aspects, and forces of life.
Literary schools, fashions, and modalities of expression will not unduly concern us. They harbor a sort of Mandarinism which cannot suit a way of thinking that is young and marvelling at its own growth, and for which no beauty
can surpass the Beauty of Action, the Philosophy of Strength and Movement,
which we do not have the presumptuousness to have discovered, but which
it seems necessary and opportune to us to place in the forefront of the French
art of Algeria.

By the application of these principles, we will consider as our own
the entire moving domain of Algeria: General Politics, political economy,
ethnic relations, the struggles of souls, the street, the city and the hinterland, Man, Earth and Sea, the Algeria of Icosium and the Algeria of
El-Djezair.][41]

The first part of the text does everything it can to differentiate itself and
the movement that produced it from literary or philosophical movements in France. Like the manifestos of the historic avant-garde, it
seeks both to attract attention and to reject the competition. Pomier
nonetheless allusively admits the debts of the movement to Futurism,
after which the Algerianists could indeed scarcely pretend to have discovered the appeal of youth, strength, and motion. In short, *Afrique* will
record the youthful phase of a culture by paying close attention to the
local, the particular, and the "forces of life," forces situated somewhere
between the political and the biological, a fascination among Algerianists following Randau.

The text, however, does not follow Randau literally or without modification. First, where Randau would simply have spoken of "Algerian
art" to contrast it with the French, Pomier calls for the development of
"the French art of Algeria." There really never was any doubt that even

Randau's artistic regionalism in fact would preserve a dominant French literary culture. His home-grown Cassard is a Rabelaisian hero transplanted to North Africa, rather than anything wholly outside the French tradition. Second, Pomier gets more specific than Randau about the historical and urban elements the Association writers wished to combine in order truly to "work Algerianly." His culminating litany of topics privileges the city and comes to rest on historical interpretations of the city to represent the entire colony. Icosium, the Roman colony sited near Algiers, and El-Djezair, the Arab city, represented respectively Latin and Arab Africa; the latter city had received had received comparatively little attention in the initial phases of a movement that saw exoticism as its primary enemy. In arguing "nihil algeriani a me alienum," "nothing Algerian is foreign to me," Pomier and the Association seem at least initially to push this to its logical conclusion of inclusiveness: the Muslims were part of Algeria, so an *"oeuvre algérienne"* could legitimately include them.[42] In fact some did, albeit in a restricted fashion, as we shall see in the upcoming chapter on the *roman indigène*. Although the ideological needs of colonialism would determine the terms of that inclusion, it did represent a significant departure from earlier criteria for the selection of worthy subject matter.

Significantly, Pomier's logic slips slightly when speaking of Icosium and El-Djezair: the terms seem to refer only to the city of Algiers itself, but Pomier connects them with Algeria as a whole. These two conflicting historical visions of the city (perhaps reconcilable in Pomier's thought) stand in for the entire country as the Association's literary construct. "El-Djezair," however, is a synecdoche across two languages. The Arabic "Al-Jazā'ir," which originally referred to the city itself, came also to be applied to the whole country as the back-translation of the French invention "Algérie," a term which did not exist until well after the conquest. In Arabic, one could argue, the same word does indeed apply to the entire country as well as to the city.[43] However, it has at various times been received, especially by Amazigh activists, as a label stuck on artificially; in any case, the simple conflation of terms obscures the real difficulties of naming a city to represent historically an entire country.[44] Furthermore, "El-Djezair" is only present in Pomier's text as a transcription. This, too, obscures difficulties, if only of pronunciation, by glossing over the glottal stop which makes the Arabic word so distinctive to a foreign ear, and which renders it a strain on the French tongue and a quandary for its alphabet. In fact, the writers of the Association would consistently impose the screen of transcription invoked in the phrase "l'Algérie d'El-Djezair" on the Arab and Amazigh presence in their works. Transcriptions, potentially only a simple expediency, would represent the heavy mediation always produced when writers portrayed Muslim characters; inclusiveness in their historical paradigms for the city did not necessarily make the Association much more friendly to the colonized, even after it had acknowledged their existence.

Afrique continued to advocate assimilation long after it had ceased to be official French policy; the authors it published tended to adopt the classic (and rather tired) affect of assimilationist generosity: "l'Algérianisme propose avant tout une politique de large et compréhensive assimilation. Il demande à la France de devenir vraiment la tutrice de ce peuple en montée. Alors elle aura fait preuve, une fois de plus, de puissance civilisatrice." [Algerianism proposes, first and foremost, a policy of broad and comprehensive assimilation. It asks that France truly become the guardian of this up-and-coming people. She will then have proven once more her civilizing power.][45] Here we see a departure from the quasi-separatist rhetoric of so many of the Association's positions. Assimilation, after all, meant assimilation of the colonized to the French; even if we substitute "Français d'Algérie" for "Français de France" in this equation, the final term remains the same, ultimately still mainland France. For all that, the Association did not toe any official government line; for example, in the same article dispensing these platitudes, the author declares that wrong-headed French government policy had prevented true assimilation thus far, and echoes growing complaints in the opposition press about Arab and Amazigh notables exploiting their own people, with government support and French landowners' collusion. Pomier and his friends did not hesitate to denounce the colonial government when they saw a threat to Algeria's prospects for a coherent cultural future, or simply when they saw its reputation, or that of colonial literature, suffering in France.

Afrique had a very direct style; its temperament makes for lively reading. It gave considerable attention to the status of colonial literature in France and reacted harshly to novels which purported to be colonial without living up to the Association's standards for well-informed, vigorous prose vindicating the colony as a self-sufficient cultural unit. Peter Dunwoodie has argued that the Algerianists held accurate realist portrayal of colonial affairs as the highest criteria of value for colonial literature.[46] Here Jean Pomier characterizes the majority of his contemporaries' novels set in Africa and describes ironically how to write a "colonial novel" for Parisian tastes:

Autant que possible, prenez une petite histoire scandaleuse, recueillie au cours d'une "mission" et que vous aurez tenue d'un journaliste mécontente, d'un indigène ambitieux ou d'un fonctionnaire limogé. Ajoutez-y un décor de paletuviers, de bananes et de tam-tam, commentez Kant, Bacon ou Jean de Lafontaine en décortiquant des cacahuètes, et quand vous tirez la moustiquaire, annotez Michel Eyquem de Montaigne. Sur ce, éteignez et baisez la négrillonne, à l'épaule, en pensant à Mme Aurel, par exemple.

Moyennant quoi, et si vous veinulez votre pâte d'une légère marbrure de salacité (blanc sur noire, noir sur blanche, au choix), vous aurez une réalisation suffisante de roman très colonial, et qui vous assurera le cinquantième mille, dès le tirage.

[Whenever possible, start with a scandalous little story gathered in the course of a "mission" and which you will have gleaned from a malcontented journalist, an ambitious *indigène*, or a fired civil servant. Add a decor of mangrove swamps, bananas, and tam-tams, hold forth on Kant, Bacon, or Jean de Lafontaine while shelling peanuts, and when you draw the mosquito netting, annotate Michel Eyquem de Montaigne. With that, kiss the little negro girl— on the shoulder—while thinking about Mme. Aurel, for example.

With all this, and if you spice your stew with a light dusting of salaciousness (white man on black woman, black man on white woman), you will have a sufficient approximation of a very colonial novel, which will guarantee you sales of fifty thousand copies in the first printing.][47]

Of course Pomier names no names and leaves readers to guess at the authors he has in mind. Stories of love between French men and colonial subject women immediately recall Loti, "le chimérique Loti lui-même" [the chimerical Loti himself], as another *Afrique* article called him, who came in for considerable criticism there for having more or less defined the colonial novel as the genre of tragic mixed-race love stories.[48] In Pomier's view, however, the real harm comes from the subject matter of such novels, drawn from stories of colonial scandal. We will get a taste of this when we examine the novels and journalism of the Algerian centenary year, but for the moment we might think of someone like André Gide: though we cannot read this passage as an explicit attack on him, we may reasonably consider him as the embodiment of what Association writers opposed.[49] As a homosexual, psychologizing aesthete of the *NRF*, he already fell into several categories reviled by the Algerianists. His writings on Algiers in *Amyntas* hardly seemed likely to win him friends among colony boosters; nor for that matter did his characterization of Algeria as the site of the protagonist Michel's moral corruption in *L'Immoraliste*. As if these turn-of-the-century texts did not suffice to condemn Gide in the eyes of the colonialists, his then-recent *Voyage au Congo* (1925) had done in a sober report exactly what Pomier complained about in novels, formulating explicit criticism of the colonial regime by exposing a scandal gleaned from journalists and administration malcontents, but also from first-hand investigation.

At other times, the critics of the *Afrique* group did name their targets, and one particular set of writers took the brunt of their fulminations: those who showed an "unhealthy" fascination with Islam. Among them, we find a few surprises, apart from the conventional exoticists who typically served as targets of Algerianist critique, and who at any rate scarcely understood the religion that enraptured them. The other cases stand out, in the articles leading up to the Centenary: the painter and writer Étienne Dinet, the brothers Jean and Jérôme Tharaud, Lyautey's quasi-official authors in Morocco (and successors to Bertrand at the Académie Française), and Isabelle Eberhardt, the (in)famous "âme du désert."[50] Pomier and his friends attacked all of these writers for destabilizing the colonial regime by criticizing its accomplishments (or else simply ignoring them) or for having "sold out" to the enemy, Islam. Pomier would recant his criticisms of Eberhardt, known in the early twenties mostly as a wild-living "Islamophile" through the portion of her writings that Victor Barrucand, her correspondent and editor in Algiers, had seen fit to publish. Raoul Stephen's 1930 biography of Eberhardt may have romanticized her, but it also defused some of the scandal attached to her person, and Pomier had to revise his earlier opinion of her as stricken with what he called "Orientalitis," a sickness he likened to "Bovarytis." Faced with new evidence, he admitted that "je doute presque de moi-même, et de la vérité de ma pensée, de la solidité de la position intellectuelle que j'essaye de tenir à l'égard des choses et des gens de ce pays" [I almost doubted myself and the truth of my thinking, and the solidity of the intellectual position I try to hold regarding the people and objects of this country].[51]

Pomier "almost doubted" his own views, but not quite: he quickly found ways of shoring up the positions the journal had previously expressed, notably in articles on Etienne Dinet and the Tharaud brothers, earlier that same year. Dinet, who died at the very beginning of the Centenary year, had lived, painted, and written for several decades in the oasis town of Bou Saada, assisted by his longtime companion Sliman ben Ibrahim Baamer. He represented the continuation of a tradition of romanticized Orientalist painting in France; an article on his death in the Algiers *Presse libre* used the neologism *nostalgérie* [nostalgeria] to describe the overall tone of his work (and incidentally attested to the word's existence more than sixty years before nostalgic *pieds-noirs* began using it again).[52] Together, Dinet and Baamer wrote several books, in which Dinet sought to minimize his role as essentially a translator and illustrator, in order to emphasize his coauthor's credibility as a Muslim writing about Muslims, a level of legitimacy not available to most European writers, but which apparently counted little for Pomier. Their novel *Khadra, danseuse Oulad Naïl* (1926) exploits French nostalgia for a legendary (and decimated) southern Algerian clan whose name, the Oulad Naïl, had become synonymous with exotic dancing and prostitution:[53] "Voyageurs, il faut vous résigner! Vous ne verrez jamais ce que vous rêviez, parce que cela n'est plus! . . . Mais votre déception nous afflige, et pour l'atténuer, nous allons chercher à vous montrer ce qu'elles étaient il y a quelques années, lorsque l'alcool n'avait pas encore triomphé de l'amour." [Travelers, you will have to resign yourselves to giving up your illusions! You will never see what you were dreaming of, because it no longer exists! . . . But your disappointment saddens us, and to lessen it, we will try to show you what these women were a few years ago, when alcohol had not yet triumphed over love.][54] The story itself, the spectacularization of a sexually self-possessed prostitute's career up through her miserable end as a beggar, contains nothing as shocking as Zola's *Nana*. Furthermore, in the context of colonial literature, even the absence of any European characters does not suffice to set it apart from any number of other *"indigène* novels." So why did Dinet's role in producing this and other texts infuriate the *Afrique* critics?

Most importantly for the Algerianists, Dinet had converted to Islam. To them, this signified a moral failing, the collapse of the robustness they so valued under the pressure exerted by African or Oriental torpor. As Pomier put it in his article on Dinet's death, "Dès que l'on est transplanté ici, on la sent bien, cette emprise du pays et du milieu, qui fait que les réactions de la sensibilité et les processus de la raison ne sont plus tout à fait les mêmes que là-bas. L'on se sent capturé dans un rets invisible qui vous ligote, rétrécit et limite vos réflexes, et fait que votre attitude mentale n'est plus celle que vous aviez. En France, vous aviez vue sur l'humain. Ici, on ne considère que l'individuel. Et les figurations de l'individu sont placées sous le signe de la Race, de la Religion, de l'Histoire. D'où il suit que les relations ne sont pas des liaisons mais des heurts, des chocs, des froissements." [As soon as you are transplanted here, you truly feel the hold of the country and the environment, which means that the reactions of your senses and the processes of your reason are no longer quite the same as they were back in France. You feel trapped in an invisible snare that binds you, reduces and limits your reflexes, and makes your mental attitude not what it had been. In France, you have perspective on the human; here, one only considers the individual. And the figures of that individual are bound up with Race, Religion, and History. From this it follows that relations are no longer links but impacts, shocks, and friction.][55] Initially, this analysis of what happens to a transplanted European in Algeria seems quite sensible; we do generally expect that exposure to another culture change one's attitudes. Furthermore, even today, foreigners in North Africa can find their personal relations poisoned by history and power relations, to the point where their dealings indeed seem to consist mainly of confrontations. However, it becomes clear in this article condemning Dinet (dead less than two months) that Pomier's "mental attitude" has not changed: rather, Pomier sees his own inborn abilities as a French intellectual under siege, invaded by the colony. The transplanted intellectual's "âme ouverte et douce de France" [sweet and open French soul] senses that "une infiltration nocive a sourdement goutté ses sucs d'Asie dans le beton d'Occident qui fait sa structure, sa robustesse, son grain loyal, sa valeur dans le temps" [a harmful infiltration of Asian sap has quietly seeped into the Western concrete that constitutes its structure, robustness, loyal character, and value over time].[56] Pomier equates the "robustness" of the French North African soul with its French pretension to value and validity in any time or place. These qualities, which he implies give the French intellectual his universal "view of all that is human," must resist the attacks of race, religion, and history, all of which would limit its universality. History seems somehow stronger, both more invasive and more pervasive in the colony than in mainland France, not because it actually is, but simply because one must deal with it differently, resisting it in order to attain a universal impact for one's art in spite of the limitations of the colonial setting. This struggle has moral consequences, "giving in" means selling out: in Dinet's case, losing one's Frenchness to the Muslim enemy. Pomier declares "Je suis de ceux qui résistent. Etienne Dinet fut de ceux qui capitulèrent" [I am among those who resist. Etienne Dinet was among those who capitulated].[57] For Pomier, confident that he and his friends will do more for the colony's cultural development than any renegade or turncoat (*m'tourni* in Algerian Arabic), such a capitulation represents treachery: "Je récuse l'exemple d'Hadj Nacr er Din [sic], 'M'tourni de la France', et tout d'abord, 'M'tourni' de l'Algérie" [I reject the example of Hadj Nacr er Din, 'M'tourni' of France, and first and foremost, 'M'tourni' of Algeria].[58] The verbs mark the historical progression from the exoticist's "capitulation" before his subjects' enticements in the past, to the Algerianist's robust, male resistance in the present. The present and future belong to the living, to the builders of the colony's next century.

Neither did the *Afrique* critics spare colonial writers outside Algeria, if they found them doing disservice to colonialism, as some believed Dinet had done. Morocco, and the French methods in the Protectorate established there, constituted a preferred target. Lyautey, though still considered by metropolitan writers the very personification of French colonialism, represented a vision of the French role in North Africa at odds with the Algerianists, and his quasi-official writers suffered vigorous attacks from *Afrique*. Lyautey had never hidden his desire to avoid at all costs turning Morocco into another Algeria; he rejected the ideas of filling it with working-class or petty bourgeois immigrants, and of razing and rebuilding the old cities to meet French standards. He favored a kind of indirect political rule and a feudal cultural conservatism, with the goal of preserving as much as possible of Moroccan Islam and its cultural productions. Jean and Jérôme Tharaud, coauthors of exotic travel books, became Lyautey's favorite writers on the Protectorate and received quasi-official approbation for the series of description-and-travel narratives they published, one for every major city in the French zone, a sort of literate guidebook series for Lyautey's Morocco. They did not impress the Algerianists, who predictably objected when the Tharauds wrote that "En Algérie, pendant un siècle, nous nous sommes organisés sans tenir compte de l'Islam, et nous avons détruit trop de choses, de celles qu'on ne remplace jamais" [In Algeria, for a century, we arranged matters without taking Islam into consideration, and we destroyed too many of the sort of things one can never replace].[59] The author and critic Claude-Maurice Robert, a frequent commentator on colonial Algerian literature, found that this passage attacked not just France's past policies in Algeria, but the very basis of its colonial future everywhere: "c'est le procès sans appel de l'oeuvre française en Afrique, et je ne pense pas que Loti, le chimérique Loti lui-même, ni son succédané Farrère aient écrit plus injurieuse ni plus gratuite sottise" [this is an unappealable judgment of the French work in Africa, and I do not believe that Loti, the chimerical Loti himself, nor his substitute Farrère has ever written anything more perniciously or gratuitously stupid].[60] Naturally, the Algerianists would not stand for writers who advanced an essentially exoticist appreciation of North African culture before the "adulteration" brought on by colonialism. Though the Tharaud's essentialized notions of cultural preservation in Morocco are difficult to defend, so is *Afrique*'s criticism; objections to exoticism can come from a variety of angles, some of which contain doxa every bit as restrictive as what they oppose. "Lorsque nous aurons dit que les auteurs fraternels furent documentés par l'apostat Hadj Dinet, on s'expliquera le caractère de partialité islamophile" [Once we know that the brother authors got their documentation from the apostate Hadj Dinet, the Islamophilic prejudice is no longer surprising] in their books, declares the critic.[61] The title of the article, "Un livre impie" [An impious book], together with the qualification of Dinet as an "apostate," foreground *Afrique*'s desire to chastise. For its proponents, Algerianism had become a religion, with a program of excommunicating colonial writers who did not support its orthodoxy. Although the Algerianists affected to pay no attention to literary quarrels and did not formally exclude members for contrary opinions, they nonetheless had as clear an idea of doctrine and heresy as their contemporaries in other literary movements.

POLITICS, PROMOTION, AND PRIZES

Having done their best to establish policies for coherent colonial promotion in literature, the Algerianists set about rewarding themselves. The Association had encouraged the establishment in 1921 of the Grand Prix Littéraire de l'Algérie, with a government subsidy of five thousand francs. In the inaugural issue of *Afrique* in 1924, Pomier declared the Association's intention to insist on the "maintien, envers et contre tous, de notre délégation au Comité du Prix Littéraire de l'Algérie, fondé sur notre initiative" [maintenance, come what may, of our representation on the Committee of the Prix Littéraire de l'Algérie, founded at our initiative].[62] For the Association's members, the prize and their sway over its selection represented an important means of influencing the Algerian literary scene; they intended to use it to "mener à bien l'oeuvre de collaboration à laquelle nous convions la pensée française en Algérie" [accomplish the work of collaboration to which we invite French thought in Algeria].[63] They did not always succeed in imposing this influence without struggle, and at several moments in the following decade, the very goals of the prize seemed open to debate.

Considerable controversy existed around the prize's criteria: these at times appeared to have as much to do with promotion of the colony as with literary value. The Association itself furthered this confusion, when Pomier addressed the prize committee in a 1924 article: "Messieurs, c'est en vue d'une propagande pour l'Algérie que vous est donnée la subvention de 5.000 francs dont vous avez à disposer. Il y a là une indication capitale, dont je veux voir tout de suite les conséquences" [Messieurs, you were given the subsidy you have in hand of 5,000 francs for propaganda for Algeria. This is a clear instruction, the consequences of which I want to see immediately].[64] We see once again the necessary link between colonial literature and promotion of the colony, for people who found their interests simply forgotten or overlooked by a metropolitan public frequently indifferent to colonial affairs. Pomier's exhortation to the Committee has a clear subtext: the prize should serve to promote colonial literature, as well as the colony in general. Some promotional function traditionally marked the ritual of literary prizes, all the more necessary in the case of Algerian literature, still at best a subcategory of literary consumption in France. Pomier applies this agenda in commenting on the works considered for the prize, about which he regrets two things: their low quality and the inclusion among them of works of history. Gabriel Esquer, the director of the Algerian archives to whom modern researchers are still grateful for his early catalogues, won the prize that same year for his history of the conquest of Algiers. Pomier found this distressing, he claimed, for commercial reasons: the prize would waste its potential promotional effect on a historical monograph, which the public would never buy in any case.[65] Whether the French public would have bought an Algerian novel which had won the prize remains debatable; unlike the French literary prizes, the Algerian prize seems to have had only an occasional effect on the print runs of the works it honored. Several times, the committee chose a work still in manuscript (in 1921 with Ferdinand Duchêne and in 1927 with Charles Courtin); it remains unclear whether these authors had already found publishers, or whether the prize helped them do so. At least in the case of Courtin's *La Brousse qui mangea l'homme* [The Brush that Ate the Man], it does not seem to have speeded publication, as the book did not appear in print for another two years. Duchêne's novels achieved greater sales, but were not reprinted until long after they had won their prize.[66]

With such a dubious record of promotion, the prize served more as a demonstration of Algerian literature's self-definition in the face of critics' doubts, than as a defense and illustration of the colony for French audiences. By 1931 the critic Pierre Martino, an administrator at the Université d'Alger, felt obliged to note the difficulty the prize committee had experienced in finding worthy books to honor in the preceding years, even after admitting for consideration any work on any subject by a long-term resident of Algeria. "Aurait-on couronné tout ce qui était couronnable?" [Could we have rewarded everything that deserved rewarding?] he wondered.[67] Far more awkward for the Algerianists, however, were Martino's musings on why the committee had never given the prize to Auguste Robinet, who, as "Musette," wrote a long series of sketches at the turn of the century about Cagayous, a mixed-blood street tough of Algiers.[68] Critics on all sides agreed that the Cagayous stories brilliantly recorded the dialect of Algiers and provided lively and subtle satire of Algerian society and politics before World War I.[69] It is striking, said Martino, himself a fan, that

> le jury du grand prix littéraire n'ait pas, malgré la proposition d'un de ses membres au moins, désigné l'oeuvre la plus remarquable peut-être de ces vingt dernières années, la plus algérienne en tout cas: le Cagayous de Musette. . . . La raison pour laquelle le jury s'est refusé à couronner cette oeuvre que tout le monde loue hautement est fort significative. Cagayous n'est pas écrit en français; il est trop local, il ne saurait être lu sans préparation par un public parisien: seuls, en dehors d'Alger, les philologues peuvent s'y intéresser. Je crois que ce véto est significatif et donne un clair témoignage sur les ambitions et les possibilités de la littérature algérienne. Elle est et elle veut être avant tout française; elle est à l'image même de la colonie, si proche de la métropole, liée à elle par tant de liens matériels, moraux, familiaux.

> [despite the proposal of at least one of its members, the grand prize jury has not singled out perhaps the most remarkable work of the last twenty years, and certainly the most Algerian: Musette's Cagayous. . . . The reason for which the jury has refused to reward this work which everyone praises highly is quite significant. Cagayous is not written in French, it is too local, and can not be read without preparation by a Parisian audience. Outside Algeria, only philologists could find it interesting. I believe that this veto is meaningful, and provides clear evidence about the ambitions and possibili-

ties of Algerian literature. Above all, it is and wishes to be French; it is in the very image of the colony, linked to the mainland by so many material, moral, and familial ties.][70]

In short, to win the prize, it did not suffice to "work Algerianly," despite the constantly repeated watchword of the Association critics. To be selected, the writer had also to produce a text marketable in Paris. In this case, Gaston Gallimard settled the question very practically, by publishing the collected Cagayous stories with introduction and notes by Gabriel Audisio to provide the necessary cultural and linguistic background. To readers today, the real interest of the problem lies elsewhere, in the reception of the Cagayous stories in Algiers. Martino suggests that the Algerianists had effectively rejected Cagayous on commercial grounds, well before Gallimard showed how wrong they were. Pomier could indeed have used Cagayous to justify his point contrasting the colonial local with the metropolitan universal; through an endless series of individual confrontations and affronts, Cagayous vigorously asserts his allegiance to a single city, and even to a single neighborhood (Bab-el-Oued) within it, and systematically ridicules ideas of a higher level of abstraction. Nonetheless, neither Pomier nor the Algerianists disowned him in the way Martino supposed they were in the process of doing. In fact, Pomier asked in an article on Musette's death in 1930 if his "Parisian friends" might not propose a luxury edition in addition to the Gallimard collection.[71] Despite Pomier's earlier reservations, he would continue to support a literary school devoted to local particularity. However, the tension remained over the artistic possibilities and commercial appeal of the local. The Association writers seemed to believe that local and regional literature could appeal to a Parisian audience, and if promoted energetically with publicity tools like the Grand Prix Littéraire, could integrate itself into the grand scheme of literature in the French empire. Martino, however, claimed that in order to accomplish this integration, Algerian writers would and should lose at least some of their local specificity. Regional literature exists in France, he says, but one nonetheless speaks only of *littérature française*, and not of *littérature bourguignonne* or *dauphinoise*.[72] His final sentence leaves no doubt about his vision of the path Algerian literature had chosen for itself, almost denying the existence of the very *littérature algérienne* Robert Randau had promoted so vigorously.

REGIONALISM VS. SEPARATISM

What then did it mean for an Algerianist to talk about "Algerian literature" and "French culture" in the same context? In July of 1929, Randau capitalized on the approach of the Centenary and the heightening interest in Paris for things Algerian to publish a brief retrospective on colonial literature in the *Revue des deux mondes*. He rehearses the well-known history of that literature's exoticist beginnings and their subsequent rejection by writers interested in the colony "for its own sake," a drastic improvement in his view. He admits that "la haute critique n'a guère encore que dédain" [high literary criticism still has little more than disdain] for colonial literature, "qui n'a point obtenu jusqu'à ce jour l'intronisation officielle au temple des belles lettres françaises" [which has up to now not been officially enthroned in the temple of French *belles lettres*].[73] In other words, the public did not accept the colonial writer's "local" in the way it accepts the metropolitan writer's; readers were not ready to receive the colonial, let alone the colonized, as part of the French cultural universe. The observation had serious consequences for the colonial writers: "Aussi les amours du beau spahi blanc et de la seniare ne l'impressionne [le lecteur] qu'à fleur de chair. Et l'intrigue du fonctionnaire européen avec la congai en Indochine relève-t-elle pour lui moins de la psychologie que du roman-feuilleton d'aventures." [So the love affair of the handsome white *spahi* and the *seniare* impresses the reader only marginally. To him, the plot of the European civil servant and the *congai* in Indochina is a matter less of psychology than of a serial adventure novel.][74] Randau explicitly alludes to Loti, the arch-exoticist, and his *Roman d'un spahi*. However, he does not conclude that this problem of reception only arises for exoticist novels. Instead, he contrasts the demands of the public, unevolved since Loti's day, with the program of the Algerianists, in order to explain why audiences appreciated only those colonial novels it could read as sensationalist adventure tales, rather than as "psychological" love stories: "le roman colonial, tel que nous l'entendons, présente au profane, non des fantoches ou des personnages de théâtre mais des êtres de chair et d'os, nous. Il dégage des valeurs d'humanité" [the colonial novel, as we understand it, does not present straw men or theatrical characters to the uninitiated, but rather humans in flesh and blood: us. It carries the values of humanity].[75] The colonial novel can participate in French universalist culture as a whole, because its characters should not be taken as exotic foreigners but as part of "us," the great colonial nation of 100 million Frenchmen. Randau ends by citing Roland Lebel, to say that "la littérature produite par la colonie exprime la colonie" [the literature produced in the colony expresses the colony], and therefore expresses part of France as well; furthermore, "c'est là . . . le but suprême de l'effort du nouvel esprit français: créer dans nos possessions, même lointaines, des centres de rayonnement intellectuel de langue et d'âme française. Ceci n'est pas du séparatisme: c'est de la décentralisation" [that is the final goal toward which the new French spirit strives: to create even in our distant possessions centers of intellectual influence for the French language and soul. This is not separatism; it is decentralization].[76] The Algerianists never stated their goals more clearly. Randau manages here to incorporate much of the rhetoric of the movement since its beginnings: "effort," "nouvel esprit," and "rayonnement" all recall Cassard's program in *Les Colons*. Randau's final declaration nonetheless betrays the extreme slipperiness of his labels: surely his "decentralization" might be another's "separatism." The program he has evoked, however, does not necessarily imply either, since "rayonnement de la culture," even from several sources, might really be more a gesture of gathering in, of attaching far-flung "possessions" more firmly to Paris. This, though, was where Randau and the Algerianists differed from proponents of other contemporary rhetorics of Frenchness: while they usually stopped short of separatism and paid more than lipservice to spreading French culture, they also recognized their local particularities in ways which went beyond Barrèsian regionalism. Barrès had never spoken of an independent *littérature lorraine*; by contrast, the Algerianists insisted on the development of *la littérature algérienne*, both within and alongside *la littérature française*. For them, "rayonnement intellectuel" necessarily passed through (when it did not originate in) layers of local difference. For Algeria to come truly into its own, and gain the place it deserved in French cultural and political life, the public would have to recognize this specificity. That it never did may today seem like a foreshadowing of 1962, when a majority in mainland France concurred in simply not wishing to hear about French Algeria any longer.[77] The European Algerians of Randau's day could not have imagined such an eventuality, and continued to do their best to instruct the mainland public on the political and cultural realities of the colony. Although one might certainly view their efforts as condemned by history, they are more compellingly seen as attempts to hammer out the connections between the local and the national in French identity, at a time when that identity was the center of vigorous debate in both France and its colonies.

NOTES

1. Another work of his, temptingly titled *Les Algérianistes*, routinely appears listed among his publications, often immediately after *Les Colons*. The Bibliothèque Nationale (BN) does not own it, and I have been unable to consult a copy elsewhere.

2. Robert Randau, *Les Colons: roman de la patrie algérienne* (Paris: E. Sansot, 1907), 40.

3. Robert Randau, *Cassard le Berbère* (1922; Algiers: Jules Carbonel, 1926), preface, n.p. I cite from the odd in-4th edition of 1926, the only one easily consultable

at the BN. It apparently reproduces a handwritten copy Randau made for the occasion, with pen-and-ink illustrations.

4. Randau, *Cassard le Berbère*, 19.

5. Ibid., 160.

6. Ibid.

7. Peter Dunwoodie, *Writing French Algeria* (Oxford: Clarendon Press, 1998), 144.

8. Jean Déjeux, "Introduction," in *Espagne et Algérie au XXe siècle: Contacts culturels et création littéraire*, ed. Jean Déjeux (Paris: L'Harmattan, 1985), 9.

9. Robert Randau, *Les Colons* (1907; Paris: Albin-Michel, 1926), 7.

10. *Moukère* is not Arabic, but a *sabir* (nineteenth-century Mediterranean patois) word for woman, derived from Spanish *mujer*. The *Trésor de la langue française* attests to its use from virtually the beginning of the occupation of Algiers. *Kahoua* and its variants (Ar. *qahwa*, coffee) see occasional use in contemporary spoken French.

11. Eugène Pujarniscle, *Philoxène ou de la littérature coloniale* (Paris: Firmin-Didot, 1931), 177.

12. Ibid.

13. Randau, *Les Colons*, 27. "Numéro ouhad," numero uno; "chbab," perhaps derived from Arabic *shabb*, pl. *shabab*, young unmarried person.

14. Randau, *Les Colons*, 48. "Béni kelb," son of a dog; "çof," Kabyle clan; "cahouète," probably from the Arabic *qawwad*, pimp.

15. Randau, *Les Colons*, 19.

16. Ibid., preface, 8.

17. Many historians have documented these dealings; see for example David Prochaska's chapters on the acquisition of land for cork-oak plantations and mines in *Making Algeria French*.

18. Randau, *Les Colons*, 311.

19. Ibid., 314.

20. Randau, *Cassard le Berbère*, 114.

21. Randau, *Les Colons*, 8.

22. Ibid., 284.

23. Ibid., 193.

24. Ibid., 209.

25. Randau, *Les Colons*, 197. For "mentules genates," I supect Randau meant "mentules géantes," giant phalluses, even if the *Trésor de la langue française* does not recognize any French word derived from the Latin *mentula*, penis.

26. Randau, *Les Colons*, 187–8. In "mokotte" we might hear a derivative of "moukère" and "cocotte."

27. Randau, *Les Colons*, preface, 8.

28. For a recent example, see Ali Behdad's *Belated Travelers*, or the work of Lisa Lowe on colonial exoticism.

29. Randau, *Les Colons*, 289.

30. Randau, *Cassard le Berbère*, 265.

31. Pujarniscle, *Philoxène ou de la littérature coloniale*, 8.

32. Ibid.

33. Jean Pomier, "Robert Randau, son art, sa pensée," *Afrique*, no. 52 (July 1929): 1.

34. Roland Lebel, *Histoire de la littérature coloniale en France* (Paris: Larose, 1931), 212.

35. Jean Pomier, "Agir," in *A cause d'Alger* (Toulouse: Edouard Privat, 1966). The collection gives no date for the poem, and I have not discovered which Randau novel Pomier meant it to preface.

36. Jean Pomier, "Chez les poètes," *Afrique*, no. 55 (January 1930): 2.

37. The citizenship law of 1889 granted automatic naturalization to all ethnic European children born in Algeria or in France. Charles-Robert Ageron says that "La loi de 1889 devait donner annuellement environ 3,500 Français dans les premières années puis, environ 4,000 et quelque 5,000 dans la période 1901–1907. Avec un contingent moyen de 500–600 naturalisés volontaires, on voit que plus de 4,000 et bientôt 5,529 (moyenne 1901–1907) étrangers vivant en Algérie devenaient chaque année citoyens. Ces chiffres ne pouvaient aller qu'en augmentant puisque naissaient annuellement quelque 8,500 enfants d'étrangers, plus de la moité des naissances européennes, et que l'immigration étrangère continuait, représentant en moyenne annuelle 1,700 personnes de plus que l'immigration fraçaise. Rétrospectivement, on a pu estimer que la loi de 1889 avait créé entre 160,000 et 170,000 citoyens français en trente ans" [The law of 1889 annually produced about 3,500 French citizens in the first years, and then 4–5,000 between 1901 and 1907. With an average contingent of 500 to 600 voluntary naturalizations each year, we can see that more than 4,000 and soon 5,529 foreigners (the average over 1901–1907) living in Algeria became citizens each year. These figures could only grow, since 8,500 children of foreigners were born each year, more than half the European births in the colony, and since foreign immigration continued, amounting every year to 1,700 more than the French immigration. Retrospectively, it was estimated that the law of 1889 created between 160,000 and 170,000 French citizens over 30 years] (*Histoire de l'Algérie contemporaine*, 120).

38. Favre twice reworked and lengthened her *Tout l'inconnu de la Casbah d'Alger* (Algiers: Baconnier, 1933), first as *Dans la Casbah* (Paris: Grasset, 1937), and then as *Dans la Casbah 1937–1948* (Paris: Ed. Colette d'Halloin, 1949).

39. Jean Pomier, "Algériennement," *Afrique*, no. 1 (April 1924): 1.

40. The phrase occurred several more times in print in *Afrique*, as late as November 1930.

41. Pomier, "Algériennement," 1.

42. Ibid.

43. Contemporary newscasters use "madinat al-jazā'ir," the city of Algiers, to refer to the capital.

44. In a 1987 interview, Kateb Yacine commented on the Arabocentric thinking evidenced in naming the entire country "L'Algérie":

Kateb Yacine: 'L'Algérie', ce n'est pas le vrai nom de notre pays. C'est un terme touristique. *Ldjazaïr*, c'est quoi?

Tassadit Yacine: 'Les Iles' . . .

Kateb Yacine: Vous avez vu un pays s'appeler 'Les Iles'? Ce sont les Arabes qui l'ont appelé ainsi.

[**Kateb Yacine:** 'L'Algérie' is not the real name of our country. It's a tourist term. What's *Ldjazaïr*?

Tassadit Yacine: 'The Islands' . . .

Kateb Yacine: Have you ever heard of a country called 'The Islands'? The Arabs are the ones who called it that.] ("C'est africain qu'il faut se dire," interview by Tassadit Yacine, in *Le Poète comme un boxeur* [Paris: Seuil, 1994], 101).

45. Charles Akoun, "Nécessité des méthodes algérianistes," *Afrique*, no. 51 (June 1929): 8.

46. Dunwoodie, *Writing French Algeria*, 147, 302.

47. Pomier, "Robert Randau, son art, sa pensée," 2.

48. Claude-Maurice Robert, "Un livre impie," *Afrique*, no. 58 (April 1930).

49. Robert Randau later published several criticisms of Gide, including "Inactualité d'André Gide," *Afrique*, no. 195 (June 1944): 14–16. There, he reproaches Gide for something he found even more objectionable than homosexuality: his lack of involvement in current events in France, and notably the absence of any evidence of suffering in Gide's latest book, *Attendu que . . .* (Algiers: Charlot, 1944). Guy Dugas reproduces this and other articles by Algerian writers from the thirties and forties in "Les Algérianistes et Gide," *Bulletin des Amis d'André Gide* 22, no. 102 (April 1994): 287–311. In private correspondance Randau would not be nearly so reserved about Gide's homosexuality, which he saw as the negation of the colonial and national reinvigoration Algerian literature needed to provide for France. Dugas cites from Randau's correspondance in "André Gide en Algérie: Les Ecrivains d'Algérie face à la morale gidienne," *Bulletin des Amis d'André Gide* 22, no. 102 (April 1994): 249–68.

50. In an earlier phase of their careers, the Tharaud brothers had been successively employed by Maurice Barrès as his personal secretaries. Jérôme, the elder, was elected to the Académie in 1941, and Jean received Bertrand's seat (formerly Barrès's) in 1947.

51. Jean Pomier, "[Notice sur Stephan]," *Afrique*, no. 61 (July–August 1930): 7. Stephan's work, a whitewashed portrait which feminist scholars have found no less objectionable than the earlier moralizing rejection of Eberhardt, was called *Isabelle Eberhardt ou la passion du désert* (Paris: Flammarion, 1930).

52. "Étienne Dinet," *La Presse libre*, 6 January 1930.

53. During the pre- and early colonial period, a number of women of the Oulad Nail clans went to desert oasis towns (and some to the coast as well) to work as entertainers and prostitutes. Having amassed a dowry, they then returned to their villages, according to the legend, and married respectably. Dinet points out in the preface to *Khadra* that the detail of the dowry, at least, cannot have been true since among the Oulad Nail, as elsewhere in the Muslim world, the groom provided the dowry. The terms "Oulad Nail," "Nailette," or their variations signified "prostitute" in colonial fiction and travel writing. The term gained such currency that the label "Quartier des Oulad Nail" on city plans in guidebooks told tourists where to find the red light district. A study of the legend elaborated around the Oulad Nail by the French in the years immediately following the conquest remains to be undertaken.

54. Sliman ben Ibrahim Baamer, *Khadra, danseuse Ouled Nail*, illus. Étienne Dinet (Paris: H. Piazza, 1926), x–xi.

55. Jean Pomier, "Attitudes devant l'Islam: celle d'Étienne Dinet," *Afrique*, no. 56 (February 1930): 2.

56. Ibid., 4.

57. Ibid.

58. The spelling "Nacr er Din" is impossible, even in French transcription; the Arabic article al- assimilates to the d, to give "Nāṣir ad-dīn," "victor (or helper or friend) of the religion," Dinet's Islamicized name (Pomier, "Attitudes devant l'Islam: celle d'Étienne Dinet," 5).

59. Jean and Jérôme Thauraud, *Les Heures marocaines*, cited by Robert, "Un Livre impie," 5.

60. Robert, "Un Livre impie," 6.

61. Ibid., 6, note.

62. Pomier, "Algériennement," 1.

63. Ibid.

64. Jean Pomier, "Le Prix Littéraire Algérien et la politique du prix," *Afrique*, no. 3 (June 1924): 1.

65. Ibid., 2.

66. Prizewinners from 1921 to 1939, as reconstituted from review articles and given in an appendix to Ahmed Lanasri, *La littérature algérienne de l'entre-deux-guerres: génèse et fonctionnement* (Paris: Publisud, 1995), 533–34.

1921—Ferdinand Duchêne, *Au pas lent des caravanes* (Paris: Albin Michel, 1922), *Thamil'la* (Paris: Albin Michel, 1923), and *Au pied des monts éternels* (Paris: Albin Michel, 1925).

1922—Maximilienne Heller, *La Mer rouge*.

1923—Gabriel Esquer, *La Prise d'Alger* (Paris: Larose, 1929) (reedition of a historical study).

1924—Louis Lecoq, *Cinq dans ton oeil* (Paris: Rieder, 1925).

1925—Gabriel Audisio, *Trois hommes et un minaret* (Paris: Rieder, 1926).

1926—Albert Tustes, for eight collections of poetry, known as *Les Méditerrannéennes*, 1906–1926.

1927—Charles Courtin, *La Brousse qui mangea l'homme* (Paris: Editions de France, 1929).

1928—No prize given.

1929—Robert Randau, for his complete works.

1930—Charles Hagel, *Drames africaines* (Algiers: Soubiron, 1930).

1931—Jeanne Faure-Sardet, *Deux femmes* (Paris: La Jeune Académie, 1930) (does not figure in the collection of the Bibliothèque Nationale); and Lucienne Favre, for her complete works.

1932—No prize given.

1933—A. Tony Zannet, *Carmélo* (Paris: Taillandier, 1934).

1934—Claude-Maurice Robert, *La Couronne des ronces* (Algiers: Soubiron, 1932) (poems),—*L'Envoûtement du Sud* (Algiers: 1934), and *Dans le silence et la lumière* (Algiers: Soubiron, 1934).

1935—Magali Boisnard, for her complete works (mostly historical novels).

1936—General Paul Azan, for his complete historical works.

1937—Paul Achard, *L'Homme de mer* (Paris: Editions de France, 1931).

1938—René Lespès, *Oran* (Paris: Alcan, 1938) (urban study).

1939—No prize given.

67. Pierre Martino, "La Littérature algérienne," in *Histoire et historiens de l'Algérie*, Collection du Centenaire (Paris: Félix Alcan, 1931), 346.

68. On Cagayous, see David Prochaska, "History as Literature, Literature as History," *American Historical Review* 101, no. 3 (Fall 1996).

69. The Franco-Algerian writer and critic Gabriel Audisio prefaced a collection of the stories for Gallimard in 1931.

70. Martino, "La Littérature algérienne," 346–47.

71. Jean Pomier, "[Sur la mort de Musette]," *Afrique*, no. 62 (September–October 1930): 2.

72. Martino, "La Littérature algérienne," 347.

73. Robert Randau, "La Littérature coloniale, hier et aujourd'hui," *Revue des deux mondes*, 15 July 1929, 429.

74. Randau, "La Littérature coloniale, hier et aujourd'hui," 431. A *seniare* (more commonly *signare*) was a Senegalese woman of mixed race, originally from Gorée or Saint-Louis, and *congai* seems to have been virtually synonymous with "concubine" in Indochina.

75. Randau, "La Littérature coloniale, hier et aujourd'hui," 432.

76. Ibid.

77. Benjamin Stora notes the haste with which French politicians (and notably de Gaulle) rid themselves of Algeria, once they had decided to do so, and attributes this haste to the sense among the public that the Algerian war was a "trouble-fête" in the midst of the "trente glorieuses" (*La Gangrène et l'oubli: la mémoire de la guerre d'Algérie* [Paris: La Découverte, 1991]).

3

The *Roman indigène*: Anthropological Fiction and Its Consequences

Since the work of Edward Said and the critiques it triggered, critics of colonial literature have often been particularly interested in searching for the ways in which the pro-colonial discourses of the literature they study break down, or in locating the spaces in which literary acts of resistance to the dominant order take place. Carried out within the genres of literature produced in French Algeria, such a search might disappoint those determined to find shows of resistance, but an examination of a few places likely to harbor aporia in the colonial discourse nonetheless provides lessons for reading resistance in colonial texts. This chapter will examine a genre of the 1920s which contemporaries labeled *romans indigènes*: novels about or by Arabs and Imazighen. We might expect that giving voice to colonized protagonists would provide a potential opening for an alternative view of the colonial project. Novels by ethnic European writers about non-European protagonists may seem to promise such a view, since they frequently stressed the failure of the assimilationist project. Not surprisingly, however, they generally proposed a conservative rehash of stereotypes justifying the French *mission civilisatrice*. The other novels labelled as *romans indigènes*, those actually written by Arabs and Imazighen, do provide a counterdiscourse to that mission, but they do so, of necessity, in such a muted tone as to read rather ambiguously today. The very first Arab or Amazigh writers to publish in French, Mohammed Ben Cherif (1879–1921), Chukri Khodja (1891–1967), and Mohammed Ould Cheikh (1906–1938), whose works predate by thirty years the canonical firsts of Mouloud Feraoun, Mohammed Dib, and Mouloud Mammeri, may not in fact fit neatly into our current notion of how

counterdiscourses to colonial ideology should sound. Literary critic
Richard Terdiman has identified the task of counterdiscourse as a "mapping of the internal incoherence of the seemingly univocal and monumental institution of dominant discourse."[1] What happens, however,
when the dominant discourse has the power to recuperate its own
"internal incoherence"? What happens in situations like Algeria in the
twenties, with a heavier discursive policing than Terdiman's example of
nineteenth-century France, where a counterdiscourse can scarcely find the
space to exist?[2] As practiced by Europeans, the *indigène* novel points to an
incoherence (the failure of assimilation) that turns out to be only an apparent crack in the dominant discourse. The introduction of new voices
gives way to univocality and demonstrates that the dominant discourse
could incorporate seemingly contradictory material while neither changing its overall direction or losing its dominance. By contrast, in the works
by Algerians, the counterdiscourse proposed had to be extremely subtle,
and inevitably participated in an array of contingent arguments and discursive compromises. We should remember here just how early this moment was in what would in retrospect become the history of counterdiscourses to colonialism. Algeria, like other parts of the French colonial
empire, would begin to hear much more explicit talk about the end of
French rule in the 1940s and '50s. None of the conditions that allowed this
development (occasional support of Paris intellectuals, recent French military defeats, publishers interested in literature questioning imperialism)
were present in the 1920s. Algeria moreover was the site of an outpouring
of colonialist rhetoric without parallel elsewhere in the French empire,
which nowhere saw the same quantity, quality, or diversity of books published supporting the development of colonial culture and the ideology
with which we are now familiar.

We have seen how the literary movements of Latin Africa and early Algerianism reacted initially against portrayals of the colonized; one could
read a dozen early Algerianist novels without encountering a single significant Arab or Amazigh character. In the 1920s, however, the program of
the *Association des Ecrivains Algériens* did not advise novelists against using Muslim characters or from presenting ethnographic details they
thought relevant. The declaration of its president and leading critic Jean
Pomier that "we must work Algerianly" explicitly included Algeria's
Arab heritage along with the Latin, and the Arabs and Imazighen along
with those of European origin. Here we will see in greater detail the restrictive terms of what would prove a limited inclusion.

A number of treatments of French colonial literature have suggested
that the apotheosis of colonialism came in the 1931 Exposition Coloniale
Internationale. The historian Charles-Robert Ageron, however, remarks
that if 1930–1931 truly marked the apogee of the colonial ideal, it was an

imperialist rather than a republican one: Ageron situates the true peak of republican interest in the colonies later, and, noting that the valorization of 1930–1931 occurred after decolonization, suspects that it came about due to a political choice of the promoters of pro-colonial nostalgia. In Algeria, it was precisely around 1930 that relations among ethnic groups in Algeria reemerged as a point of contention.[3] Even as the Gouvernement Général was establishing, well in advance, the commission charged with preparing the celebrations for the Centenary, it found itself confronted with demands for reform coming from several quarters. Kabyle and Arab elected officials, together with a number of French politicians, demanded representation in the Assemblée Nationale for the vast majority of Arab and Amazigh Algerians who were not naturalized French citizens. This argument developed especially near the end of the 1920s, in the writings of leftist pamphleteers like Jean Mélia and Victor Spielmann, and of Maurice Violette, former Governor General, in his widely commented polemic, *L'Algérie vivra-t-elle?* [Will Algeria Live?], and most of all in the Arab and European press.[4] The problem of elected representation for the colonized hinged on their citizenship: Algerian Arabs and Imazighen were French subjects, not enjoying the rights of citizens.[5] In the early twentieth century, only the Jewish portion of the non-European population held the rights of French citizens, following the *décret Crémieux* of 1870. Colonial apologists routinely declared that Muslim Algerians could become citizens as soon as they chose, as long as they gave up the status of *Français musulmans* which gave them exemption from a number of French laws, notably those regulating marriage, inheritance, and family matters, even as it subjected them to the humiliations of the laws directed specifically at Muslims. A few did (several hundred annually), especially those who worked for the railway or in other jobs granting attractive pension plans to citizen employees. The rest did not, partly because they saw renouncing their Muslim personal status as tantamount to apostasy. Several journals in the Muslim press did what they could to combat this belief, which, writers claimed, had little precedent in most interpretations of the *Qur'an* and *shari`a*.[6] The real problem lay with the colonial administration, which did everything it could to keep the number of requests to a minimum, and to delay or refuse those it received. Under these conditions, most members of the Muslim political opposition and their French friends demanded representation for nonnaturalized *Français musulmans* as the only means of democratizing Algeria. By 1930, Muslims had already for some years been elected to Algerian offices, including to the powerful Délégations financières, and to city councils throughout the colony, though most Muslim candidates were more or less promoted to their positions by the colonial administration. The vast majority of the French political class, however, successfully opposed their election to the

Sénat and the Assemblée, ostensibly on Constitutional grounds: nonciti-
zens could not be electors. A number of politicians sympathetic to the
Muslim opposition proposed ways of dealing with this problem, ranging
from ignoring it and allowing them to vote anyway, to naturalizing selected portions of the population: Imazighen, army veterans, or the formally educated.[7] Representatives of the *colons* opposed these schemes. At
the same time, they demanded restrictions on the Muslims' right to seek
work in France, hoping to stem the outward flow of workers who would
no longer be available for farm employment in the colony. All these issues
decisively influenced the literature examined in this chapter, beginning
with a question the French never resolved: to what extent should they
adopt a special policy toward the Imazighen?

French Berber policy had already undergone several transformations
since the initial conquest of Kabylia in the 1840s.[8] By 1844, General Daumas had outlined an early inventory of knowledge on the Amazigh world
in *La Grande Kabylia, études historiques* [Greater Kabylia, Historical Stud-
ies].[9] Daumas was the first major proponent of a rigid binary opposition
between Arab and Kabyle cultures and peoples, an idea which he continued to support in his *Moeurs et coutumes de l'Algérie* [Manners and Customs of Algeria], published in 1853, and reprinted several times; his work
informed that of several generations of French travelers writing about Algeria.[10] At the time, the hypothesis of an Arab-Berber dichotomy carried
with it an essentially racist valorization of the "good Kabyle" (sedentary,
secularist, perhaps descended from ancient Christian or European origins, and susceptible to assimilation) over the "bad Arab" (nomadic, fa-
natically Muslim, Semitic, and hostile to any assimilation with the
French). This idea would persist well beyond the "discovery period" of
initial contacts, a period ending with the Kabyle revolt of 1871 and the
publication of General Adolphe Hanoteau and A. Letourneux's monumental *Kabylia et les coutumes kabyles* [Kabylia and Kabyle Customs] the
following year.[11] The "Berber myth" is an excellent example of the persistence of discredited beliefs despite constant negative reinforcement,
when the beliefs in question can be mobilized to support diverse political
causes.

Writing at the end of the 1860s, the General and his jurist coauthor had
nonetheless declared that they could not share what they called the "illusions" of secularism and aptitude for assimilation of the Kabyles: "As-
surément, aux yeux d'un vrai croyant, les Kabyles peuvent ne pas être des
musulmans irréprochables. . . . Mais, en tout ce qui concerne le dogme et
les croyances religieuses, leur foi est aussi naïve, aussi entière; aussi aveugle que celle des musulmans les plus rigides. Loin de les regarder comme
plus favorables que d'autres à notre domination, nous les croyons, au contraire, plus hostiles, parce que cette domination ne froisse pas seulement

leurs préjugés religieux, mais blesse profondément le sentiment, si vivace chez eux, d'indépendance." [Assuredly the Kabyles may not be irre-proachable Muslims in the eyes of a true believer. . . . However, in matters of dogma and religious beliefs, their faith is just as naive, whole, and blind as that of the most rigid Muslims. Far from viewing them as more favor-able than others to our domination, we believe them on the contrary to be more hostile to it, because this domination not only offends their religious prejudices, but also deeply wounds the sentiment of independence that is very strong among them.][12] This seems only sensible, but few people writ-ing about Berber policy took it to heart. Ten years and more later, colonial authorities and apologists still wanted to believe the opposite. Almost all later writers on the Imazighen repeatedly cite Hanoteau and Letourneux, all the while writing as if these primary authorities had never once ques-tioned the myth of assimilation. The enthusiastic assimilationists Émile Guimet or Camille Sabatier, or the zealous missionaries Charmetant and Dugas, all publishing well after the appearance of *Kabylie et les coutumes kabyles*, ignored its cautions about assimilation.[13] Most of them had polit-ical aims: Sabatier, for example, could use the Berber's supposed in-difference to religion for his own extremely anticlerical agenda. Pseudo-scientific discourses on the Kabyles could differ significantly from those of ethnologists. Fifteen years later, another constantly cited ethnological authority, Émile Masqueray, would be treated by his successors in the same way as Hanoteau and Letourneux, despite the differences between his theses and theirs.[14] Other writers praised his work, but continued to ignore if not obscure his most important ideas. Masqueray's principle contribution to the field was his observation of the changeability of Kabyle social groups and of the mobility and flexibility of their institu-tions; his was the very opposite of the stationary view which subsequent authors adopted.[15] Thirty-five years later, the successful novelist Ferdi-nand Duchêne would publish a series of nine novels in which questions of Berber anthropology figure very prominently, and in which he would frequently refer to the ethnological literature on Kabylia. In these novels, the Kabyles would appear static, fixed in time and in their "eternal cus-toms," exactly as if Masqueray's work on Kabyle anthropology had had no impact whatever.

Duchêne, a French-born magistrate in Dellys on the Kabyle coast, later became a *conseiller* at the Algiers appeals court. Trying his hand at litera-ture around 1920, he turned to the Kabyles for subject matter. He was not the first to do so and did not singlehandedly invent the *indigène* novel in its European-authored form. The versatile novelist Charles Géniaux had already published stories with Arab or Kabyle settings, but was clearly less concerned with depicting the milieu than with exoticist *dépaysement*.[16] The painter Etienne Dinet was collaborating with Sliman ben Ibrahim

Baamer on a series of novels and short stories portraying a highly exoti-
cized version of desert life. Whatever critics said of Dinet the man (suspect, as we saw in the last chapter, for his conversion to Islam), his collaboration with an Arab and his own extensive experience in Algeria
forced them to accept his descriptions as ethnographically accurate.[17] This
reception was the real hallmark of a *indigène* novel: books that participated fully in the genre were read as containing accurate anthropological
details on the *indigènes*. Here Duchêne clearly surpassed his colleagues.
His novels, he repeatedly declares, were largely inspired by his experience as a colonial magistrate; for him, they derive most of their value from
their "real-life" origins, just as any colonial novel should, according to the
Algerianists. His career successes as a judge appear respectable if not brilliant, but he managed to publish nine novels with the Paris editor Albin
Michel between 1922 and 1930.[18] Albin Michel brought his work out in
one of their more successful collections, edited by Henri de Régnier of the
Académie Française, "Le Roman littéraire" a label expressing the editor's
expectations for Duchêne's work: middle-brow respectability leading to
significant sales figures. The promoters of Algerian literature rewarded
three of his novels with the first Grand Prix Littéraire de l'Algérie in 1921,
amid admiring commentary on the accuracy of their representation of
Berber reality.[19] Finally, as we will see, a number of his novels, especially
those he called "Kabyle" or "Berbère," received official consecration in the
1920s as authoritative texts in the Berber policy debate.

A sample of Duchêne's novels will outline some of his favorite dramatic
situations, as well as the *topoi* of his cultural commentary. *Thamil'la* (1923)
stages the tragic melodrama of the eponymous heroine, a Kabyle girl. Her
father marries her to Akli, interpreter at the Dellys magistrate's court, and
she discovers to everyone's surprise that she loves her husband. Meziane,
the shrewd and mean-spirited father, spoils everything by sequestering
her at his house and forcing her to ask for a separation from her husband,
in a complicated scheme to make Akli forgive one of Meziane's debts in
order to get his wife back. Once back with her husband, Thamil'la lives in
fear of a curse placed on him by a marabout paid off by her father, who
had told her Akli planned to force her to convert to Christianity and bap-
tize her daughter. This sours her relationship with her husband, who
takes another wife and repudiates Thamil'la. Meziane "sells" her again (a
constantly recurring event in Duchêne's novels) to a disgusting and brutal merchant. When the French imprison the man for having killed
his own son, Meziane refuses to let Thamil'la come back to live with him.
She wanders into the mountains, where a gang of thieves rape her and
sell her into prostitution. She escapes and limps back to Dellys, where
she finds her husband again, but too late; she dies miserably in the public
hospital.

Duchêne persists in the same vein in the more complicated plot of *La Rek'ba, histoire d'une vendetta kabyle* (1927). Mansour ben Ahmed sells his prepubescent daughter Baya to Khalil ben Larbi, who repudiates her when his family persuades him she brings bad luck. The "bad luck" consisted in Khelil's prosecution by the French for the statutory rape of Baya herself when he consummates the marriage. Rejected by her family as well, Baya wanders into the mountains where she is raped again. Her attacker marries her to avoid scandal; later, however, when he becomes impotent after an illness, he kills her by cutting off one of her breasts, in an effort to cure himself. His family and Baya's then exterminate one another in a gory and repetitive vendetta. The French judicial system manages only to send one family member to the penal colony at Cayenne and to guillotine another. The vendetta ends when an itinerant marabout preaches a sermon calling for revolt and holy war against the Christians. The two sole survivors exchange daggers and bury their animosity before rearming to face the common enemy, the French. The stereotype of the docile and assimilable Berber found no favor with Duchêne.

Vendettas and Kabyle injustice dominate two other novels, *Le Berger d'Akfadou* [The Shepherd of Akfadou] (1928), and *L'Aventure de Sidi Flouss* [The Adventure of Sidi Flouss] (1929). In the first, the protagonist, thwarted in his plan to raise the money to buy the hand of the girl he loves, finds his actions taken as an excuse for a vendetta, of which he is the last, innocent victim. A note to the text cites the historian Augustin Bernard: "Ce sont les querelles de çofs qui sont le fondement même de l'âme berbère" [the quarrels of factions are the very foundation of the Berber soul].[20] In the second novel, a rich Kabyle, educated and partially assimilated in the French school system, finds himself reduced to matching wits with corrupt Berber notables and forced to gather an armed band of family members to protect himself from a vendetta he inherited along with his father's money. Only after deflecting the brutality and corruption of his fellow Berbers can he marry and live the life of an *évolué*, a modernized and assimilated colonial subject. This happy ending is almost unique in Duchêne's work: for him, life in Kabylia is nasty, brutish, and short.

Such bloody subject matter contrasts vividly with the official propaganda of the day, which held up the image of a peaceful and modern colony in which all ethnic groups lived in harmony. Was Duchêne attempting to suggest, in this apparent counterdiscourse, that there was something wrong in the colony, and that colonialism had not fulfilled its promises? We will shortly see some reasons why he might have been doing so. Even if he were, it is by no means clear that his work evidences anything like the counterdiscourse to colonialism that some postcolonial critics have attempted to find in problematizing the literature and film from the period. In a 1984 article on what they identify as contradictions between the triumphant discourses of the Algerian centenary celebrations and the representation of Arab and Berber characters in colonial novels, the critics Christiane Achour and Simone Rezzoug admit the literary defects of the novels they examine, but look to them nonetheless for aporias and fissures in the official discourse. Any text that frankly and openly presented the difficulties of assimilation, or contained *indigène* characters not docilely acquiescent to the cultural projects of French Algeria, would for them participate in a more positive discourse of resistance to colonialism.[21] This seems like a dangerous assumption: in our desire to find something other than pure domination, it is unwise to forget the capacity of the colonialist discourse to recuperate opposing arguments and turn them to its advantage. Despite the wish of some recent critics to see some hints of resistance in the complexities of certain colonial texts, Duchêne's novels remain above all proponents of the system their magistrate author helped perpetuate.

Admittedly, a first look at Ferdinand Duchêne's work suggests that it occasionally fulfills Achour and Rezzoug's criteria for the formation of a counterdiscourse, since his assimilated characters have nothing but trouble, and his traditionalist characters are anything but docile to the French administration. In *La Rek'ba*, the characters pursuing their vendetta try hard to avoid involving the French criminal justice system, for which they have only scorn. Though well-educated, Sidi Flouss, whose name might be translated as "Mr. Money," still has to lower himself to the use of force, threats, and trickery, all habits, according to Duchêne, of "unevolved" Berbers. In another novel, a French-educated Berber official cannot govern his village until he abandons his enlightened French principles, and in the end Kabyle customs, "éternelles, tolérées par dieu . . . reprenaient tout leur empire" [eternal, tolerated by God . . . reasserted their full hold].[22] The novels hold out little hope of improving the morals, condition, or disposition of the colonized, and thereby justify the violence of what colonial administratiors called "energetic measures" in dealing with them. Duchêne usually proves incapable of speaking of "customs" without qualifying them as "eternal": everywhere he accentuates the enormous gulf which separated the Kabyles from the French and the strength of the Kabyle traditions which made any hope for assimilation seem ridiculously utopian.

For all that, Duchêne hardly produces a counterdiscourse to the official one boasting of colonialism's triumphs. His work ultimately demonstrates the diversity of the dominant discourse, capable of gathering strength exactly where later critics like Achour and Rezzoug hope to find it destabilized. Although triumphalism and assimilation were the dominant features of colonialist writing at the time, they were not the only features. They did not rule out other modes of writing with rather different impact, that were nonetheless equally pro-colonial. Citations from two very different examples of the Algerian press in 1930 make this clear. First, a lyric from l'*Afrique du Nord illustrée*, the *Life* magazine of Algeria between the wars:

> Le 14 juin 1830, les Armées de Charles X débarquaient sur la plage de Sidi-Ferruch pour venir pacifier la terre barbaresque. Un siècle plus tard jour pour jour, les représentants de la France et des indigènes, libérés du joug des deys d'Alger, sont venus communier dans le même amour de la Patrie et la même lutte pour le Progrès.

> [On the 14 June 1830, the armies of Charles X landed on the beach of Sidi-Ferruch to come pacify the Barbary lands. A century later to the day, the representatives of the French and of the *indigènes*, freed from the yoke of the deys of Algiers, came to commune in the same love of their country and the same struggle for progress.][23]

Second, a diatribe from *L'Evolution nord-africaine*, which an Algerian Communist once called "l'organe officiel des arabophobes" [the official organ of the Arabophobic]:[24]

> La France ne parachèvera son oeuvre grandiose que si elle sait demeurer suffisamment longtemps la bienfaisante tutrice des populations qu'elle a arrachées à l'obscurantisme et à la tyrannie turque. . . . L'oublier serait compromettre l'avenir de toutes les populations qui vivent sur la terre algérienne et ruiner vainement cent ans de sacrifices et d'efforts français . . . IL Y A DANS LA COLONIE, 500.000 FRANÇAIS, MAIS IL Y A CINQ MILLIONS INDIGÈNES.
> CETTE MASSE MUSULMANE—PAR FANATISME ET PAR IGNORANCE —SES ÉLUS PAR SPÉCULATION POLITIQUE—DEMEURENT EN TRÈS GRANDE PARTIE HOSTILE À NOTRE CIVILISATION ET À NOTRE NATIONALITÉ.

> [France will not finish its grandiose work unless it is capable of remaining for long enough the beneficent guardian of the populations which it tore from obscurantism and Turkish tyranny. . . . To forget this would be to compromise the future of all the populations living on Algerian soil and to ruin, for nothing, a hundred years of French sacrifices and efforts . . . IN THE COLONY, THERE ARE 500,000 FRENCH PEOPLE, BUT THERE ARE FIVE MILLION INDIGÈNES.
> THE GREAT MAJORITY AMONG THESE MUSLIM MASSES AND THEIR ELECTED REPRESENTATIVES, THE FORMER OUT OF FANATICISM AND IGNORANCE, THE LATTER OUT OF POLITICAL CONSIDERATIONS, REMAIN HOSTILE TO OUR CIVILIZATION AND NATIONALITY.][25]

The first quote illustrates the dominant triumphalism mixed with professions of peaceful intentions which characterized the official optimism

of the time. All combats are in the past, and, communing with the colonizers in faith in the Fatherland, the colonized stand on the threshold of
assimilation. The second quote derides this Polyanna-ish idea, but
nonetheless does not provide the least escape from colonialist discourse.
For Charles-Collomb, editor of *l'Evolution*, the colony's alleged brilliant
success does not obscure the limited progression of assimilation. For
many polemicists like him, assimilation represented a trap, not for the
Muslims, who risked alienation, but for the European Algerians, who
risked deception by false appearances of acculturation among the colonized. The ethnological idea underlying Charles-Collomb's venom holds
that the Muslims remained for the most part as backward as when the
French arrived; this idea informed a great many of the articles coming
from all parts of the political spectrum. The idea that assimilation was a
failure did not necessarily lead to any real questioning of colonialism's
morality or progress, nor anything like a counterdiscourse to it. In this
context, the political impact of Duchêne's work becomes clear when we
consider an article in *Annales nord-africaines* in which an anonymous author declared that people might be less enthusiastic about giving political
representation to the *indigènes* if they heard recent "histoires du bled"
[stories from the hinterland], reports of barbarism in the countryside.[26]
Duchêne gave a conservative public exactly that, stories from the hinterland in which barbarism and nonassimilation dominate, rendering impossible the idea of according political responsibility to such unworthy
subjects. The features of his work with the greatest apparent potential for
subversion (the revelation that assimilation has failed) turn out to carry
the most conservative message, due partly to the political context, and
partly to the way the novels themselves demanded that readers interpret
them.

What Duchêne called his *romans berbères* constitute a striking example
of a body of fiction which succeeded in dictating the manner of
its interpretation. They called very clearly for a documentary reception
by engaging explicitly with scholarly anthropological texts, and by
producing their own network of footnotes, references, and interpretive
commentary. This documentary apparatus, absent in the first of the "Barbaresques," appears quickly enough in *Thamil'la*, the second, where
Duchêne starts in on his favorite subject, the Berbers of Kabylia. Prefaces,
introductions, explanatory notes, and references increased in frequency
and length as the series progressed, and as Duchêne's conviction of his
status as an authority grew. *La Rek'ba*, for example, opens with this "Déc-
laration": "Tout ce que j'ai écrit sur les Barbaresques est vrai ou possible.
À propos de chaque épisode de n'importe lequel de mes livres, je pour-
rais citer des références, des témoignages, des écrits, des jugements. Mes
personnages ont eu pour la plupart, dans la vie, un sosie ou un parent de

caractère, d'attitude. Et il n'est pas une phrase, placée dans la bouche d'un indigène, qui ne puisse être traduite en arabe usuel, presque mot pour mot." [Everything I have written on the Barbaresques is true or possible. Regarding every episode in each one of my books, I could cite references, eyewitness accounts, writings, and court judgments. For their personalities and attitudes, most of my characters have had a double or a close relative in real life. And there is not one sentence, placed in the mouth of an *indigène*, that could not be translated almost word for word into vernacular Arabic.]²⁷ These propositions range from banal (his characters have real-life doubles) to questionable (he could find citations to support his assertions) to bizarre (every phrase of dialogue could be translated word-for-word into Arabic). When all the characters are Kabyles, presumably speakers of Kabylia's variety of Tamazight, what could this last assertion mean?²⁸ As for the real-life doubles and the supporting citations, Duchêne attempts to provide the proof with notes. The narrator of *L'Aventure de Sidi Flouss*, commenting on the "tenue de primitif noble" [bearing of a noble primitive] of a Berber, cites "un de nos grands administrateurs" [one of our great administrators], whom he does not name, as saying that "parmi les Berbères, il y a des voleurs, des assassins; il n'y a pas de mufles" [among the Berbers, there are thieves and murderers, but there are no louts].²⁹ To him, even a possibly apocryphal citation is better than nothing, but where available, real examples are best. Duchêne often adds them in notes at the bottom of the page, as if he wished to prove by documented example that however unlikely the foregoing plot development might seem, it has an actual precedent in Kabyle society.

The relation between note and text, however, can present difficulties. Once again in *Sidi Flouss*, the narrator feels obliged to prove that a Kabyle could in fact win first prize in French at the Algiers *lycée*, as the protagonist did; he informs us in a note that "En 1928, un jeune Kabyle du Djurdjura, élève du Lycée d'Alger, a été reçu à la fois aux concours de trois grandes écoles. Il a choisi Polytechnique" [in 1928, a young Kabyle from the Djurdjura studying at the Lycée d'Alger passed the entrance examinations of three of the Grandes Ecoles. He chose the Polytechnique].³⁰ However, the text to which this note is appended describes the completely different fate of a young, educated Berber: "Depuis son retour à la Tribu, l'ancien élève de Bab-el-Oued, prix de français en premier, avait plongé dans une atmosphère morale différente et reçu un lot de directives d'une toute autre orientation . . . en présence de quoi le fils kabyle, que sa culture européenne ne l'empêchait pas de demeurer, n'avait pu que replier ses préférences." [Since his return to the Tribe, the former student of Bab-el-Oued, winner of first prize in French, had been plunged into a different moral atmosphere and had received a very differently oriented set of directives . . . to which this son of Kabylia, which his European culture did not prevent him from remaining, could only submit, despite his own preferences.][31] Events in the text will support this assertion, undermining the possibility of assimilation proudly declared in the note. Other notes prove even more contradictory. In *La Rek'ba*, a footnote attempts to suggest that Baya's extremely young marriage was common practice, in order to show once more how primitive the Berbers supposedly were by citing an even more extreme precedent: "un jugement du 11 août 1865, cité par Sautayra et Cherbonneau, statue sur le cas d'une fille kabyle mariée avant sa naissance" [a decision of 11 August 1865, cited by Sautayra and Cherbonneau, judges the case of a Kabyle girl married before her birth].[32] The reference cites a well-known compendium of case law that does indeed record the case, but only to say that Berber common law itself banned such marriages.[33] The evidence thus suggests exactly the opposite of what Duchêne was trying to prove by citing it. Contradictions between textual and paratextual elements (notes, prefaces, etc.) suggest the difficulty of constructing a coherent argument about the Imazighen, if the starting point was some version of the Berber myth, mixed with an array of other colonial stereotypes. The requirements of a colonial plot and the preconceptions of colonial anthropology did not easily cohabit.

"Anthropological" remarks by the narrator proliferate in parallel with these notes. In *Thamil'la*, early in the series, the narrator relies on the melodramatic presentation of events to convey his message, but by the time he gets to *L'Aventure de Sidi Flouss* and *La Rek'ba*, he resorts to simply dictating his own anthropological interpretation of events. For example, "parmi l'évolution européenne, à laquelle il s'était adapté en partie seulement au mieux de son intérêt" [amidst the European evolution, to which he had partially adapted solely in order to further his own interests], Zemmour, Sidi Flouss's father "demeurait au fond . . . le Berbère attaché au vieux roc nord-africain sur lequel, symboliquement, ses Kanouns, c'est-à-dire sa loi, restent gravés" [remained at bottom a Berber attached to the old North African stones, on which his Kanouns, that is, his law, were still symbolically engraved].[34] Elsewhere the narrator expressly calls attention to "l'indestructible malice berbère" [the indestructible Berber malice].[35] In short, the text does everything it can to force readers to share its conclusion: "Au vrai, que de divergences, parmi les gestes et les conceptions, entre nous et nos voisins Arabo-Berbères!" [In truth, what disparities in acts and beliefs separate us from our Arabo-Berber neighbors!].[36] When anthropology entered the novel, it no longer stood on the merits of its observations, but on the ability of the narrator's rhetoric to foreclose alternate interpretations.

This imposition of tendentious cultural interpretations typifies novels late in the series. Since Duchêne's earlier novels were not so overdetermined by extranarrative interventions, we might wonder why he radically intensified his efforts at guiding the interpretation of his works. His success did not seem to depend on it. His first novel, with no notes and little extranarrative commentary, sold well enough for Albin Michel to reprint it for the Centenary. His second, also without notes but with events so shocking that only one interpretation seemed possible, attracted more comment than any other. The proliferation of notes and commentary in the later novels was as much the result of the corpus's reception as cultural documents as its cause. In fact, when Duchêne composed the later novels of the series, he was already aware of their recognition as anthropological documents by critics, scholars, and government officials. As we will see, in 1925, on the strength of *Thamil'la*, he already passed for an expert on Berber customs, and the progressive takeover of his novels by *soi-disant* anthropological description marks his installation in the role his texts had prepared for him, and which the public had obligingly accorded him. Much of this role consisted in promoting himself as a self-appointed defender of Kabyle women, whom the French perceived as occupying a less-than-enviable position in their society. Faulting Duchêne here does not imply that any concern over the fate of Kabyle women would have been misplaced. Nonetheless, French attempts to reform the status of women in a culture they believed themselves to be civilizing had serious complications. Camile Sabatier, administrator in the Kabyle town of Tizi-Ouzou, declared openly his motivation for proposing reforms to the condition of Kabyle women: "C'est par les femmes qu'on peut s'emparer de l'âme d'un peuple" [It is via the women that one can take hold of a people's soul].[37] In Duchêne's case, his rhetoric for the good cause of respect for women clearly addressed the French and their cultural preoccupations rather than the Kabyles and theirs. It aimed to promote French intervention in Kabyle society, and also to aggrandize Duchêne himself. His extreme conservatism will become very clear later, in the light of the reforms he actually proposed, which were likely irrelevant to the actual status of Kabyle women, and probably did more to impede progress than to further it.

Duchêne's integration into the anthropological tradition may best be followed in his prefaces, which also provide clues regarding the reception he expected. Although he addresses most of his prefaces to French audiences in France and Algeria, and speaks of the Kabyles in the third person, the preface to *Thamil'la* addresses the men of Kabylia themselves: "Louange à Dieu! Qu'il soit exalté!" [Praise be to God! May He be exalted!] it begins, awkwardly imitating the opening formulae of a speech in Arabic. The preface makes a plea on behalf of Kabyle women, insisting that the "misères, parfois atroces" [sometimes horrible miseries] they suffered were "pour la plupart la conséquence de l'observation stricte, souvent aussi abusive, je dois le dire, de vos Kanouns" [for the most part the consequence of strict, and I must say, often also abusive, observance of your Kanouns] or common-law traditions.[38] He continues his indictment, inscribing himself in the grand tradition of Kabyle studies:

> Voulez-vous que je vous les rappelle, ces Kanouns? Je vais le faire en résumant le titre IV du 2e volume d'un ouvrage que vous connaissez bien, vous aussi, qui est un véritable code en matière kabyle et qui fait autorité en justice: La Kabylie, de MM. le général Hanoteau et Letourneux, conseiller à la Cour d'appel d'Alger. Ecoutez bien! Voici la loi que subissent vos femmes, loi qui, je m'empresse de le reconnaître, n'est pas édictée uniformément dans toutes vos tribus, ni partout avec la même rigueur, mais qui n'en est pas moins la loi applicable dans la plupart de vos villages:
> La femme kabyle n'a pas de droits héréditaires.
> Elle n'a aucun droit de propriété sauf sur les vêtements qu'elle porte.
> Mariage: Elle est vendue par son père, à défaut par son parent mâle le plus proche, qui touchent le prix (toutchit, "le manger"). "Ils mangent d'elle." (sic).
> Elle n'a pas à formuler de consentement. Le mariage peut lui être imposé, même avec emploi de la force, par le mâle ayant autorité sur elle.
> Elle n'a pas le droit de répudier son mari; et elle ne peut, dans aucun cas, sous aucun prétexte, demander le divorce à la Justice. . .
> Et cet adage qui résume tout ce qui précède, dont je respecte la traduction littérale et que vous connaissez certainement tous:
> TU PEUX FAIRE DE TA FEMME CE QU'IL TE PLAIT, HORMIS UN CADAVRE. Maintenant, réfléchissez!

[Would you like for me to remind you of those Kanouns? I will do so by summarizing volume two, title IV of a work which you, too, know well, which is a veritable code in Kabyle affairs, and which is authoritative in the courts: *La Kabylie*, by MM. le général Hanoteau and Letourneux, counselor at the Algiers appeals court. Listen closely! This is the law under which your women live—a law which, I hasten to add, is not handed down uniformly in all your tribes, nor applied everywhere with the same rigor, but which is nonetheless the law applicable in most of your villages:
The Kabyle woman has no inheritance rights.
She has no right to hold property, except for the clothes she wears.
Marriage: she is sold by her father, or lacking a father, by her closest male relative, who receives her purchase price (*toutchit*, "food"). "They eat her." (sic)
She does not need to pronounce her consent. The marriage may be imposed on her, even by force, by the male having authority over her.
She does not have the right to repudiate her husband, and she can in no case, for any pretext, request a divorce from the courts. . . .
And finally, this adage that summarizes everything I have said, the literal translation of which I have respected, and that you all certainly know.
YOU CAN MAKE ANYTHING YOU WANT OF YOUR WIFE, EXCEPT A CORPSE. Now, think!][39]

This preface forms the basis of Duchêne's self-insertion into the academic and legal canons on Kabylia and typifies his use and abuse of Hanoteau and Letourneux's work. It also helped shape the reception of his work as "anthropological," on the border between academic and popular discourse. Duchêne positions himself as the interpreter of academic rigor for the benefit of his addressees. Despite the invocation of the Kabyle elders, the pronoun "you" cannot really refer to them. Few of them would have read it, and fewer still would have needed Hanoteau and Letourneux's work to tell them about their own legal traditions. The imagined audience here seems to consist of people who did know the work in question, or more probably, those whom Duchêne felt should know it: non-Kabyle jurists, politicians, administrators, journalists, armchair exoticists, and anyone else interested in humanitarian justifications for intervention in Kabyle society. Duchêne writes at once as a scholar who must summarize a great predecessor's findings, and as a popularizer who spares his readers the trouble of consulting a three-volume work.

His summary of Hanoteau and Letourneux's volume two, title IV, is nonetheless problematic. In reducing thirty pages to ten lines, and then ten lines to one proverb, Duchêne eliminates all the detail of his predecessors' discussion. Though recent scholarship has blamed the two earlier *qanūn* compilers for oversimplifying and rigidly fixing a changing body of law, Duchêne certainly never accused them of this.[40] In fact, in the places where his predecessors distinguish wide variation among various clans' *qanūns*, Duchêne himself generalizes bluntly: the two sentences in which he asserts the total passivity and powerlessness of Kabyle women in marriage replace an entire page of exceptions in the original.[41] Nonetheless, this crude summary and the novel that illustrates it point by point ensured Duchêne's reputation and authority on Kabyle policy. It also upholds the tradition in literature about Kabylia of citing predecessors in an argument that either ignores or contradicts their observations. Almost ten years later, the former Governor General of Algeria Maurice Violette, a liberal and ardent assimilationist, needed an authority to cite to support his assertions about the conditions of Kabyle women. He found that Duchêne, "dans une série d'ouvrages qui sont autant de documents sur le sort de la femme kabyle, a traduit de façon saisissante ce que lui avait enseigné la pratique des choses de l'audience et du parquet d'Alger et aussi son observation directe des moeurs kabyles" [in a series of novels which constitute so many documents on the fate of the Kabyle woman, has strikingly translated what he learned from the practical realities of the Algiers courtroom and also from direct observation of Kabyle customs].[42] Violette did not mind at all that a magistrate had "translated" this experience into novels.

Violette had a precedent for ignoring the question of literary genre: Duchêne's novels positioned themselves for reception in genres far removed from the novel. The preface of *La Rek'ba* reported the entrance of the Kabyle novel into the official discourse of social reform: "pourquoi ne pourrais-je noter ici qu'en 1922, aux premières pages de *Thamil'la*, j'avais placé un appel aux fiers et intelligents montagnards du Djurdjura en faveur de la femme kabyle; pourquoi ne dirais-je pas que cet appel, joint à d'autres voix généreuses commençant alors à s'élever, a été entendu en Kabylie, écouté en très haut lieu; pourquoi n'aurai-je pas la fierté et la joie de constater qu'aujourd'hui quatre ans après, l'amélioration juridique et sociale du sort de la femme kabyle, grâce à l'action du Gouverneur Général de l'Algérie, en 1926, est en voie de consécration législative?" [Why should I not note here that in 1922, in the first pages of *Thamil'la*, I placed an appeal to the proud and intelligent mountain-dwellers of the Djurdjura, in favor of the Kabyle woman? Why not mention that, together with the generous voices then beginning to be raised, this appeal was heard in Kabylia and listened to in very high places? Why should I not take pride and joy in noting that four years later, thanks to the actions of the Gouverneur Général of Algeria in 1926, the judicial and social improvement of the fate of the Kabyle woman is today on the way to legislative approval?][43] Duchêne may seem to give himself a good deal of credit here; relatively few novels can boast of changing government policy. Yet regardless of the literal truth of its assertions, the preface, patronizing to the Kabyles and reverential to the "très haut lieu" of policy-making, did help place the novel for reception as a document as serious, factual, and influential as a government report.

A number of articles in the scholarly and colonial press allow us to follow Duchêne's rise to the status of government expert. In 1925, Governor General Steeg established a commission "chargée de rechercher les mesures législatives et réglementaires, juridiques et administratives qu'il conviendrait de prendre pour l'amélioration de la condition de la femme kabyle" [charged with investigating the legislative regulatory, judicial, and administrative measures appropriate to take in order to improve the condition of the Kabyle woman].[44] It produced a report rather rapidly, thanks to the "dévouement éclairé de son rapporteur" [enlightened devotion of its secretary], M. le Conseiller Ferdinand Duchêne.[45] The minutes of the commission's meetings, published in the *Revue des études islamiques*, confirm Duchêne's active participation in the debate. The commission's conversations betray a sense of urgency in their tone, given the situation of the women it was supposed to help: a situation constantly dramatized by testimony from a variety of sources, but especially from Duchêne's own novels. Said one Kabyle member of the commission, "il importe d'apporter un remède immédiat à une situation présente qui est des plus déplorables. Il faut secourir la femme matériellement" [it is essential to remedy immediately the current situation, which is most deplorable. It is necessary to help the women materially].[46] This particular remark, however, came out in an unexpected context: the speaker was describing as inadequate a proposal for an extremely slow and conservative reform, coming from none other than Ferdinand Duchêne. For him, enlightened devotion to reform meant slowing it down, at least in the context of the commission debates.

The debate unfolded exactly as if all the participants had carefully studied their Duchêne novels to get a clear idea of the supposed "conservatism" of Kabylia. Genuinely reform-minded Muslims, however, accused the administration of trying to keep Kabyle society underdeveloped by averting changes to customary law.[47] Proposals for reforms were supposed to come from the Kabyles themselves, but the commission pushed aside every idea coming from a Kabyle member, especially if other members thought it might tend to "Islamicize" the Kabyles.[48] The conclusions of fifty years of ethnology proving that the Kabyles were already convinced Muslims could still go ignored, partly at least as a result of writings like Duchêne's. Serious thinkers could still believe the Kabyles to be assimilable, if only the French took care to protect them from further Islamic influence. The commission therefore refused to consider any reform with a basis in *shari`a* law. Duchêne himself stressed once again the opposition between "Qur'anic" and Berber customs, in his report to the commission cited *in extenso* in the minutes:

> La femme kabyle n'a pas de droits héréditaires. Elle n'a, dans beaucoup de tribus, aucun droit de propriété, à part sur les vêtements qu'elle porte.
>
> Elle est mariée, plus exactement vendue par son père, à défaut par son parent mâle le plus proche, qui touchent le prix (touchit, le manger). Littéralement: "Ils mangent d'elle".
>
> Elle n'a pas à formuler de consentement. Le mariage peut lui être imposé, même avec emploi de la force, par le mâle ayant autorité sur elle . . .

> [The Kabyle woman has no inheritance rights. In many tribes, she has no right to hold property, except for the clothes she wears.
>
> She is married off, or more accurately, sold by her father, or lacking a father, by her closest male relative, who receives her purchase price (*toutchit*, "food"). Literally: "They eat her."
>
> She does not need to pronounce her consent. The marriage may be imposed on her, even by the use of force, by the male having authority over her . . .][49]

These remarks sound familiar: Duchêne is citing, word for word, his own preface to *Thamil'la*, which itself cited the venerable Hanoteau and Letourneux. Text published between the covers of a novel, and claiming justification from events narrated in it, has suddenly become part of an official policy document. In doing so, it also manages to enlist the support of scholarly predecessors for characterizations of the Kabyles that they in fact refute. Finally, Duchêne's text achieves consecration as scholarly discourse, appearing as a citation in an article called "Le Statut de la femme kabyle et la réforme des coutumes berbères" [The Status of the Kabyle Woman and the Reform of Berber Customs] in the *Revue des études islamiques*, edited by Louis Massignon, the most eminent French scholar of Islam in the twentieth century.

The commission would eventually adopt a parcel of reforms (made law in 1930) so conservative that they may actually have slowed the pace of social change. For instance, divorce for Kabyle women was gradually acquiring legal precedent in courts of the sort Duchêne had presided, but his reform limited it to women married to absconders or felons.[50] The commission's refusal to take account of historical change in some ways determined its proposals: it designed its "reforms" based ultimately on evidence from Hanoteau and Letourneux's work from 1868, which itself described the situation as changing; moreover, before reaching the commission, this evidence had been filtered, generalized, and above all fictionalized and petrified in a series of novels composed between 1905 and 1920. Duchêne published his first novel, *Au Pas lents des caravanes* [In the Slow Strides of the Caravans], in 1922 and set it in 1914. His later novels, however, describe situations identical to those of the first, even though Duchêne admits he had to set them before the turn of the century, in order to obtain a semblance of historical verisimilitude. In fact, Duchêne remains intentionally vague about the exact timing of most of his novels, and makes apparent his view that Kabylia remained essentially impervious to historical progress. Duchêne's novels exhibit a curious form of nostalgia by presenting their version of the Kabyle world as if nothing had changed since before the arrival of French ethnographers and administrators. Their overwhelming desire not to have to acknowledge that Kabyle society had changed amounts nearly to an admission that it had, as Duchêne occasionally admits in minimal caveats. The real unspoken nostalgia in the text, however, is for a time when the French could deal as summarily with the Kabyles as the supposed primitiveness of their customs justified. The text seems to wish to pretend that that time is now, despite the protests of certain Kabyles. The extremely conservative tone of Duchêne's speeches to the commission fell in line with this vision of resistance to progress in Kabylia: "D'autres retouches des kanouns . . . ont été proposées, par quelques uns de ses membres. Il lui a semblé qu'en les souhaitant pour plus tard, elle était fondée à croire que l'heure n'était pas venue de les accueillir, parce que, à son avis, elles apparaîtraient à la grande majorité des Kabyles, trop contraires à leurs conceptions actuelles, à leurs intérêts du moment . . . ce serait là, croyons-nous, à leurs yeux, non des éléments d'évolution, mais des ferments de Révolution." [Other alternations to the kanouns were proposed to the commission by some of its members. It seemed to the commission that while it hoped to see them implemented later, it was justified in believing that the time had not come to embrace them, because in its view, they would appear to the great majority of Kabyles too contrary to their current ideas and their interests of the moment . . . we believe that in their eyes these reforms would not be elements of evolution, but rather ferments of Revolution.][51] Revolution for whom? The real conservative on the commission was Duchêne, not the Kabyle delegates; a revolution in Kabyle culture would have destroyed his conception of the Berber world. It would also have ended his usefulness as a producer of anthropological fiction interpreting that culture for policy makers and the general public.

The development of the Duchêne case warn us effectively of the pitfalls of reading novels as anthropology. Yet they also demonstrate the value for critics today of reading novels *with* anthropology, the ethnological discourses of their time, to go beyond the usual view of the impact of colonial literature which characterizes it as producing images of the periphery for people in the center. Duchêne's variety of *roman indigène* novel clearly had readers at both center and periphery who used it for very particular and concrete political purposes in Kabylia. These purposes were anything but revolutionary, or even evolutionary in the usual sense adopted by social progressives. Novels by Europeans with colonial subjects as characters suffered from the colonial situation that made it impossible for them to propose any coherent way forward. Rather than suggesting that this might mean that something was wrong with the system, however, the texts used this impossibility to solidify the status quo.

THE POLITICS OF ASSIMILATION

As I indicated earlier in this chapter, there is no particular reason to look for resistance to colonialism in these novels. Another set of texts, also labeled *romans indigènes*, though because of their authors rather than their content, appears far more likely to offer potential alternatives to colonial immobilism. In the years leading up to the 1930 Centenary, and then in the somewhat disillusioned climate following it, a small handful of Arab and Amazigh writers published novels with political concerns which, for today's critic, distinguishes them sharply from the other so-called *romans indigènes* I have so far been discussing.

Most accounts of the origins of the Maghribi novel in French place its debut in the political and historical conjunction of the 1950s and the Algerian war of independence. Born amidst the violence and polarization of a war of decolonization, the Francophone Algerian novel (as construed by the current canon) necessarily reflected its contestatory and confrontational origins. The arguments attaching Mouloud Feraoun's *Le Fils du pauvre* [The Poor Man's Son] (1954) or Kateb Yacine's *Nedjma* (1956) to the political and emotional context of the "savage war of peace" have been repeatedly rehearsed to explain certain qualities most readers concur in attributing to the genre.[52] These include a political consciousness of oppression, an ever-present textual and physical violence, and a sense of cultural alienation from those in power, whether French, in early works, or Algerian, in later ones. Compelling arguments trace these elements back to the 1950s in representative novels, and situate there the origins of the genre itself.

There exists, however, an earlier set of texts with a prior historical claim to the status of "origins" of the Algerian novel in French. While authors like Kateb, Feraoun, and Mammeri indeed founded the genre as we know it, they nonetheless had important predecessors. Ahmed Bouri's *Musulmans et Chrétiennes* [Muslims and Christian Women], possibly the very first, appeared in serial form in 1912.[53] The first significant crop of novels in French by Algerians appeared between the wars. These novels were few and scattered, perhaps numbering ten altogether; the three I will discuss here, Mohammed Ben Cherif's *Ahmed ben Mostapha, goumier* [Ahmed ben Mostapha, Trooper] (1920), Khodja Chukri's *El Euldj, captif des barbaresques* [El Euldj, Captive of the Barbary Pirates] (1929), and Mohammed Ould Cheikh's *Myriem dans les palmes* [Myriem among the Palms] (1936) appeared over a period of sixteen years, and to some extent resist grouping.[54] Taken together, however, the obvious political consciousness and concern with cultural alienation of these "other" *indigène* novels suggest that the origins of these phenomena in the Algerian novel go back considerably farther than the independence era. These novels, too, enter into dialogue with the discourses of colonialism; however, their positions are considerably more difficult to place than those of their successors.

As Terdiman has argued, writers struggling to change a dominant discourse (in this case, one that excluded them from almost all political participation) discover its capacity to ignore or absorb subversion, but also its contingence and permeability.[55] The three writers I will discuss here proceed from this discovery to a highly selective counterdiscourse, picking their battles carefully, and leaving other issues, even important ones, aside. Under the government's heavy policing of all expressions of dissension, counterdiscourses became problematic for very immediate legal reasons. The colonial authorities could and did shut down by decree any newspaper they felt objectionable, and under this pressure, the *indigène* press, both source and outlet for these writers, dwindled from approximately twenty titles before World War I to three or four in the thirties.[56] Selectivity in deciding where to apply discreet pressure on the dominant discourse became both necessary, to get their message across at all, and inevitable, to deal with the complicated political investments of the period.

All three of these novels quickly fell into relative obscurity; Chukri's, perhaps the most compelling from a stylistic perspective, does not even seem to have been reviewed in any of the Algerian literary journals.[57] They also received little sustained critical attention until Peter Duwoodie's recent work, and remain sufficiently unknown to make useful the following plot summaries.[58] The Caid Ben Cherif was a captain in the French army during World War I, thus outranking the protagonist of *Ahmed ben Mostapha, goumier,* who joins the army with dreams of glory and fulfills them fighting Moroccans and proselytizing for the expansion of the French empire among the clans he is sent to subjugate. Page after page details his bravery and devotion, attracting the attention of his captain, a young Arabic-speaking French officer who teaches him the glorious history of Arab military conquest. After a respite at home, spent in picturesque falcon-hunting and feasting episodes, Ahmed insists on volunteering to serve in Europe, the moment France enters World War I. The Germans soon capture and intern him with other Algerian troops. Tunisian and Moroccan agents of the Kaiser fail to convince him of the evils of French colonialism, which he defends with very sophisticated political arguments, and his loyalty to France earns him harsh treatment. He falls ill and has the good fortune to be sent to internment in Switzerland, where his charm earns him social success. The climate, however, does not agree with him, and after a series of touching but chaste letters to a French woman he had met in Paris, he dies, far from home, of pneumonia.

Khodja Chukri reaches much further back in history for the setting of *El Euldj, captif des barbaresques,* and chooses the early sixteenth century, the height of the pirate regime of Algiers. The "Barbaresques" capture a French vessel and crew, including the young Bernard Ledieux. He and his comrades suffer many misdeeds and tortures at the hands of Algerians, themselves subject to the arbitrary cruelty of Barbarousse. Years pass; the young man forgets his wife in France and marries his master's daughter, after committing the unthinkable, converting to Islam. He immediately finds himself cut off from his fellow European slaves and begins to regret his decision, despite his increase in status with his captors. To add to his distress, his son by his new wife grows up to become imam of the Ketchaoua mosque (the same one the French would transform into the Cathedral of Algiers three hundred years later). Ledieux grows taciturn and disaffected, becomes convinced he is a traitor, and dies miserable and insane shortly after Charles V's failed conquest of Algiers in 1541.

Finally, Mohammed Ould Cheikh took his inspiration from more recent history for *Myriem dans les palmes*. Myriem Debussy, rich heiress from Oran, has a Muslim mother, alive, a French officer father, dead, two suitors, one Arab and worthy, another Russian and scheming, a villa, and an airplane, which she pilots on a visit to her brother, an officer in the French army "pacifying" the Tafilalet in southeastern Morocco. After a forced landing, she becomes the prisoner of Belqacem, leader of the unsubjugated territory. He of course wishes to include her in his harem, but Ivan Ipateff, an unscrupulous Russian arms dealer (and her former fiancé), challenges him to single combat for her. Too cowardly to fight, Ivan hires a dashing cavalier who wins the joust, but carries Myriem off to her brother and the safety of the French army, for he is none other than Ahmed, her worthy Arabic professor and admirer from Oran. Belqacem flees into the desert with his concubines, and Ahmed and Myriem return to civilized marital bliss in the city.

These books at first seem positively to glorify French rule: Arabs are often barbarians, while French people usually appear as enlightened gentlefolk. The novels initially seem to present no alternatives to the status quo: they apparently envision no change in Algeria's colonial status. However, we must realize that the political demands of the colonized would only begin to affirm the existence of an Algerian nation around 1930; about that time the leaders of the political opposition (the Emir Khaled Ibn al-Hachemi, Cheikh `Abdelhamid Ben Bādīs, and Messali Hadj, for example) began to speak openly of a French withdrawal from Algeria. The Emir Khaled, a former Army captain and grandson of the legendary nineteenth-century Emir Abdelkader, was among the founders of the *Étoile Nord-Africaine*, the first party to demand independence. Cheikh Ben Bādīs founded the *Association des Ulémas algériens*, an explicitly Islamic and pro-Arab opposition group, in May 1931. He also edited a review called *Al-Shihāb*, which strongly advocated resurrecting an "Arab personality" and culture in Algeria. As for Messali Hadj, he would found a succession of highly influential militant nationalist parties until his marginalization during the Algerian War and the purge of his supporters by the FLN. Messali in particular would radicalize his position in the mid thirties, whereas earlier oppositon rhetoric generally stopped short of demands for independance. In the late twenties, the Emir Khaled denounced the irony that "des centaines de milliers des nôtres sont morts pour un pays qui les considère toujours comme 'sujets'. Pourtant, ils durent lutter pour défendre des droits qu'ils n'ont jamais possédés" [hundreds of thousands of ours died for a country that still considers them "subjects." Even so, they had to struggle to defend rights they never possessed].[59] At that time, he demanded political rights rather than independence. The first newspapers in Algeria to support Arab nationalism wholeheartedly, *El Ouma* and Khaled's *Ikdām*, began publishing between 1928 and 1930.[60] Given the novelty and marginality of radical nationalism at the time, it would be unrealistic to hold works from the twenties and thirties to a standard of radicalism from the fifties.

Before and after *El Ouma*, most significant opposition newspapers in French or Arabic concentrated their attention on other matters, notably pay equity, fair elections, and educational opportunity. Reformist papers with considerable followings among educated Muslims (for example, the *Voix des indigènes* and the *Voix des humbles*, as well as *El Hack*) fought for the abolition of the *régime d'indigénat* [native code], a set of laws prescribing separate legal treatments for *indigènes* and Europeans, and for the extension of citizenship and political representation to at least part of the five million *Français musulmans* who enjoyed neither.[61] The historian Charles-Robert Ageron has argued that "La vieille chanson assimilationniste, peu à peu transformée en berceuse apaisante dans le ronronnement du discours politique, reprenait parfois valeur concrète de chant révolutionnaire. Ce n'était pas rien, dans le contexte de la colonie, que de réclamer les droits du citoyen pour 'nos sujets' algériens ou malgaches, l'abolition du régime de l'indigénat et le droit des élites autochtones à la gestion des affaires publiques, locales ou nationales; c'était demander l'Égalité" [The old assimilationist song, transformed little by little into a calming lullaby in the droning of political speech, occasionally took on the value of a revolutionary chant. It was not nothing, in the colonial context, to demand citizen's rights for "our subjects" the Algerians or Malgache, the abolition of the native code, and the right of local elites to manage public affairs either local or national: it was a demand of equality.][62] These demands, which in fact predate the postwar developments Ageron discusses, found support in several arguments: the service provided by Arab and Amazigh soldiers fighting and dying for France in World War I, and the "evolution" and acculturation to French thinking which the editors and readers of opposition journals could easily display. At least until the early 1930s, most of these journals favored political assimilation, in that they demanded equal status within the French nation for Arabs and Berbers. With some notable exceptions, such as Ben Bādīs's journal *Al-Shihāb*, they often also favored cultural assimilation, asserting that the way forward for all Algerians lay in better education and integration in the French mold. In the *Voix des humbles*, Ait Kaci wrote that "Le développement des indigènes dans leur propre milieu et leur civilisation est une impossibilité. . . . La civilisation occidentale est la maîtresse du monde et quiconque n'évolue pas dans son sein est voué à l'immobilité et l'immobilité c'est la mort. La politique assimilationiste est donc la seule logique, la seule possible et la seule viable en Afrique du Nord française."

[The development of the *indigènes* in their own environment and civilization is impossible. . . . Western civilization is master of the world, and whoever does not advance in its heart is doomed to immobility, and immobility is death. Assimilation is therefore the only logical policy, and the only one that is possible and viable in French North Africa.][63] Despite its advocacy of an "Arab personality," even Ben Bādīs's journal also supported the campaign for political rights within the French nation.

The contemporary ramifications of some otherwise inexplicable developments in the novels of Ben Cherif, Choukri, and Ould Cheikh becomes much clearer to today's readers when interpreted in conjunction with this political rhetoric. While such a reading does not eliminate all political ambiguity, the ideological context of the 1920s and 1930s reframes in a much more positive light motivations which might otherwise appear suspect, even arguably pro-colonial. What can it mean, for example, that Ahmed ben Mostapha shows diehard bravery in supporting the French cause, fighting and humiliating "backward" Moroccans? In the struggle for enfranchisement of the *indigènes*, many proponents of citizenship declared that decorated veterans should be the first so rewarded.[64] Proving one's valor and loyalty thus had extremely concrete political rewards. Ben Cherif's novel had a further purpose as well, that of answering hostile propaganda. It responded to *L'Islam dans l'armée française*, published in Constantinople in 1916 by R. Bou Kabouya, a deserter working for the Turks by attempting to spread dissension among Muslim officers. Ben Cherif's positioning of his protagonist represented more than mere toadyism: Muslim army veterans were among the few non-Europeans with the moral authority to address the French on matters regarding treatment of the *Français musulmans*, and the early opposition movements frequently placed them in the foreground of their agitations. Readers today may certainly choose to blame the protagonist Ahmed for his lack of solidarity with other colonized people, but we will not advance far without understanding all that the early political rights movements quite reasonably hoped to gain through demonstrations of loyalty immediately after World War I.

This would soon change, as it became apparent even to the most sanguine that they had little to hope for from French goodwill. The 1930 defeat in the Paris Assemblée of the proposal to give political representation to the *Français musulmans* demonstrated how little cooperation they could expect from the French either in the colony or in the metropole, and prepared the way for more overt nationalism.[65] Ben Cherif anticipates this at the very moment his brave Ahmed is haranguing the Moroccans, supposedly about the benefits of belonging to the French empire:

Pendant des siècles nous avons lutté pour l'honneur, pour venger nos morts, pour jouir d'un paturage ou éloigner l'ennemi de nos douars. Aujourd'hui tout cela est résumé, pensée unique, en un seul mot: "el Ouatan."
—El ouatan? répète le Marocain stupéfait.
—Oui, el ouatan! Et cela signifie le culte de la terre où reposent nos pères, l'amour de ceux qui nous aident à la garantir contre nos ennmis d'où qu'ils viennent; oui, l'amour sans limites pour les protecteurs de nos biens et de notre religion.

[For centuries we have fought for honor, to avenge our dead, to use pasture land, or to drive the enemy away from our villages. Today all this is summarized as a single idea, in one word: "al-waṭṭan."
—"Al-waṭṭan"? repeated the Moroccan, amazed.
—Yes, "al-waṭṭan"! It means the cult of the ground in which our fathers are laid to rest, and love for those who help us secure it against our enemies, wherever they may come from; yes, love without limits for the protectors of our possessions and our religion.][66]

Ben Cherif published his novel one year after the Egyptian revolution of 1919, whose leader Saad Zaghloul had done a great deal to popularize the word *"al-waṭṭan,"* the nation, in modern Arabic. Zaghloul might not have appreciated the speedy slippage in Ben Cherif's text toward the notion of the French as protectors of Islam. However, one of the most highly charged words in the history of Arab nationalism has nonetheless "slipped out" and been hammered in by a most unaccidental repetition in a speech connecting it with love of the homeland, military security, and private property. Ben Cherif's hero also links the word with the Arab literary tradition; no situation finds him at a loss for a classical citation or reference to the canon of heroic poetry, in which his favorite references are the pre-Islamic poets and the Antar epic.[67] He thus evokes an alternative historical tradition to the French, one that stresses the longevity of a literate culture. Despite the window-dressing of casting the French as necessary defenders of the Arabs, Ben Cherif hardly wins converts to colonialism by sketching a history of bravery reaching from the sixth century to contemporary Egypt.[68] Modern Egypt constituted a powerful reference, as the site of the *nahḍa ʿarabiya,* or Arab renaissance in letters, and Mohammad ʿAbduh's modernizations in Islam. Already in 1911, the Oran weekly *El Hack* [The Truth] subtitled itself "Le Jeune Egyptien." In 1920, with the eyes of every educated Arab on Egypt's independence struggle, the word *waṭṭan* could scarcely have left anyone as stupefied as it did Ahmed's Moroccan. The mask of loyalty to France lets Ben Cherif use the word "nation" a decade before the newspapers supporting the rights of the colonized would mention the term.[69]

   Khodja Chukri seems to respond to the growing radicalization of political demands around 1930 anticipated by Ben Cherif, as democratic reform began to seem less likely.[70] His tale, like Ben Cherif's, also admits of several readings: the theme of barbarous pirates causing the physical and emotional ruin of a young Frenchman sounds at once sinister and pro-colonial. It could imply both self-satisfiedness ("thank goodness the French have come to put an end to this") and pessimism ("we French make enormous sacrifices here; this country still ruins us to this day").[71] Chukri, however, ensures that we read his historical novel as a parable of failed assimilation.

Assimilate is exactly what the protagonist Ledieux cannot do, despite his apostasy. He works hard for his Muslim master, learns to speak his language, and marries his daughter, the ultimate assimilation a colonial subject could covet or a colonizer could revile. In order to do this he must convert to Islam, thus shedding his chains and becoming the slave overseer himself. This earns him the traditional label of "renegade," the ostracism of his former comrades, and the assurance of eternal damnation from the slaves' chaplain. It represents a point of no return: diplomatic convention traditionally barred renegades from inclusion among the slaves ransomed every year by European governments and charities. Wholly cut off from his cultural background, Omar Lediousse, ex-Bernard Ledieux, goes slowly mad. The parallels between the impossible asked of Ledieux, and that asked of any Arab or Amazigh wishing to assimilate to French colonial society, underscore the warning Chukri sought to convey. Assimilation, he says to his fellow Muslim intellectuals, is a trap, in which you will lose everything. Other elements of the story complicate this warning, however. With his Algerian wife Zineb, Omar Lediousse has a son Youssef, who becomes an imam preaching and answering the questions of the faithful. His sixteenth-century questioners seem preoccupied with topics strikingly relevant to Chukri's time: one asks "Que diriez-vous d'un musulman qui, sans renier sa religion, arborerait un chapeau après adoption du costume européen" [What would you say of a Muslim who, without denying his religion, wore a hat, after adopting European dress?][72] In response, Youssef predicts the fever of "Europeanization" which would strike the Arab world following the French invasion of Egypt, and declares "j'aime à croire que cette vie nouvelle sera d'un effet salutaire sur les esprits" [I like to think that this new life will have a salutary effect on people's minds].[73] Youssef carries the standard of Europeanization and what colonial intellectuals of all ethnicities called "évolution des moeurs": little by little, through the effects of education and contact with Europeans, the Arab and Berber populations would lose their rough edges and backward ways. Chukri's Youssef proposes doing so without any loss of cultural identity. Consensus among intellectuals in the colony was only apparent, however: the French would, with some exceptions, insist on complete cultural assimilation to a standard always set to be unattainable.

As a kind of compromise with assimilationism, Youssef's idea could appeal to people like Chukri who clearly saw the danger of trying to become French. It certainly appealed to Youssef, who as it happens speaks perfect French, having tasted "les fruits du jardin de la rhétorique française" [the fruits of the garden of French rhetoric].[74] Paradoxically, the narrator reveals Youssef's inexplicably unaccented French just after he rescues his reapostasizing father from an angry crowd of Muslims, which he does with a flourish of rhetoric, presumably in Arabic. As he explains to his surprised father, "Dieu a voulu que le fils musulman d'un père redevenu chrétien ait en lui le mélange altier de la fierté arabe conjugée à l'esprit chevaleresque français, grâce auquel il a su te protéger contre le mauvais coup que tous les croyants étaient décidés de te faire." [God willed that the Muslim son of a father who had returned to Christianity have in him the august mixture of Arab pride and French chivalrous spirit, thanks to which he was able to protect you from the harm that the believers were determined to do you.][75] Some mysterious cultural alchemy is apparently necessary so that overzealous and (to use Chukri's word) barbarous Muslims may restrain themselves from intolerant violence. Although Omar Lediousse's forced assimilation fails miserably, his son's voluntary rapprochement with French culture works wonders.

Despite the Algerian historian Abdelkader Djeghloul's effort to characterize Chukri as categorically rejecting assimilation in favor of retaining a "true" Algerian identity, *El Euldj* presents a double discourse.[76] Djeghloul speaks of assimilation as "le marché qu'aucun écrivain algérien de langue française n'acceptera" [the deal which no Algerian writer in French would accept].[77] No doubt; however, the refusal was not always categorical. Some, like Chukri, tried to modify the terms of the deal. Assimilation as then defined might indeed constitute no more than a lure, but Chukri nonetheless tries to change its terms to give it substance and the possibility of becoming a tenable position: "il parle français, donc il est français" [he speaks French, therefore he is French], says Omar/Bernard of his son.[78] If assimilation were simply a matter of language and cultural knowledge, Chukri might accept the deal; at any rate, he seems somewhat wistfully to propose it. Though Omar/Bernard dies insane and rejected, the flower of French influence lives on unexpectedly in Algiers in the guise of an imam *rhétoriqueur*, transmitting an essential modicum of Frenchness to future generations. For the cosmopolitan Chukri, hoping for a positive and flexible cultural understanding among French, Arab, and Amazigh Algerians, this represents the predestination of a Mediterranean compromise. The success of his model remains questionable. It seems at least possible that the son, if projected forward into Chukri's era, might yet suffer the fate of the father. Chukri's novel does not resolve the problem of assimilation: his subtlety lies in proposing at least a potential model, but nudging his readers to conclude that the colonial situation rendered the problem definitively insoluble.

Double discourse continues to work through Mohammed Ould Cheikh's *Myriem dans les palmes*, the only one of these three novels published in Algeria, and the one most approaching popular melodrama. Abdelkader Djeghloul has called Ould Cheikh "un bon exemple de cette double tendance au mimétisme procolonial et affirmation de l'identité algérienne" [a good example of the double tendency of pro-colonial mimicry and affirmation of the Algerian identity].[79] On the one hand, Ould Cheikh, like Chukri, does seem to push aside the temptation of excessive Europeanization. His heroine marries her Arabic teacher, a good Muslim named Ahmed, making her Muslim mother happy. On the other hand, he also seems to endorse the presence of the French Army. In the novel, the French wipe out the last stronghold of military opposition in North Africa, Morocco's Tafilalet (actually subdued in 1936, the year of *Myriem's* publication), thus ensuring peace, prosperity, and progress for all. The Algerian critic Ahmed Lanasri makes a cogent argument for a further disjunction between discourse and story: although the narrator ostensibly supports the French conquerors, he describes the pre-colonial Tafilalet region as a prelapsarian paradise. The descriptions Lanasri cites, however, could have been drawn from any of the classic sources of exoticist nostalgia, a descriptive tradition rarely liberating for the countries and peoples it treated.[80] In other words, the narrative conveys exactly the mixed message that Muslim novelists of the period were so good at sending. Myriem's penchant for aviation and her objections to veiling might simply come as progressive icing on the cake for liberal readers. Progress can coexist with adherence to tradition; her Ahmed, if not an *évolué*, seems like exactly the sort of figure Ben Bādīs hoped would advance the Algerian political personality: well educated, certain of his rights, and respectful yet open-minded about the Islamic tradition.

This account of Ould Cheikh's mixed but ultimately unsurprising message leaves out two important problems which complicate it significantly: the political implications of rapprochement and Myriem's mixed identity in it. First, in the political discourses of the twenties and thirties, where we hear few hints of real separatism, there was as yet little notion among supporters of the Muslims of the political significance of affirming a separate Arab Algerian cultural identity. Since the system of colonial domination depended on keeping cultural separation rigidly intact, Arab and Amazigh writers typically responded by taking an opposite tack, and basing their claims on political (and if necessary cultural) rapprochement between colonized and colonizers. Rather than "we are different, and demand a country of our own," they tended to say "we are more like you than you think, and demand rights like yours." Generally, those in favor of rapprochement turned out to be progressive Muslim intellectuals for whom mixing in all its forms had great potential political benefits. At that time, those who believed in the radical difference of a definable Arabo-Berber identity largely fell on the other side and supported the status quo of a separate and oppressive legal regime for Muslims.[81] Unless we are willing to make the autodidact Mohammed Ould Cheikh into a prophetic figure reversing the political charges of these positions, it is difficult to envision him as a champion of Arabo-Berber identity victorious in the struggle against assimilationism. Abdelkader Djeghloul argues precisely this, probably because he wishes again to see in these writers precursors of the Algerian nationalist struggle. Their status of precursors, however, need not depend on their doubtful affirmation of some sort of essential Arabo-Berber identity.

Such an argument might prove tenable if Myriem's identity, and therefore her marriage, did not present considerable complications. Her father, we recall, was a rich French officer who struggled mightily with his Muslim wife over the children's religion; their Muslim identity is merely a name in Myriem's case, and a name and a circumcision in her brother's.[82] In fact, the story makes clear, Myriem and her brother "ne fréquentent ni l'Eglise ni la Mosquée" [frequent neither Church nor Mosque]; according to their mother, "ils s'occupent du 'modernisme' qui est l'ennemi de toute religion parce qu'il corrompt ceux qui en abusent et les conduit souvent à leur perte" [they are interested in 'modernism,' which is the enemy of all religion because it corrupts those who abuse it, and often leads them to bad ends].[83] We sense where this might lead: Myriem literally crashes to earth, realizes her mother is right, and chooses a sensible marriage with a man of her ethnicity and religion.

The story never gets there, however, as the narration cannot decisively specify Myriem's identity. From the beginning, the narrator insists he is presenting the "idylle de deux jeunes Algériens du vingtième siècle: un Arabe évolué et une Française" [idyll of two young Algerians of the twentieth century: an Arab *évolué* and a French woman].[84] According to Lanasri, "la fiction apporte une sérieuse corrective aux propos liminaire de l'auteur" [the fiction brings a serious correction to the preliminary words of the author]: Myriem studies Arabic, and Ahmed looks more and more like a traditionally educated Arab than an *évolué*.[85] However, every character in the book who refers to her in the third person calls her "the French woman," "the foreigner," or "la roumia," suggesting that in the context of the story, her identity remains foreign; at the very least, she is unreadable to the other characters (or at least misread).[86] Further emphasizing the theme of *mixité*, Ahmed declares his love in these terms: "Je

vous aime, Myriem, depuis longtemps je vous aime. . . . Mais une diffi-
culté se dresse devant nous: la race!" [I love you, Myriem; I've loved you
for a long time. But there is a problem ahead of us: race!] To which his
beloved replies "Que nous importent ces préjugés absurdes si nous nous
aimons. . . . Ma mère n'est-elle pas musulmane? Ne suis-je pas libre
d'aimer et d'épouser qui me plaît? . . . N'avons nous pas la même communauté de sentiments et d'habitudes?" [What are these absurd prejudices to us, if we love each other . . . is my mother not a Muslim? Am I not
free to love and marry whomever I please? Do we not share the same
commonality of sentiments and habits?][87] The texts sounds as if it were
trying to imagine not a straying Arab returning to the fold, but an enlightened métisse asserting her right to a mixed marriage. These somewhat stilted vows of eternal love hardly plead for the recognition of a
"pure" Algerian identity in the way some postindependence criticism
would like to see it. Rather than responding to postindependence needs
for political affirmation, Ould Cheikh responds to his contemporaries'
need for a response to unmeetable demands for assimilation. We might
object that Myriem's plea glosses over some serious issues: in reality, prejudice absurd or otherwise kept in place almost insurmountable barriers
to mixed marriages in Algeria, and "commonality of sentiments" sounds
like just the sort of completely ineffectual conventional piety cited by the
bien-pensant of the colony, careful not to propose any concrete compromise, much less any common sacrifices. The implicit criticism of purist
conceptions of identity here applies to the view of assimilation which defined it as the seamless adoption of a pure French identity by all Algerians, and set it up as the only (and impossible) means of fully joining colonial Algerian society.

  This may seem considerably more conservative than Chukri's position,
and it is at least possible that Ould Cheikh was; he published articles in
the extremely conservative (borderline fascist) paper *Oran matin*.[88] However, if we believe that he placed an impossible precondition on his cooperation (i.e., modifying the terms of assimilation), we might read his
text as a veiled refusal to assimilate. Alternatively, the novel may represent a fairly sophisticated view of the multiple possibilities for Algerian
identity, accepting at least the historical fact of French presence, and beginning from the notion of the elusiveness and counterproductivity of
cultural purity. With this in mind, we should listen to the rhetoric of his
preface:

> Après un siècle d'occupation, l'Algérie se réveille de sa torpeur. . . . L'éduca-
> tion occidentale ayant portée ses fruits, les nouvelles générations françaises
> et musulmanes, contrairement aux 'anciennes' restées longtemps hostiles
> l'une à l'autre, commencent à se comprendre et à s'aimer.

Et cela grâce à l'instruction, à cette lumière chérie qui éclaire les hommes, les rapproche et les guide vers la paix, la vie et le bonheur.

Toutefois, je n'ai aucune prétension d'avoir écrit un livre à thèse.

Au contraire, j'ai essayé simplement de faire plaisir aux pionniers du rapprochement franco-musulman en leur dédiant ce modeste ouvrage, auquel j'ai donné une allure romancée.

[After a century of occupation, Algeria is awakening from its torpor . . . western education having born its fruits, the new generation of Muslims and French, unlike the previous ones which remained for a long time hostile to one another, are beginning to understand and love each other.

This is thanks to education, that cherished light which enlightens men, brings them together, and guides them toward peace, life, and happiness.

However, I do not pretend to have written an ideological book [livre à thèse].

On the contrary, I have simply tired to please the pioneers of the Franco-Muslim rapprochement by dedicating to them this modest work, to which I have given a romanticized style.][89]

This statement begins with a hymn to French Algeria that could have come from any of the colony's many apologists at the time of the Centenary. However, it manages to undercut its apparent conservatism in several ways. First, it emphasizes the importance of education, and thereby aligns the author against the many conservatives who argued that schools for Muslims were a waste of money. Second, in saying the country is awakening under the influence of Western education, Ould Cheikh also hints that the formerly acquiescent *indigènes* are at last rising to demand the rights their French-style formation has led them to expect. Finally comes the disavowal at the end, abandoning the ostensible hymn to French-inspired progress: "but I do not pretend to have written a *livre à thèse*"—or at least, not a book with that *thèse*. Instead, Ould Cheikh declares his wish to further the cause of the pioneers of rapprochement, a goal certainly consistent with the novel's ending. In a context where rapprochement would have meant undeniable political progress for the Muslims, allowing them effective opposition, and where a successful mixed marriage represented a clear threat to rigidly drawn ethnic boundaries, Ould Cheikh's ideological commitment, while veiled, is not nearly as conservative as it first seems. It represents a carefully drawn, selective counterdiscourse, striving to find an audience that might hear it.

It is intriguing to ponder whether the founders of the genre of the Francophone novel in the Maghrib read any of the works of their predecessors. The novelist and anthropologist Mouloud Mammeri has said that he at least discovered their existence only rather late, and we have no evidence that other members of the "génération de '52" knew much of their work.[90] The argument here is not one of literary influence in a traditional sense, but of literary interpretation that devolves upon the reader, who must be aware of the fortunes and the principles operative in the history of decolonization. Reading anticolonialist commitment in the colonial novel requires us to consider disavowals, cross-purposes, and ambivalences of myriad origins. In reading works by colonized authors, we cannot satisfy ourselves with generalized arguments about political commitments in the anticolonialist struggle. To reach real understanding, we need to ask questions less about global ideological strategy than about local political tactics. The importance of these novels lies less in their influence, or even in their founding a proto-nationalist movement, than in their lessons for readings of the complex counterdiscourses of their more famous successors. Examining particular genres and specific historical situations on the periphery of colonial power (and of literary studies) demonstrates the way fiction can intertwine with political and anthropological writing to produce results both more complicated and more concrete than critics have imagined.

NOTES

1. Richard Terdiman, *Discourse/Counter-Discourse: Theory and Practice of Symbolic Resistance in Nineteenth-Century France* (Ithaca, NY: Cornell University Press, 1985), 77.

2. Later in this chapter, I will outline the practical means at the disposal of the colonial administration for preventing counterdiscourses from gaining wide audiences.

3. Charles-Robert Ageron, "L'Exposition coloniale de 1931: Mythe républicain ou mythe impérial?" in *Les Lieux de Mémoire: I, La République*, Ed. Pierre Nora (Paris: Gallimard, 1984), 590.

4. Maurice Violette, *L'Algérie vivra-t-elle?* (Paris: Félix Alcan, 1931). Others in favor of citizenship wrote mostly in *La Voix indigène, La Voix des Humbles,* and *La Presse libre*; those against, in *La Dépeche algérienne, L'Écho d'Alger,* and of course in all the right-wing papers.

5. For a full treatment of the citizenship question, see Louis-Augustin Barrière, "Le Puzzle de la citoyenneté en Algérie," *Plein droit,* no. 29–30 (November 1995).

6. Hadj Cadi, "De la naturalisation," *La Voix indigène,* 24 October 1929, and others.

7. The Third Republic never accepted any of these schemes. The *Français musulmans* became voting citizens 1947, but tampering by the Gouvernement Général ensured that no free elections ever took place.

8. Patricia Lorcin's *Imperial Identities: Stereotyping, prejudice and race in colonial Algeria* (London: I. B. Tauris, 1995) provides the best extended analysis of French Berber policy to date and furnished a framework for the present discussion.

9. Eugène Daumas, *La Grande Kabylie, études historiques* (Paris, 1844).

10. Eugène Daumas, *Moeurs et coutumes de l'Algérie: Tell—Kabylie—Sahara,* 1853 (Paris: L. Hachette, 1858). This work was reprinted in 1864. Given the demo-

graphic preponderance of Kabyles in the Algerian Amazigh population, the French had a tendency to subsitute one term for another, and to speak of "Berbères" and "Kabyles" as if the words were synonymous. Early ethnologists were not immune to this confusion of terms.

11. Gen. Adolphe Hanoteau and A. Letourneux, *La Kabylie et les coutumes kabyles* (Paris, 1872–73). The first preface dates from September 1868.

12. Hanoteau and Letourneux, *La Kabylie et les coutumes kabyles,* vol. 1, 310.

13. Charmetant, *Les Peuplades kabyles et les tribus nomades du Sahara* (Montreal, 1875); Père Joseph Dugas, *La Kabylie et le peuple kabyle* (Paris, 1877); Émile Guimet, *Arabes et Kabyles: pasteurs et agriculteurs* (Lyon, 1873); Camille Sabatier, *Étude sociologique sur les Kabyles,* Comptes rendus de l'Association française pour l'avancement des sciences (1881). The ensemble of Sabatier's works is of a much greater magnitude and quality from that of the other three authors' pamphlets.

14. The most interesting of Masqueray's works are his *Formation des cités chez les populations sédentaires de l'Algérie,* a basic text in the history of Kabyle ethnology, as well as his travel narratives in *Voyage dans l'Aurès: études historiques* (Paris, n.d.) and *Souvenirs et visions d'Afrique* (Paris: E. Dentu, 1894).

15. Camille Lacoste-Dujardin, "Génèse et évolution d'une représentation géopolitique: l'imagerie kabyle à travers la production bibliographique de 1840 à 1891," in *Connaissances du Maghreb: Sciences sociales et colonisation,* ed. Jean-Claude Vatin (Paris: CNRS, 1984), 270.

16. Charles Géniaux, *Sous les figuiers de Kabylie: Scènes de la vie berbère* (Paris: Flammarion, 1917). Most of Géniaux's other works have nothing to do with North Africa.

17. See the preface to Dinet and Baamer's *Khadra, danseuse Ouled Nail* (Paris: H. Fiazza, 1926), and the critic Jean Pomier's article following Dinet's death, "Attitudes devant l'Islam: celle d'Etienne Dinet," Afrique, no. 56 (February 1930): 2.

18. Duchêne's complete bibliography: *Au pas lent des caravanes,* 1922 (Paris: Albin-Michel, 1931) *Thamil'la* (Paris: Albin-Michel, 1923); *Le Roman du Meddah* (Paris: Albin-Michel, 1924); *Au pied des monts éternels: roman berbère* (Paris: Albin-Michel, 1925); *Kamir, roman d'une femme arabe* (Paris: Albin-Michel, 1926); *La Rek'ba, histoire d'une vendetta kabyle* (Paris: Albin-Michel, 1927); *Le Berger d'Akfadou, roman kabyle* (Paris: Albin-Michel, 1928); *Les Barbaresques: L'aventure de Sidi Flouss* (Paris: Albin-Michel, 1929); *Ceux d'Algerie: Types et coutumes* (Paris: Editions des Horizons de France, 1929); *Mouna, cachir, et couscouss* (Paris, Albin-Michel, 1930); *L'Incroyable histoire de Tali-Tho, la décolorée* (Paris, 1932); *Les Fantaisies du Docteur Mysti* (1934); *Siroco, fièvre algérienne* (Algiers: Baconnier, 1946); *Becavin* (1947).

19. The three manuscripts were *Au pas lent des caravanes, Thamil'la,* and *Au pied des monts éternels.* See the preceding chapter for a discussion of the circumstances and policies of attribution of the Grand Prix Littéraire.

20. Duchêne, *Le Berger d'Akfadou,* 70, citing Bernard, *Les Confins algéro-marocains,* 190.

21. Christiane Achour and Simone Rezzoug, "Brisure dans une cohérence discursive: l'autochtone dans les textes coloniaux de 1930 en Algérie," in *Des années trente: groupes et ruptures,* ed. Anne Roche and Christian Tarting (Paris: Éditions du CNRS, 1984), 80. Writing in 1984, they could not cite Terdiman explicitly, but their

model of the potential of literature for qualified subversion of the dominant discourse mirrors his in simplified form.

22. Duchêne, *Au pied des monts Eternels,* 247.

23. "Les Grandes fêtes de l'union Franco-Musulmane à Sidi-Ferruch," *l'Afrique du Nord illustrée,* 21 June 1930, 11.

24. Victor Spielmann, "En marge du Centenaire," *Demain,* 31 May 1930.

25. Charles-Collomb, "[Editorial]," *L'Évolution nord-africaine,* 1 January 1930, 2; emphasis in the original.

26. "Le Rapprochement est-il sincère ou factice?" *Annales nord-africaines,* 1 June 1930.

27. Duchêne, *La Rek'ba,* 3.

28. The term "Tamazight" is a recuperation of contemporary Amazigh cultural activists, intended to designate the ensemble of the North African indigenous linguistic stock, without signifying any particular dialect. The most widely spoken dialect in Algeria was and is more often referred to as *Taqbalit,* the language of the Kabyles. This term has the political disadvantage of its derivation from an Arabic word, *qabayl,* tribe, with derogatory overtones.

29. Duchêne, *L'Aventure de Sidi Flouss,* 101.

30. Ibid., 35.

31. Ibid.

32. Duchêne, *La Rek'ba,* 21.

33. Sautayra and Eugène Cherbonneau, *Droit musulman du statut personnel et des successions* (Paris: Maisonneuve et Cie., 1873–74), vol. 1, 60–61.

34. Duchêne, *L'Aventure de Sidi Flouss,* 38.

35. Ibid., 88.

36. Ibid., 100.

37. Ageron, *Histoire de l'Algérie contemporaine,* 142. Ageron notes that Sabatier also proposed forbidding facial tattoos for young women because it made them repulsive to European men. His chimerical scheme to perpetuate what he called "our race" with children fathered on Kabyle mothers attracted scorn in the press. The Egyptian historian Leila Ahmed notes similarly dubious motivations among *soi-disant* reformers in colonial Egypt in *Women and Gender in Islam: Historical Roots of a Modern Debate* (New Haven, CT: Yale University Press, 1992), 153.

38. Duchêne, *Thamil'la,* ix.

39. Duchêne, *Thamil'la,* ix-x. Emphasis and "sic" in the original.

40. Lacoste-Dujardin, "Génèse et évolution," 267.

41. Hanoteau and Letourneux, *La Kabylie et les coutumes kabyles,* vol. 2, 150–51.

42. Violette, *L'Algérie vivra-t-elle?* 413.

43. Duchêne, *La Rek'ba,* 3.

44. Marcel Morand, "Le Statut de la femme kabyle et la réforme des coutumes berbères," *Revue des études islamiques* 1 (1927): 49.

45. Ibid.

46. Ibid., 56.

47. Ageron, *Histoire de l'Algérie contemporaine,* 148.

48. Morand, "Le Statut de la femme kabyle," 48, 54.

49. Ibid., 64–5.

50. In fact, Duchêne even intervened to limit a proposed reform from the commission, which sought to grant divorces for physical maltreatment; Duchêne's version of the law would only have allowed divorces in cases of maltreatment which had resulted in criminal convictions. The commission overruled him, retaining their version (Morand, "Le Statut de la femme kabyle," 65, 83).

51. Morand, "Le Statut de la femme kabyle," 67.

52. "Savage wars of peace" is Rudyard Kipling's epithet for campaigns of colonial "pacification," recalled by the title of the British historian Alistair Horne's recently revised study of the Algerian war, *A Savage War of Peace : Algeria 1954–1962*, 1977 (London: Papermac, 1996).

53. *Musulmans et Chrétiennes* appeared in the Oran weekly *El Hack* ("Le Petit Egyptien. Organe de défense des intérêts musulmans"), beginning in April of that year. No bibliographic tool indicates that it ever appeared in volume form, and the (incomplete) collection of *El Hack* at the BN seems to support Déjeux's assertion that it was never finished. Déjeux gives another serial publication, "Ali, oh mon frère," in *El Hack* in 1893 by Zeid ben Dieb as a still-earlier "first." I have not managed to locate a copy or ascertain even the scope of the work (Jean Déjeux, *Maghreb littératures de langue française* [Paris: Arcantère, 1993], 31).

54. Khodja Chukri was the pseudonym of Hassan Khodja Hamdan. Other very early published writers include Hadj Hamou Abdelkader, author of a novel, *Zohra la femme d'un mineur* (Paris: Editions du monde moderne, 1925), and a number of short stories published in reviews in the 1920s and 1930s.

55. Terdiman, *Discourse/Counter-Discourse*, 13.

56. Zahir Ihaddaden, "L'Histoire de la presse 'indigène' en Algérie, des origines jusqu'en 1930," Thèse de doctorat du 3eme cycle (Université de Paris II, n.d.), 124–25.

57. It did rate mention in Roland Lebel's landmark study of colonial literature, purely to illustrate the existence of works by Algerian *indigènes*, but with no discussion (*Histoire de la littérature coloniale en France* (Paris: Larose, 1931), 104).

58. Peter Dunwoodie, *Francophone Writing in Transition: Algeria 1900–1945* (Bern: Peter Lang, 2005).

59. Emir Khaled Ibn al-Hachemi, *La Situation des Musulmans d'Algérie: Conférences faites à Paris les 12 et 19 juillet 1924*, 1924 (Algiers: Editions du Trait d'Union, Victor Spielmann, 1930), 41.

60. *El Ouma*, with the larger circulation, proclaimed nationalism in its title, Arabic for *nation* as well as for *community of believers*. The government rapidly suppressed both these papers. The physical deterioration of much of the BN's collection of Algerian newspapers, the most substantial outside Algeria, severely limits research on the *presse indigène*. The collection at the Archives d'Outre Mer in Aix is also respectable, but has major gaps as well.

61. Considerable divergences separated Rabah Zenati's assimilationist *Voix des humbles* and Bouri's *El Hack*, more separatist in its outlook.

62. Charles-Robert Ageron, *France coloniale ou parti colonial?* (Paris: PUF, 1978), 199.

63. Ait-Kaci, "La Représentation des indigènes au Parlement," *La Voix des humbles* 74 (May 1929): 3.

64. "Le Centenaire: revendications politiques," *La Voix indigène*, 21 November 1929.

65. Labiod, "Désillusion et espérance," *La Voix indigène*, 10 July 1930.

66. A. Ben Cherif, *Ahmed ben Mostapha, goumier* (Paris: Payot, 1920), 86–87.

67. Khodja Chukri, *El Euldj, captif des barbaresques* (Paris: Editions de la Revue des Indépendants, 1929), 42, 139.

68. Dunwoodie, *Francophone Writing in Transition: Algeria 1900–1945*, 266–67.

69. The first paper to adopt national independance in its platform was *El Ouma*, in 1930. On the radicalization of 1930, see Abdelkader Djeghloul's chapter on "Les Revendications de indépendance au début du XXe siècle" in *Éléments d'histoire culturelle algérienne* (Algiers: ENAL, 1984). Ageron discusses briefly the vocabulary of the opposition in *Histoire de l'Algérie contemporaine*, 241.

70. The Blum-Violette reform of the status of the *indigènes* in Algeria was definitively pushed aside in 1935; it represented the last serious possibility for reform coming from the government. Most observers trace the birth of an explicitly nationalist opposition to this period.

71. For the first message, compare Henriette Celarié's *Esclave à Alger* (1930), a rosy captivity narrative ending optimistically with the conquest of 1830. For the second, see Charles Courtin's *La Brousse qui mangea l'homme* (1929), in which a young man loses his fortune and his life in a pointless, doomed, and above all unheroic effort to establish himself as a *colon*.

72. Chukri, *El Euldj, captif des barbaresques*, 114.

73. Ibid., 116.

74. Ibid., 133.

75. Ibid.

76. The phrase "double discourse" is Djeghloul's (*Éléments d'histoire culturelle algérienne*, 107).

77. Djeghloul, *Éléments d'histoire culturelle algérienne*, 107.

78. Chukri, *El Euldj, captif des barbaresques*, 135.

79. Djeghloul, *Éléments d'histoire culturelle algérienne*, 34.

80. Ahmed Lanasri, *La Littérature algérienne de l'entre-deux-guerres: génèse et fonctionnement* (Paris: Publisud, 1995), 182–84.

81. Rabah Zenati, the assimilationist editor of the *Voix des humbles*, and Charles-Collomb, the rabid "arabophobe" editor of the *Évolution nord-africaine*, embodied these two opposed positions. Ben Bādīs and Messali Hadj were only just then beginning to reverse the political charges of these poles.

82. Mohammed Ould Cheikh, *Myriem dans les palmes* (Oran: Editions Plaza, 1936), 22.

83. Ibid.

84. Ibid., cover page.

85. Lanasri, *La Littérature algérienne de l'entre-deux-guerres: génèse et fonctionnement*, 178.

86. Ould Cheikh, *Myriem dans les palmes*, 196. "Roumia" is the feminine of "roumi," etymologically a person from Rome, but generically (and to this day) any European-looking foreigner in the Maghrib.

87. Ould Cheikh, *Myriem dans les palmes*, 212.

88. Djeghloul calls this paper "proche des milieux fascistes de Doriot" [close to the Fascist millieu of Doriot] (Djeghloul, *Éléments d'histoire culturelle algérienne,* 36).

89. Ould Cheikh, *Myriem dans les palmes,* preface.

90. Mammeri spoke at a discussion of colonial Algerian literature recorded in Paul Siblot, ed., *Vie culturelle à Alger, 1900–1950* (Montpellier: Praxiling, Université de Montpellier III, 1996), 32.

4

✝

1930: The Cult of Memory

The year 1930 marked a number of historical anniversaries, and the French found ways of observing most of them, with a taste for public remembrance undiminished since. "L'année des Centenaires," as an exhibition catalogue appearing that year called it, included the centenary of Victor Hugo's *Hernani* and the scandal of Romanticism; the centenary of Greek independence, Europe's *cause célèbre* of the early nineteenth century; the centenary of the July Revolution and the end of legitimist monarchy; and the centenary of the conquest of Algiers.[1] In addition, in the colony, the year saw the deaths of the journalist Musette, inventor of the Algerian Gavroche, Cagayous, and first observer of the new urban ethnic mix in Algiers, and of the painter Étienne Dinet, perhaps the last exemplar of the grand tradition of exoticist Orientalism in French art, and a symbol of "l'union franco-musulmane, sous le signe de l'Art" [Franco-Muslim unity, under the aegis of Art].[2] As a major anniversary of French Algeria's founding act, 1930 represented the colony's renewed presence in public discourses of history, the moment of self-consciousness of its own past as history. The fact that France had no colonial project or goals in attacking Algiers in 1830 received only limited attention in commemorations, and official discourse supported the idea of a full century of colonialism. The weekly *Annales Africaines* wrote in October 1929 that "Ce qu'il y a de particulier, de prenant, dans l'oeuvre accomplie par nous en Algérie, c'est que, datant de près d'un siècle, elle se présente, à qui veut la contempler dans son ensemble, avec un recul suffisant. Elle n'a pas seulement pour elle la force, mais déjà la durée, signe infaillible auquel se reconnaît la force véritable. L'Algérie française, et c'est un de ses charmes, possède déjà un passé." [What is most striking in the work we have accomplished in Algeria is that, since it dates back nearly a century, it presents itself with sufficient distance to anyone looking at it overall. It has in its favor not only strength, but also longevity, the infallible sign by which true strength is recognized. French Algeria already possesses a past, and this is one of its charms.][3] To have a centenary is to have a past, an object for nostalgia and an entry into the historical "ensemble" which lent dignity and charm to France as a whole. The connection between that history and the colonial urban fabric continued undiminished; the *Annales* journalist could think of no better way to illustrate the colony's newly visible historical dignity and charm than by following up immediately with a comment on the appearance of its cities: "Laissons les grandes et magnifiques villes de la côte, Alger, dont la prospérité, le développement marchent au rythme des plus riches cités américaines, Alger qui est à la fois Marseille et Nice; laissons Oran, florissante elle aussi; Bône, Philippeville; arrêtons-nous aux petites villes de l'intérieur, Blida, Medea, Mascara, Tlemcen qui ont le charme vieillot des sous-préfectures de France, je ne sais quel air Louis-Philippe, qui sont un vrai morceau de notre terre, miraculeusement transporté sur la terre d'Afrique." [Let us leave the grand and magnificent cities of the coast: Algiers, where prosperity and development advance at the pace of the richest American cities, and which is at once Marseille and Nice; Oran, also flourishing; Bône and Philippeville. Let us stop in the little towns of the interior, Blida, Medea, Mascara, and Tlemcen, which have the superannuated charm of *sous-prefectures* in France, a certain air of Louis-Philippe about them, and which are a true piece of our soil, miraculously transported to the soil of Africa.][4] To readers remembering Louis Bertrand's 1930 call for an archaeology of the colonial city, akin to the one he said could be practiced in Spain's former colonies in the New World, it might appear that he was getting his wish before even formulating it.[5] Colonial intellectuals valued Algeria's second-rank cities because they displayed their history in the same way France did, and on a comparable time line.[6] Algiers, on which we will continue to focus, seemed almost too modern for this journalist; we will see why urban archaeology began to be problematic in the capital.

The first centenary of French Algeria was also the last; we cannot look at it with the eyes of those who organized the parades, delivered the speeches, wrote the novels, and published the albums, nor even of those who criticized the very project of commemoration in the press. Their declarations ring rather hollow, and not only when they make pious or triumphant predictions about the celebration of a hypothetical second centenary of French Algeria, which they knew they would not see themselves, but could not imagine that no one else would, either. The enterprise of commemoration, insofar as it entails choices of what to commemorate and how, seems suspect almost by definition: public commemorations are always the product of political choices, reflecting at best a consensus, and at worst, an imposition of a historical worldview from above. In the days of the post-colony, moreover, our suspicions grow ever more as we examine the self-proclaimed commemorative apotheosis of colonial Algeria. Without letting go of that suspicion, we can nonetheless consider what it meant to celebrate together, as France and Algeria did, the "cult of memory": "Le culte du souvenir a toujours été une vertu française" [the cult of memory has always been a French virtue], wrote Gustave Mercier, head of the Commissariat du Centenaire.[7] Is there something particularly French about this new, or newly old, religion? If so, how did the very Frenchness of the forms of public remembrance play out in the colony struggling to identify itself as French, and therefore worthy of consideration, but also Algerian, and worthy of respect? Clearly the *culte du souvenir* would involve the sanctification of certain monuments and the canonization of certain saints, so the hagiographic tone of much of the material published around the Centenary should not surprise us. Yet readers might wonder why, if the *culte du souvenir* were one of France's eternal virtues, colonial publicists and others devoted so much time, money, and energy to promoting it. The promoters wrote as if memory were not a *culte*, any religion, but a cult, one that required endless indoctrination and firm discipline because the value of the object worshipped is not obvious or long-accepted, or because the people leading it demand absolute deference. In the terms of this study, the commemorations of 1930 constituted a spectacular episode of restorative nostalgia, purpose-built rather than preexisting.

Debating what to commemorate raised the question of what was truly important to the Algerian identity, both as Algerians of various ethnicities wished to see themselves, and as they wished to be seen, in France and abroad. Many Algerian writers, journalists, and politicians accused the government of misrepresenting the colony, of projecting a false image to the French at home, and of letting slip an opportunity to correct the misperceptions of colonial exoticism, barbarism, and oppression that they found prevalent in mainland France.[8] In this context, the notion of "opposition" takes on a variety of nuances difficult to appreciate today. First, it included opposition to the official image of harmony between Muslims and European Algerians, from those on the right (e.g., the *Arabophobe* journalist Charles-Collomb), who would have preferred vigorous repression of the Muslims and complete rejection of their participation in the elaboration of the colonial image.[9] Second, it also included those on the left, whose pronouncements may today seem condescending, naive, or simply tepid. The *Presse libre*, the Algiers leftist daily, frequently criticized government waste and occasionally denounced egregious abuse of Muslims; in 1930, it was clearly an antigovernment paper, albeit one whose criticisms of the colonial order debated only its daily functioning and never its premises. Although by 1930, a very few Arab and Amazigh leaders (notably the Emir Khaled) had begun to express complete rejection of the colonial regime, no European writing in Algeria at the time openly questioned the very legitimacy of the North African colonies. Victor Spielmann, the Communist pamphleteer, wished to abolish its bases with radical agrarian reforms; Maurice Violette, former Governor General, and his former chief of staff Jean Mélia, "le pape des indigènes" [pope of the natives] wished to reform it from within, by abolishing the *code d'indigénat* [native code] and other abuses of the *régime d'exception* [irregular rule].[10] Another factor rendered unlikely the development of significant opposition to colonialism in the print production of the Centenary: its source and funding. A great deal of it, especially the newspaper and magazine articles and the *Cahiers du Centenaire*, was funded and sometimes actually written by various services of the Gouvernement Général in Algiers. The Commission du Centenaire declared that it spent 2,075,971 francs on press subventions to place over 300 articles in French newspapers between January and July 1930.[11] Evidently none of these, nor any of the hundreds of other articles cribbed from them, were likely to question the colonial status quo. That no writer or politician of European origin in Algeria actually challenged the very existence of the colony does not make any less oppositional the writings of reformers or others discontented with government policy: their tone, and that of government supporters combating them, demonstrates their radically divergent views of the colony's history and identity. In this context, the literature of the Centenary could not be the vehicle for discourses opposing colonialism as such; however, it was fertile ground for developing and debating divergent views on what the colony was and should become, debates which frequently challenged the official representations of colonial history.

FANTASIAS AND FIREWORKS: HISTORICAL COMMEMORATION AS COSTUME PARTY

The authorities spared no effort or expense to make a truly grandiose spectacle of the celebrations, concentrated in the spring to capitalize on good weather and to culminate with the anniversary of the landing at Sidi-Ferruch on 14 June 1830. The foundation of the *Commissariat Général du Centenaire*, five years in advance, and the budgets at its disposition, totaling 100 million francs, testify to the government's high expectations. Leaving nothing to chance, an order dated 27 December 1927 established an additional *Conseil Supérieur du Centenaire*, which included Gustave Mercier, head of the Commissariat, the Mayor of Algiers, and the Governor General; it met at least sixty times over the following three years.[12] The community of Algerian journalists and intellectuals (both European and Muslim) largely shared these expectations, or wished to do so at least initially. Almost everyone agreed that the Centenary should place Algeria in the forefront of the French consciousness, at least for a time. From this focalization of public attention, carefully orchestrated by the Commissariat and other government agencies, Algerians of all ethnic groups hoped to gain a wide variety of benefits from the metropole: moral support, favorable tariffs, new immigrants, and even political reform. When these failed to materialize, many hastened to accuse the government of having promoted a chimera and of raising expectations unreasonably. Before looking at these expectations and complaints, however, we should first examine the context provided by the official events of 1930. Relatively little that was published that year actually differed much from the years before or after, but the context of commemoration itself gave the year's complicated weave of events and texts their particular flavor.

The official "Programme du Centenaire," published, revised, and republished in various formats in every major newspaper and popular review, could claim true comprehensiveness: virtually no medium, venue,

Figure 4.1.   Poster for the centenary of French Algeria. Archives d'Outre-Mer, Aix-en-Province. Reproduced by permission of Editions Baconnier.

or variety of event escaped the attention of the organizers. (See figure 4.1.) Dozens of sporting events, several motor rallies including one across the Sahara, an extraordinary array of conferences and professional meetings, a concert premiering a specially composed *Cantate du Centenaire,* and any number of theatrical productions made for a very full calendar in the four months leading up to the official celebrations in May and June. These included a rolling schedule of visits from *députés* (arranged so as not to empty the chamber completely, since virtually every legislator in the *Assemblée* took advantage of this junket), military parades, official ceremonies, and a visit by President Gaston Doumergue. Many of the events and displays subsidized, though not organized, by the government had little to do with historical commemoration: the meetings of the Association des Anciens Combattants, the Association des Avocats, or the Congrès de la Presse (along with dozens of others) had no substantive content related to the Centenary, and their presence in Algiers that year had as much to do with the colonial government's wish to fill the hundreds of extra hotel rooms it had encouraged building, than with the wish, equally real, and much more often admitted, to promote the colony in the French press. Numerous local journalists complained about the *humiliante platitude* of the celebration calendar which, in response to criticism, had merely added "Nouvelles fantasias et nouveaux feux d'artifices" [new fantasias and new fireworks] as Jean Mélia headlined one of his articles.[13] Their objections seem justified by the hodgepodge of events loudly proclaimed as part of the commemoration, but often more publicity-seeking than anything else. Nothing suggests that the Commissariat wanted anything else from them: 1930 constituted *the* year of avowed self-promotion for the entire colony.

The official events themselves represented something else, and had another character (or at least another promotional thrust) altogether. Here the government had a free hand to select the time, manner, and object of promotion and commemoration. While other events gave free publicity to vineyards, automakers, or hotels, the official ceremonies publicized history itself, as officially conceived. One event stood out: the march through Algiers of a recreated regiment of the *Armée d'Afrique,* troops costumed and equipped like those who conquered Algiers in 1830, and of identically reconstituted early regiments of Spahis, Zouaves, and Chasseurs d'Afrique. A great deal of historical research went into this military costume party. Those in charge wanted to reproduce everything, from weapons down to buttons on the uniforms. In a military review on 19 April 1930, several weeks before President Doumergue's arrival and almost two months before the actual anniversary of the landing, the troops paraded through the streets of Algiers, to arrive via the waterfront boulevards at the Place du Gouvernement (formerly the Place d'Armes) and massed around the equestrian statue of the Duc d'Orléans. There, they formed up to receive the salute of the modern versions of each regiment. Nothing in the press coverage suggests that anyone wondered what justified the mix of pre-colonial troops (the *Armée d'Afrique*) with colonial (the North African regiments); apparently it seemed logical to have a whole range of the early military history on display at once, and to combine it with modern troops. The Army restricted itself to an accurate reconstitution, without delving into the logic of the representation, and by all accounts they attained impeccable representational accuracy. To the untrained eye, the recreated troops did not miss the slightest detail. The inclusion of other colonial regiments helped them compress the story of a fortnight's assaults in 1830, and of twenty years of heavy campaigning which followed, into a two-hour show. Parade goers and visitors could take home their image on the parade program, as well as in lavishly illustrated weeklies; the troops constituted a historical souvenir.

Dozens of articles attested to the recreated troops' success, very nearly as many as reported Doumergue's arrival in May. The iconography of the Centenary likewise reserves a large place for them; they provided one of the most memorable images of the celebrations. Observers attributed to them the power of transporting them back, almost literally, to the conquest, and spent considerable rhetorical energy describing the depth of their emotions on seeing them. When the troops marched in the July 14th parade in Paris that year, *Le Journal* carried the comments of a member of the colorful and imposing group of Muslim notables imported for the occasion to march with them:

> Je suis cent ans en arrière. . . . C'était vrai. Ces soldats, revêtus d'uniformes de jadis, ces voltigeurs, ces turcos, ces spahis de Charles X et de Louis-Philippe, faisaient surgir l'épopée de cet autrefois, qui, lui aussi, fut grand.
>
> C'est l'Histoire même qui prenait corps tout à coup près de nous.
>
> Et après cent ans, notre présence dans cette revue, qui était comme un anniversaire, symbolisait la communauté d'esprit et de coeur, sanctionnée hier encore dans les combats, qui nous lie pour toujours à notre mère, la France. Nous étions ses soldats, nous aussi.

> [I am a hundred years in the past. . . . It was true. These soldiers, clothed in the uniforms of the past, these *voltigeurs*, *turcos*, and *spahis* of Charles X and Louis-Philippe, revived the epic of that past, another great moment of French history.
>
> It was History itself suddenly embodied next to us.
>
> After a hundred years, our presence in that parade, which was like an anniversary, symbolized the community of hearts and spirits, sanctioned only yesterday in combat, which links us forever to our mother, France. We, too, were her soldiers.][14]

The author, the factitiously titled "cheik el-Arab" Bouaziz ben Gana, had just before alluded to his ancestor's submission to Bugeaud; here, one paragraph later, he seems to have forgotten that anyone could have been on the other side, except possibly the Germans, the common enemy in the most recent unifying struggle, "only yesterday."[15] Furthermore, Ben Gana's "it was true" suggests several interpretations: it seems to attest to the truth not only of the troops' power to evoke history, but also to the truth-value of that history itself. However, even though the recreated troops embody history, in a curious way they erase it as well: in their presence, and in the absence of any recreated enemies for them to pretend to fight, the *indigènes* and the French were friends and had never been anything else. Interestingly, the press reports no Arab dignitaries marching in Algiers in the first parade. Did the organizers fear that the power of the recreated troops to "embody" history might work more ambiguously there, or that it might not have this impressive effect of erasure? The notables may simply have wished to stay away. At home, even the French-decorated (and created) *bachaghas* may have felt it impolitic to show their faces at this particular parade.

The troop reconstitution effaced other conflicts besides the twenty-year fight against the Arabs and Imazighen. The *Revue des Vivants*, a veterans' journal, declared that "Les générations actuelles sont assez loin des querelles anciennes pour ne pas s'inquiéter de savoir si les troupes qui ont conquis Alger marchaient sous les plis du drapeau tricolore ou du drapeau blanc fleur-delysé; c'est le coeur de la France qui battait sous leurs uniformes." [the current generation is far enough removed from the old quarrels not to worry over whether the troops which conquered Algiers marched under the tricolor or the white flag with fleur-de-lys; it was the heart of France which beat under their uniforms.][16] At least, so thought General Paul Azan, author of the violent suppression of several riots in Tunisia in the 1920s, as well as of the article and several military histories of North Africa. That he mentioned the question of the monarchy at all should raise questions, about both his statement's accuracy and its motivation. Apparently, others believed that the possibility of disagreement between monarchists and republicans nonetheless existed, and had taken steps to preempt it. The recreated versions of the troops who took Algiers marched under the tricolor, despite the anachronism apparent to anyone aware that the conquering troops of early July 1830 could not have anticipated the change in flag that occured two weeks after they entered the city. If the organizers wished to avoid controversy, they certainly succeeded; the only journalist to remark on this substitution of flags thought it a useless precaution:

> Je me permettrais de leur signaler [aux organisateurs] néanmoins un petit anachronisme. Le drapeau des troupes de débarquement de 1830 (pas plus

que les cocardes des shakos) n'était point tricolore mais bien blanc fleur-delisé.

Cette entorse à la vérité historique a été fait intentionnellement sans doute et pour éviter de froisser certaines sensibilités, mais la lutte des partis n'est pas tellement tendue, de ce côté de la Méditerranée, qu'elle ait dicté pareille décision.

[I will nonetheless allow myself to mention to the organizers one small anachronism. The flag of the troops of the invasion of 1830 (as well as the ribbons on the shakos) was not tricolor, but in fact white with fleurs-de-lys.

This twisting of historical truth was no doubt intentional, to avoid offending certain sensibilities, but the struggle between parties is not so tense on this side of the Mediterranean as to dictate such a decision.][17]

This from a journalist from the *Dépêche Algérienne*, the colony's daily of record, who had every reason to know that party struggles divided Algeria as much as France. However, he was right in the sense that these conflicts indeed did not center around republican or monarchic forms of government. By focusing attention on lack of conflict in this particular area, the article makes Algeria appear politically united and peaceful. After the ceremonies, the question arose of what to do with the uniforms so painstakingly and expensively recreated for the reconstituted troops; the government considered selling them to private individuals. Mercier, head of the Commissariat, would not hear of this. He warned that "si on les cède à un particulier, il est à craindre que nous les retrouvions plus tard sur des scènes de théâtre ou les tréteaux de foires" [if we sell them to a private individual, it is to be feared that we would find them later on the stages of theaters and fairs].[18] To sell the uniforms was to cede the capacity to create public historical entertainment, and to give up the monopoly on creating nostalgia.

Although most of the Algerian press refrained from direct criticism of the rituals promoting nostalgia as the national affect for the months of April, May, and June, objections had arisen earlier.[19] Bitter arguments had broken out over the nature of the celebrations, especially in a series of lengthy diatribes from both government and opposition in the *Presse libre*. Jean Mélia, author of several tracts favoring political representation for the Muslims, repeatedly attacked the Commissariat du Centenaire for wasting taxpayers' money, ignoring the Muslims, and having a conception of the Centenary, and therefore of the colony, that did not measure up to its true dignity. Mélia found easier targets for his wrath than the official speeches and ceremonies, and in essence conceded the government's role in promoting restorative nostalgia. He preferred to attack the relatively hollow season of public partying with which the Commissariat padded the calendar. At least one official must have regretted the day he approved a poster with the following description of public festivities in an oasis town south of Oran: "Centenaire de l'Algérie, Béni Ounif de Figuig. Grandes fêtes sahariennes 1er avril–10 avril 1930. Fantasias . . . Courses de chevaux et de chameaux. Danses arabes et danses guerrières, Attaque de caravanes et de douars, Pillage et incendie de tentes. Rapt de femmes. Manifestations sportives, etc." [Centenary of Algeria, Béni Ounif de Figuig. Grand Saharan Festival, 1 April–10 April 1930. Fantasias . . . Horse and camel races. Arab dances and war dances, attacks on caravans and villages, pillage and burning of tents. Kidnapping of women. Sporting events, etc.][20] Even in 1930, the juxtapositions in the list of festivities seemed ridiculous. It did to Mélia, but his response is totally humorless, and scarcely more attractive than the obliviousness to irony represented by the original poster: "Ainsi voilà, sous l'égide du Gouvernement Général de l'Algérie, ce que l'on trouve pour célébrer, à Béni-Ounif, où la presque unanimité des habitants est indigène et parfois de moeurs primitives, tout ce que la France a fait de bien en Algérie, depuis cent ans! . . . Mais cela est licite, penseront les gens simples de certains tribus, puisque, pour fêter le caractère licite de la conquête française, le Commissariat Général du Centenaire le reconstitue officiellement dans toute sa précision." [So, under the auspices of the Gouvernement Général de l'Algérie, this is what they found to celebrate in Béni-Ounif, where almost all the inhabitants are *indigènes*, sometimes with primitive customs: all the good France did in Algeria, in a hundred years! . . . But this is legal, the simple people of certain tribes will think, because, to celebrate the legitimate nature of the French conquest, the Commissariat Général du Centenaire is officially reconstituting it in every detail.][21] Mélia feels slighted, as an earnest promoter of the *mission civilisatrice* against the proponents of an exclusively mercantile and exoticist vision of French Algeria, the vision represented here by proposals to reenact some of the more vivid aspects of the conquest. Razzias might be more entertaining than school building, one of Mélia's favorite topics, but he does not want amusement: he wants credit where he feels it due. His earlier article had already summarized his view: "Nouvelles fantasias et nouveux feux d'artifice.—Rien en l'honneur de l'Oeuvre de francisation de l'Algérie" [New fantasias and new fireworks.—Nothing in honor of the Work of Frenchification of Algeria]. We might read his specific criticism as exactly the opposite of the *Dépêche* journalist's complaint about a slight defect in the verisimilitude of the imagery presented in official commemorations. Mélia, here, complains instead about excessive accuracy: the government is reconstituting the conquest "dans toute sa précision," where it should instead leave certain things out. He feels such details are unnecessary, painful, and dangerous, not because they risk offending Muslims who did not wish to see their humiliation reenacted, but because such exciting spectacles might incite the still-primitive clans of some desert regions to revert to their old ways and imitate this government-endorsed spectacle.

Both Mélia and the author of the article in the *Dépêche* believe that historical details hold the potential for both social division and reconciliation, depending on the audience to which one presents them. European citizens of Algiers rally round the anachronistic tricolor, paradoxically by finding it not really necessary to their social cohesion; they were mature enough not to find embarrassing the unpalatable details of monarchy's role in the foundation of Republican Algeria. The *indigènes* of the Sud Oranais, however, allegedly had no such mature historical judgment to distinguish between behavior appropriate in the past and behavior appropriate now: "Ils viendront . . . se surexcitant l'esprit, sentant grandir en eux tous les désirs de l'or à obtenir par n'importe quel moyen, les yeux de plus en plus emplis de convoitises . . . Ah! la belle leçon de choses qu'ils recevront" [they will come . . . and get overexcited, feeling the desire growing in them for gold obtained by any means, their eyes full of greed. . . . A fine object-lesson they will receive!][22] Greedy by nature, they might be moved to act as the *colons* had, using force to confiscate property and inflict punitive damage on those who had held it. This insidious *leçon de choses* would legitimate for the Muslims in 1930 what the *colons* legitimated for themselves and their army beginning in 1830; it constitutes a clear threat to the "Work of Frenchification" Mélia so wanted to glorify, and which the Commissariat, angrily retorting to his articles, asserted it would.[23] It seems historical accuracy should have been marked "for mature audiences only"; in the wrong hands, it threatened the very government which had the power to represent it to its subjects. Glorifying the conquest in an act of (literally) restorative, in fact reconstitutive, nostalgia seemed to threaten the security of the conquest itself.

Despite Mélia's imagined scenario, these subjects did not sit passively by, absorbing the *leçons de choses* afforded by the various festivities. Rather, they were busily presenting demands for parliamentary representation and an end to the *régime d'indigénat*, the separate-and-unequal justice system applied to Muslims. More prosaically, they also demanded that the government use the money voted by the Assemblée to celebrate the Centenary more constructively. The *Voix indigène* expressed its desiderata as follows:

> Des crédits importants sont entre des mains expertes et qui sauront donner satisfaction à tout le monde. Nous déclarons que les expositions ne nous intéressent pas beaucoup, car nous donnons à l'Idée du Centenaire un sens qui signifie l'union entre tous les peuples en contact dans ce pays, la collaboration loyale, la pensée d'un travail effectif en vue du bonheur des populations entières et de la grandeur de la France.

Pour réconcilier tous les coeurs, pour donner libre cours aux sentiments de légitime fierté pour l'oeuvre accomplie par les Français, aidés des Indigènes, pour donner aux manifestations qui se préparent toute la dignité et toute la joie que mérite un pareil événement, nous demandons instamment la création de beaucoup d'écoles.

[Large sums of money are in the expert hands of people who will manage to satisfy everyone. We declare that expositions do not interest us very much, because we attribute to the Idea of the Centenary a meaning which signifies the union among all the peoples in contact in this country, loyal collaboration, and the idea of effective work for the happiness of entire populations and the greatness of France.

To reconcile all hearts, to give free rein to feelings of legitimate pride in the work accomplished by the French, helped by the *Indigènes*, and to lend the planned events all the dignity and joy such an occasion merits, we strongly insist on the creation of a large number of schools.][24]

As articles in the *Presse libre* make clear, it remained difficult, despite several public accountings, to determine exactly how much of the Assemblée's 93 million francs went into building projects and durable infrastructure; a great deal no doubt financed one-time events.[25] This article, however, differs from those in the Franco-Algerian press, which all routinely assured the public that the loyalty of the *indigènes* and their adherence to France were henceforth a certainty. Most papers devoted a good deal of space to coverage of speeches or actions by *indigène* notables "proving" their loyalty; the *Voix indigène* suggests on the contrary that this reconciliation, though near, is still to come. For its editors, a school building program would do far more to "reconcile all hearts" and to justify French pride (which they cleverly contrive to suggest needed justification) than any series of fairs and expositions.

Although the Muslim political opposition gained one of its goals, the end of the *régime d'indigénat*, declared at the height of commemorative celebrations in the spring of 1930, opposition writers quickly began to suspect they would have no success with their other major goal, elected representation on the national level.[26] On 1 May the *Voix indigène* published a sort of *cahier de doléances* for the Centenary (demands for generalized naturalizations, administrative reforms, and parliamentary representation) under the headline "*Cahier du Centenaire*, ou ensemble des réformes que les Indigènes algériens attendaient pour le Centenaire" [*Cahier du Centenaire*, or collection of reforms which the Algerian *Indigènes* were expecting for the Centenary."[27] The imperfect of the verb conveys the suspicion that the Muslim political class was still waiting for satisfaction slow to come. Already on 5 June, nine days before the climax of the official celebrations, the paper's editors knew that the "loi Soulier" granting the Muslims the right to elect *députés* would not pass; in responding to a climate of promises made to be broken, they wrote, "Le Centenaire aura le sort d'un grand feu de joie qui ne laisse que des cendres bientôt dispersés par les vents . . . cet effort est sans résultat palpable" [the Centenary will have the effect of a large firework which leaves only cinders, soon dispersed by the wind . . . this effort remains without palpable result].[28] The *députés* did in fact defeat the bill, leaving one writer to regret the "cortège interminable de fêtes" [interminable succession of parties] and hollow commemorations without durable results.[29] The disabused tone of these articles indicates their authors' views of the context of commemorations offered during the official Centenary; months before, another writer had said that in glorifying the past, "on ne met pas suffisament en relief le rôle de l'Indigène qui, quoi qu'on en dise, a pris une large part à la fécondité et à la prosperité de ce pays" [they are not sufficiently emphasizing the role of the *Indigène* who, whatever they say, has played a large part in the fertility and prosperity of this country].[30] In other words, the problem lay once more in the vision of the colony's history chosen for promotion. Perceptive Muslim observers had quickly noted their absence (not to say exclusion) from official commemoration, except as ceremonial pawns, and had foreseen the inevitable conclusion: if they had contributed nothing to colonial history, why grant them citizenship or political representation? The narrative of restorative nostalgia had no significant role for them.

We should understand by now that complainers about the official celebrations of the Centenary constituted a vocal minority, but a minority nonetheless. For the most part, the press showed itself remarkably easy on the government, even after thinly veiled accusations of fraud (and entirely overt allegations of mismanagement).[31] Most of the press adopted the government's position on celebrating the understanding between Muslims and European Algerians that was allegedly bringing Algeria into the modern world and enriching it in the process. Jean Mélia had an uphill battle to convince anyone that anything was missing from this vision of the colony; his four-column open letter to André Tardieu in the *Presse libre* in early January spends a great deal of time driving at the cultural void of the Centenary as the Commissariat conceived it. For Mélia, the Commissariat had no visible plan of cultural promotion: "A-t-il montré quelque sollicitude pour ces écrivains qui, nés en Algérie même, se sont appliqués à la langue et au génie de leur patrie métropolitaine, qui ont traduit leur pensée et leur flamme par des ouvrages que la France a remarqués et auxquelles elle a applaudi dans la fière et légitime constation que les vrais fils du terroir africain s'élevaient, eux aussi, dans sa propre littérature?" [Has it shown any solicitude for those writers born in Algeria itself, who have applied themselves to the language and spirit of their French fatherland, and who have translated their thought and their flame into works which France has remarked upon and applauded, proudly and legitimately noting that the true sons of the African soil were rising in the tradition of its own literature?][32] The "Exposition du livre français" scheduled for March had already fallen through due, journalists thought, to lack of diligence among the organizers; in not supporting literary and artistic events, the Commissariat committed the heresy, in Mélia's view, of deemphasizing Algeria's irrevocable Frenchness.

What, after all, could have proven this Frenchness better than a good crop of literary writers in the colony, all writing in a French as worthy of recognition as Mélia suggests? Everyone agreed that the Centenary represented a unique opportunity for proving Algeria's worth, and the only question was how to do so, and in what domain. For Mélia and others, this worth resided largely in the Frenchness of the colony:

> Il faut, en effet, montrer au monde entier qu'après cent ans d'occupation, [l'Algérie] est quelque chose de plus qu'un comptoir, qu'elle est la France elle-même dans sa vie spirituelle, dans ses lettres, dans son génie, dans tout ce qui fait la grandeur immortelle de sa culture et son idéal.
> Algériens, nous en avons assez de ce bluff qui consiste à dire que l'Algérie est uniquement un pays immensément riche . . . nous ne voulons pas de cette surenchère mensongère qui nous voue aux plus bas appétits d'égoisme et de lucre. Algériens, nous sommes Français dans l'âme même de la France.

> [We really must show the entire world that after a hundred years of occupation, Algeria is something more than a trading post, that it is France itself in its spiritual life, its letters, its genius, and in everything which makes the immortal grandeur and ideals of a culture.
> As Algerians, we have had enough of this bluff which consists of saying that Algeria is only an immensely rich country . . . we want nothing to do with this extravagant lie, which consigns us to the lowest appetites of egotism and lucre. As Algerians, we are French, in the very soul of France.][33]

For Mélia, promotion of Algerian literature in French would prove (especially, one suspects, to Parisians) that Algerians were capable of producing something other than the wine that competed well with France's own vintages. Even more importantly, it would show that Algeria was "l'âme même de la France." We shall see in what measure the literature of the Centenary actually did this, and investigate in what way it supported or complicated the commemorative projects in nostalgia.

THE LITERATURE OF COMMEMORATION

The Algerian government subsidized a fairly ambitious publishing program, "Les Publications du Centenaire," a series of approximately thirty-five scholarly studies covering most aspects of the colony's history, geology, colonization, and public institutions. In addition, the Comité national métropolitain du Centenaire de l'Algérie, in Paris, published a twelve-volume set duplicating much of this coverage, which in both series varied between dry scholarship and popularization. Both projects ran into difficulties. Charles Tailliart, rector of the Université d'Alger and coordinator of the "Publications du Centenaire," found himself explaining to Governor Bordes and a worried Conseil supérieur du Centenaire that these works were not simple brochures, but necessitated time-consuming research; in May 1929, only two had actually appeared.[34] The "Collection du Centenaire de l'Algérie," as it was also known, included no literary works at all; the various funding agencies seem to have granted little money for literature, though the government occasionally agreed to buy a number of copies of expensive art books in advance of publication.[35] The twelve-volume set of *Cahiers du Centenaire*, a series wholly managed by the Gouvernement Général, received more widespread official distribution: 70,000 copies went to the ministry of education alone.[36]

This did not mean that the Centenary and the years immediately preceding and following it suffered from any lack of fiction on Algeria by either French or Algerian writers. On the contrary, 1930 saw a boom in publication of fiction by Algerians or with Algerian themes.[37] Publication and reprinting of Algerian-authored or -themed fiction nearly tripled from 1929 to 1930; the numbers for the years preceding and following fall on a highly symmetrical bell curve peaking at the Centenary. The year 1930 represented a major opportunity to publish or reprint fiction on Algeria, so much so that a number of books listed in the *Bibliographie de la France* at the end of 1929 or the beginning of 1931 made a slight adjustment on the copyright notices printed in them, in order to claim publication in the more prestigious year of the Centenary. The anniversary had a similarly galvanizing effect on reeditions, and on publications of works which had languished in manuscript for years before. Ferdinand Duchêne owed far more reprints to the Centenary publishing boom than to his literary prize; Charles Courtin's prize-winning *La Brousse qui mangea l'homme* [The Brush that Ate the Man] sat in manuscript for two years after winning the Grand Prix Littéraire de l'Algérie, until the Éditions de France published it late in 1929. Clearly Paris and Algiers publishers needed no government-promoted program to encourage them to capitalize on the occasion by bringing out a much larger number of works on Algeria than usual. The concentration of literary production in 1930 gives us an opportunity to observe what visions of Algeria publishers thought would sell to a broad audience, and also what perspectives on the colony writers thought worthy of promotion on both sides of the Mediterranean.

Some publishers at least attempted to market colonial history, much as the Algerian authorities tried to do so with the commemorations. In the year of the Centenary, the mainland-French historical novelist Henriette Celarié, as well as the *Académicien* Louis Bertrand, wrote historical novels set in Algiers in or around 1830. A rather kind reviewer in the *Dépêche Algérienne* said of Celarié's *Esclave en Alger* [Slave in Algiers] (1929) that "la prise d'Alger se compose sous la plume de Mme Henriette Celarié comme une marche militaire bien rythmée. L'auteur a simplifié, déblayé, romancé les scènes et les dialogues; il ne manque pas un bouton de guêtre à ses uniformes . . . ce petit livre peut se lire en deux heures et nos visiteurs du Centenaire le glisseront facilement dans leur valise" [by the pen of Mme. Henriette Celarié, the conquest of Algiers takes the form of a well rhythmed military march. The author has simplified, clarified, and romanticized scenes and dialogs; her uniforms are not missing so much as a button on a gaiter. . . . This little book can be read in two hours, and our Centenary visitors will slip it easily into their suitcases].[38] In the elaboration of the "culte de souvenir" around 1830, the book played a significant part in providing both an encapsulated history and a novelistic counterpoint to the official historical recreations. The Library of Congress cataloguers assigned Celarié's book a call number in the DT series, classing it among works of Algerian history, while the Bibliothèque Nationale relegated it to Y2, novels. The plot lent itself quite well to both readings. In 1825, the young narrator, Désiré, borrows money from Nathan, an evil Jew of Toulon, thus incurring the wrath of his hot-tempered father, who sends him to sea to work off his debt and repent his folly. This he has ample time to do, as Algiers corsairs take his ship and sell its crew on the slave market in the city's Badistan, a small square whose location the French would later enjoy pointing out in the Marine quarter. The rest of the book details his captivity, which the reader knows can only last five years, when the French invasion foremost in the audience's mind would infallibly deliver him. This takes a great deal away from the book's potential drama, even with two failed escapes by Désiré, who obviously cannot know of his impending rescue at the hands of History.

Five years does give Celarié time to assert repeatedly the resentment the city felt against its Turkish rulers, and to include several of the usual descriptions of the Casbah before French intervention: "Je ne me lassais pas de la regarder; j'en avais tant entendu parler! Je m'en étais fait une idée dans ma tête et voilà qu'elle était tout différente de ce que j'avais imaginé" [I did not tire of looking at it; I had heard so much about it! I had gotten an idea in my head, and here it was quite different from what I had imagined].[39] What purpose does the narrator serve by echoing, for a 1930 audience, the sentiment so commonly expressed over the preceding century, that Algiers, while completely fascinating, did not conform to preconceived images? Désiré's lines function most importantly as a warning to metropolitan readers, the ones the *Dépêche* reviewer imagined slipping *Esclave en Alger* in their suitcases before embarking for Algeria. Received wisdom represented such visitors as themselves slaves to preconceptions about all things Algerian, and one of the major salutary effects hoped for from masses of visitors during the Centenary was the chance to correct such errors among the metropolitan population. Celarié begins to do this by warning her readers that even precolonial visitors had to revise their ideas of the city's physical appearance on arrival, thus changing their conception of the country, its people, and its history.

A tragic romance figures Désiré's relation with the city. Before the French fleet's arrival, he falls in love with a Circassian slave whom he has heard singing French songs on the other side of the garden wall. During the chaos of the French takeover of the city, the girl's master, a Turk, dies, and his henchman kills her, in accordance with the Turk's wishes. The invasion for Désiré thus means freedom and return home, but also loss. The narration makes it rather flat-footedly obvious that colonialism kills the exotic object of desire, just as it had for Fromentin or Gautier. However, an alternative reading may prove more appropriate to the context of 1930. Désiré, by his very name, embodies the object of desire himself. The city, figured in contrasting personifications of Désiré's kind and equitable master and the cruel and unfair Dey, has a rocky love relationship with him. Furthermore, Celarié's Arabs are distinctly effeminate; from a city desiring its French prisoner to a city inviting invasion by his countrymen is but a step. A further historical detail links Désiré to the invaders: like Désiré, the French occupiers supposedly "desired" by the city were sent there at the issue of a murky story of a debt owed to Jewish creditors. The book imagines the Jews as cruel and undeserving patriarchs, not unlike the Dey, whose insult to the French provided the immediate justification for the invasion. The arbitrary spite of these bad fathers must first be appeased; ultimately, however, wrongs are redressed and turn out to lead to happy conclusions: Désiré returns home and the French keep Algiers. By the end of the novel, the bad fathers are happily forgotten, replaced with good paternal authority. The feminized city, formerly restive under the Dey, has what it supposedly desired, the firm guidance and patronage of French rule.

In Celarié's somewhat thin fiction, readers of 1930 knew the outcome as soon as they saw the date of the novel's opening; likewise, we know the story of Bertrand's *Roman de la Conquête* [Novel of the Conquest] before beginning. The context of the Centenary makes some interpretations foregone conclusions: what other *conquête* could Bertrand possibly write about, in 1930? The act of historical commemoration thus places limits on our reading. This restriction seems entirely deliberate on the author's part; on the title page, he even connects with a long dash the word *conquête* with the date "1830," further overdetermining the title's historical reference. Having thus insisted so heavily, Bertrand feels no need to justify this part of his title, and concentrates instead in his preface on explaining its first word, *Roman*. Why *roman*, when *histoire* might seem more appropriate, especially considering the number of histories coming out in the two government-sponsored series? Bertrand attempts to answer:

> Le livre que voici est, au sens propre du mot, un roman, une oeuvre d'imagination. Mais c'est un roman d'histoire, c'est-à-dire une aventure romanesque et de pure invention insérée dans un cadre strictement historique. A côté des personnages purement imaginaires comme Messaoud, Khadidja, ou la fiancée d'Amédée de Bourmont, j'en ai placé d'autres, comme le maréchal de Bourmont, qui sont absolument conformes à l'histoire. Pour tout l'essentiel de l'expédition de 1830, les choses se sont passées comme je les raconte. En même temps que le roman, c'est bien l'histoire de la conquête que j'ai essayé de raconter.

> [The present book is a novel in the true sense of the word, a work of imagination. However, it is a novel of history, that is, a novelistic adventure of pure invention inserted in a strictly historical frame. Next to purely imaginary characters like Messaoud, Khadidja, or Amédée de Bourmont's fiancée, I have placed others, like the Maréchal de Bourmont, who are absolutely historically accurate. As for the essentials of the expedition of 1830, events occurred as I relate them. At the same time as the novel, I have in fact tried to recount the history of the conquest.][40]

In other words, there exists both an *histoire* and a *roman* of the conquest, and the former can happily find its place in the latter. Bertrand sees no difficulty in attributing words to Bourmont for which no historical source can exist, for instance, when the supposedly "historical" Maréchal (actually, his "romanesque" avatar) is speaking to a character of the novel with no counterpart in history. This occurs frequently in the novel, in Bourmont's conversations with Messaoud, or in Amédée's letters to his fiancée, but also in speech "reported" between historical characters. So much for "absolument conformes à l'histoire" (though this, too, was probably a foregone conclusion). Most novelists wishing to include "genuine" historical personages grapple with this problem, and it may seem small-minded to mount literalist challenges to Bertrand's insistence that "things happened the way I tell them." What happens if instead of thinking about *histoire* in the *roman*, we consider the *roman* in *histoire*? Just as the colony's history has an important (albeit occasionally distorted) place in Bertrand's novelistic discourse, the novel comes to take a place in the popular historical discourse surrounding the events of 1830.

We might begin by asking where and when it is appropriate, or even possible, to insert fictional events among historical ones. The Centenary claimed to celebrate the entire span of the century of French occupation and its achievements. From the point of view of a French military historian, the lengthy campaigns to pacify Algeria would rank high among these successes. Bertrand keeps his focus much more narrow, however, even though his novel runs over three hundred pages. To justify his choice he says

> qu'on ne se méprenne pas sur le sens que j'attribue à ce mot de "conquête." Je m'en suis tenu ici, à la Prise d'Alger, comme à l'acte capital qui a déterminé toute la suite de la conquête. Celle-ci a demandé près d'une vingtaine d'années . . . pendant près d'un quart de siècle, ce fut, en Algérie, une succession d'aventures et d'exploits héroiques, dont le souvenir est presque perdu, aujourd'hui.
>
> S'il y a dans la Prise d'Alger, dans l'Expédition de 1830, quelque chose de merveilleux qui confine au romanesque, la suite de la conquête—non exempte, d'ailleurs, d'une certaine poésie—est d'un réalisme plus âpre. Le roman ne convient plus pour raconter cette tragique et magnifique histoire qui touche à l'épopée. L'imagination ne peut rien y ajouter.
>
> Si, quelque jour, j'essaie, à mon tour, de la raconter, ce sera en historien et non plus en romancier.
>
> [let no one mistake the meaning I give to the word "conquest." I have restricted myself to the taking of Algiers, as the chief act which determined the entire series of events of the conquest, which took nearly twenty years. . . . For almost a quarter century, Algeria saw a succession of adventures and heroic exploits the memory of which is almost lost today.
>
> If there is something marvelous in the Expedition of 1830 and the taking of Algiers that approaches the novelistic, the rest of the conquest (which is not without a certain poetry) is of a more bitter realism. The novel is no longer suitable for recounting this tragic and magnificent history, which approaches epic. The imagination can add nothing to it.
>
> If one day I take my turn at narrating it, it will be as a historian, and no longer as a novelist.][41]

Bertrand prefers a two-week local campaign to the twenty-year, countrywide drama that other novelists would have seized upon.[42] His hesitation at first seems to stem from a sense of decorum: some events, he states, are simply too tragic or sublime to make suitable material for historical novels. Other qualifications apply as well. Despite the excitement and interest of the events post-1830, they have nearly slipped from public memory, according to Bertrand, who depicts this as almost more hindrance than help. A public that has forgotten the events on which a writer bases a historical novel will be a hard sell; the novel will look more like minor military history, or a simple adventure story with a colonial background of a sort already abundant on the market. Some subjects in Algerian history seem to admit more readily than others of novelistic treatment and the production of saleable fiction.

More importantly than either decorum or sales, however, is Bertrand's distinction between the romantic imagination and the realist, oddly phrased for someone who a moment ago assured readers that everything "really" happened as he told it. Heroism and adventure do not suffice; the event must have "something marvelous . . . that approaches the novelistic." There must be something of the *roman* already inherent in the *histoire*. Above all, the *histoire* must stimulate the imagination, and allow it to insert its creations in the chain of verifiable events. Bertrand's confession that his imagination could add nothing to the epic of the wars of conquest has a certain wrenching quality. He has in the intervening passage listed the generals who would have figured as its characters (Bugeaud, Larmoricière, Pélissier, Randon, Saint-Arnaud); each name calls up horrific episodes which indeed render the twenty years following the invasion of Algiers "a more bitter realism." It is difficult to imagine anything to add to Pélissier's and Saint-Arnaud's *enfumades*, episodes in which they ordered, on two separate occasions, the building of fires in front of caves in which whole clans had taken refuge, killing hundreds of noncombatants by asphyxiation. In 1992 Assia Djébar would succeed in using episodes like these in a nonlinear novelistic treatment of Algerian history, but in 1930, Bertrand, with neither Djebar's formal innovation nor her desire to expose violence, does not see fit to do so. For the purposes of the Centenary, some realities are simply too bitter. Such events could not easily fit into the fictionalized history of Bertrand's day.

Bertrand's 1929–1930 publications (including both the novel and descriptive trilogies) therefore eschew both realism and bitterness. The sentimental plot of *Le Roman de la conquête* contains two tragic love stories in the romantic tradition: that of Amédée de Bourmont and his fiancée, and that of Khadidja, one of the Dey Hussein's concubines, and a young official named Messaoud. The background for the first story had already been fixed in the colony's popular memory. According to the popular histories, Amédée de Bourmont refused to use his father's position as general commanding the expeditionary force to get himself a safe posting; on principle, he fought where his rank placed him and suffered a fatal wound in one of the first battles. His father received the news of his death the day he negotiated Algiers's capitulation, according to the legend, and returned to France with Amédée's heart in a silver casket. In Bertrand's version, Amédée's fictional fiancée does not hear the news until after the revolution which destroyed her almost-father-in-law politically, and ended her position as lady-in-waiting at court. Bertrand does nothing new with this story by adding the fiancée. The theme of young, high-minded self-sacrifice for a greater colonial France emerges equally well from half a dozen earlier versions in history books, even though Bourmont could not have thought he was fighting for a colonial ideal, since France had no such projects for Algiers in 1830. Most historians in 1930 and today agree that the French government had no idea what to do with the newly conquered *Régence d'Alger*. A considerable debate in the Chambre des débutés over the next five years eventually concluded by keeping the new possession. However, those in favor of abandoning Algeria continued to speak up loudly throughout the July Monarchy. Thus the tragic romance serves solely as poignant foil to the book's more gripping love story, that of Khadidja and Messaoud.

Khadidja constitutes Bertrand's most interesting addition to an otherwise unenlivened tale of battles whose lopsided odds produced the obvious outcome of the war. Bertrand occasionally lets show a secret affinity for romanticism, despite his contempt for the exoticism to which it usually led in the colony. Here he describes his novel's love interest: "En pantalon bouffant, en veste lamé d'or, dans les gazes pailletées de ses écharpes et des voiles trainant à ses pieds, elle était la houri qui hantait alors les imaginations des jeunes lecteurs des *Orientales*." [In puffed trousers and a gold lamé vest, with the sequined gauze of her scarves and veils trailing at her feet, she was the houri who at the time haunted the imaginations of the young readers of the *Orientales*.][43] Khadidja is in fact half French and relatively cultured; she has more than one way of seducing the reader, left cold by Amédée's somewhat cloistered fiancée. Given her casting in the doomed role of exotic African temptress, the disaster that befalls her surprises no one. Despite the clever plotter Messaoud's attempt to bargain with him, General de Bourmont decides that the terms of the Dey Hussein's surrender allow the former ruler to take her with him into exile, with the rest of his women. Arrested in her hiding place by French soldiers enforcing the treaty obligations, she commits suicide. Killing her off has the effect of severing the connection between precolonial Algiers and Orientalist fantasy: General de Bourmont has much more serious cares, and even the bereaved Messaoud consoles himself with French backing to put him in power as a regional governor. Consolidation of France's still-shaky conquest takes precedence over *Orientales*-style romantic idylls. More importantly, though, Khadidja's disappearance, as an effect of the *Roman de la conquête*, permits her replacement with the new sort of concubines more suitable to Bertrand's vision of the colony's history: the "ritual" prostitutes of which he dreamed in *Nuits d'Alger*. What I would here call the move from *Les Orientales* to *Salammbô* shows what one can accomplish by interpolating a *roman* into *histoire*. Cutting off thirty years of French literary history by a jump forward (incidentally, to the time corresponding to Bertrand's "heroic" period of

Algerian colonization) allows a jump back several millennia in terms of the historical period valorized. Bertrand thus replaces the unseemly complications of Khadidja's mixed Mediterranean identity with something he understands much better, the far simpler bases of Latin Africa, resurrected for the Centenary.

THE COMMEMORATED CITY AND ITS ARTIFACTS

None of the other novels appearing in 1929–1931 deal as explicitly as these with 1830; they generally have much more diffuse relationships with the rhetoric of commemoration so prevalent in the press and official discourse. Many look like potboilers written for the occasion by metropolitan writers with little connection to Algeria, and few have the ideological sweep (or even the narrative power) of early Randau novels. Despite the claims of the Algerianists, writers who concentrated on the *colons* produced novels no more aesthetically effective than those still fascinated by the Muslims. No artistic criteria valorize Léon Adoue's *Un Poète chez les colons* or Henriette Waltz's *Ceux de ma rue* over a pulpy *roman indigène* like Jean Not's *Zinah! Aux portes du harem*. All three of these 1930 novels were their authors' first (and in some cases, last) works with no more centenary-related content than the sporting events sponsored by the government. Their appearance in a relatively tight publishing market testifies to the appeal of any Algerian content at all in novels for mass consumption appearing that year. The tripling in volume of Algerian-themed books published in 1930 may have come at the cost of quality, as noted by the cautious critic Pierre Martino. One such potboiler, whose interest will become apparent in the context of promoting and manufacturing nostalgia in the Algiers of the Centenary, nevertheless merits study.

From an aesthetic point of view, Antoine Chollier's *Drusilla, dame d'Alger* [Drusilla, Lady of Algiers] (1930) may at first seem to have little more to recommend it than Not's *Zinah!*, the fantastic tale of the daughter of a Muslim woman and a French general, who fights plotters and sorcerers to marry the head of her clan, or Waltz's *Ceux de ma rue*, the story of an exploited maid and abused single mother who drinks, loses her child, and kills herself in despair. Historically, however, quite a lot more is at stake in Chollier's novel than in those of many of his contemporaries. As the author of several descriptive works on Algeria, he had already demonstrated a much more active engagement with the problems of representing Algerian history than most other Parisian *littérateurs*. Stephan Audric, Chollier's protagonist, travels to Algiers as a reporter assigned to write a feature story on the Centenary celebrations for the Parisian daily *Le Matin*. On the boat, he meets a cast of suspicious international characters worthy of Agatha Christie: Lord Creakwell, an English peer, and Lady Creakwell, his aristocratic French child-wife; Gravilos, a Greek banker and collector of antiquities; and Luigi Spaldini, an amateur painter, going to Algiers to gather orientalist material. In Algiers, Stephan meets and falls in love with Drusilla Ben Zafir, the young widow of a rich Arab. After an encounter at her villa, complete with harem couches, caged asps, sinister slaves, and impressive views over Algiers, she confirms the rumor Stephan has heard: she descends directly from Juba II, the Amazigh king of Numidia, and Cleopatra Selena, herself daughter of the more famous Cleopatra and Mark Antony. Drusilla gives him a rendezvous at the Tombeau de la Chrétienne, an ancient tumulus outside the city, where she shows him into a secret bed chamber full of relics, drugs him with pearls dissolved in wine, and walls him in, abandoning him to die. The tomb mysteriously reopens, however, and Stephan escapes back to Algiers, where he discovers that Drusilla, on that very same night, was bitten by one of her pet asps, and has died; Lord Creakwell, her old lover, has committed suicide; and Gravilos has been arrested for plundering artifacts from the tumulus (where his raid inadvertently rescued Stephan) by Spaldini, an undercover agent of the Sureté. Stephan finds himself on the boat back to France; he has failed to reenter the tumulus by himself, but succeeded in getting a date with the book's new young widow, the much less dangerous Lady Creakwell, back in Paris.

Bertrand, we recall, began with the stereotypically exotic Arab concubine, only to eliminate and replace her with the "ritual" prostitute-priestess of Latin Africa. Chollier for his part begins with the *Afrique latine* paradigm, with Lady Creakwell declaring on the boat that "il me semble que cette Méditerranée fait partie intégrante de ma patrie, comme je suppose que cette terre d'Algérie doit être le prolongement en quelque sorte de notre Côte d'Azur!" [it seems to me that the Mediterranean is an integral part of my homeland, just as, I suppose, the soil of Algeria must in some way be the extension of our Riviera!][44] Stephan sees past the silliness of this pronouncement of a French socialite saying essentially that Algeria could be an annex of France's holiday destination for people like her, and approves the ideological and historical view underlying it: "Vous avez raison, répondit Stephan, cette mer, comme tout le nord de l'Afrique, est essentiellement latine. Notre civilisation a gravité autour d'elle et nous y retrouvons les traces de notre race à chaque instant." [You are right, responded Stephen. This sea, like all of North Africa, is essentially Latin. Our civilization has gravitated around it and at every moment we find in it the traces of our race.][45] When Stephan meets Drusilla, he immediately understands that her direct family connection to Cleopatra, together with her Europeanized life, make her the living representative of Latin Africa: "Avec sa tunique blanche, ses pieds chaussées de babouches, ses bracelets tintinabulants sur ses poignets et ses chevilles nues, elle paraissait, dans le cadre de ce palais arabe, l'incarnation vivante de ce passé qu'évoquaient tous ces souvenirs" [With her white tunic, her feet shod in slippers, and bracelets clinking on her bare ankles and wrists, she appeared in the setting of the Arab palace as the living incarnation of the past that all these souvenirs evoked].[46] In fact, by going right back to Ptolemaic Egypt, Chollier cuts out one of Bertrand's steps, getting his Greek and Roman heritage without the detours and somewhat free associations necessitated by passing through Carthage. Drusilla has just shown Stephan the classical treasures of her private museum, displayed, as she herself is, in her Arab mansion. For Stephan, this constitutes a privileged form of sightseeing to complement the Musée des Antiquités et de l'Art Musulman which he has just visited. Furthermore, his liaison with Drusilla will provide a culminating moment of historical sex tourism. Where nineteenth-century travelers wishing to "penetrate the Arab soul" sought out "Moorish" prostitutes in the Casbah to consummate their connection with Oriental Algeria, Stephan will try to penetrate the secrets of Latin Africa by sleeping with its sexy and liberated modern representative.

He finds, however, that Drusilla has no secrets worth knowing. Despite all the trappings surrounding her, so appealing to the tourist of Latin Africa, the direct female-line descendant of Cleopatra is high priestess of the wrong *culte du souvenir*. Stephan can marvel at the Tombeau de la Chrétienne, and at Drusilla's knowledge of its secret treasure chamber, passed from mother to daughter for several millennia, but the secret turns first to horror, and then to farce. The enormous span of time is itself part of the problem: Drusilla admits that the treasure has disappeared, prosaically enough to meet the financial needs of several hundred generations of the family's women. That they would have done better to invest in something else does not discourage Stephan from investing a great deal in the now frankly dilapidated historical stock of Latin Africa. The tomb, which represents it and the presence of Christian rulers in North Africa, also has the distinction of having inspired Pierre Benoît (as the text notes) to write his wildly successful 1919 novel of Atlantis in the Sahara, *L'Atlantide*. Nonetheless, all that actually remains in the treasure chamber does not inspire Stephan to write anything like the kind of bestseller which would win him a place in the Académie Française, as *L'Atlantide* had done for Benoit. Drusilla, then, is left with a Roman bed and stool, and some faded crimson draperies: Empire kitsch. Furthermore, the inner sanctum of this "Latin" monument will become Stephan's prison, and very nearly his tomb; Drusilla, like Benoît's Antinéa, has the sinister habit of killing off her European lovers one by one.[47]

Drusilla's story may be understood on several levels. First, it figures the colony and the whole of North Africa as a rapacious and threatening femme fatale, a sexually aggressive counterthreat to the colonial conquerors. The modern colony can hardly afford to let her continue as such, and the plot that creates her handily does away with her, bitten by the nightmarish creature with which she seemed to have an uncanny affinity. Yet death by snakebite also links Drusilla to her illustrious ancestor Cleopatra, suggesting a second reading. More than just another feminized incarnation of African horrors to be repressed, Drusilla represents a vision of the colony's (and continent's) history, and a well-known one at that. Her history, the Latin Africa represented by the objects the narrator has called "souvenirs," has fangs to cut down the unwary reporter straying from the official path of receptions, parades, and interviews. Behind the tomb chamber where Stephan thought to consummate his historical discovery in bed with Drusilla, he finds a deep well, an oubliette in which, he surmises, his lover must have thrown her past victims. The epicenter of Latin Africa's piously guarded memory contains its opposite, the forgetting enforced by the oubliette. The plot makes clear to what this forgetting applies: in this case, it nearly swallowed up one of Algeria's modern visitors. Nothing could better express the capacity of the "Latin" vision of North African history to devour all other views. Drusilla, metaphorically swallowing up her lovers, also buries more modern perspectives of colonial history in her oubliette; it is this that the colonial plot (and even more the colony itself, celebrating its history at that very moment) cannot tolerate. Stephan feels that his story has no place in the contemporary colony; recovering from his shock with friends in a bar in downtown Algiers, he asks himself "C'était au milieu d'une semblable atmosphère qu'il allait oser raconter son aventure? Qui donc pourrait ajouter foi à une histoire digne des 'Mille et Une Nuits'?" [Was it in the midst of such an atmosphere that he would dare recount his adventure? Whoever could believe a story worthy of the *1001 Nights*?][48] As a final irony, we learn on hearing of the smuggler Gravilos's arrest for trafficking in antiquities, the *souvenirs* of Latin Africa, that the *sanctum sanctorum* of that ancient Africa yielded nothing of value: all the artifacts the Greek stole from Drusilla's seduction den were fakes.

In ridding Algiers of Drusilla, it might seem that Chollier creates a void, but in reality he has already advanced a substitute, just as Bertrand already had his ritual prostitutes waiting in the wings to evoke Latin Africa the moment Khadidja's demise cleared space for them. Drusilla's disappearance does not leave Chollier struggling to advance a new historical vision of the city to replace the one she represented: the Centenary has already provided him with one. Unfortunately for the sake of this argument, it does not come packaged as another vivid and emblematic character, but appears in conversations between Stephan and his sculptor friend Bonjan, a resident of modern Algiers. Chollier wholeheartedly adopts the official discourses regarding the colony's modernity, both here and in his travel narrative, *Alger et sa région* [Algiers and its Region], published the year before. In this vision, the city's accessibility by car, the way it lends itself to driving or being driven in, accentuates a discourse the Centenary organizers would have approved. Algeria really does have everything it needs to enter the modern world, went the argument; it has left the darker, precolonial portion of its history well behind. It is part of France; in fact, it *is* France, and not merely in the administrative sense of three French *départements*.

Cars and their European drivers dominate Chollier's novel. Characters constantly dash about the city in distinctive automobiles: Lord Creakwell in his Daimler, specially brought over on the boat, Gravilos in his two-seater, Stephan and Bonjan in a recent (and *très pratique*) Citroën. On the boat, Lord Creakwell asserts that a car is essential for seeing the country; even run-of-the-mill tourists rush through the city on their way up to luxurious Mustapha in cars owned by the Hotel Algeria.[49] It seems a car is also necessary to see the city itself; linear recitals of streets replace the panoramic city views that orient most Algiers novels. To see the city properly from a car, we must go to *Alger et sa région*, from which Chollier banishes the usual description of arrival in Algiers by sea, in favor of a passage describing his ride from pier to hotel:

> Par une glace baissée je peux regarder le mouvement de la rue. Large rue, plantée d'arbres dont les feuillages sombres, lavés de pluie, brillent à la lumière des magasins et des premiers réverbères qui commencent de s'allumer; rue animée, comme le boulevard à cinq heures du soir, par le double courant montant et descendant de piétons sur le trottoir et la chaîne ininterrompue des autos sur la chaussée. On pourrait se croire facilement dans quelque coin de Paris ou mieux, de Marseille, s'il n'y avait, au milieu de tous les costumes européens, ces arabes qui marchent pour la plupart pieds nus dans la boue, la tête abritée de l'étrange petit capuchon de leur burnous de laine et aussi ces femmes, toutes blanches, qui passent voilées et mystérieuses. Et quelle quantité stupéfiante d'automobiles!
>
> A mesure que nous avançons, mon ami me cite les rues que nous prenons, Square Bresson, rue Dumont-d'Urville, rue d'Isly, rue Michelet!
>
> Mais la pluie recommence en trombe qui nous oblige à remonter la glace de la voiture et jette son voile crépitant sur ce premier aperçu de la cité africaine.

> [Through the lowered window I can see the movement on the street. A broad street, planted with trees whose dark leaves washed with rain shine in the light of stores and of the first street lamps beginning to light; a street animated, like the boulevards at five in the evening, by the double stream of pedestrians going up and down on the sidewalk, and the uninterrupted

string of cars in the road. One could easily believe oneself to be in some corner of Paris or, better, Marseille, if among all the European suits there were
not the Arabs walking mostly barefoot in the mud, heads covered with the
strange little hood of their wool burnous, and the women passing, all white,
veiled, and mysterious. And what a stupefying quantity of automobiles!

As we go along, my friend names the streets we take: Square Bresson,
Rue Dumont-d'Urville, Rue d'Isly, Rue Michelet!

But the rain begins again in a downpour which obliges us to raise the
car window, and which throws its spattering veil over the first perception of
the African city.][50]

The city promenade by car through the financial and administrative
heart of Algiers, substantially the same as the walk I described in chapter 2, passes here in the blink of a reader's eye, with the street names
succeeding one another before the narrator can mention any of the
buildings that made them distinctive. As names alone, and at this speed,
they bear out Chollier's pronouncement that a visitor to Algiers could
mistake the city for Paris or Marseille; in fact, such street names could
be anywhere in the French-dominated world. Only the presence of the
Arabs makes the city unique; as barefoot pedestrians, they contrast radically with the new order of speed embodied by the narrator. The sheer
numbers of cars overwhelm them, reinforcing their minority status. Furthermore, speed and the framing effect of the car window seems to affect the "mystery" veiled women traditionally present to first-time European visitors. Though they retain some degree of it, in the last
paragraph we have the clear impression that the viewer who raised the
water-spotted window will be able to lower it again to reveal the city
and its inhabitants completely. This he does a few pages later, noting
that "ces femmes voilées . . . n'ont plus rien des fabuleuses odalisques
des contes des Mille et une Nuits; ce sont tout simplement de braves petites mauresques, femmes de ménage ou servantes" [these veiled
women . . . are no longer anything like the fabled odalisques of the stories in the *1001 Nights*; they are simply worthy little Moorish women,
maids or servants].[51] Passing rapidly in a car somehow permits Chollier
to do away with mysterious speculations, and facilitates quick deflation
with easy and practical-sounding remarks like these. An element of the
city's ethnic makeup and history, part of what makes it unique, gets reduced to simple domestic help going to work to satisfy the prosaic
needs of the European population, otherwise occupied behind the
wheel. Chollier's discourse fits easily into the official view of partner-
ship (practical and rigidly hierarchized) between Muslims and Europeans for the smooth development of a rich colony. This view of the
city's functional relations neatly pigeonholed the Arab population, and
extended to the use-value of their neighborhood as well.

Algiers retains one neighborhood inaccessible by car, and yet emblematic of the city as a whole: the Casbah, still and ever a required visit for all travel writers, and the city's only predominantly Arab quarter at the time.[52] The official discourse of the Centenary reduces the Casbah to its use value for attracting tourists, the last in its series of conquerors. Chollier makes no secret of his affiliation with conquerors, whether armed with rifles or cameras. Visiting the Casbah, "J'ai emporté avec moi l'âme d'un des plus simples soldats du Général de Bourmont qui, le 19 juin 1830, pénétra dans la grande cité conquise et c'est avec cette âme ignorante et non prévenue que je veux prendre contact avec la ville" [I took with me the soul of one of the simplest soldiers of General de Bourmont who, on 19 June 1830, penetrated the great conquered city, and it is with this ignorant and unforewarned spirit that I wish to make contact with the city].[53] In regaining his ignorance by "forgetting" everything he has ever read about the Casbah, he may or may not approach the state of mind of the soldiers of 1830, but he does not forget one essential piece of information, the conquest itself and its fetishized date. Readers even suspect he knows as well as they the impossibility of innocence. He is far too aware of how the Casbah fits into the itinerary of the tourist on a schedule, and into the symbolic schema of Centenary Algiers:

> Le voyageur pressé classera [la Casbah] dans ses notes de voyage, s'il en prend, à côté d'une visite au quartier réservé de Marseille ou de Toulon.
>
> Ce qui m'attire ici et me pousse à gravir péniblement cette rue de la Casbah, artère principale de la sombre ruche, c'est moins le cadre lui-même que toutes les pensées qu'il suscite à mon esprit. C'est malgré tout entre ces murs lépreux que demeurent les dernières vestiges de l'Orient à Alger. Je ne dis pas qu'une ingénieuse publicité n'ait pas exploité cela pour satisfaire au goût de curiosité de quelques étrangers en mal d'orientalisme. Il n'empêche que la plupart de ces ruelles n'ont pas changé d'aspect depuis la conquête. . . . Il y a bien dans ce quartier une population qui vit d'une existence personnelle. . . . Certes le voyageur passe sans encombre à travers les rues, il regarde avec étonnement, mais c'est bien lui l'étranger et on ne fait que le supporter avec indifférence.

[The hurried traveler will file the Casbah in his travel notes, if he takes any, next to a visit to the red-light district of Marseille or Toulon.

What attracts me here and pushes me to climb laboriously this Casbah street, the main artery of the dark beehive, is less the setting than all the thoughts it brings to mind. It is, after all, inside these peeling walls that remain the last vestiges of the Orient in Algiers. I do not deny that ingenious publicity has exploited this in order to satisfy the taste for curiosity of a few foreigners suffering from orientalism. Nonetheless, most of the streets have not changed their appearance since the conquest. . . . There really is a population in this neighborhood which lives a personal and private existence. . . . Certainly the traveler may pass without hindrance through the streets; he looks with astonishment, but it is he who is the stranger here, and they only tolerate him with indifference.][54]

For a hurried traveler, the species represented if not by Chollier himself, then certainly by his whirlwind tourist Stephan, the most distinctive part of Algiers might fit into the space of a few lines in a notebook devoted to prostitution in France's southern ports; after such a statement the narrator cannot do much to rescue the Casbah except by making it once again a set piece for visitors. There does remain a small quantity of local color, the very last vestiges of the Orient, well exploited by the tourist propaganda of a city keen to put on a show. Yet it remained a show without historical significance, despite Chollier's earlier comparison of himself to Bourmont's invading soldiers. The residents of the Casbah have a "personal" existence, private and ahistorical, interesting only insofar as the place they inhabit has resisted historical change. The photos accompanying the text show Casbah buildings in alarming states of dilapidation, yet Chollier does not comment much on this: decay is the natural and unremarkable state of historical backwaters, and by effacing history from the neighborhood, the author leaves readers to imagine that it had looked like that even at the best of times. A number of observers and urbanists (including Bertrand, as we saw in chapter 1) recommended razing the Casbah and replacing it with a sort of Muslim theme-park parody of itself. Chollier suggests one reason, apart from lack of finances and political will why the city did not do this: the change from living neighborhood to tourist set piece had already occurred for him. (After all, he did not have to live there.) Chollier's Casbah, like that of many other writers, was somehow always the place where visitors could see what was ahistorical about the colony. The already ahistorical requires no intervention to make it more so.

COMMEMORATION AND SUBVERSION: THE INADVERTENT RESISTANCE OF CHARLES COURTIN

Not all the novels published around the Centenary supported points of view so close to that of the government. At least a few seriously complicated the dominant discourses, and occasionally opposed them covertly; Khodja Chukri's refusal of the endlessly extended and retracted promise of assimilation provides a good example of this. As an exemplar of subtle opposition, Chukri's text gives clues for reading complicated webs of political exigencies and ideological commitments, with strands pulling in contrary directions in many of colonial Algeria's more interesting literary productions. Among the novels of the Centenary, Charles Courtin's *La*

Brousse qui mangea l'homme (1929) is one of the very few as evocative of these complexities as Chukri's. Charles Courtin was born in Blida in 1884, and pursued a very successful career as an administrator in the system of *communes mixtes*, the local adminstrations in municipalities where large non-European populations made the French wary of installing ordinary town councils with full powers. In 1934 he was transferred to Algiers, where he eventually worked in the office of the Gouverneur Général, holding positions of responsibility for policy regarding the Muslims. It may seem at first paradoxical to consider Courtin as an opposition novelist at all: he was a bureaucrat in the upper echelons of the administration of the *indigènes*, and his work was in many ways one of the most "officially approved" of colonial Algeria. He took care to submit his manuscripts to the *Direction des Affaires indigènes* before sending them to a publisher; he won the Grand Prix Littéraire de l'Algérie, a prize generally given to works in harmony with the colonial government's promotional objectives.[55] The critic Jean-Louis Planche says that Courtin was "un des écrivains les mieux en consonance avec le discours intérieur de la haute administration coloniale, avec cette réflexion interne dont le discours public se nourrit mais qu'il voile, et que la fiction romanesque permet, consciemment ou non, d'avancer au grand jour" [one of the writers most in concordance with the internal discourse of the upper levels of colonial administration, with the internal thinking that public discourse feeds on but veils, and that fiction permits, consciously or unconsciously, to appear in broad daylight].[56] Courtin certainly was in tune with government discourse, but his first novel proves very difficult to insert into any single ideological perspective. Placing it in a framework of disguised commitments and contradictory agendas demonstrates how difficult it was to write wholeheartedly and unambiguously in favor of the official discourse of Centenary optimism, despite the capacity of that discourse to diffuse most attacks from its opposition.

La Brousse qui mangea l'homme tells the story of a young *colon* arriving in Algeria immediately before World War I, probably too late to hope to accumulate the land necessary to build an agricultural fortune in grain or wine production. Leroux, Courtin's *colon*, buys a farm on the Hauts Plateaux near the village of Raspail from an enterprising farmer eager to sell a poor piece of property. Leroux served in Algeria with a regiment of *spahis*, and therefore thinks he knows everything he needs to know about life in the colony in order to move himself and his mother onto the new farm with every confidence of success. He rapidly runs afoul of the Muslims who resent his ownership of land once theirs; they accuse him of murdering a young girl of their clan. When a clear-sighted judge throws the trumped-up charges out of court, they gradually sabotage Leroux's farm. In the meantime, Leroux becomes lazy and does little to oppose them; sensing his weakness, they attack his house at night and murder him. The book ends with his mother, incapable of action, watching over his body lying where it fell, as flies buzz about the corpse.

Courtin hardly presents a rousing tale for the promotion of *l'Algérie française*, and any prospective immigrant farmer would hear a dangerously clear message to stay away. There were relatively few new immigrants to rural Algeria by the 1920s, when birth had long since overtaken immigration as the principal source of new Algerians, so this message might seem less dangerous to the colony's future then than forty years earlier, but the colony's promoters hardly felt that way.[57] Algerianist writers and critics of colonial literature frequently demanded that literature about the colony promote it: usefulness as a marketing tool had become an important guide to perceived literary quality. This book's plot seems to say quite the opposite of a promotional slogan: come to Algeria, get cheated buying a hopeless farm, slowly go to pieces, and get yourself murdered. Courtin underlines the inevitability of his plot's conclusion: "Un de plus. Une fois de plus, la vieille terre africaine a dévoré l'homme d'Europe. A travers les siècles, elle demeurait le Moloch monstrueux et sournois, jamais repu, aux mâchoires refermées sans cesse sur de nouvelles victimes." [One more. One more time the old African soil had devoured the man of Europe. Through the centuries, she remained the monstrous and cunning Moloch, never satisfied, her jaws constantly closing on new victims.][58] Promoters commonly called Algeria "the granary of Rome," nourishing Europe with grain, produce, and wine. "Algérie, pays de grande production agricole" [Algeria, country of great agricultural production] said the 1930 poster, with the *colon* standing looking over his fields, one arm over the shoulder of a handsomely dressed *indigène* (see figure 4.2).[59] For Chollier, however, Europe feeds Algeria, instead of the other way around; there is no cash fortune to make, but a blood tribute to pay.

Apart from mythical conceits such as the extended Moloch metaphor, Courtin has other very specific reproaches against both Africa in general and French Algeria in particular. From the beginning, the pro-colonial publicity mill cranks out a propaganda bound to deceive, promoting a reality certain to disappoint: the man who cons Leroux into buying his farm "ramassait des clichés usés par des milliers de lèvres, pareils, au toucher, à de vieux sous: l'avenir de la France était de l'autre côté de la Méditerranée, la race poussant là-bas de rejets vigoureux, de magnifiques cèpes. Il parla de fortunes fabuleuses, édifiées en un clin d'oeil" [picked up clichés worn out by thousands of lips, like old coins to the touch: the future of France lay on the other shore of the Mediterranean, and the race grew vigorous shoots and magnificent stock there. He spoke of fabulous fortunes, built in the twinkling of an eye].[60] Courtin's rhetoric tells his

**Figure 4.2.   Poster for the centenary
of French Algeria. Archives d'Outre-
Mer, Aix-en-Provínce.**

readers what to think of this sort of talk, the quasi-official discourse of Algeria's riches and opportunities. In his review of Courtin's work, the novelist Louis Lecoq said ironically that its tone was not exactly that of official speeches.[61] The text's heteroglossia allows those official discourses to enter, only to be rejected immediately; Leroux, who does not see their ridicule, plunges headfirst into disaster.

His confidence comes from platitudes and self-aggrandizing tales he had himself told to credulous audiences back in France after his tour of duty with the *spahis*; what he hears on arrival differs radically. He had half-remembered, half-imagined loyal Arabs of noble attitude, and he hears tales of a venomous race, the plague of Algeria.[62] The narrator forces the reader to listen as well to the awful stories of Leroux's neighbors, and then to watch as the Muslims themselves prove, as if wilfuly, the "truth" of every scurrilous stereotype imaginable. The experienced *colons* call them greedy, lying, lazy, cowardly, and murderous; the plot will show them, by turns, all of these and more. Courtin attributes the only more positive discourse to Leroux, whom ignorance and incapacity rob of any credibility. The novel thus makes it difficult for its readers to see in it any position other than the one for which it offers such a superabundance of evidence. Courtin undercuts all notions of colonialist progress or optimism by saying that the Muslims are far worse than any stereotype.

At this point I must introduce a very significant "but . . .," or risk losing the reader's patience with a novel with idiosyncrasies beyond its enumerations of colonialist prejudice. Courtin says all these things about the Muslims, *but* shows them justified in acting this way. They do so only in order to get their land back from Leroux, who has inherited a claim usurped from them by the nefarious Dubard, his predecessor. They view the arrival of the *colons* as "an ill" constantly "eating away" their heritage; in this novel, at least, Courtin never suggests they are wrong.[63] Here, the author begins to show a more complicated attitude in his language, making it hard to reduce his work to an ideological alibi. Without losing credibility and getting labelled a firebrand, revolutionary, or blind *indigénophile*, Courtin cannot come out openly to say he opposes cheating the *indigènes* of their land.[64] Yet by never saying they should not struggle, and, even more, by showing the moral bankruptcy of their *colon* opponent, he certainly pushes his audience to see the abuse inherent in colonial land transfers, the cornerstone of the government's colonization policy in Algeria. From there to opposing such transactions actively represents a major step that Courtin, in his government position, could scarcely have taken had he wanted. Nonetheless, his text continues to undermine colonialism with pessimism. Better than an open attack in the name of liberation or human rights, this tactic demonstrates the complexities in the colonial context of producing even documents very favorable to Empire.

He performs this undermining mostly by insisting on French Algeria's failure to change the character of North Africa. In his view, certain highly essentialized qualities of the Maghrib remain unaltered and will continue to resist change from outside. The Berber population has always succeeded in overwhelming its invaders, beginning with the Arabs. The Latinization of Africa seems irrelevant to him; he describes only the Mediterranean Sea itself as Latin, since for him the Roman invasions of Africa constituted only another failed attempt to impose a culture on the Berbers from outside. As characteristic traits of the Berbers, he finds those adumbrated above: duplicity, flexibility, and resistance, all capable of overcoming French honesty, legalism, and rigidity. In fact, the Berbers do more than resist, according to Courtin: they corrupt. They oblige their conquerors to adopt their methods to fight them, and even so,

> Submergés par les Berbères prolifiques, il leur [les colons] faudrait biaiser tous les jours, fourbir des armes perfides pour sauver leur domination chancelante, qui ne pourrait plus s'appuyer sur le sabre. Cette ruse qu'ils avaient affrontée témérairement, elle faisait tâche d'huile, déjà, gagnait les plus faibles, les gens de négoce, habitués à d'artificieux compromis avec la rigidité des lois.

Etait-ce pour cela, pour que la mentalité de la race se déformât, perdit sur un sol neuf le plus clair de sa grandeur, que la France avait conquis cette terre hostile? Le temps coulerait, finirait par amalgamer les métaux jetés au hasard, dans ce creuset battu par la mer latine. Insensiblement, insidieusement, la race serve, souple d'avoir subi d'innombrables dominations, imposerait son empreinte aux étrangers. Toujours, dans cette partie de l'Afrique, la ruse berbère serait la plus forte, inoculerait son virus aux cerveaux rebelles, que débilitait le climat. La revanche de cette race, courbée pendant des millénaires sous des jougs différents, sans cesse opprimée et sans cesse renaissante et qui traverse les âges, intacte, pareille à une flexible lame d'acier qu'on ne peut rompre.

[Drowning among the prolific Berbers, they would have to compromise every day, and sharpen treacherous weapons in order to save their shaky domination, which could no longer depend on the sword. The trickery which they had confronted fearlessly was already spreading like an oil spot, overcoming the weakest, the compromisers, used to tricky dealings with legal rigidity.

Was it for this, so that the mentality of the race could be deformed and lose the greater part of its grandeur on the new soil, that France had conquered this hostile ground? Time would pass, and would end up amalgamating the metals thrown at random into this crucible washed by the Latin sea. With the flexibility coming from having lived through innumerable dominations, the servile race would insidiously and imperceptibly place its imprint on the foreigners. In this part of Africa, Berber trickery would always come out on top, and would infect with its vices obstinate minds debilitated by the climate: the revenge of this race, bent for millennia under various yokes, constantly oppressed and constantly renewed, traversing the centuries intact, like a flexible steel blade that no one can break.][65]

The *colons* will never manage to overcome the indigenous population without exterminating them, an alternative Courtin does not imagine.[66] Rather, in an inexorable historical process in which the supposedly subservient race will come to dominate, they will slowly become *indigènes* themselves. Is this anticolonialism, and if so, what kind? Although we may not recognize it as such, the undercurrent of Courtin's text is in fact anticolonial. His discourse radically destabilizes colonial certainties, though in the end, most readers today will find his rhetoric pessimistic and racist.

The failure of the colony represents a failure of assimilation: Courtin reveals as pure hubris the assimilationist project, in which a relatively small number of French people hoped to bring an entire population with a radically different culture into compliance with French norms. French pretensions to rigidly and universally applying their law (both the *Code civil* and the law of assimilation) appear ridiculous. Surely the reverse will happen, as in most similar cases in history: the conquered population will not only assimilate its victors, but absorb them altogether. The *tâche d'huile* metaphor figured highly in colonialist discourse, describing the slow and certain spread of French ideals and influence through North Africa; here colonialism is in effect working in reverse, as the oil spot of Berber trickery begins instead to stain the French character. For Courtin, this constitutes a moral failing of the *colons*; his thinking recalls the colonial critic Jean Pomier's characterization of Africa's poisonousness to the French moral fiber.

As in Pomier's article, the metaphor of liquid describes Africa's aqueous and lubricious infiltration into Europe's rigid mass. Alternatively, Courtin sees Africa's influence in epidemiologic terms: the country would infect the brains of its immigrants with an untreatable virus, and the climate would do the rest. In recycling a nineteenth-century discourse on Africa as the site of infectious diseases particularly lethal among Europeans, Courtin contradicts one of the major doctrines of French Algeria. French officials and writers delighted in pointing out (and endlessly repeating) how wrongly the early pessimists had diagnosed the country's climate. Despite dire predictions and truly awful beginnings, French determination had won out, sanitizing the very ground of the colony, making it fit for human habitation (incidentally, implying the nonexistence of any previous, non-French population, a fallacy repeated elsewhere). The Mitidja plain and the village of Boufarik, supposedly transformed from unhealthy wasteland to prosperous farm country, became the boosters' favorite case in the massive effort to promote Algeria's healthiness, not as something inherent or natural, but created and secured by French hard work and sacrifice.[67] In setting his novel near a dusty and smelly town on the Hauts Plateaux, far from "Boufarik, jewel of the Mitidja," with its "Monument au colon" inaugurated in 1930, Courtin makes it all the easier to present an Algeria largely untouched, and entirely unchanged, by a scanty French presence.

In the same passage Courtin commits further colonial heresies. The French role in "liberating" North Africa from the Turks, a commonplace of official rhetoric, even repeated by Muslim speakers at Centenary ceremonies, gets short shrift.[68] The Berber race has been "bent for millennia under various yokes, constantly oppressed"; Courtin says nothing about liberation, even in a village named for the noted republican Raspail. The Muslims' unchanging fate, furthermore, owes far more to their ethnic characteristics than to any intervention from the French. The text presents no hope whatsoever of amicable cooperation between them and the *colons*; that cooperation rested largely on French domination dependent in turn on the sword, and would disappear with it. Even Robert Randau, entirely unsqueamish about *colons* adopting Berber tactics, did not imagine that all cooperation would end as soon as the Europeans stopped threatening violence.

Neither did Randau conceive of abjection so complete among the *colons*, abjection that in Leroux works through sexual means. Whereas for Randau, Algeria seems to spur men to virile heights of effort and sexual potency, here it operates like a succubus, sapping them of their energy. The narrator describes a group of men watching the dance of prostitutes who are successfully separating them from their hard-earned cash: "La passion vidait les cerveaux déjà déshabitués de l'effort. La race s'abêtissait, guettée par des fièvres sournoises, enlisée dans le sommeil qui suit l'extase amoureuse. . . . Leroux s'hallucinait sur ce ventre nu qui lui promettait des ivresses savoureuses. Il se sentait une âme de barbare où s'ancrait le désir du rapt. . . . Dans ses veines circulait les poisons d'Asie." [Passion emptied their brains, already out of the habit of mental effort. The race was becoming stupefied, prey to insidious fevers, sinking into the sleep which follows amorous exstacy. . . . Leroux was hallucinating about the bare midriff that promised him delicious intoxication. He felt within himself a barbarous soul, in which rapacious desires took hold. . . . In his veins flowed the poisons of Asia.][69] The same "Asian" poisons, we recall, kept Barrès's hero Sturel from effective political action in *Le Roman de l'énergie nationale*: while they represent a dangerous contagion in France, they are positively deadly in its home territory. Thirty pages later, Leroux will be dead; bullets rather than sexual exhaustion kill him, but sexual poison nonetheless prefigures the end, both of Leroux and of the dream of energetic colony-building that men like him were supposed to realize. Leroux can do nothing to counter his infection, a sort of sleeping sickness brought on by passion. In contrast to Randau's thinking about Cassard as a *barbare*" Leroux's "barbarian soul" is precisely what prevents him from reflecting clearly or constructively. "Asia" (more readily associated with Islam than Africa) has stupefied him with greedy and libidinous desires which get in the way of their own satisfaction by rendering him incapable of work. He will die neither satisfied nor rich.

The comparison with Conrad's *Heart of Darkness* seems inevitable, and to some extent compelling: even if the dominant characteristic of Courtin's Africa is dust rather than darkness, the continent and its climate still have the same debilitating effects on European thought and moral fiber. The "natives" show similar features of moral degeneracy, and their emulation brings about the downfall of European protagonists. The Nigerian novelist Chinua Achebe famously denounced Conrad's pro-colonialism; an Algerian intellectual could easily do the same for Courtin, whose work cannot even pretend to the foregiveness sometimes granted to extraordinary literary quality. Yet at the end of *La Brousse qui mangea l'homme*, no one declares "Mr. Leroux, he dead." The lack of any such pronouncement implies Leroux's symbolic insignificance and points to important differences between the two works. Leroux has none of the qualities of Conrad's Kurtz, and Courtin does everything to make certain that we never sympathize with him, even to the limited extent of equating him with European-style progress gone bad, as readers might still do with Kurtz. Courtin provides no enthralled Marlowe as a foil for our interest in his degenerate protagonist; he gives readers no reason to feel anything but uninterested aversion for his character. Leroux was never anyone's best or brightest, tragically "gone native" in the bush: he is a venal, mediocre, and unintelligent man easily disposed of in a land conflict in which his side stands in the wrong.

The novel's context further undermines any possible parallel between Leroux's and Kurtz's descents into barbarism. Kurtz has gone out to the very edge of European civilization, and beyond, a sort of pioneer into the "heart of darkness." Leroux, on the contrary, has gone almost nowhere: to an unproductive farm on the Hauts Plateaux, just before World War I. The author in no way considers him a pioneer, but at best a faulty cog in the clumsy machine of French colonial domination. Several other books described the experiences of pioneering French colonizers in uncompromising terms, apparently similar to Courtin's: the title of Maxime Rasteil's collection of memoirs, *À l'aube de l'Algérie française: le calvaire des colons de 48* [At the Dawn of French Algeria: The Calvary of the Colonists of '48] (1931), sets the tone its firsthand reports will take and situates their *calvaire* comfortably far in the past.[70] In the eastern province of Constantine, Rasteil's heroes succeed only with great difficulty and at substantial human cost, due to government neglect and occasional hostility; his book hardly presents an inspiring picture of How the East was Won. His tone differs from Courtin's, however, imparting an epic quality to the pioneers' sufferings. Official speeches in 1930 sometimes adopted this tone, and ultimately a work like Rasteil's fit in rather well with the discourse of Algeria's difficult founding, past struggles, and current greatness. Rasteil's work clearly appreciates the pioneers' laudable self-sacrifice and the hard-earned progress the country has made since then. However, his memoirs date from 1848, and not 1914, as in Leroux's case; what should we make of Leroux's trials and tribulations, set so oddly close in time to Courtin's contemporaries? The sixty intervening years dull significantly the impact of Leroux's exploits: simple passage of time since the period of colonization that Courtin's contemporaries identified as the heroic golden age robs Leroux of any heroism his original initiative might have given him. A shift in historical context deprives him of the significance even his failures might have held. Failing miserably and dying in 1850, Rasteil's narrator's family become martyrs to the cause; doing the same in 1914, Leroux becomes an embarrassing statistic, *un de plus*, another dissipated Frenchman frying in the sun at a time when "progress" should have prevented it.

Though Courtin provides the very opposite of pro-colonial propaganda, his book nonetheless won Algeria's official literary prize. We have few substantive reviews and, given the novel's ideological complexities, it is far from clear that reviews would reflect what readers saw in it. Most notices contented themselves with praising its style, which indeed shows complexities absent in virtually all the other novels of the immediate period (and especially from most discussed in this chapter). The only substantial review, from *Afrique*, also comments on the book's stylistic merits, but then devotes much of its space to an analysis of how *La Brousse* differs from other Algerian literature. Courtin's radical difference in tone, and the violence of his novel's tragedy, may have indicated serious literary innovation to the prize committee. The novelist Louis Lecoq's review does not neglect Courtin's pessimism, but it speedily zeros in on something else: his truthful representation of the cultural isolation and disruption in which a large number of *colons* allegedly subsisted: "On a bien cru pouvoir prédire que [la littérature algérienne] serait une littérature d'action, une littérature de force et d'optimisme comme en ont les peuples jeunes. Cela est possible. On a oublié toutefois de faire sa part à l'impression de déracinement. Celle-ci est peu vive chez ceux des Européens qui séjournent dans les villes du littoral extrêmement occidentalisées, mais elle est, par contre, assez forte et ressentie d'une façon inéluctable par les Français qui—comme c'est le cas de Courtin—vivent dans le bled depuis des années, en plein pays arabe, et tout baignés, tout cernés par une race étrangère." [Some critics have thought it possible to predict that Algerian literature will be a literature of action, a literature showing the strength and optimism possessed by youthful peoples. This is possible. Nonetheless, some have forgotten to take into consideration the impression of uprooting. This sensation is weak among the Europeans who live in the very westernized coastal cities, but it is on the contrary very strong, ineluctably felt by the French who like Courtin have lived in the hinterland for years, deep in Arab country, entirely surrounded by and immersed in a foreign race.][71] The link to Barrés's *Déracinés* seems evident, though here, *déracinement* may be experienced in the farming provinces, even more than in the city. Though immigration had swollen the urban working class and petty bourgeoisie, French Algeria wished to believe itself a young country of *colon* farmers, and Lecoq's reminder thus goes to the heart of the European Algerians' image of themselves. Lecoq reminds them of something they may never have experienced firsthand, the uprootedness and isolation of those who live without the support of a European community. In other words, he is attempting to rehabilitate a pessimistic tale for use, à la Rasteil, as a demonstration of how trying life can be for hardscrabble *colons*. He never mentions Leroux's degeneracy; he manages to suggest that if only the country possessed a critical mass of *colons*, everyone's feeling of uprootedness would go away, taking Courtin's pessimism with it.

In this way, a highly conservative writer like Lecoq can recuperate Courtin's inadvertently implied opposition, to make it approach his own pro-*colon* sympathies. Lecoq supported, among other things, measures to prevent the colonized from travelling, thus giving an economic boost to the *colons*, and barring people he considered potentially violent from mainland France.[72] To someone like him, Courtin's book had a message requiring careful handling, and the power of pro-colonial discourse at the time seems to have been equal to the task. Pessimism indeed suffuses the book, went the argument, yet this pessimism does not stem from the "labeur d'Europe mangé par la brousse d'un autre continent" [labor of Europe eaten up by the brush of another continent] but rather from "toute l'atmosphère du livre, sa constatation, fluide et diluée comme une vapeur, qui baigne les choses et les êtres, de notre impuissance humaine" [the whole atmosphere of the book, and its recognition, fluid and diluted like a vapor bathing objects and characters, of our human impotence].[73] The threatened *impuissance coloniale* becomes a relatively banal and general human malaise. In attributing an extremely broad impact to the book, Lecoq not only argues for its literary significance beyond the colonial context, but also divests it of its particular meaning within that context. Under these circumstances, we can see the difficulties of writing even a clearly stated pro-colonialist novel. Courtin seems to have set out to write a story about the realities of colonial existence around 1914, hardly an oppositional project for an administration policy maker. Yet his rhetoric betrays his ambivalence and exposes the shaky foundations of pro-colonial optimism. Readers could ignore his odd sort of anticolonialist pessimism, but his most thoughtful reviewer did not miss Courtin's point altogether: Lecoq admits that one *could* get the idea that the colonial effort was all in vain. That he did not understand it this way results thus from a conscious decision to read the book in another register. His espousal of the Centenary's official rhetoric gave him a way to reconstruct Courtin's meaning into something palatable to *Afrique*'s readers, an audience evoked as ready to accept a book that deviated from the tone of commercial promotion or colonial boosterism, but not prepared to swallow all of its ambiguities.

THE FATE OF LITERARY COMMEMORATION

The ideological and historical richness of the literary production of 1930 more than compensates for its aesthetic limits, not to mention its ephemeral presence: a substantially increased production of novels disappearing from view once the festivities had passed. The books of the Centenary, with very few exceptions, constituted a publishing flurry akin to the spate of agitation for political reform remarked on in the weekly *Voix indigène*, "fireworks" leaving few lasting results. In the first third of the twentieth century, colonial Algeria produced very few works of fiction that found their way into the front ranks of their metropolitan contemporaries; this state of affairs probably owes much to the relatively low numbers of Algerians writing. One might therefore argue that the fate of the books of 1930 was not exceptional. Nonetheless, prolific and often-reprinted authors do give indications of success relative to their peers, and the vast majority of the Centenary books came from authors who were neither. Nor did the few Centenary works by well established authors (Randau, Bertrand, or Duchêne, for example) achieve much lasting success. Even the "valeur durable d'un beau livre comme celui de Courtin" [lasting value of a beautiful book like Courtin's], as Lecoq put it, proved ephemeral: *La Brousse qui mangea l'homme* appears to have sunk into the same unreprinted oblivion as the rest of its cohort of novels. However, the traces they left on the cultural scene of colonial Algeria did not pass as quickly as they; this will become obvious in the following chapter on novels produced before and during the Algerian war.

The importance of these works lies not in their less-than-stunning literary success, but in their reflection on and construction of the discourse of the Algerian Centenary. We have seen how they and their readers demonstrated the surprising resilience of that discourse. If it had consisted entirely of the officially stated clichés, it would have collapsed under the assaults of writers like Jean Mélia, who made a virtue of attacking the purely mercantile view of the colony, or even of Louis Bertrand, who relentlessly exposed exoticist perceptions, regardless of the position of those espousing them. If anything, people like Mélia and Courtin strengthened the colonialist discourse by forcing it to adapt to their difference.

Readers today cannot help but feel that the authors of the Centenary, and the views of history they supported, missed some essential and basic features of the Algerian political and cultural landscape. Overall, with the clear exception of occasional works by the tiny group of Arab and Amazigh writers, these books give an impression of omission, despite their significant revelations concerning the colonialist view of Algerian history. Unlike the believers in Latin Africa, the novelists of 1930 did not simply remove the Muslims; instead they included them, without imagining the possibility of real opposition from them. Surely it is not merely hindsight that makes readers today find this lacking. We have seen enough of the Muslim press, and heard enough from opposition figures like Chukri and Mélia, to know that while opposition to the colonialist order was never easy, obvious, or unqualified, it nonetheless existed in forms visible at least to some. More often, we have seen variations and contestations within the dominant discourse, which exercised the power to recuperate veiled opposition and turn it into support, as in Lecoq's review of Courtin's novel. The context of the 1930 commemoration made it very difficult to receive such subtle opposition as clear contestation, and reading resistance, for the few so inclined, became at least as delicate as writing it.

In the preceding chapter, I reproached critics for believing naively that anyone who wrote about assimilation's failures provided a discourse of resistance, by quoting a vehement colonialist whose pessimism about assimilation led only to more rabid views of French racial superiority. In this chapter, however, I find Courtin's deep pessimism subversive, despite my earlier warning that we should not look to colonial literature by French or Franco-Algerian writers from this period for significant resistance to the dominant discourses. In reality, the contradiction may be only apparent; as I showed, Courtin offers no direct resistance, and his contemporaries did manage at least partially to recuperate his subversive pessimism. On the one hand, just because some were able to do this does not mean that the message was wholly inaudible: witness the comments that Courtin's tone was "not exactly that of official speeches." Contemporary readers could detect slight differences in tone within the official discourse, and Courtin's divergences were anything but slight. On the other hand, the same readers could be stunningly oblivious to the very existence of those who really did resist a bit more; Chukri, Ould Cheikh, and Ben Cherif went unreviewed and for all we know, unread.

The real problem in reading and writing resistance was one of history, its representation, and its reception. We have seen in considerable detail how creatively (not to say aberrantly) Algerian writers could use history to promote the colony. Access to history gave writers of European descent a substantial edge over their Arab and Amazigh colleagues, the effects of whose grasp on their country's history we have yet to see. This near-monopoly on history allowed the European Algerians to maintain a basic pro-colonial coherence and crush serious opposition, all the while diverging considerably among themselves. Creating a collective memory from a tendentiously reconstructed history led to rhetoric that effectively shut the Muslims out of it. This exclusion was by no means watertight: the imprint of the colonized could return in the form of significant holes in the narrative that the European Algerians used to convert historical events into collective memory. This did not prevent them from using their narration as a promotional device at home and in France. However, the "cult of memory," predicated on the nostalgic ritualization of history, would prove itself sufficiently inflexible to prevent most Europeans from imagining a truly inclusive history of Algeria. 1930 was a missed opportunity not only for reform in colonial policy, but also for creativity in collective memory.

NOTES

1. Palais des Beaux-Arts de la Ville de Paris, *Exposition du Centenaire de la Conquête de l'Algérie, 1830–1930*, preface by Camille Gronkowski (Paris: Impr. de Fraiser-Soye, 1930), i.

2. Ibid., iv.

3. Raymond Recouly, "La France et l'Algérie: un glorieux centenaire," *Annales Africaines*, 15 October 1929.

4. Ibid.

5. Louis Bertrand, *D'Alger la romantique à Fés la mysterieuse* (Paris: Editions des Portiques, 1930), 24.

6. On the special case of Oran in the eyes of Albert Camus, see the next chapter.

7. Mercier's speech was reproduced *Terre d'Afrique illustrée* 136 (October 1929), and also in the *Livre d'or du Centenaire de l'Algérie française. Son histoire. L'oeuvre française d'un siècle. Les manifestations du Centenaire. 1830–1930* (Algiers: Fontana, 1931). The phrase *culte du souvenir* also occurs in several other newspaper articles (e.g., the *Presse libre*'s article on *bidonvilles* and shoddy planning, "[Le Musée des beaux arts et les bidonvilles]," *La Presse libre*, 18 June 1930).

8. I discuss this perception of an image problem needing correction in "'Unknown and Unloved': The Politics of French Ignorance in Algeria, 1860–1930," in *Identitiy, Memory, and Nostalgia: Algeria 1800–2000*, Ed. Patricia Lorcin (Syracuse, NY: Syracuse University Press, 2005).

9. *Vérités nord-africaines* (Algiers: Deltrieux et Joyeux, 1932) contains a collection of Charles-Collomb's editorials. The label "Arabophobe" was in regular use beginning around the turn of the century, if not before, while "Arabofous," its opposite, appeared rather less often.

10. The term *régime d'exception* referred to the ensemble of decrees and policies which subjected the *Français musulmans* to unconstitutionally repressive treatment. The term was most often used to denounce the status quo by those who wished to see French laws extended (and actually applied) in Algeria, to the benefit of the Muslims. See Violette's *L'Algérie vivra-t-elle?* (Paris: Felix Alcan, 1931) and Mélia's *Le Centenaire de la conquête de l'Algérie et les réformes indigènes* (Paris: Ligue française en faveur des indigènes musulmans d'Algérie, 1929). Mélia was president of the organization publishing the pamphlet.

11. Charles Robert Ageron, *Histoire de l'Algérie contemporaine* (Paris: PUF, 1979), 404.

12. The AOM preserves minutes of some of this body's meetings in the *Fonds du Gouvernement Général de l'Algérie* (GGA 8-X-8).

13. Jean Mélia, "L'Humiliante platitude," *La Presse libre*, 2 February 1930.

14. *Le Journal*, 17 July 1930, cited in René Weiss, *Le Centenaire de l'Algérie française (1830–1930)* (Paris: Imprimerie nationale, 1930), vol. 1, 530–31.

15. "Cheik el-Arab," "Agha," and "Bach-Agha" were among the Turkish-style titles the French revived to gratify notables loyal to the colonial regime; they aroused considerable scorn among the opposition press in Algeria, both *indigène* and *colon*, who called them a sign of feudalism.

16. Gen. Paul Azan, "Le Centenaire de 1830," *Revue des vivants* Special issue, "Le Centenaire de l'Algérie" (1929): 24.

17. "Défilé des troupes de l'Armée d'Afrique," *La Dépêche algérienne*, 19 April 1930, 7.

18. "Procès-verbal de la réunion du Conseil Supérieur du Centenaire du 11 octobre 1930," Gouvernement Général de l'Algérie (Aix-en-Provence: Archives d'Outre Mer, 1930), GGA Carton 8-X-8. A number of the uniforms ended up in the newly-created Musée Franchet d'Esperey, the Algiers military museum, but archival documents leave the vast majority of them unaccounted for.

19. The only significant complaints in the colonial press appeared in the communist weekly *Demain*, e.g., Victor Spielmann, "Le Wagon Présidentiel," *Demain*, 3 June 1930. Other scathing editorials appeared in Paris, notably in *L'Humanité*.

20. Jean Mélia, "L'Oeuvre néfaste: la plus dangereuse erreur du Commissariat Général du Centenaire," *La Presse libre*, 4 March 1930.

21. Ibid.

22. Ibid.

23. "[Réponse du Commissariat du Centenaire à Jean Mélia]," *La Presse libre*, 17 January 1930, 1, responding to an earlier letter, covering four columns of the front page, that Mélia had addressed to the Président du Conseil Général: "Une lettre de M. Jean Mélia à M. André Tardieu. L'oeuvre néfaste du Commissariat général du Centenaire de l'Algérie," *La Presse libre*, 11 January 1930, 1.

24. Labiod, "À propos du Centenaire," *La Voix indigène*, 6 February 1930.

25. "[Note de la rédaction]," *La Presse libre*, 30 April 1930. Ageron says that of 93 million francs spent, the *colons* controlling the *Délégations financières* (and thereby the allocation of the colonial budget) allowed only five million for schools and other projects for the Muslim population. They rejected a further 100 million proposed in Paris for that purpose, ostensibly to defend their privilege of deciding how the government's money should be spent in Algeria. Ageron, *Histoire de l'Algérie contemporaine*, 410.

26. It is unclear what practical effect the decreed end of the *régime d'indigénat* actually had. One of the major problems for historians of colonial Algeria lies in determining how laws or government decrees were implemented. This is especially true of measures attempting to institute reforms favorable to the Muslims. Administrators at all levels routinely ignored, circumvented, or disobeyed them.

27. "Le Cahier du Centenaire," *La Voix indigène*, 1 May 1930.

28. "Après le Centenaire," *La Voix indigène*, 5 June 1930.

29. Labiod, "Désillusion et espérance," *La Voix indigène*, 10 July 1030.

30. *La Voix indigène*, 15 May 1930.

31. "[Note de la rédaction]," *La Presse libre*, 30 April 1930.

32. Mélia, "Une lettre de M. Jean Mélia à M. André Tardieu."

33. Ibid.

34. "Procès-verbal de la réunion du Conseil Supérieur du Centenaire du 29 mai 1929," Gouvernement Général de l'Algérie (Aix-en-Provence: Archives d'Outre

Mer, 1930), GGA Carton 8-X-8. The archives do not tell us how radically the sponsors had to scale back their series, but unoccupied call numbers in the Bibliothèque Nationale's card-file entries for it suggest that at least thirty percent of the volumes originally expected never appeared. The BN cataloguers divided the projected volumes (as announced in a number of prospectuses in the front-matter of the books themselves) in an elaborate structure of subclasses (*sous-côtes*) under the main call number assigned to the series. Thirty-six volumes share this call number, and the subclasses leave out about seventeen numbers. Some of these books, whose titles were announced in earlier publications, are held at other libraries, but many appear never to have been published at all.

35. "Procès-verbal de la 35e séance du Conseil Supérieur du Centenaire," Gouvernement Général de l'Algérie (Aix-en-Provence: Archives d'Outre Mer), GGA Carton 8-X-8; at the 36th meeting on 9 January 1930, Governor Bordes noted the difficulty of satisfying the large number of requests for book subsidies, and proposed that the Conseil examine all such requests at a meeting in May. We have no record of this meeting.

36. Ageron, *Histoire de l'Algérie contemporaine*, 405.

37. Few bibliographers can claim total coverage, but a comprehensive search of the major preexisting bibliographies by Jean Déjeux, and a fairly exhaustive examination of publishers' catalogues and book reviews, reveals a striking trend. Déjeux's *Situation de la littérature maghébine de langue française: approche historique, approche critique, bibliographie méthodique des oeuvres maghrébines de fiction 1920–1978* (Algiers: Office des Publications Universitaires, 1982) provides an invaluable starting point for any work of this sort on Algeria, as does his 650-page *Maghreb: littératures de langue française* (Paris: Arcantère, 1993).

38. "'Esclave en Alger' par Henriette Celarié," *La Dépêche algérienne*, 10 January 1930.

39. Henriette Célarié, *Esclave en Alger* (Paris: Hachette, 1930), 45.

40. Louis Bertrand, *Le Roman de la conquête* (Paris: Arthème Fayard, 1930), 7.

41. Ibid., 7–8.

42. Jules Roy's five-volume saga *Les Chevaux du soleil* (Paris: Grasset, 1967–72) takes this other option.

43. Bertrand, *Le Roman de la conquête*, 197.

44. Antoine Chollier, *Drusilla, dame d'Alger* (Algiers: Soubiron, 1930), 31.

45. Ibid.

46. Ibid., 184.

47. This idea seems to have occurred to another colonial writer, in another colonial empire. In Rider Haggard's *She*, the very white Greco-Egyptian queen of an African kingdom threatens to marry (and bury) the protagonist in her underground realm.

48. Chollier, *Drusilla*, 264.

49. Ibid., 30.

50. Antoine Chollier, *Alger et sa région* (Grenable B. Arthand, 1929), 17–18.

51. Ibid., 29.

52. In 1930 approximately 100,000 Arabs and Imazighen lived in the city, half or more in the already overcrowded Casbah, while the European majority numbered about 150,000 (figures interpolated from Farouk Benaita's data in *Alger: agrégat ou cité: l'intégration citadine de 1919 à 1979* [Algiers: SNED, 1980], 37).

53. Chollier, *Alger et sa région*, 28.

54. Ibid., 73.

55. Jean-Louis Planche, "Charles Courtin, romancier de l'affrontement colonial," *Revue de l'Occident Musulman et de la Méditerranée*, no. 37 (1985): 38.

56. Ibid.

57. Those born in Algeria began to outnumber immigrants just before the turn of the century.

58. Charles Courtin, *La Brousse qui mangea l'homme: images de la vie africaine* (Paris: Editions de France, 1929), 266.

59. "L'Algérie 1930: pays de grande production agricole" (Paris: Imp. Marx Dormoy, 1930), AOM Fonds iconographique.

60. Courtin, *La Brousse*, 8–9.

61. Louis Lecoq, "[Notice sur *La Brousse qui mangea l'homme*]," *Afrique*, no. 55 (January 1930): 11.

62. Courtin, *La Brousse*, 7, 13.

63. Courtin, *La Brousse*, 32. According to Planche, Courtin legitimates the *loi du plus fort*: in this case, however, the *plus fort* are certainly the colonized. In other novels, Courtin would nonetheless find other excuses for dispossessing them (Planche, "Charles Courtin," 43).

64. The Communist Victor Spielmann, one of very few Europeans to speak out against expropriations, was called just that. See, for example, his pamphlet *En Algérie: le centenaire au point de vue indigène* (Algiers: Editions du Trait-d'Union, 1930). *Trait-d'Union* was also the name of his Communist, Muslim-friendly review, suppressed on several occasions.

65. Courtin, *La Brousse*, 218–9.

66. Other writers did, notably Louis Bertrand.

67. On Boufarik and its monument, see "Au coeur de la colonisation française," *Terre d'Afrique illustrée*, no. 143 (June 1930). Other writers tended to view Boufarik as the very soul and illustration of French colonialism at work. See, for example, Jean Leune's much appreciated and frequently quoted *Le Miracle algérien* (Paris: Berger-Levrault, 1930), 23. The Mitidja was, according to colonial legend, an infamous swamp when the colonists arrived. This appears to have been true, but only because the Army had driven out the Arab farmers who had previously maintained it as prosperous farmland.

68. Compare the speeches by representatives of the Muslims at the dedication ceremony of the monument at Sidi Ferruch on 14 June 1930, as reported in "Les grandes fêtes de l'union Franco-Musulmane à Sidi-Ferruch," 11. Hadj Hamou Abdelkader, a founding member of Pomier's AEA speaking on behalf of the corps of Muslim schoolteachers, felt compelled to mention the freedoms embodied in the French Republic, freedoms which everyone present knew that the vast majority of Muslims did not enjoy.

69. Courtin, *La Brousse*, 233.

70. Maxime Rasteil, *À l'aube de l'Algérie française: le calvaire des colons de 48* (Paris: Eugène Figuière, 1931).

71. Lecoq, "[Notice sur *La Brousse qui mangea l'homme*]," 10.

72. Louis Lecoq, "[L'immigration]," *Afrique*, no. 2 (May 1924): 13.

73. Lecoq, "[Notice sur *La Brousse qui mangea l'homme*]," 10.

5

+

Broken Idylls:
Audisio, Camus, and Roblès

Although nothing could ostensibly have been further from the official pronouncements of the 1930 Centenary, desperation often seems close behind the reiterated declarations of triumphalist colonialism. Were the Europeans in Algeria proclaiming their force because they feared they would have to use it? Shortly after the Centenary, an anxiety previously held at bay in the colony began to gain hold. The gradualist experiments in political enfranchisement for the colonized ran into obstructions from European Algerians convinced that the trickle would become a flood. By the late thirties such projects had failed. World War II would bring another mass recruitment of Algerians to fight for France, with its concomitant consciousness-raising effects. It would also bring the *Manifeste du Peuple Algérien,* in which Arabs and Imazighen openly demanded full participation in Algerian politics in accordance with their demographic strength. When the French government established the Fédération of its colonies in 1947, Muslims could theoretically vote for representatives in the National Assembly, but opposition from Eurcopean Algerians supported by the Gouvernement Général used massive election fraud to neutralize yet another potential legal opposition.

In this political impasse, worsened by the slaughter of thousands of Muslims by the army and *colon* vigilante groups following riots on 8 May 1945, a number of European Algerian intellectuals loosely grouped as the École d'Alger tried to find an antidote for anxiety in the creation of a collective, Mediterranean identity and historical narrative, with which Algerians of all ethnic backgrounds could identify. The three writers I will focus on here, Gabriel Audisio, Albert Camus, and Emmanuel Roblès, all

191

participated in the elaboration of this ideal, and in the subsequent break-downs and attempted revivals of the Mediterranean idyll. Their polemics and their fictions, in works as diverse as Audisio's *Jeunesse de la Méditer-ranée* [Youth of the Mediterranean], Camus's *La Peste* [The Plague] and *Le Premier homme* [The First Man], and Roblès's *Saison violente* [Violent Sea-son], indicate that the nervousness underlying Algeria's apparent calm was an anxiety about history even if it was also worry about the future. All three writers suspected at different moments that the official version of Algerian history as expressed in the Centenary celebrations had been based on flawed premises and feared that it might be too late to do any-thing decisive to change them. Their mostly unsuccessful attempts to re-orient the narrative of Algerian history implied a failure to rethink the colony's future direction in a way that could both answer the demands of the colonized and conserve something of the culture of the colonizers. In-timations of this failure as imminent or, worse, as already happened, led to a certain nostalgia in some of their works. In others, however, it also led to the realization that they had very little for which to be nostalgic. Once they discovered the undersides of the traditional objects of *colon* nostalgia (e.g., the wagoneers of the wild south, or the first "martyr" settlers of the Mitidja) they also began to question the figures they themselves had ear-lier advanced for nostalgic valorization. Audisio laid the foundation for a "Mediterranean" Algeria, and Roblès radically revised the concept; be-tween them stood Camus, the primary example of a Franco-Algerian in-tellectual grappling with the past and present of colonialism. He com-bines compelling literature with problematic politics, in ways more difficult to analyze than the work of Audisio and Roblès, who nonetheless give us a framework for reading him. In all three cases, major parts of their work consisted of an analysis of where French Algeria had gone wrong, and of what history they might construct as part of their effort to set it right. This chapter will show to what extent they succeeded, and how they analyzed their inevitable failures.

GABRIEL AUDISIO AND MEDITERRANEAN NOSTALGIA

Si je fais . . . quelque stage téméraire au-dessus d'un certain parallèle, en Bourgogne par exemple, ou plus loin dans le nord exotique, je me découvre une mélancolie de colonial: mes voeux et mes pensées, comme dit Laerte en Danemark, se tournent vers la France, je veux dire vers Marseille.

[If I undertake . . . some daring trip north of a certain latitude, that of Bour-gogne for example, or farther into the exotic North, I discover in myself a colonial's melancholy. My thoughts and hopes, as Laertes said in Denmark, turn toward France, I mean, toward Marseille.][1]

Perhaps the southern orientation of Audisio's "colonial's melancholy" was preordained by geopolitics, which situated colonies more often in the south than elsewhere. However, there remains something odd about Audisio's French geography. First, the reversal of terms: the south is "home," at least spiritually; the north (anything above Burgundy) is "exotic." Second, the siting of France: when in the "north" (even in Ile-de-France?), one looks elsewhere to find the nation, apparently centered around Marseille. Even if we read the last clause as a specification rather than a substitution, Audisio has still concentrated his homeland on the shores of the Mediterranean. This promotion of the Mediterranean as central to France allows him to redefine both metropole and colony and recast the literary production of the colony into that of the Mare Nostrum, "la mer du milieu" [the middle sea], as Audisio called it, using a calque of the Arabic *al-bahr al-mutawaṣiṭ*. As the gesture to Arabic implies, Audisio's views represented a significant change from Louis Bertrand's notion of Latin Africa. Much younger than Bertrand and Randau, Audisio had time to evolve a position away from the intimations of fascism in the literary pronouncements coming out of Algeria in the twenties, to a much more progressive view of what Algerian (and Mediterranean) literature should be.

Gabriel Audisio was born in 1900 into a family of actors and musicians based primarily in Paris. His father Victor Audisio was named director of the Théâtre Municipal (later the Opéra) of Algiers in 1910, and the family spent part of each year there; after an extended absence for *lycée*, the young Audisio got a job with the Gouvernement Général, a position enabling him to return to Algiers shortly after World War I.[2] As the organizer of a long series of invited lectures by French authors in Algiers and the author of a small *oeuvre* of poetry, novels, and criticism, he cut a significant figure among the Algerian literati, not least because he published with Gallimard. Before Camus's arrival on the Paris scene, Audisio represented Algerian literature in mainland France, embodying the trans-Mediterranean existence between Algiers and Paris led by writers he identified as the École d'Alger: Max-Pol Fouchet, Emmanuel Roblès, Marcel Moussy, Claude de Fréminville, and for a while Camus himself. During World War II Audisio spent time in both places, and during the *épuration*, was called to sit on a commission to examine writers suspected of collaboration; he resigned when asked to judge Henri de Montherlant, once a fellow resident in Algiers. The two wars, world and Algerian, were periods of rethinking the positions on Algerian literature that he developed in sporadic critical essays. Audisio left Algeria more or less for good after World War II, and lived (in France) until 1978, but his literary production fell off in the 1950s, eclipsed by that of Camus. Before Camus's ascendency, however, he had laid out a seductive program for Algeria's evolution in a Mediterranean context in essays that evolved significantly with the colony's changing political scene. By the time of Algeria's independence in 1962, he had more or less taken his literary retirement, returning to write his nostalgic memoirs in *L'Opéra fabuleux* (1970). These memoirs echo an idea from his earlier work: an awkward suspicion that his evolution had been too slow. Although he had been twenty years ahead of most other European writers in Algeria in the thirties, he was twenty years behind the thinking of people like Kateb Yacine, Mouloud Feraoun, and Mohammed Dib in the fifties. Part of his nostalgia may have come from his sense of being perpetually too late in relation to Algerian culture and politics.

His tardiness appears the least in his early writings, *Héliotrope* (1928), *Jeunesse de la Méditerranée* (1935), and *Sel de mer* (1936).[3] In *Héliotrope*, Audisio's second novel, a very thin narrative links together a series of evocative prose poems on various aspects of the Mediterranean and its people, as typified by a cast of characters drawn from the port and proletariat of Algiers. The hero, Sauveur, rebaptized Héliotrope to reflect his taste for sun, is a young Algiers fisherman of indeterminate Mediterranean origins, who attains mythic status as a sort of demigod of sea, sex, and sun. Nude, Sauveur leads his followers in a Bacchic procession through Algiers, ending with communion on the beach, celebrated in the ancestral Mediterranean libations of olive oil, tomatoes, and salt.[4] The book has no closure; once enthroned, the young demigod announces his intention to "continuer, pardi!" [continue, by God!], presumably with heroic and erotic celebrations of the male body and the overflowing sexuality generated by proximity to the sea.[5] The sea, for Audisio, represents a sexual satisfaction as available as the "loges qui n'ont rien de clandestin" [holes-in-the-wall with nothing hidden about them] in the "quartiers si peu réservés" [red-light districts so open] of Mediterranean ports.[6] The sea becomes a female lover, the real "Savior" of the novel; diving or playing in it nude, the Mediterranean male consummates his marriage to his native landscape. The overwhelming heterosexuality of Audisio's metaphor frames homoerotic description of young men in his hymns to youth; this worship of youth takes on considerable cultural importance in the essays following *Héliotrope*.

At the beginning of this novel-*cum*-prose poem, Audisio declares "je parle de la Mer, l'Unique, la mienne. Ou la nôtre, j'y consens. Car je suis provençal, sarde, catalan; je suis, peu m'importe, de tous les rivages de cette mer où j'ai vécu . . . [et qui] montre son beau ventre de déesse largement plissé et qui couche avec l'univers navigateur depuis Bizerte jusqu'à Port-Bou, d'Algesiras à La Spézia" [I speak of the Sea, the Unique Sea, my Sea. Or ours: fine with me. For I am Provençal, Sardinian, Catalan; I am from all the shores, any shore, of this sea where I have lived and which shows off its beautiful goddess's torso, well-contoured, which sleeps with the navigating universe from Bizerte to Port-Bou, from Algeciras to La Spézia].[7] The sea is nothing if not promiscuous, both sexually and ethnically, and the author's identification with its peoples (those of its western shores, at least) follows suit. This identification already breaks significantly with Bertrand's *latinité*. Bertrand portrayed very little actual mixing of the "Latin" peoples he saw in Algeria, and kept them strictly hierarchized: French on top, and then Spanish, Majorcans, and Italians, followed distantly by the half-Arab Maltese. Audisio dispenses with this notion immediately, though he takes some time to add Arabs to the list of people with whom he claims to identify.

Jeunesse de la Méditerranée begins where *Héliotrope* left off, with another description of male bodies intertwined in the sun in the port of Toulon, waiting for the boat to Africa. This suggested physical union leads Audisio to conclude a moral one: once they start talking about their respective countries, he and his fellow Mediterraneans are "tous frères depuis Algesiras jusqu'à Messine, en passant par Marseille" [all brothers, from Algeciras to Messine, by way of Marseille].[8] This embrace, whether fraternal or erotic, omits the Arabs by choosing the north shore; in addition, with the narrator's interlocutors coming from Tuscany and Campagnia, it has a distinctly Italian flavor. At various points in the book, Audisio's endlessly restated valorization of youthful vigor, often attributed to virile men, will lead directly to appreciative considerations of the wonders of Mussolini's Italy. "C'était à Naples," says an enthusiastic Audisio, "que j'ai vu les premiers enfantements de ces travaux d'éternelle structure . . . dont la nation fasciste veut être fier" [that I saw the first productions of those works of eternal structure . . . in which the fascist nation wants to take pride].[9] Audisio may not have been taken in by the claim of Italian fascism to be building for eternity, with ancient Rome as its example. However, he did wonder what the future would make of the constructions of the beautiful and youthful race he admires:

> Je ne sais ce que pourront éprouver les gens qui verront nos cités méditerranéennes et nos pays "latins" quand nous n'y serons plus: cette Italie nouvelle, galvanisée, parcourue de jeunes dieux d'acier (et il n'est pas indifférent qu'un de ses hymnes soit 'jeunesse, printemps de beauté'),—cette Espagne qui resurgit d'elle-même en mille endroits comme les fontaines du sable,— l'Afrique du Nord qui ne fait que commencer. Et l'Egypte, et la Turquie. . . . La vieille Méditerranée n'a pas fini d'etre jeune: déjà quels exemples de jouvence! J'en sais qui n'ont pas peur de croire encore à quelque 'empire romain' . . . librement consenti.
>
> [I do not know what those who will see our Mediterranean cities and our "Latin" countries when we are gone will feel. This new, galvanized Italy, trodden by young gods of steel (it is not coincidental that one of its hymns is "youth, beauty's spring"),—this Spain regenerating itself in a thousand

places like springs from the sand,—and North Africa, which is only just beginning. And Egypt, and Turkey. . . . The old Mediterranean has not ceased
to be young: already, what amazing examples of youthfulness we see! I know
some who still unabashedly believe in a sort of freely agreed-upon Roman
Empire.][10]

Young fascists get the same praise as Young Turks; Audisio's enthusiasm
for youth and building programs leads him to indulgence toward political acts readers today might see as dangerous, and he was not always
very discriminating in distributing praise for Mediterranean virility. This
passage, from before the Spanish Civil War, will be the last of his flirta-
tions with fascism; elsewhere in *Jeunesse* he places Mussolini in the larger
context of the sweep of Mediterranean history, and calls him "transitory,"
too insignificant for further consideration.[11] Ultimately, Audisio is less interested in fascism than in Mediterranean rebirth.

Audisio's admiration of fascist building projects and his fascination
with its youthful energy may not have gone much further than this; rebirth and rebuilding went hand in hand all over the Mediterranean regardless, he thought, of political climate.[12] He promptly transfers his
attention to Algiers, in order to prove how young people and new constructions brought Algeria into the Mediterranean circle. For him, understanding its place in that circle implied rejecting previous literature on the
colony so as to arrive in North Africa

innocement, c'est-à-dire ayant oublié la littérature des temps révolus, aussi
bien celle de la "latinité" que celle de "l'orientalisme".

J'arrive en rade, je suis encore sur le bateau, par quoi suis-je frappé
d'abord? Par l'exotisme? Non, mais par cet immense immeuble de béton, le
palais du Gouvernement Général, qui domine une partie de la ville, et par
l'entassement des grandes bâtisses aux multiples étages, en un mot par le
modernisme.

Autre vue: quiconque débarque ici (le témoignage de nombre d'écrivains
et d'artistes est probant) ce qui le touche au vif, dès la rue, c'est la jeunesse
de la race, la beauté des filles, la force des garçons.

[innocently, that is, having forgotten the literature of bygone ages: the literature of *Latinité* as well as that of Orientalism.

I arrive in port, and am still on the boat, and by what am I struck at first?
By exoticism? No, but by the immense concrete building, the palace of the
Gouvernement Général, which dominates part of the city, and by the crowd
of large multi-story constructions; in a word, by modernism.

Another view: anyone who arrives here (the accounts of numerous writers
and artists prove it) is struck to the core the moment they set foot in the street
by the youth of the race, the beauty of the girls, and the strength of the
boys.][13]

The new Algiers will require a new literature to recast its history and description in Mediterranean terms. Having gotten rid of his literary precursors for this arrival scene, however, Audisio immediately needs to call them back to prove his point about the "youth of the race": try as they might, almost no one, French or Algerian, could arrive in Algiers without invoking predecessors. However, Audisio's description is unique in substituting the massive rectangle of the new Gouvernement Général building for the clichéd triangle of the Casbah. He also omits the Santé maritime pavilion and the Peñon lighthouse, the "Carthaginian" constructions Bertrand found so evocative; finally, he even leaves out the early colonial edifices of the lower Casbah.

All disappear in favor of the overwhelming modernity of the new government headquarters, an imposing office block that owed much of its panache to its size and prestigious site on a plateau high above the commercial streets of central Algiers.[14] Audisio implicitly acknowledges that modernity comes with a new symbolism of power, in which the building symbolic of bureaucratic administration comes to dominate the new city center in the same way the prison and artillery of the Casbah fort continue to dominate the old. Exemplifying a new view of urban space and a new architectural trend (the multistory concrete office-block), the new "G-G" elicited criticism which Audisio dismisses as "cortèges de pleureuses antiques et vociferatrices" [funeral processions of ancient and vociferous professional mourners], asserting that "dans vingt ans ils y verront tous un honneur de leur cité. Cette ville, que doit-elle à son passé? Presque rien. Que peut-elle attendre de son avenir? Presque tout. Son présent? Quelque chose. Et quelque chose de fort, de vivant: Alger qui bâtit" [in twenty years they will all see the building as an honor to the city. What does that city owe to its past? Almost nothing. What can it hope for from its future? Almost everything. Its present? Something, something strong and vital: Algiers, building].[15] This "ruche" [hive] or "usine d'architecture puissante" [factory of powerful architecture] heralds the future of a city which, Audisio paradoxically asserts, owed almost nothing to its past.[16] This was easy to say when the construction of the G-G involved no destruction of picturesque local color; it, the boulevard Laferrière leading up to it, and the Monument aux Morts inaugurated in 1930 were all built on the site of former French fortifications. Ironically, twenty years later, the G-G, its plateau, and the boulevards leading up to it would indeed become symbols of the city, though not in a way a moderate liberal like Audisio would appreciate. There the *pied-noir* crowds gathered at tense moments in the Algerian war: pelting Prime Minister Guy Mollet with tomatoes, when he attempted to suggest anything less than crushing the rebels, or erecting barricades and rallying to support the two putsches, one to bring de Gaulle in, the other to throw him out. The "hive of bureaucrats" became a hive of contention, the place for the hard-liners of *Algérie française* to air complaints about the present and fears about the future.

In addition to unwittingly foreshadowing later historical and political polemics, Audisio's arrival in Algiers also represents a new view of the colony's history and the identity of its people, a view explicitly opposed to Louis Bertrand's. Like Bertrand, Audisio attacks the exoticists, but in a blasé tone, as if that battle were already won. He inveighs only briefly against those captivated by "des séductions trop faciles" [too easy seductions]: the white Casbah, veiled "Mauresque" women, camels, and oases.[17] However, such authors are not his main prey; that honor he reserves for Bertrand himself. If exoticism seems too easy, so does *latinité*: Audisio calls it a simplified vision based on the elimination of a major period of history:

> Ah! que l'on nous fasse grâce de la trop facile latinité! La politique, la littérature, le sentiment se la disputent. On sait avec quelle allégresse l'éminent hagiographe d'Augustin d'Hippone, M. Louis Bertrand, supprime les douze siècles d'Islam qui ont pesé sur le Maghreb, avec quelle foi il fait appel à la conscience latine des musulmans nord-africains. Je n'ai guère plus d'indulgence pour les autres généralisations qu'on impose à ma mer, l'hellenique, la byzantine ou la phénicienne: pour moi, les thalassocraties orientales, le miracle grec et ses amphictonies, l'empire romain, la catholicité et, plus près de nous, les chimères d'un Charles-Quint, d'un Napoléon, d'un Mussolini lui-même, ne sont que des "moments", des aspects transitoires de l'éternelle Méditerranée.
>
> Mais c'est à cette latinité surtout que j'en ai, polémique et provocante. Je regarde bien ma race et je trouve qu'elle n'en conserve pas grand'chose.
>
> [Spare us the all too easy *latinité*! Politics, literature, and sentiment all fight for its possession. We know with what ease the eminent hagiographer of Saint Augustine, M. Louis Bertrand, does away with the twelve centuries of Islam which have weighed on the Maghreb, and how earnestly he appeals to the Latin consciousness of North African Muslims. I have scarcely more indulgence for the other generalizations people impose on my sea: the Hellenic, the Byzantine, or the Phonecian: for me, the Oriental sea-kingdoms, the Greek miracle, the Roman Empire, Catholicism, and, closer to our day, the chimeras of Charles V, Napoleon, or Mussolini himself are only "moments," transient aspects of the eternal Mediterranean.
>
> But I have a special grudge against this provoking and polemical *latinité*. On looking closely, I find that my race has preserved very little of it.][18]

Audisio does no more than suggest that the centuries of Islam which "weighed" on North Africa might have produced something worthy of consideration, and he was not the first writer to raise this objection to Latin Africa. Nonetheless, he reconsiders the precolonial history he had cast aside in his pronouncement on the future of Algiers. He also begins a

critique of essentialist history, rejecting one after the other the generaliza-
tions that historians proposed for the Mediterranean, Procrustean beds
that he finds too small for its grandeur and youthful strength. From this
point on, he will consistently reject the Roman model as a reductive and
constrictive view of Mediterranean vitality: "Je ne cesserai pas de distinguer la Rome provisoire de l'éternelle Méditerranée, de dire que Rome
ne fut qu'un moment la Méditerranée, d'opposer à la piétaille de Rome et
son sac au dos les matelots d'Ulysse et leur barda, à la latinité terrienne,
dure et conservatrice, l'universalité mouvante et vivante de la mer." [I
will continue to make a distinction between the provisional Rome and the
eternal Mediterranean, to say that Rome was only a moment of Mediterranean history, and to mark the contrast between the foot-soldiers of
Rome with their knapsacks, and Ulysses' sailors with their sea-bags, and
between land-bound, hard, conservative *latinité* and the vital, moving
universality of the sea.][19] In rejecting the conservatism of *latinité* Audisio
discounts the importance of its focus on the land, a natural focal point for
a discourse seeking above all to justify occupation of territory taken from
its previous possessors. Peter Dunwoodie characterizes Audisio's own
ideological move as one from land to sea, one which allows him to attain
the universal (or at least the Greco-Roman) from the local, with Mediterranean man "a geographically and culturally redrawn figure cutting
across (imperialist) national and cultural boundaries."[20] In addition, his
move avoids the question (embarrassing only for some) of who owned
the land before the arrival of the French. Despite earlier talk about it as a
"French lake," no one claimed sovereignty over the entire Mediterranean;
and it seems more difficult, both metaphysically and practically, to appropriate a sea than a piece of land. Unfortunately for Audisio, the question of who took the land from whom could not simply disappear in reality as it did in his rhetoric.

In addition to attempting to destabilize the metaphysics of possession,
Audisio questions the racial basis of the Algerianist view of North Africa.
In doing so, his argument passes via exactly the same sites as Bertrand's:
first Algiers, then the ancient sites of Roman Algeria, and finally the archaeological confusion of Tunisia.[21] Audisio invokes Carthaginian god-
desses and goes into transports over ruined cities, but his enthusiasm
sends him in a different direction from Bertrand's.[22] Rather than stressing
purity of form in the ruins, he prefers the places where Punic, Roman, and
Arab forms succeeded each other, each one burying or swallowing up the
last. When he evokes a Mediterranean race, he hastens to qualify: "mais
c'est le type de la race impure, faite de tous les apports et de tous les
mélanges: exactement le contraire de ces entités ethniques qui voudraient,
se croyant spécifiques, en tirer la raison d'une imposition universelle. Vos
Latins, grattez un peu: le Juif, le Maure, et parfois le Noir ne sont pas loin"

[but it is the archetypal impure race, made of every kind of contribution and mixture: exactly the opposite of those ethnicities that, believing themselves specific, want to make that into a reason for imposing themselves universally. Scrape a bit at your Latins: the Jew, the Moor, and sometimes the Black are not far].[23] Unlike his predecessors, Audisio seems truly convinced of the value of ethnic mixing; he also knows that it is not a project for the future, but a process that has already occurred. However, his rejection of purity does not imply a rejection of the notion of race itself, since groups based on phenotype still hold on to some sort of metaphysical existence for him. There may be no pure Latins, but for Audisio the *Juif*, the *Maure*, and the *Noir* nonetheless exist in definable groups; he never suggests that the idea of *le Noir* might be quite separate from the existence of people with dark skin. He deplores the limits of humanism invented by and for whites only, but rather than embark on any radical critique of that humanism, he prefers to see it extended to universality: he will happily claim citizenship in the Mediterranean, "à condition d'avoir pour concitoyens tous les peuples de la mer, y compris les Juifs, les Arabes, les Berbères et les Noirs" [on the condition that I would have as fellow citizens all the peoples of the sea, including the Jews, the Arabs, the Berbers, and the Blacks].[24] Moving from the land-based Latin Africa to the seagoing *Algérie méditerranéenne*, Audisio creates the humanist utopia he still wishes to believe possible in 1936.

Audisio quickly drew the literary conclusions implicit in creating his idyll. When critics tell North African writers they are "the inheritors of Rome," he finds this a "vue sommaire, inexacte, une prime à la paresse d'esprit et d'invention. Je ne méconnais pas l'importance de l'oeuvre romaine en Tunisie mais je tiens que le mélange des races, Français, Arabes, Maltais, Italiens, Juifs, Grecs, Russes (et j'en passe sans doute), je tiens que le mélange des croyances et des disciplines, que l'amalgame qui constitue ce peuple étonnant *vaut mieux*" [summary and inexact viewpoint, an encouragement for mental laziness. I am not unaware of the importance of Roman accomplishments in Tunisia, but I hold that the mix of races, French, Arab, Maltese, Italian, Jews, Greek, Russian (no doubt I am leaving some out)—I hold that the mix of beliefs and disciplines, the amalgam constituted by this amazing people *is worth more*.][25] Audisio would like to believe in the possibility of a genuine literary *métissage* on the Mediterranean's southern shore. He has significantly extended Bertrand and Randau's rhetoric of ethnic mixing and changed the basic components of the mix. His list of ingredients is longer, less white, and more inclusive than those of his predecessors. It may, however, be almost too inclusive in its eagerness ("no doubt I am leaving some out") to find every possible minority group to counterbalance the Arab and Amazigh dominance in North Africa. Asserting an exaggerated scope of ethnic diversity was a common tactic to undermine Arab and Amazigh political demands by claiming that other ethnic groups (Jews, Turks, Italians, even Greeks) had as much right to political recognition as they.[26] Moreover, Audisio's rhetoric is simply another list of ingredients and does not provide anything like a recipe. The reality of cultural and political domination will prevent this mix (or any other) from getting past a bare enumeration of the peoples and cultures deserving inclusion.

Power dynamics already implicit in Audisio's French Mediterranean will allow those in Algeria to obey only the first two terms of his triple exhortation to "bâtir, agir, s'amalgamer" [build, act, amalgamate yourselves].[27] Though prepared to live with Arabs as his fellow citizens, Audisio has difficulty considering them his cultural equals, speaking of the Arab domination as "plusieurs siècles d'absence de civilisation" [several centuries of absence of civilization] in North Africa.[28] In stating his wishful belief that modern Algeria is less the result of an idea than of a "naturelle confusion des sangs" [natural confusion of blood] he feels the need to specify: "je ne dis pas l'Algérie conquise mais l'Algérie colonisée" [I do not mean conquered Algeria, but rather colonized Algeria].[29] For him, these were two different and separable countries which diverged historically. Audisio could not imagine that for the colonized, the difference between the conquered country and the colonized one was minuscule; concrete practices of power inherent in both prevented any real amalgamation of peoples from taking place in Algeria.

The literary difficulties of Mediterranean mixing indicate the practical and ideological sticking points of Audisio's ideas, and it soon became clear that his vision was implicitly a utopia presented in order to be proven impossible. Describing "L'Algérie littéraire" in 1946 for the *Encyclopédie coloniale et maritime*, Audisio writes

> Sans nation, sans race, sans langue, comment donc parler de littérature?
> Essayons de situer le problème dans le temps et l'espace, en partant de l'époque contemporaine. Si artificielle que soit l'Algérie, aujourd'hui elle existe, telle que la France l'a faite. Parlerons-nous pour autant d'une littérature algérienne? Pour faire une littérature, il faut *une* langue. Or l'Algérie en parle au moins trois: le français, l'arabe et le berbère. Il y aurait donc des littératures algériennes, ou, à la rigueur, des chapitres algériens des littératures française, arabe et berbère.

> [Without a nation, a race, or a language, how can we speak of a literature?
> Let us try to situate the problem in time and space, starting from the contemporary period. As artificial as it may be, Algeria exists today, as France has made it. Nonetheless, will we speak of an Algerian literature? To make a literature you need *a* language. Algeria speaks at least three: French, Arabic, and Berber. There could therefore be several Algerian literatures, or perhaps Algerian chapters of French, Arabic, and Berber literatures.][30]

Audisio begins his encyclopedia article with a levelheaded explanation of the complexities of Algeria's linguistic and historic cartography. He notes the coexistence of Arabic and Tamazight without asserting, as many of his predecessors had done, that ethnic diversity and historical incoherencies made any unifying cultural treatment impossible. Nonetheless, his assertion, (true on a purely pragmatic level), that Algeria existed as France made it leads him to revert quickly to consideration solely of the colony's Francophone literature: "On oscillera toujours entre ces deux pôles: une littérature faite *par* l'Algérie ou *sur* l'Algérie, par des indigènes ou par des exotiques, dans un idiome local ou dans une exogène. On se trouve devant des états de fait. Force nous sera de dresser un tableau littéraire de l'Algérie par approximations et à peu près, exactement comme l'administration française a constitué l'Algérie elle-même." [We will always oscillate between two poles: literature created *by* Algeria or *about* Algeria, by natives or by outsiders, in a local idiom or an exogenous one. We find ourselves confronted with practical realities, and we will be obliged to draw a literary picture of Algeria by approximations and imprecisions, exactly the way the French administration created Algeria itself.][31] Audisio chooses a telling model for his analytical work by comparing his job to that of the French colonial administrators. His essay wavers but comes down in favor of a literature *"by* Algeria," or at least by the people of European origin then calling themselves *Algériens*, and in French, the "exogenous language" whose foreignness to the colony he implicitly acknowledges. Arabic, he says, was just as foreign to North Africa, an eighth-century introduction with no greater pretension to local rootedness than French. He takes advantage of the status of Tamazight, which then had no system of writing in common use, to argue that even the locals wrote in foreign languages: Amazigh writers had composed in Greek, Punic, Latin, and Arabic, and now French.[32] Once one removes oral literature from consideration, Amazigh cultures suddenly have no literary language of their own, and their spoken language is thus demoted to a purely "local idiom." Audisio does his best to deduce that there had been, up to then at least, no Algerian literature at all. This does indeed constitute an "imprecision" of exactly the sort the colonial administration routinely committed.

Having thus dismissed the country's literary production in Arabic and Tamazight, and shown that lack of nationhood led to lack of literature, Audisio turns to the colony's literature in French, the corpus he had no wish to explain away. Audisio says he wrote this article before the Allied landing in North Africa, and first published it in 1943. He uses this fact to explain his discretion on certain points of his argument, notably concerning Algeria's role in French literature between the end of Vichy rule south of the Mediterranean in November 1942 and the end of the occupation of

France in August 1944. During that time, he tells us in an afterword, he could not freely state the *mission spirituelle* of Algeria in maintaining the French national consciousness and in furthering the perennial "rayonnement de la littérature française dans le monde" [influence of French literature around the world].[33] Algiers was a well-known rendezvous for French writers fleeing the Occupation and the home of resistance literary journals like Max-Pol Fouchet's *Fontaine*, distributed illegally in France. No doubt Audisio could not speak much, in 1943, of the Algerian work of Gide, Saint-Exupéry, or Soupault. For Audisio, the place of this literature's production was irrelevant on one level, but highly significant on another: irrelevant because the literature itself was still French, whether produced in Algiers or Paris, but significant because it became a point of honor for the colony: "jamais on n'aura vu" [never has there been seen], he says, "dans une métropole un tel apport spirituel de ses enfants d'outre-mer" [such a spiritual contribution to a mother country by her children overseas].[34] This could happen, he believes, because "la littérature française prend son bien où elle le trouve, mais il n'y a qu'une littérature française, à Gonesse comme au Japon, à Bruxelles comme à Alger. Le jour où nous viendrait d'Algérie un *nouveau Discours de la méthode*, nous ne nous soucierions pas plus de le tenir pour algérien que l'autre pour hollandais." [French literature takes what it can where it can, but there is only one French literature, in Gonesse as in Japan, in Brussels as in Algiers. The day a new *Discourse on Method* comes to us from Algeria, we will no more think of considering it Algerian than we would consider the first one Dutch.][35] Audisio believes that national coherence is at once a precondition and a consequence of national literature. However, he also feels considerable ambivalence about what shape national literature might take (or even whether it might take shape at all) in Algeria. A suspicion of incoherence lurks behind the rhetoric of colonial Algeria as a "fusion of races"; his "proof" that there has been no real Algerian literature so far may result from his inability to talk about any mechanism for moving toward the fusion he proposed.

As he did with the semiclandestine literary production of wartime Algiers, Audisio chooses to annex Algerian literature to French: "de même que cette Histoire [de l'Algérie], comme il advint, avait osé figurer dans une collection des provinces de France, je veux espérer qu'on pourra découvrir ici les grands traits d'une province algérienne de *la* littérature" [just as this History of Algeria, as it happened, dared to figure in a collection of the provinces of France, I would like to hope that we will be able to discover here the outline of an Algerian province of Literature].[36] Algerian history is closely tied to the fate of Algerian literature, for it was in literature, as I have been arguing, that Algerian historiography took shape. Here, however, the discourses of colonial literature and history move toward different ends. Adisio's point is predicated on an Algerian history wholly subsumed into French history. The colony's history ends up taking a place among the histories of the regions making up France; Algerian literature, while still a province, may hope to end up part of *"la* littérature," the universal Literature that French writing supposedly represented. The question of national belonging is essential here. Audisio rejects the particularism of the Algerianist school, implying that it is based on parochialism, an "esprit de clocher ou de minaret": "Le temps de 'l'Algérie aux Algériens' est révolu. Il faut tout attendre du libre-échangisme dans les commerces de l'esprit." [The time of "Algeria for the Algerians" is over. We must hope for great things from free trade in the commerce of the mind.][37] A new generation of writers, Audisio hoped, was taking part in a humanist and universalist free-trade zone in the Mediterranean basin. This hope, more than any desire to belittle Algerian writing, led him to declare "des écrivains algériens, oui, une littérature algérienne, non" [Algerian writers, yes; an Algerian literature, no].[38] Regionalism, in his view, was over; it was time for French literature, led by its Algerian province, to enter into the currents of the Mediterranean.

This project does not exclude Arabs and Berbers writing in French: the line about the absence of "esprit de clocher ou de minaret" applies to them as much as to the Europeans. However, Audisio admits that there were still very few Muslims writing in French, and he suggests that blame for this lay with France's laxity in pursuing its alleged goal of cultural assimilation. However, his terms for evaluating literature by Arabs and Berbers pose problems from the outset. "Qui songerait sérieusement" [Who would seriously think], he asks, "à faire remonter une 'littérature algérienne' à l'écrivain arabe Ibn-Khaldoun, à l'écrivain latin Apulée, à l'écrivain grec Juba, à l'écrivain punique Hiempsal?" [of tracing an "Algerian literature" back to the Arabic writer Ibn Khaldūn, the Latin writer Apulius, the Greek writer Juba, or the Punic writer Hiempsal?][39] Although (pace Bertrand) there were no Latins, Greeks, or Punic people in Algeria to claim literary descendance from the Imazighen Apulius, Juba, or Hiempsal, quite a few Arabs and Imazighen writing in both French and Arabic would in fact consider all of them among the founders of their tradition. The failure of imagination represented by this rhetorical question would prevent Audisio from fully appreciating the work of even so widely recognized a writer as Gide's protégé, the Amazigh poet Jean Amrouche. Ultimately, Audisio himself would realize that the blindness he shared with many other Franco-Algerian intellectuals (not to mention *colons*) had already doomed the Algerian "fusion des races" by ignoring the cultural contributions of the largest group involved in it.

In one of his last "Mediterranean" publications, *Algérie méditerranée: feux vivants 1957*, Audisio reconsiders his literary positions in the midst of the Algerian war. He becomes convinced he has been behind the times in hoping for racial fusion during World War II; even in 1938, he had already been late since, he now realizes, the Centenary of 1930 was the last opportunity to solve the "moral problem" of Algeria.[40] Now he must admit defeat: "Si triste que m'en soit l'aveu, il me faut dissiper une illusion que j'ai longtemps partagée: l'illusion de ce qu'on appelle, ou appelait, la communauté algérienne. Quarante ans d'expérience et de réflexions aboutissent à cette conclusion décevante: la communauté algérienne n'a pratiquement jamais existé." [Sad as I am to admit it, I must dispel an illusion which I shared for a long time, the illusion of what we call, or rather called, the Algerian community. Forty years of experience and reflection lead to this disappointing conclusion: the Algerian community has practically never existed.][41] With the allusion to forty years of experience in Algeria, he seems to say "we knew, but it was always already too late" rather than "I told you so." He enumerates the causes of this failure (racial separation, and lack of mixed marriages or a common language) and reproaches the power dynamics blinding the European Algerians, himself perhaps included, who genuinely believed in the chimerical community: "je crains qu'ils l'aient confondue avec le paternalisme du bon patron" [I fear they confused it with the paternalism of the good boss].[42]

Despite this failure, when faced with the violence of the Algerian war and the other Mediterranean conflicts of the late 1940s and '50s (Greece, Cyprus, Israel, Egypt, Suez), Audisio continues to insist on a theme apparently no less chimerical than the "Algerian community": the power of the Mediterranean to "opérer la synthèse entre les croyances contradictoires, celle d'établir l'équilibre entre les forces opposées" [bring about a synthesis between contradictory beliefs, and to establish an equilibrium between opposing forces].[43] He appeals to people of good will, North African artists and intellectuals, to create the Mediterranean community for which he has hoped for forty years; his list of participants includes Assia Djebar, Jean Sénac, Taos Amrouche, Albert Memmi, Emmanuel Roblès, Mouloud Mammeri, Mohamed Dib, Kateb Yacine, and Driss Chraibi. He thus has the honor of being the first European critic to imagine Maghribi literature mostly by Maghribis, and to draw a cultural map of the region that reflected the actual makeup of the cohort of Algerian authors that had recently emerged. Despite his earlier inclusiveness, his conception of Mediterranean culture remained based on a binary opposition between East and West, exemplified by his maxim stated as late as 1958, "ex oriente lux, ex occidente lex" [out of the Orient, light; out of the Occident, law], a formula that seems to justify continued European rule.[44] Four years into the Algerian war and two years after Moroccan and Tunisian independence, he was once again too late; Ben Bella, Mohammed V, and Bourguiba were busily organizing a new political order on the south side of the Mediterranean. Ultimately, Audisio's Mediterranean could not survive much longer than Randau's Algeria; the advent of Arab nations with real power caused the collapse of a community unimaginable (at least by its inventor) without French cultural and political leadership. Moving France's center from Paris to Marseille was one thing; moving the Mediterranean's center from Marseille to Tunis or Cairo was quite another. At that point, Algerian literature would have truly ceased to be French, and that Audisio could not conceive.

ALBERT CAMUS AND THE COLLAPSE OF COLONIAL HISTORY

In *Algérie méditerranée*, Audisio's reference for insisting that the Greco-Roman Mediterranean still constituted the center of the world was a lecture by none other than Albert Camus. The lecture dated back to 1937 (another example of Audisio's tardiness), but the anachronism may not have been apparent: twenty years later, Camus still conceived of the Mediterranean and of Algeria in a French-dominated context. The preeminent thinker of his generation of Algerian-born writers, Camus grappled throughout his life with his relationship to the country, and his country's relationship to France. He possessed the lucidity never to pretend these relationships were anything other than painful. Despite his extreme sensitivity to other historic troubles, ranging from the Nazi Occupation to the Communist purges, he found that Algeria constituted the major source of pain and nostalgia in his life: "En ce qui concerne l'Algérie, j'ai toujours peur d'appuyer sur cette corde intérieure qui lui correspond en moi et dont je connais le chant aveugle et grave. Mais je puis bien dire au moins qu'elle est ma vraie patrie et qu'en n'importe quel lieu du monde, je reconnais ses fils et mes frères à ce rire d'amitié qui me prend devant eux." [In the case of Algeria, I am always afraid to touch the internal chord which corresponds to it in me, with a deep, blind sound I know. But I can at least say that it is my true country, and that no matter where I am in the world, I recognize her sons and my brothers by the laughter of friendship that seizes me with them.][45]

Several critics have noted Camus's silence regarding the Algerian war; this silence was more a matter of declared intentions than actual fact. Although he never addressed the war itself directly in a magisterial polemic or novel of the impact of *L'Homme révolté* [The Rebel] or *L'Étranger* [The Stranger] (both of which evoke the Algerian situation allusively), his silence regarding colonial politics and history was only relative. Well before the revolt he had published several short texts presenting his country in both evocative and argumentative terms: *L'Envers et l'endroit, Noces, Été,* and the famous investigative journalism of *Misère de la Kabylie.* The critic Alec Hargreaves points out that Camus's real silence came in the ten years between his World War II-era journalism (*Misère de la Kabylie* and his reports on Algeria's economic and political crisis in May of 1945 in *Combat*) and his polemics of 1955–1958.[46] Camus emerged from this first silence in the midst of the Algerian war to publish a short and combative series of articles, in *L'Express*; he complemented this journalistic activity with a serious political effort to bring about a "civil truce" to spare the lives of non-combatants by putting an end to terrorism by both sides.[47] When this effort came to nothing early in 1957, he collected all his articles on Algeria in *Actuelles III* (1958) and announced his silence in the Algerian debate. He nevertheless maintained a vigorous private campaign on behalf of Algerians sentenced to death or prison for political violence. Only in 1995 could the reading public discover what he had been working on from 1956 to his death in 1960: *Le Premier homme,* a novel specifically addressing the Algerian war and its antecedents.

Camus's politics in and out of Algeria have elicited a great deal of comment since Conor Cruise O'Brien's indictment of his silence; O'Brien argues that Camus could have helped rally antiwar opinion decisively, had he spoken out, especially with the international authority accorded him with the Nobel Prize in 1957.[48] David Carroll finds this an exaggeration of Camus's power, though he and most other critics agree that despite (or perhaps because of) his progressive calls for reform and his eventual demand for suppression of the colonial regime, Camus could not imagine an Algeria other than French.[49] Alec Hargreaves suggests that Camus's first silence resulted from his simply not having anything constructive to offer once assimilation had failed, as the riots of May 1945 clearly proved it had.[50] Whatever else one can say about Camus's position during the war, he was certainly very involved with both day-to-day events and far-reaching projects; his silences, the moments when he disappoints those looking for political solutions, stem from genuine pain and sense of loss, more than from any lack of courage or engagement. In a formulation all the more painful coming from a man suffering from tuberculosis, he wrote in 1955 that "j'ai mal à l'Algérie, en ce moment, comme d'autres ont mal aux poumons" [I have a pain in my Algeria at the moment, the way other people have pains in their lungs].[51] Of all the critics, certain post-independence Algerian scholars feel the disappointment in Camus the most acutely. Abdelkader Djeghloul notes that "On exige beaucoup de ceux qu'on aime" [One demands a great deal from those one loves], and explains his reproach: "si quelqu'un pouvait alors produire une réflexion assumant et intégrant le nationalisme algérien, c'était bien lui. Lui seul pouvait assurer la jonction avec les nationalistes. Il ne l'a pas fait. Voilà pourquoi notre rapport à lui est un rapport d'amour déçu" [if anyone could then have produced a position assuming and integrating Algerian nationalism, it was surely he. He alone could have made the connection with the nationalists. He did not do it. This is why our relationship with him is a relationship of disappointed love].[52] Camus, however, could have done no such thing; for systemic reasons he was incapable of producing any such reflection, and he knew it. His writings on Algeria constitute an investigation into the reasons behind this impossibility, reasons that also caused the failure of a culture unable to integrate the nationalist thinking of the majority.

Camus began his thinking on Algerian culture in the context of the colonial humanism embodied by the Mediterranean as conceived by Audisio and others. His commitment to Mediterranean cultural issues appeared as early as 1937 when he was earning a meager living as literary director of Edmond Charlot's publishing venture in Algiers. There, Camus and Emmanuel Roblès, a young novelist from Oran, edited a collection called "Méditerranéennes," reflecting in its title the heritage they wished to revive, or perhaps more accurately, to create. Charlot published a number of important texts in the development of Mediterranean humanism, notably works by Roblès and Camus themselves, as well as *Santa-Cruz*, by Camus's philosophy professor at the Lycée d'Alger, Jean Grenier.[53] Mediterranean humanism was distinctly fashionable: Grenier had opened Camus's eyes to it with *Les Iles*, Paul Valéry had just given a lecture in Algiers in April 1936 called "Impressions de Méditerranéen," and Audisio was in the middle of his most influential series of essays.[54] In the same year, 1937, Camus delivered a lecture as general secretary of the Maison de la Culture in Algiers, newly founded with money from the Communist Party. The lecture, Camus's first contribution to the debates around Mediterranean culture, appeared in the *Bulletin* of the Maison de la Culture, an ephemeral journal appropriately titled *Jeune Méditerranée*.

In laying out in his lecture the schematic of a cultural program he ascribes to the young group of artists and authors animating the Maison de la Culture, Camus shows considerably more political awareness than Audisio. Where *Jeunesse de la Méditerranée* had described the Mediterranean culture in terms fascists could easily recognize and appropriate, Camus specifically addresses and forestalls recuperation by the right wing. He notes the incongruity of leftist intellectuals speaking out in favor of a cultural project right-wing ideologues had already seized upon, and clarifies the true goals of his program:

Servir la cause d'un régionalisme méditerranéen peut sembler, en effet, restau-
rer un traditionalisme vain et sans avenir, ou encore exalter la supériorité d'une
culture par rapport à une autre et, par exemple reprenant le fascisme à rebours,
dresser les peuples latins contre les peuples nordiques. Il y a là un malentendu
perpétuel. Le but de cette conférence est d'essayer de l'éclaircir. Toute l'erreur
vient de ce qu'on confond Méditerranée et Latinité et de ce qu'on place à Rome
ce qui commença dans Athènes. Pour nous la chose est évidente, il ne peut s'a-
gir d'une sorte de nationalisme du soleil. Nous ne saurions nous asservir à des
traditions et lier notre avenir vivant à des exploits déjà morts.

[Serving the cause of Mediterranean regionalism may indeed seem to be
restoring a pointless and doomed traditionalism, or to be proclaiming the superiority of one culture in relation to another, and for example, taking up fascism in reverse, setting up the Latin peoples against the Nordic. This is a persistent misunderstanding. The goal of this lecture is to attempt to clarify it.
The whole problem comes from confusing Mediterranean and *Latinité*, and
from situating in Rome what began in Athens. For us the matter is clear, and
it cannot consist of a sort of sun-based nationalism. We cannot enslave ourselves to traditions, and tie our living future to exploits already dead.][55]

Camus follows Audisio in rejecting the conflation of Rome with the
Mediterranean, but he explains much more clearly his reasons for doing
so. He saw that this confusion allowed the Right to subvert a perfectly
credible leftist project intended to develop what he considers the true goal
of Mediterranean humanism: not the imposition of Latin values, but the
meeting of east and west in "Mediterranean collectivism." For Camus, the
Mediterranean constitutes an avenue toward a particular kind of collectivism that would differ significantly from the Soviet version. Everything
rests on this regional difference. Under Camus's secretariat, the Maison de
la Culture aimed to work regionally; Camus declares that "Nous voulons
seulement aider un pays à s'exprimer lui-même. Localement." [We only
want to help a country express itself. Locally.][56] Camus's biographer
Roger Grenier suggests that the author's "Mediterranean collectivism"
was probably an early sign of his deviation from the Communist line; Camus left the Party shortly thereafter, so Grenier's argument is certainly
tenable.[57] Camus's lecture, however, seems unconcerned with Communist orthodoxy or heresy. In his view, the Mediterranean rises above ideologies, overpowering and transforming them into local products:
"Chaque fois qu'une doctrine a rencontré le bassin méditerranéen, dans le
choc d'idées qui en est résulté, c'est toujours la Méditerranée qui est restée
intacte, le pays qui a vaincu la doctrine." [Every time a doctrine has met
the Mediterranean basin, it is always the Mediterranean which has remained intact in the clash of ideas which resulted; the country has
vanquished the doctrine.][58] As evidence for this claim, Camus cites two

examples, both in the enemy camp, from a Communist point of view: Christianity and Fascism. While never showing the slightest sympathy for the ideologies themselves, he finds that Roman Catholicism and Italian Fascism, humanized by contact with the Mediterranean, at least allow citizens of the basin to live full and colorful lives, unlike Nazism, which only crushed the people.

Camus could have cited another ideology in this context, but chose not to: Islam. His silence regarding Algeria's major religion may result more from a sense of ignorance regarding Islamic history than anything else. Camus does not consider Islam as a coherent and free-standing ideology of its own, but rather as part of the Mediterranean atmosphere, an unlocalizable "feeling" he tries to capture in evocative details of Mediterranean cities: "[La Méditerranée] n'est pas classique et ordonnée, elle est diffuse et turbulente, comme ces quartiers arabes ou ces ports de Gênes et de Tunisie. Ce goût triomphant de la vie, ce sens de l'écrasement et de l'ennui, les places désertes à midi en Espagne, la sieste, voilà la vraie Méditerranée et c'est de l'Orient qu'elle se rapproche. Non de l'Occident latin. L'Afrique du Nord est un des seuls pays ou l'Orient et l'Occident cohabitent" [The Mediterranean is neither classical nor ordered; it is diffuse and turbulent, like the Arab quarters or the ports of Genoa or Tunisia. This triumphant taste for life, this sense of ennui and of being crushed, the deserted squares at midday in Spain, the siesta, this is the true Mediterranean, and it comes close to the Orient. Not to the Latin West. North Africa is one of the only countries where the West cohabits with the Orient.][59] Peter Dunwoodie notes that cohabitation does not mean fusion, and in fact Camus sheds little light on the terms of this cohabitation.[60] He simply asserts that North Africans (*nous*) are all the more prepared for the task of rehabilitating the Mediterranean after its usurpation by the political right, because "nous sommes en contact immédiat de cet Orient qui peut tant nous apprendre à cet égard" [we are in immediate contact with this orient which can teach us so much regarding this].[61] The Mediterranean "qui nous entoure de sourires, de soleil et de mer" [which surrounds us with smiles, sun, and sea] teaches Camus to "rattacher la culture à la vie" [join culture with life]; he imagines that Arabs have much more direct contact with life's essentials.[62] This idea had inspired several generations of exoticists before Camus and represents at the very least a highly essentialized (if not outright tendentious) view of one of the cultural components he advanced as part of the Mediterranean's strength. Furthermore, when Camus enumerates the places where he sees the *vérité méditerranéenne* emerging, he leaves Arab and Amazigh cultures out: "1. unité linguistique—facilité d'apprendre une langue latine lorsqu'on en sait une autre—: 2. unité d'origine—collectivisme prodigieux du Moyen-Age—ordre des chevaliers, ordre des religieux, féodalités, etc." [1. Linguistic unity—ease of learning one Romance language when one knows another—: 2. unity of origin—prodigious collectivism of the Middle Ages —order of knights, order of monks, feudalisms, etc.][63] Here, Mediterranean history contains no Muslims, except as the unmentioned historic enemy of the knights and monks; furthermore, excluding the difficulties of learning Arabic or Tamazight certainly facilitates linguistic unity. Clearly, the Muslims who take part in this Mediterranean culture will have to become French Muslims.[64] Camus and the Maison de la Culture had as much trouble as Audisio proposing workable bases for a Mediterranean unity as inclusive as they hoped in their initial rhetoric.

In spite of these limitations, the Mediterranean would act as a useful rallying point for progressives of several flavors. It offered a way of rethinking the *cité*, in the French sense, that of the civic unit. The idea of a Mediterranean Algeria led its proponents to reconsider who had *droit de cité*, the right to be present in the civic space. This reconsideration came with a perception of the need for common ground in the Mediterranean cityscape. The second number of *Jeune Méditerranée* contains an appeal and petition in favor of the Projet Blum-Violette (already defeated in the Assemblée), which would have granted civil rights to some nonnaturalized Muslims. Here at least the project of Mediterranean unity demanded the political participation of Arabs and Imazighen. The inaugural issue of the review also reflected the trend of rethinking the *cité*, both in its ethnic content and in its urban fabric. Camus's essay appeared under the rubric "Culture indigène," as if the editors (or Camus himself) meant it as a contribution to the study or promotion of that culture, even though it did little to advance the Arabs or Imazighen. Read differently, the heading might also suggest a broadening of the notion of *indigène* to include anybody born around the shores of the Mediterranean. Twenty years later, Camus would declare that the *pieds-noirs* were just as much *indigènes* as the Arabs and Imazighen.[65] The contestatory context of that assertion made during the war renders difficult its retroactive application in 1937, when *indigène* still unquestionably meant non-Europeans; however, calling Camus's essay a work on *culture indigène* at least invites a reconsideration of the ethnic makeup of the Mediterranean *cité*.

The editors of *Jeune Méditerranée* had something to say about that city's physical texture as well. Camus's article followed immediately an interview with the architect Le Corbusier, presented in the following terms: "La Maison de la culture a décidé d'appuyer de toutes ses forces la campagne du grand architecte Le Corbusier en faveur de l'habitat méditerranéen'" [The Maison de la culture has decided to give its full support to the campaign of the great architect Le Corbusier in favor of the 'Mediterranean habitat'].[66] In the interview they reprint, Le Corbusier responds to a question about what contemporary political system was most favorable to the architect by asserting that all systems and ideologies are irrelevant if only the architect can draw up a compelling and technically feasible plan. In his desire to generalize his own system, he does not mention Mediterranean specificity. His assertion of the irrelevance of politics reminds readers of Audisio's statement that Mediterranean dynamism could flourish under almost any political regime; unfortunately, we do not have any direct response to the architect's ideas from Camus. The architectural historian Michèle Lamprakos has shown how Le Corbusier, in promotional drawings for the Obus plans for restructuring Algiers, placed the city at the intersection of two axes: that of the Mediterranean, and that of Greater France, running from Dunkerque to Tamanrasset.[67] His designs provided the architectural echo to the literary projects of the young Algiers intellectuals. The Obus plans supported a view of Algiers and the Mediterranean as parts of the French cultural domain, making little concession to Arab needs. Le Corbusier tended to propose grand and apparently inclusive plans, such as his idea for an enormous viaduct looping gracefully along the crest of the ridge above Algiers and linking isometrically sited housing blocks, but his designs took little account of the colonized majority. His viaduct would have crushed the Casbah visually and isolated it physically; Le Corbusier's concept of Mediterranean culture may have been considerably more dominated by Europeans than Camus's. It certainly contained next to no concession whatever to history, whether in architectural idioms or in local patterns of use of space, both of which would become important for Camus.

HISTORY AND THE CITIES WITHOUT A PAST

Camus's other texts of the 1935–1938 period (coincident with his beginnings in the theater, and before the composition of *L'Étranger* as published) take up the Mediterranean cultural construction almost as regularly as Audisio, and in much more complex ways. Camus uses reflections on the Mediterranean to think through the early phases of a long argument against the notion of orderly or teleological historical progress, part of the argument which would help separate him first from the Communists and later from Sartre. In considering his own relationship to the Mediterranean, Camus comes to muse on his personal history, which he considers formative, and on national history, which he finds more arbitrary than teleological. Whereas Audisio suggests a Greek thesis, Roman antithesis, and Algero-Mediterranean synthesis, Camus rejects any notion of progress or ends for history. For him, a personal relationship to the landscape and its past quickly becomes far more important. This does not mean that he disengaged in any way from historical processes going on in Algeria in the late thirties; on the contrary, Mediterranean introspection seems to have favored Camus's energetic Algerian engagement, in which his commitment to social causes first emerged. In addition to *L'Envers et l'endroit*, *Noces*, and the early essays of *L'Été*, Camus also published articles in *Alger Républicain* defending the Cheikh el-Okbi, accused of complicity in the murder of the imam of Algiers, and the civil servant Hodent, accused of corruption in a trumped-up affair to discredit progressive reforms in rural administration.[68] Following these two affairs, Camus wrote *Misère de la Kabylie*, a trenchant and accusatory series of investigative articles that the Algerian administration would not forgive. After closing down *Alger Républicain* and its ephemeral younger sibling *Le Soir Républicain*, the administration made it very difficult for Camus to find work in the colony; after a short stay in Oran, he embarked for France on the eve of World War II, in search of a cure for his tuberculosis and underemployment. His engagement with the Algerian politics had resulted directly in exile from his personal Mediterranean.

For Camus, the Mediterranean represented a constant tension between exile from and repatriation to his childhood. His first sense of this would come during a trip away from the Mediterranean basin, the disastrous holiday in central Europe in 1936 during which he and his first wife separated; "La Mort dans l'âme" describes his sense of estrangement and exile in Prague, before returning thankfully to the Mediterranean.[69] The city of his youth, still inhabited by his mother, becomes the regional locus of nostalgia for Camus, who situates his longing between exile and return: "S'il est vrai que les seuls paradis sont ceux qu'on a perdus, je sais comment nommer ce quelque chose de tendre et d'inhumain qui m'habite aujourd'hui. Un émigrant revient dans sa patrie. Et moi, je me souviens. Ironie, raidissement, tout se tait et me voici rapatrié." [If it is true that the only paradises are those that we have lost, I know what to call this tender and inhuman thing which lives in me today. An emigrant returns to his country. And I remember. Irony, stiffening, everything falls silent, and here I am, repatriated.][70] This passage introduces a much longer one repeating the formula "here I am, repatriated," as the narrator sits in an Arab coffee shop "tout au bout de la ville arabe" [at the very end of the Arab city], looking out over the port and its lighthouses, and recalling his childhood home in Belcourt, at the opposite end of the city.[71] Like several generations of exoticists, Camus chose the heavily used setting of a *café maure* for his nostalgia; however, his sensations are those of identification rather than of the social estrangement which romantically inspired exoticists felt when frequenting such places. His regrets focus not on the paradise lost of exotic dreams, but on his own childhood, which the port of Algiers brings back in a very concrete way, beckoning to him with its beacons to a returning emigrant. His nostalgia is not at all restorative: he never mentions wishing to bring back the paradise he has lost.

In his emigrant's return, Camus finds his memory taking physical shape in the port and waterfront, in his old neighborhood, and in the building in which he grew up. The closer he gets to home, his mother's apartment in the rue de Lyon, the closer he comes literally to incorporating the memories evoked:

> Et me voici rapatrié. Je pense à un enfant qui vécut dans un quartier pauvre. Ce quartier, cette maison! Il n'y avait qu'un étage et les escaliers n'étaient pas éclairés. Maintenant encore, après de longues années, il pourrait y retourner en pleine nuit. Il sait qu'il grimperait l'escalier à toute vitesse sans trébucher une seule fois. Son corps même est imprégné de cette maison. Ses jambes conservent en elles la mesure exacte de la hauteur des marches. Sa main, l'horreur instinctive, jamais vaincue, de la rampe d'escalier. Et c'était à cause des cafards.

> [Here I am, repatriated. I am thinking of a child who lived in a poor neighborhood. This neighborhood, this house! It had only one upper floor, and the stairs were not lit. Even now, after many years, he could return there in the middle of the night. He knows that he could climb the stair at full speed without even once stumbling. His very body is impregnated with this house. His legs remember the exact measure of the height of the steps. His hand, the instinctive, never-vanquished horror of the handrail. It was because of the cockroaches.][72]

The repetition of the first sentence suggests a doubled repatriation, a mirror effect of a dream in two stages: the return first to the city and the *patrie*, and second, to the home and the mother. Even the final grotesque details find their expression in the narrator's body, "impregnated" and made fertile by the physical memory of his childhood home in all its particularities. Physical space thus becomes lodged in memory via its presence in the body.

Camus was quite as fascinated with the physical beauty and pleasures of the body as Audisio; he links the idealized body of the young Mediterranean man both to physical memory—as at the apartment in Belcourt—and to the physical city, as in the houses in the Casbah:

> Quand on va pendant l'été aux bains du port, on prend conscience, d'un passage simultané de toutes les peaux du blanc au doré, puis au brun, et pour finir à une couleur tabac qui est à la limite extrême de l'effort de transformation dont le corps est capable. Le port est dominé par le jeu de cubes blancs de la Kasbah. Quand on est au niveau de l'eau, sur le fond blanc cru de la ville arabe, les corps déroulent une frise cuivrée. Et, à mesure qu'on avance dans le mois d'août et que le soleil grandit, le blanc des maisons se fait plus aveuglant et les peaux prennent une chaleur plus sombre. Comment alors ne pas s'identifier à ce dialogue de la pierre et de la chair à la mesure du soleil et des saisons?

[When you go to swim at the port in summer you become aware of a simultaneous progression of all skins from white to golden to tanned, ending up in a tobacco color which marks the extreme limit of the effort of transformation of which the body is capable. Above the harbor stands the set of white cubes of the Kasbah. When you are at water level, against the sharp white background of the Arab town the bodies form a copper-colored frieze. And as one moves into the month of August and the sun grows, the white of the houses becomes more blinding and skins take on a darker warmth. How can one fail to identify, then, with that dialogue of stone and flesh in tune with the sun and the seasons?][73]

Seen from the water level of the Mediterranean, these bodies unified by the effects of the sun become an architectural feature, a frieze displayed across the Casbah; the reference to classicism and the association of stark white and bronze calls to mind Greece, the root of the Mediterranean tradition for the Algiers intellectuals. Yet in 1939 readers still knew the Casbah as the focal point of exoticist description, still the symbol of the ethnic and cultural alterity of Algiers.[74] To integrate this intrusion of Arab history, the bodies of European Algerians must tan and darken to the limit of their pigmentation, to become "typically" Mediterranean, the stereotypical olive-skinned men. They also become more like the imagined complexion of the Arabs; at the outer limit of its transformation under the Mediterranean sun, the European boys can figure, indeed replace, the Arabs, otherwise absent from the description. Camus avoids any notion of the specificity of the people who might actually inhabit the Casbah; he lets the reader believe that the working-class boys swimming in the harbor are undifferentiated, simply citizens of Algiers. Like the earlier passages of corporal identification with physical space, this paragraph is about nostalgia for the city of childhood, and not about the power relations necessarily involved in history. Elsewhere Camus speaks of the Mediterranean's "terres antiques où tout est à la mesure de l'homme" [ancient lands where everything is to the measure of man]; yet in the city measured against the (transformed) European body, there is no sense of the antique.[75] The passage of time registers instead like changing seasons, in a mode if anything the very opposite of history.

A more specific engagement with history nonetheless appears in other texts written around 1938–1939 but not published in volume until 1954, in the collection *L'Été*.[76] Camus, choosing a city in which to meditate on history in the essays in *L'Été*, picks Oran, the city where he finds no visible history. He was not the first to register this void; Oran's neglect by visitors looking for picturesque remnants of the past began in the mid-nineteenth century with its first French visitors.[77] Urban archaeologists would have found as much to do in Oran as in any other Algerian city, but most writers treated it as a place with no history. This may have had something to do with the relative scarcity of Arabs, a minority of the population, and of visible precolonial structures, mostly present in decorative elements and recent imitations. Colonial historiography often denied Arabs any historical evolution, embodying a sort of preoriginal state of colonial society, a "before" to colonialism's "after." Yet despite their status as an ahistorical people, colonial history needed them as a precondition to its discourse of progress. Progress, after all, must be measured against something, and this was a primary function of the Arabs in colonial histories. Lacking such measures, Oran may have presented little history to its viewers.

Camus places small faith in colonial progress, and wishing to avoid notions of historical teleology, ends up evacuating Oran of any history at all.[78] Only half ironically, Camus describes his own relationship to the city, which, like all loyal citizens of Algiers, he dislikes; he nonetheless admits to needing its very bareness, its desertlike sterility:

> où trouver la solitude nécessaire à la force, la longue respiration où l'esprit se rassemble et le courage se mesure? Il reste les grandes villes. Simplement, il y faut encore des conditions.
>
> Les villes que l'Europe nous offre sont trop pleines des rumeurs du passé. Une oreille exercée peut y percevoir des bruits d'ailes, une palpitation d'âmes. On y sent le vertige des siècles, des révolutions, de la gloire. On s'y souvient que l'Occident s'est forgé dans les clameurs. Cela ne fait pas assez de silence.
>
> Paris est souvent un désert pour le coeur, mais à certaines heures, du haut du Père-Lachaise, souffle un vent de révolution qui remplit soudain ce désert de drapeaux et de grandeurs vaincues. . . . Descartes, ayant à méditer, choisit son désert: la ville la plus commerçante de son époque. . . . On peut avoir moins d'ambition et la même nostalgie. Mais Amsterdam, depuis trois siècles, s'est couverte de musées. Pour fuir la poésie et retrouver la paix des pierres, il faut d'autres déserts, d'autres lieux sans âme et sans recours. Oran est l'un de ceux-là.

[where can one find the solitude necessary to vigor, the deep breath in which the mind collects itself and courage gauges its strength? There remain big cities. Simply, certain conditions are required.

The cities Europe offers us are too full of the din of the past. A practiced ear can make out the flapping of wings, a fluttering of souls. The giddy whirl of centuries, of revolutions, of fame can be felt there. There one cannot forget that the West was forged in a series of uproars. All that does not make for enough silence.

Paris is often a desert for the heart, but at certain moments from the heights of Père-Lachaise there blows a revolutionary wind that suddenly fills that desert with flags and fallen glories. . . . Descartes, planning to meditate, chose his desert: the most mercantile city of his era. . . . It is possible to have less ambition and the same nostalgia. But during the last three centuries Amsterdam has spawned museums. In order to flee poetry and yet recapture the peace of stones, other deserts are needed, other spots without soul and without reprieve. Oran is one of these.][79]

Camus treats history as an intrusive noise; he needs a place where the revolutions of Paris (and of Western history generally) will let him work in peace. Oran's historical silence provides such a space. Camus's relief at being in such a city may have resulted from the frustrations which vestiges of past revolutions present to a leftist from the colony, who knows that the colonial city does its best to make revolution impossible. He speaks quite literally when he refers to the "desert in Oran"; for him, the city is not the site of civilization, but of wilderness. All the details in his physical portrait (sand, rocks, dust, violent weather, heat) concur to make Oran an urban Sahara in miniature. Camus's self-inscription in the Algerian city is personal and corporeal in Algiers, and collective and historical in Oran. The city has no such *lieux de mémoire*, and seems to have nothing to remember, nor any desire for recollection. This is exactly what appeals to Camus, who distrusts the histories endorsed by museums, flags, and official commemorations.

Camus's left-handed compliment to the city so devoid of historical or cultural movement soon turns into an indictment of its overall aspect in both architecture and urban plan. He perceives Oran's ugliness in contrast with the natural beauty of a stunning site: the hills, cliffs, and sea views on which the city turns its back. Oran is less a Mediterranean city connected to an open horizon and universalizing past than its nightmarish opposite, the closed and claustrophobic space of Mediterranean architecture gone wrong, the Cretan labyrinth:

Forcés de vivre devant un admirable paysage, les Oranais ont triomphé de cette redoutable épreuve en se couvrant de constructions bien laides. On s'attend à une ville ouverte sur la mer, lavée, rafraîchie par la brise des soirs. Et, mis à part le quartier espagnol, on trouve une cité qui présente le dos à la mer, qui s'est construite en tournant sur elle-même, à la façon d'un escargot. Oran est un grand mur circulaire et jaune, recouvert d'un ciel dur. Au début, on erre dans le labyrinthe, on cherche la mer comme le signe d'Ariane. Mais on tourne en rond dans des rues fauves et oppressantes, et, à la fin, le Minotaure dévore les Oranais: c'est l'ennui. Depuis longtemps, les Oranais n'errent plus. Ils ont accepté d'être mangés.

[Obliged to live facing a wonderful landscape, the people of Oran have overcome this fearful ordeal by covering their city with very ugly constructions. One expects to find a city open to the sea, washed and refreshed by the evening breeze. And aside from the Spanish quarter, one finds a walled town that turns its back to the sea, that has been built by turning back on itself like a snail. Oran is a great circular yellow wall covered over with a leaden sky. In the beginning one wanders in the labyrinth, seeking the sea like the sign of Ariadne. But one turns round and round in pale and oppressive streets, and eventually the Minotaur devours the people of Oran: the Minotaur is boredom. For some time the citizens of Oran have given up wandering. They have accepted being eaten.][80]

Instead of evoking the ancient sources of Mediterranean culture with a hero, like Audisio's Ulysses, Camus chooses to evoke it with a horror, the labyrinth's inhuman architecture of boredom and fear, which swallowed those who entered. Oran's "circular wall" and "harsh streets" do the work of both labyrinth and Minotaur, devouring the cowed inhabitants. Audisio's Mediterranean was a vision of an open horizon and the freedom to set out from port to port; Camus's Oran is a closed city cut off both from its port (situated a few kilometers down the coast at Mers-el-Kebir) and from the sea in general, a city in which the only possible movement turns in circles.

Camus finds this environment oddly stimulating; both here and in his "Petit guide pour des villes sans passé," he shows himself ironically charmed by the kitsch and gracelessness which the absence of history seems to entail. Nonetheless, regional history does poke through the urban fabric of Oran, despite the failure of official *lieux de mémoire*. "Minotaure" records this failure of official commemorations and the substitution of a locally produced historical vision:

De monuments, Oran ne manque guère. La ville a son compte de maréchaux d'Empire, de ministres et de bienfaiteurs locaux. On les rencontre sur des petites places poussiéreuses, résignés à la pluie comme au soleil, convertis eux aussi à la pierre et à l'ennui. Mais ils représentent cependant des apports extérieurs. Dans cette heureuse barbarie, ce sont les marques regrettables de la civilisation.

Oran, au contraire, s'est élevé à elle-même ses autels et ses rostres . . . les Oranais ont médité d'y bâtir, dans le sable et la chaux, une image convaincante de leurs vertus: la Maison du Colon. Si l'on en juge par l'édifice, ces vertus sont au nombre de trois: la hardiesse dans le goût, l'amour de la violence, et le sens des synthèses historiques. L'Egypte, Byzance et Munich ont collaboré à la délicate construction d'une patisserie figurant une énorme coupe renversée. Des pierres multicolores, du plus vigoureux effet, son venues encadrer le toit. La vivacité de ces mosaiques est si persuasive qu'au premier abord on ne voit rien, qu'un éblouissement informe. Mais de plus près, et l'attention éveillée, on voit qu'elles ont un sens: un gracieux colon, à noeud papillon et à casque de liège blanc, y reçoit l'hommage d'un cortège d'esclaves vetus à l'antique.

[Oran hardly lacks monuments. The city has its quota of imperial marshals, ministers, and local benefactors. They are found on dusty little squares, resigned to rain and sun, they too converted to stone and boredom. But in any case, they represent contributions from the outside. In that happy barbary they are the regrettable marks of civilization.

Oran, on the other hand, has raised her altars and rostra to her own honor. . . . The people of Oran conceived the idea of building solidly a convincing image of their virtues: the Maison du Colon. To judge from the edifice, those virtues are three in number: boldness in taste, love of violence, and a feeling for historical syntheses. Egypt, Byzantium, and Munich collaborated in the delicate construction of a piece of pastry in the shape of an upside-down glass. Multicolored stones, most vigorous in effect, have been brought in to outline the roof. These mosaics are so exuberantly persuasive that at first you see nothing but an amorphous brilliance. But with a closer view and your attention called to it, you discover that they have a meaning: a graceful colonist, wearing a bow tie and white pith helmet, is receiving the homage of a procession of slaves dressed in classical style.][81]

We can understand the irrelevance of Empire heroes in a country replete with military men of its own; however, even the pillars of the local community are less commemorated than petrified with dust and boredom. Oran ignored both the importation of heroes and the imposition of their mode of figuration, and the city raised its own monument whose historical significance Camus gently ironizes (see figure 5.1). By highlighting the "most vigorous effect," "liveliness," and "shapeless dazzle," he points out

Figure 5.1. Oran, the Maison du Colon and its frieze of slaves. Fonds documentaire Editions J. Gandini.

kitsch with euphemism. Egypt and Byzantium suggest the architectural malapropisms on which overdone *Arabisance* design fed; the presence of Munich on the list of inspirations suggest the political overtones of this architectural nonsense. The Maison du Colon housed the agricultural cooperatives that dominated the Algerian economy; most of them were highly conservative, in a city known for right-wing politics. If the building reminded Camus of Munich, this is scarcely coincidental in 1939. The mosaics demonstrate the vision of the colony that this "historical synthesis" of ancient Mediterranean and modern fascist architecture produced: slavery, only slightly disguised by the period costume of the slaves and the ridiculous bow tie of the *colon*. Since pictorial convention had inured viewers to seeing Arabs portrayed in robes like ancient Greeks or Hebrews, these "ancient" slaves easily stood in for contemporary *indigènes*.[82] In a footnote Camus says that "Une autre des qualités de la race algérienne est, on le voit, la franchise" ["Another quality of the Algerian race is, as you see, candor"].[83] He had an opportunity to feel the effects of this frankness; Emmanuel Roblès relates that Camus carefully preserved the stack of anonymous letters and threats he received from the citizens of Oran after publishing his essay. He acknowledged these protests in a note to the 1954 edition, the last version published in his lifetime, and concluded by saying "Oran désormais n'a plus besoin d'écrivains: elle attend des touristes" ["Oran has no further need of writers: she is awaiting tourists"].[84] Several months before the outbreak of the war, the irony was not yet apparent.

In the period between 1945 and the Algerian war, Camus's inability to think of Algeria outside France began to appear more strikingly than before. In April 1945, Camus spent three weeks on private visits in Algeria, returning to Paris before 8 May, date of victory for the Allies and sign of future defeat for French Algeria.[85] That day, a march in Sétif in the province of Constantine turned into a nationalist demonstration followed by riots, in which nearly 130 European Algerians were killed. The army, air force, and vigilante groups of *colons* moved into the hill country; conservatively estimated, their victims numbered about fifteen thousand Muslims.[86] On his return to Paris, Camus published a short series of articles in *Combat*, titled "Crise en Algérie."[87] The series began on 13 May, and given the extreme reticence of the press in relating the events of the fortnight following the riot, Camus may not yet have known the extent of the tragedy. Once he did, however, he had no substantive comment. Camus does ridicule those who blamed the nationalist leader Ferhat Abbas, but he attributes the riots to Algeria's economic misery rather than to any genuine or justified nationalist sentiment. Rather than admit the presence of a national identity counter to the French, Camus declares the absence of one favorable to them: "J'ai lu dans un journal du matin que 80% des

Arabes désiraient devenir des citoyens français. Je résumerai au contraire l'état actuel de la politique algérienne en disant qu'ils le désiraient effectivement, mais qu'il ne le désirent plus." [I read in a morning paper that 80 percent of the Arabs wish to become French citizens. I will on the contrary summarize the current situation of Algerian politics by saying that indeed they used to want it, but that they do not want it anymore.][88] For Camus, this rueful realization of the failure of assimilation undoubtedly represented despair and the collapse of a dream, but it scarcely satisfies as a response to thousands of deaths by strafing, arson, torture, and summary execution. His articles make matters worse by calling for a "second conquest" of Algeria; he clearly insists on peaceful means, a campaign to improve radically the economic and political lot of Arab Algerians, but his term echoes that used by the government and admits of no genuine change in the colony's status.[89] No complete picture of Camus's Algerian writings can obscure this problem with his thinking.

COLONIAL SICKNESSES: *LA PESTE* AND HISTORICAL REPRESENTATION

The articles in *Combat*, however, were not Camus's last word on the colonial history that could draw no adequate lessons from events like those of Sétif. In *La Peste* [*The Plague*] (1947, trans. 1948), he thinks through this history much more thoroughly and radically than in his previous political journalism. Something very similar to his earlier perception of Oran as a city without history caused him to select it as the setting for *La Peste*. The narrator devotes the first two pages of his story to explaining the city's ordinariness, and the consequent sense among its inhabitants that the events of the plague "n'y étaient pas à leur place, sortant un peu de l'ordinaire" ["were misplaced there, since they deviated somewhat from the ordinary"].[90] The fictional Oran had never felt need of a historian, and the city reflected neither on its history nor the physical setting which expressed and contextualized it. The citizens of this "entirely modern" city live without a thought for the natural beauty of the site, or for the signs of time passing around them, because in Oran, these signs are practically invisible: "Comment faire imaginer, par exemple, une ville sans pigeons, sans arbres et sans jardins, ou l'on ne rencontre ni battements d'ailes ni froissements de feuilles, un lieu neutre pour tout dire? Le changement des saisons ne s'y lit que dans le ciel." ["How can one convey, for example, the idea of a town without pigeons, without trees or gardens, where you hear no beating of wings or rustling of leaves, in short, a neutral place? The change of season can only be detected in the sky."][91] Oran is the perfect "anywhere" for the historically unthinkable to happen. For that is what the plague represents: the event for which history did not prepare the observer, the event so singular and catastrophic that it cannot be witnessed and represented ordinarily, and is received as "historically impossible."[92]

Several critics have read *La Peste* as a parable about the difficulties of representing the unpredictable or unimaginable: for Roger Grenier, the Occupation, and for Shoshana Felman, the Holocaust.[93] An array of details support both ideas: the way the authorities cut Oran off from the rest of the world, the use of force to back up a well-organized and meticulous administrative machine, the establishment of camps, the trains carrying corpses, the cremation of victims, etc. Having accumulated all this detail, Camus's narrator Rieux and the other sympathetic characters must try to draw from it some understanding of the enormous event that has overtaken them. Rieux is among the first to acknowledge the reality of this unthinkable return of the plague, one of history's ghouls. He is nearly alone at first, as the authorities remain incredulous for some time, essentially denying that the series of "grave events" make up more than a day-to-day chronicle, or that they are indeed signs of history's power to impose seemingly arbitrary forces on unsuspecting populations.

Felman has called *La Peste* a "monument to witnessing," a story of how to relate the unthinkable, how to tell the untellable. Rieux, with his careful third-person "objective" voice, is convinced of the need for a survivor to relate what happened to the population of sufferers, so many of whom have been definitively silenced.[94] However, there is one "detail" neither Rieux's testimony nor the story itself can relate, one ultimate "untellable": the Arabs. *La Peste* reduces the Arab population of Oran to a detail, which it then cannot represent. Arabs, apart from one explicit reference and two allusions (again couched in terms of details, this time of the urban layout of Oran), are totally absent. These allusions, occurring in conversations often cited by critics in which Rieux's interlocutors reveal essential characteristics, refer to buildings and streets, rather than to people. Rambert asks for help in escaping the city during a walk through the "quartier nègre" ["African quarter"], "curieusement solitaire" ["oddly deserted"] and empty of inhabitants.[95] Tarrou recounts his childhood on a roof terrace adjoining its neighbors across an entire quarter in the Arab manner; the house, however, belongs to a poor pensioner of unspecified origin. The narrator makes nothing of what the Arab references of these surroundings imply; neither does he comment specifically on the emptiness they evoke. Even the one direct reference, to the journalist Rambert's investigation of public health among the Arabs, goes no further: Rambert quickly forgets his reporting in his haste to leave Oran. The Arab presence is really an absence; even the concierges in Rieux's neighborhood seem to be Spanish.

In examining the reasons and consequences of this absence, one finds few answers. True, a casual visitor to Oran's center might actually not have noticed any Arabs: the city's population contained so many Spanish residents that other ethnic groups, truly numerical minorities, tended to disappear. Recourse to this historical fact cannot explain everything, however, since the other major Franco-Algerian author writing about Oran, Camus's friend Emmanuel Roblès, did notice the Arabs and wrote about them.[96] Furthermore, *La Peste* does much more than represent the social reality of colonial Oran; everything in the introduction to the story tends to universalize the narration, and to prepare readers for a metaphysical lesson drawn from the experience of a town which is "rien de plus qu'une préfecture française de la côte algérienne" ["nothing more than a French Prefecture on the coast of Algeria"].[97] Nothing more, but also nothing less: the very fact of its setting in a French prefecture on the Algerian coast poses problems for a universalizing reading. Even allegorical readings focused on concerns far from Algeria tend to see *La Peste*'s allegory as a historical one; Felman's reading provides a good example. As such, historical allusions inevitably present difficulties. Did Camus find the Arabs too insignificant to figure in a story he wished to universalize? If we believe this, we could take slightly anachronistic advantage of the racial slur in the term *ratonnade* [rat hunt], and see the Arab presence in the story figured by the rats, who die off in droves before the European population is affected, and which the administration sees as the principal vector of infection.[98] A discourse of hygiene, infection, pest control, and policing becomes intelligible in all its sinister implications: the rats and their dangerous fleas pollute parts of town which did not tolerate their presence; as the infection moves into better neighborhoods, citizens demand that police quarantine the slums and allow only essential workers to leave them, thus conflating rats and humans. The Algerian press before World War II routinely printed complaints about "flea-ridden" Arabs "polluting" French public space; the public already knew the language of the *cordon sanitaire* evoked in *La Peste* when a navy officer describes the concentration camp for *indigènes* during an epidemic in Cairo, where guards shot at anyone who tried to cross the surrounding no-man's-land.[99]

This explanation merits consideration, in spite of its bleakness; proposing another should neither completely discredit it nor make it disappear. Nor should it disavow Felman's reading of the novel that has informed my discussion so far. The other reading indicates a serious failure of *La Peste*, by suggesting that the narration of a historical allegory is incapable of representing a group condemned to silence and subhumanity. A supplementary reading might apply David Carroll's characterization of Camus's Algerian writing as not a "failure of literature," but rather a "powerful and compelling 'literature of failure.'"[100] The only passage in which the narration mentions the Arabs by name reads as a commentary *en abyme* on their exclusion, an analysis of a failure of representation:

[Rambert] alla droit au but. Il enquêtait pour un grand journal de Paris sur les conditions de vie des Arabes et voulait des renseignements sur leur état sanitaire. Rieux lui dit que cet état n'était pas bon. Mais il voulait savoir, avant d'aller plus loin, si le journaliste pouvait dire la vérité.
—Certes, dit l'autre.
—Je veux dire: pouvez-vous porter condamnation totale?
—Totale, non, il faut bien le dire. Mais je suppose que cette condamnation serait sans fondement.
Doucement, Rieux dit qu'en effet une pareille condamnation serait sans fondement, mais qu'en posant cette question, il cherchait seulement à savoir si le témoignage de Rambert pouvait ou non être sans réserves.
—Je n'admets que les témoignages sans réserves. Je ne soutiendrai donc pas le votre de mes renseignements.

[He came straight to the point. He was doing an investigation for a large Parisian newspaper about the living conditions of the Arabs and wanted information about their state of health. Rieux told him that their health was not good; but before going further, he wanted to know if the journalist could tell the truth.
"Certainly," the other man said.
"I mean, can you make an unqualified indictment?"
"Unqualified? No, I have to say I can't. But surely there wouldn't be any grounds for unqualified criticism?"
Rieux gently answered that a total condemnation would indeed be groundless, but that he had asked the question merely because he wanted to know if Rambert's report could be made unreservedly or not.
"I can only countenance a report without reservations, so I shall not be giving you any information to contribute to yours."][101]

This conversation summarizes the problems of any liberal Franco-Algerian writing about Arabs. He could tell the truth, but what if that led him to believe that the only real answer lay in a condemnation of colonialism as a whole? This he could not abide: it would condemn his friends and family, and undermine his own moral ground. He had therefore to believe that such a position was groundless, or at least, grossly exaggerated; hence the rather pathetic picture of two liberals reassuring one another that total condemnation would be "baseless." Rieux pushes further, however, and draws conclusions from this dilemma. Committed to testimony without reserve, he will refuse to testify when reserve is unavoidable. Camus's narrator explains very cogently why he will not describe the misery the Arabs must have suffered in the plague, a misery that the author himself had investigated and denounced without compromise in *Misère de la Kabylie*. He refuses to elaborate a fiction that could not condemn the situation totally, and that in not doing so would lend credence to a colonial regime he despises. However, he cannot (and here he is very clear) construct a fiction that *would* so condemn. Caught between the two, the best he can do is portray the very impossibility from which he suffers.

If *La Peste* is about the representability of history, Camus's removal of the Arabs suggests a further point about the constitution of Algerian historiography. Colonial Algerian history as officially conceived was predicated on a dual premise regarding the Arabs: the need for their presence on the one hand and for their absence on the other. Edward Said and many others have pointed out the absence of Muslim Algerians from Camus's works situated in North Africa. Despite Said's criticism of the readings of Camus that ignore this and stress his universalism and focus on Europe, it does seem possible to keep in mind the exclusion of the Muslims while nonetheless reading *La Peste* as an argument about how to represent history, including that of the colony.[102] Arabs in colonized Algeria represented a sort of null category for historiography, that is, a group that had no history of its own, but at the same time without whom no history was possible. The official account of the colony's founding started with the insult of the Dey of Algiers to the French consul in 1827 and went on to show how the Arabs were stagnating in a chaotic and feudal backwater of history in which progress, conceived as the very possibility of history, was unimaginable. The story thus began with a Muslim's act with historical consequences, an act necessary to justify subsequent developments; however, it then wrote the Arabs out of further participation. Algerian history thus could not do without the very people it refused to represent. (Nor of course could the colony function without the labor of those it refused to enfranchise.) *La Peste* attempts to end this hypocrisy by clearly stating the conditions of historical representation in the colony. Throughout the novel, the citizens of Oran prove incapable of seeing the relationship between events in their city and the historical "plagues" of all sorts that make it impossible for contemporary readers not to think of the Occupation, the Holocaust, or colonialism. The impossibility of representing the Arabs, unlike that of representing the plague, stems neither from lack of precedent nor from a horizon of expectations that cannot comprehend what is happening, but rather from the very premises of colonial historiography.[103] The practical results of this are clear: from the beginning, the city's inhabitants do not suspect that anything might be happening larger than their own lives.[104] Their self-satisfied complacency represents a true historical stagnation, next to the false one that colonial historiography imputed to the Arabs. The lack of history does not occur before the advent of the colony, as colonial historians maintained, but after it, once the Oranais have settled into their habits in a city whose self-image erases the Arabs who make up an essential part of it.

Under these conditions, the inhabitants return to complacency after their brief scare, just as the Europeans in Algeria did after each manifestation of political will by the Arabs. Before 1945, Europeans in the colony could almost believe ethnic or anticolonialist violence was as much a thing of the past as the plague. After Sétif, however, this should no longer have been possible. The general in charge of repressing the riots declared that the massacres he had caused or countenanced had bought "la paix pour dix ans" [peace for ten years]; he was off by less than six months, as the Algerian war broke out on 1 November 1954. In 1945 (or 1947), Algerians less prescient than Camus heard "peace" and ignored the warning implicit in the time limit. They ignored what Rieux knows, that is, that "le bacille de la peste ne meurt ni ne disparait jamais, qu'il peut rester pendant des dizaines d'années endormi dans les meubles et le linge, qu'il attend patiemment dans les chambres, les caves, les malles, les mouchoirs et les paperasses, et que, peut-être, le jour viendrait où, pour le malheur et l'enseignement des hommes, la peste réveillerait ses rats et les enverrait mourir dans une cité heureuse." ["The plague bacillus never dies or vanishes entirely, that it can remain dormant for dozens of years in furniture and clothing, that it waits patiently in bedrooms, cellars, trunks, handkerchiefs old papers, and that perhaps the day will come when, for the instruction or misfortune of men, the plague will rouse its rats and send them to die in some well-contented city."][105] Whether it most closely resembles the successive upwellings of Algerian nationalism, or the historical blindness that, after being caught unawares by these convulsions, found them impossible to represent or interpret, the plague is a very colonial sickness.

POLITICAL DEAD ENDS

The colony's susceptibility to historical plagues became clear as soon as the Algerian war broke the silence of colonial history, and as Camus broke his own silence of personal distress. In "Lettre à un militant algérien" [Letter to an Algerian militant] (1955), addressed as an editorial to his friend Aziz Kessous's new journal *Communauté algérienne*, Camus announces his hope for a compromise to end the war. For him there can be no question of forcing the French to abandon the roots they have put down in Algeria; however, they must desist from cutting off the equally legitimate cultural roots of the Arabs.[106] This leads him to a call for reform, not revolution. Camus will consistently stress his own brotherly affection for liberal Algerian activists like Kessous, with whom he feels "uni dans l'amour que nous portons à notre terre" [united in the love that we feel for our land]; shades of the unifying potential of the Mediterranean landscape reappear at least momentarily.[107] Camus lays claim to the land, a claim he now wishes to share in order to avoid losing it altogether: "[Cette terre] est la nôtre et je ne peux plus l'imaginer sans vous et vos frères que sans doute vous ne pouvez la séparer de moi et de ceux qui me ressemble" [This land is ours, and I can no more imagine it without you and your brothers than you no doubt can separate it from me and those who resemble me].[108] Even supposing that a proponent of liberal compromise like Kessous shared in this failure of imagination, the majority of Arab Algerians would shortly demonstrate that they had less trouble mentally separating the land from the French than Camus thought.

Already fixed in his determination to see Algeria continue as French, whatever radical reforms might take place, Camus further binds himself with an ultimately paralyzing dedication to the principle of moral equivalency of all suffering. His constant insistence that poor Franco-Algerians were just as deserving as poor Arabs would prevent him from thinking beyond the French presence. As David Carroll says, since Camus

> demanded justice for all poor Algerians, he could never acknowledge that justice could only come for the destitute Arabs of Algeria not just with the end of colonialism and the institution of new and more equal and just relations between Arab and French peoples, but rather with Algerian independence and the departure of the French from Algeria. He could not accept that 'the sacred task' of giving back the land to the 'immense herd of the wretched,' who were 'mostly Arab,' would mean *not giving it back* to the 'few French' who were for him also 'the wretched of the earth' and thus in his terms equally sacred.[109]

In 1957, a committee of European and Arab liberals invited Camus to Algiers to address a rally in favor of a *trêve civile* intended to protect civilians on both sides from terrorism and reprisals. In his speech, delivered under tight security as a crowd of pro-*Algérie française* agitators demonstrated outside, he acknowledged historical facts, but could not rethink the realities of power which would cause the "civil truce" to fail before it began: "'Il faut choisir son camp,' crient les repus de haine. Ah! Je l'ai choisi! J'ai choisi mon pays, j'ai choisi l'Algérie de la justice, où Français et Arabes s'associeront librement!" ['You must choose your camp,' cry those gorged on hate. I have chosen it! I have chosen my country, I have chosen the Algeria of justice, where French and Arabs will associate freely!][110] In reality, history gave out only parsimoniously the possibility of exercising free choice in the colony: colonial power dynamics offered it more easily to Camus and the *Français d'Algérie* than to Arabs. The crowd outside tried to censor Camus's choice, covering his voice with chants of "Camus, ta gueule" [Camus, shut up]. With no moral position he could reconcile with historical facts, Camus would soon heed them, at least in public.[111] The year following his Nobel Prize, he gradually withdrew from public debate on Algeria, as evidenced by the subdued tone of his introduction to *Actuelles III*: "ceux qui ne connaissent pas la situation dont je parle peuvent difficilement en juger. Mais ceux qui, la connaissant, continuent de penser héroïquement que le frère doit périr plutôt que les principes, je me bornerai à les admirer de loin. Je ne suis pas de leur race." [those who do not know the situation I am speaking of can hardly judge it. But those who, knowing it, continue to believe heroically that their brothers must die before their principles, I can only admire from a distance. I am not of their race.][112] His humane withdrawal from the company of intransigents would not let him out of his political impasse: *Actuelles III* ends with "Algérie 1958," a text vehemently opposed to Algerian independence. While he demands an end to all colonialist practices, he declares that "il n'y a jamais eu de nation algérienne" [there has never been an Algerian nation].[113] He suggests that Algerians have nothing to gain from an independence that would only play into the hands of "Arab imperialists" in Cairo and Communists in Moscow, and lead to "une sorte de mort historique" [a sort of historic death] for France.[114] However, the Algerian war itself had already contradicted the basic assumptions from which he was working; the war was rapidly turning the real "Algérie 1958" into the nation that the essay refused to see.

LE PREMIER HOMME: FIRST MAN, LAST DAYS

Since the posthumous publication of Camus's unfinished novel *Le Premier homme* [*The First Man*], "Algérie 1958" no longer stands as his last word on his country. Emily Apter and David Carroll have both pointed out the disjunction between Camus's essays and his fiction; the discovery of *Le Premier homme* reveals that he never stopped thinking about Algeria.[115] In the novel, he pushes his reflections on the way history had trapped him considerably further than he had done in his polemical essays. Camus attempts to connect the memory of working-class European Algerians to the colony's history, since he feels that establishing such a correspondence would lead to a rethinking of colonial history along more humane and workable lines. In this attempt, he discovers the poverty of memory among the disinherited, which forces him to give up forging the connection for which he had hoped. In the face of the poverty of memory among the working class, nostalgia is a longing that can only be for a time when conditions would have permitted (via the retention of less fragmented memories) nostalgia for anything else. Restorative nostalgia at least would seem impossible under the conditions he describes. However, he faces another obstacle as well. In colonial Algeria, he finds, coherent historical vision is simply unattainable; he has to fall back on memory, inherently personal and subject to vacillation or radical failure. Despite his characters' local, provisional, and personal attempts to intervene in Algerian events, colonial history leaves no way out of the spiral of violence and counterterrorism. Camus illustrates how flawed premises of historiographic representation compromise not only the image of colonial history, but the colony and its future as well.

Le Premier homme has no place for pronouncements about the impossibility of Algerian independence. The narrator's only attempt at historical certainty comes in the novel's opening, an effort to recount the protagonist's birth in a heroic mode. This narration imbricates him in a perspective on the Algerian landscape that implies an omniscient view of the land and its history:

> Au-dessus de la carriole qui roulait sur une route caillouteuse, de gros et épais nuages filaient vers l'est dans le crépuscule. Trois jours auparavant, ils s'étaient gonflés au-dessus de l'Atlantique, avaient attendu le vent d'ouest, puis s'étaient ébranlés, lentement d'abord et de plus en plus vite, avaient survolé les eaux phosphorescentes de l'automne, droit vers le continent, s'étaient effilochés aux crêtes marocaines, reformés en troupeaux sur les hauts plateaux d'Algérie, et maintenant, aux approches de la frontière tunisienne, essayaient de gagner la mer Tyrrhénienne pour s'y perdre. Après une course de milliers de kilomètres au-dessus de cette sorte d'île immense, défendue par la mer mouvante au nord et au sud par les flots figés des sables, passant sur ce pays sans nom à peine plus vite que ne l'avaient fait pendant des millénaires les empires et les peuples, leur élan s'exténuait et certains fondaient déjà en grosses et rares gouttes de pluie qui commençaient de résonner sur la capote de toile au-dessus des quatre voyageurs.

> [Above the wagon rolling along a stony road, big thick clouds were hurrying to the East through the dusk. Three days ago they had inflated over the Atlantic, had waited for a wind from the West, had set out, slowly at first then faster and faster, had flown over the phosphorescent autumn waters, straight to the continent, had unraveled on the Moroccan peaks, and gathered again in flocks on the high plateaus of Algeria, and now, at the approaches to the Tunisian frontier, were trying to reach the Tyrrhenian Sea to lose themselves in it. After a journey of thousands of kilometers over what seemed to be an immense island, shielded by the moving waters to the North and to the South by the congealed waves of the sands, passing scarcely any faster above this nameless country than had empires and peoples over the millennia, their momentum was wearing out and some already were melting into occasional large raindrops that were beginning to plop on the canvas hood above the four travelers.][116]

This set piece of epic description from a narrator with head literally in the clouds conforms closely to the codes of opening descriptions for

Algerian history texts. Convention dictated that the author begin with an overview of the land, noting the mountain ranges and plateaus which divided it into farming and grazing land, and which separated the *pays sans nom* from its neighbors. Camus echoes a historiographic commonplace by evoking Algeria's neighbors in order to define the country negatively as the vague and chaotic territory falling between Morocco and Tunisia, two coherent countries with historical pedigrees. It was thus a land which had never had political consistency of its own, but in which foreign empires succeeded one another in the blink of an eye. The lay of the land cuts Algeria off from its neighbors on all four sides and transforms it into an island in history on which every successive foreign power could claim to have been the first to set foot. Jacques Cormery, the son born just after this scene in a fictional moment of great fraternity between Arabs and French, will be yet another such *premier homme*. The critic André Aciman calls this passage "embarrassingly kitschy," an oversight in bad taste; rather, it is an initial engagement with a mode of historical representation Camus will quickly find untenable.[117] The rest of the novel analyzes its inadequacies.

After only a dozen pages in this epic tone, something goes abruptly wrong. The heroic narration ends suddenly, and we jump forward forty years: Cormery is on the train from Paris to Saint-Brieuc, contemplating the unheroic, flat, and regimented countryside slipping past.[118] He is on a pilgrimage to the grave of the father he never knew, since Henri Cormery died after receiving a shell fragment in his skull at the Marne, only months after Jacques's birth. The narration moves from an omniscient voice relating the birth of a hero, to that hero's attempt, forty years later, to reconstruct his family's past and his own inheritance; in short, the story abruptly switches from history to memory. Looking back at the opening, readers find few clues as yet to understanding what exactly went wrong with this section of the novel to which Camus never returns. Clearly, its heroic mode had difficulty accounting for the individual's position in the grand panorama produced by flying over the breadth of Algeria's topography and history. Camus seems to have sensed this immediately; as he says in a note to himself, "ajouter anonymat géologique. Terre et mer" ["add geological anonymity. Land and sea"], in order to make even clearer the difficulty of humans' inserting themselves into this impersonal, topographic view of history.[119]

This, however, is not the only problem with the opening. The advent of the personal in the narration solves nothing, and ultimately results in total breakdown of the abandoned panoramic mode. At the graveside in Saint-Brieuc, the former epic hero Cormery gazes at the clouds again, but to rather different effect:

Jacques Cormery, le regard levé vers la lente navigation des nuages dans le ciel, tentait de saisir derrière l'odeur des fleurs mouillées la senteur salée qui venait en ce moment de la mer lointaine et immobile quand le tintement d'un seau contre le marbre d'une tombe le tira de sa reverie. C'est à ce moment qu'il lut sur la tombe la date de naissance de son père, dont il découvrit à cette occasion qu'il l'ignorait. Puis il lut les deux dates, "1885–1914" et fit un calcul machinal: vingt-neuf ans. Soudain une idée le frappa qui l'ébranla jusque dans son corps. Il avait quarante ans. L'homme enterré sous cette dalle, et qui avait été son père, était plus jeune que lui.

Et le flot de tendresse et de pitié qui d'un coup vint lui emplir le coeur n'était pas le mouvement d'âme qui porte le fils vers le souvenir du père disparu, mais la compassion bouleversée qu'un homme fait ressent devant l'enfant injustement assassiné—quelque chose ici n'était pas dans l'ordre naturel et, à vrai dire, il n'y avait pas d'ordre mais seulement folie et chaos là où le fils était plus âgé que le père. La suite du temps lui-même se fracassait autour de lui immobile, entre ces tombes qu'il ne voyait plus, et les années cessaient de s'ordonner suivant ce grand fleuve qui coule vers sa fin.

[Jacques Cormery, gazing up at the slow navigation of the clouds across the sky, was trying to discern, beyond the odor of damp flowers, the salty smell just then coming from the distant motionless sea when the clink of a bucket against the marble of a tombstone drew him from his reverie. At that moment he read on the tomb the date of his father's birth, which he now discovered he had not known. Then he read the two dates, "1885–1914," and automatically did the arithmetic: twenty-nine years. Suddenly he was struck by an idea that shook his very being. He was forty years old. The man buried under that slab, who had been his father, was younger than he.

And the wave of tenderness and pity that at once filled his heart was not the stirring of the soul that leads the son to the memory of the vanished father, but the overwhelming compassion that a grown man feels for an unjustly murdered child—something here was not in the natural order and, in truth, there was no order but only madness and chaos when the son was older than the father. The course of time itself was shattering around him while he remained motionless among those tombs he now no longer saw, and the years no longer kept to their places in the great river that flows to its end.][120]

A random and insignificant event, the clinking of a bucket, interrupts Cormery's sensory apprehension of the landscape and awakens him to basic facts of his family history. As the critic Raquel Salgado notes, there is no more powerful moment in Camus; the radical upheaval provoked by this revelation will have a domino effect on historical coherence (and eventually on memorial coherence as well) up to and beyond the novel's provisional end.[121] In essence, Jacques has become his own father, mourning a dead child. He precedes and supersedes his forebear, and of the two

becomes the "first" man. An unnatural order has interrupted his conception of historical succession; the years no longer follow in a linear and unidirectional stream. Cormery is cut adrift.

Immediately after the cemetery episode, his drift washes him up in Algiers. The few family memories he can draw from his mother cannot help
him reestablish order or gain access to his father's legacy, let alone to a
prelapsarian coherence. His mother exemplifies what Camus calls "la mémoire des pauvres" ["poor people's memory"], "moins nourrie que celle
des riches" ["less nourished than that of the rich"], and with "moins de
repères dans le temps d'une vie uniforme et grise. Bien sûr, il y a la mémoire du coeur dont on dit qu'elle est la plus sûre, mais le coeur s'use à
la peine et au travail, il oublie plus vite sous le poids des fatigues. Le
temps perdu ne se retrouve que chez les riches. Pour les pauvres, il marque seulement les traces vagues du chemin de la mort." ["fewer reference
points in time throughout lives that are gray and featureless. Of course
there is the memory of the heart that they say is the surest kind, but the
heart wears out with sorrow and labor, it forgets sooner under the weight
of fatigue. Remembrance of things past is just for the rich. For the poor it
only marks the faint traces on the path to death."][122] Camus's quest for
memory cannot end in bittersweet Proustian pleasure, for purely economic and political reasons. The last line could apply to the poor on either
side of the Algerian conflict; Camus is scrupulously fair in distributing the
resources and shortfalls of memory. Poverty places Cormery's family in
the undifferentiated stasis which colonial historiography assigned to the
Arabs. They cannot possibly participate in, or imagine their participation
in a heroic narrative of historic progress, the official story of building
Algeria.

Cormery quickly discovers the extent of the colonial failure of memory.
Some individuals have memories and even anecdotal knowledge of history, but no one he questions regarding his father can put together a coherent story. The characters attribute this to a bizarre trait of Algerian history: every new generation begins again, as if they were the first men; at
every point, everything must start from scratch: "Puisque vous êtes du
pays, vous savez ce que c'est" ["Since you're from here, you know how it
is"], says one of Cormery's incapable informants. "Ici, on ne garde rien.
On abat et on reconstruit. On pense à l'avenir et on oublie le reste." ["We
don't preserve anything here. We tear down and we rebuild. We think
about the future and forget the rest."][123] This applies as much to official
memory as to the private kind; Camus mentions in a note at the end of the
manuscript that "Les mairies d'Algérie *n'ont pas d'archives* la plupart du
temps" ["in most cases the town halls of Algeria *have no archives*"].[124]
Thinking of the future is hardly a panacea; the isolated *colons* occupying
his father's farm can only evoke their likely fate in apocalyptic terms, like

the farmer ordered to evacuate, who works day and night to destroy the fruit of his labor and advises his Arab employees to join the FLN. The peculiar destructiveness of colonial Algeria's cyclical history makes such acts perfectly logical, another repetition of the first phase of the "tear down and rebuild" cycle.

The heart of the problem is precisely the question of roots on which Camus had pronounced so insistently in his political writings, where he asserted the rootedness of the French Algerian population in "their" land. Here, he greatly complicates this notion, exposing the fragility and transience imposed on roots in the context of colonial occupation. Returning from his visit to his parents' former farm at Mondovi, Jacques realizes that he is like

> tous les hommes nés dans ce pays qui, un par un, essayaient d'apprendre à vivre sans racines et sans foi et qui tous ensemble aujourd'hui où ils risquaient l'anonymat définitif et la perte des seules traces sacrées de leur passage sur cette terre, les dalles illisibles que la nuit avait maintenant recouvertes dans le cimetière, devaient apprendre à naître aux autres, à l'immense cohue des conquérants maintenant évincés qui les avaient précédés sur cette terre et dont ils devaient reconnaître maintenant la fraternité de race et de destin.
>
> L'avion descendait maintenant vers Alger. Jacques pensait au petit cimetière de Saint-Brieuc où les tombes des soldats étaient mieux conservées que celles de Mondovi.

> [all the men born in this country who, one by one, try to learn to live without roots and without faith, and today all of them are threatened with eternal anonymity and the loss of the only consecrated traces of their passage on this earth, the illegible slabs in the cemetery that the night has now covered over; they had to learn how to live in relation to others, to the immense host of the conquerors, now dispossessed, who had preceded them on this land and in whom they now had to recognize the brotherhood of race and destiny.
>
> Now the plane was descending to Algiers. Jacques was thinking about the little cemetery of Saint-Brieuc where the soldiers' graves were better kept than those in Mondovi.][125]

The fluke of death in France (and in the middle of a major event of world history) preserved the physical trace of Henri Cormery's existence. Otherwise, history leaves Franco-Algerians with only "illegible slabs"; they must learn to live without the roots that decipherable signs would provide. The hard-liners of French Algeria swore they would never leave, because to do so meant leaving behind their forebears' graves.[126] These graves, however, are already illegible; a series of generations effacing one another in succession continues to erase history as rapidly as it can be created. The passage carries a sense of urgency; Cormery feels acutely that he and his fellow Franco-Algerians risk a definitive loss and need a sort of collective rebirth. They need to see their connection to the other "first men," the crowd of conquering predecessors. Camus disarms the pro-colonial thrust of this idea by remembering that these successive conquerors were all thrown out, and that if the French believed themselves to be the first men as well, they must necessarily admit "brotherhood of race and destiny" with losers, people who had not been able to maintain themselves as conquerors. Camus comes as close here as he ever would to admitting the doom of an Algeria based on conquest.

For Camus, illegible tombstones and unreadable memories lead to unwritable history. In his notes he suggests writing a "[c]hapitre *à reculons*. Otages village kabyle. Soldat émasculé—ratissage, etc., de proche en proche jusqu'au premier coup de feu de la colonisation. Mais pourquoi s'arrêter là? Cain a tué Abel. Problème technique: un seul chapitre ou en contre-chant?" ["chapter *going backwards*. Hostages Kabyle village. Emasculated soldier—roundup, etc., step by step to the first shot fired in the settlement. But why stop there? Cain killed Abel. Problem in technique: a single chapter or in countermelody?"][127] These problems are much more than technical. Tracing the history of colonization back through time, one never reaches anything but a renewed cycle of violence and forgetting. There can therefore be nothing innocent or comforting in the apparently natural replacement of one generation by the next; instead,

Des foules entières étaient venues ici depuis plus d'un siècle, avaient labouré, creusé des sillons, de plus en plus profonds en certains endroits, en certains autres de plus en plus tremblés jusqu'à ce qu'une terre légère les recouvre et la région retournait alors aux végétations sauvages, et ils avaient procréé puis disparu. Et ainsi de leurs fils. Et les fils et les petits-fils de ceux-ci s'é-taient trouvés sur cette terre comme lui-même s'y était trouvé, sans passé, sans morale, sans leçon, sans religion mais heureux de l'être et de l'être dans la lumière, angoissés devant la nuit et la mort. Toutes ces générations, tous ces hommes venus de tant de pays différents, sous ce ciel admirable où montait déjà l'annonce du crépuscule, avaient disparu sans laisser de traces, refermés sur eux-mêmes. Un immense oubli s'était étendu sur eux.

[Whole mobs had been coming here for more than a century, had plowed, dug furrows, deeper and deeper in some places, shakier and shakier in others, until the dusty earth covered them over and the place went back to its wild vegetation; and they had procreated, then disappeared. And so it was with their sons. And the sons and grandsons of these found themselves on this land as he himself had, with no past, without ethics, without guidance, without religion, but glad to be so and to be in the light, fearful in the face of night and death. All those generations, all those men come from so many nations, under this magnificent sky where the first portent of twilight was already rising, had disappeared without a trace, locked within themselves. An enormous oblivion spread over them.][128]

Algerian history from the colonizers' point of view is impossible precisely because it is predicated on the notion of the colonizer as "first
man." The idea originated as the seductive premise of a history that
wished to empty Algeria of its precolonial inhabitants, in order to give
the French right of first occupancy. Camus exposes the premise by pushing it to its logical conclusion: if each new generation of occupants is first,
the previous one must have disappeared; Camus shows how this happened. The current first man, Jacques Cormery, will himself disappear
from history, just as all previous generations have done. The *oubli* that
covers them demonstrates the impossibility of a national history based on
the exclusion stated in the first-man premise. In the end, it also demonstrates the impossibility of any conception of historical existence for the
Franco-Algerians. "Le livre *doit être* inachevé" ["The book *must be* unfinished"], notes Camus. He has just shown us why he cannot finish the
story.[129]

EMMANUEL ROBLÈS AND THE MEDITERRANEAN REVISED

Camus was not the only liberal Algerian writing out of a sense of social
justice, a sense which hindered as much as helped his attempts to imagine a solution to the Algerian crisis. Although none of the other Algerian
liberals proposed anything more effective than the brave attempt of
the *trêve civile*, a number of them did come to accept the idea of Algerian
independence. The sporadic weekly paper *Espoir Algérie*, billed as
"L'Expression des Libéraux d'Algérie" [The Expression of the Algerian
Liberals] came slowly to an editorial position recognizing the necessity of
independence; finally, in June 1962, it heralded the new nation by quoting
the question posed and answered by Emmanuel Roblès: "Quelle peut
bien être ma patrie?—Là où tu veux vivre sans subir ni infliger d'humiliation." [What country could be mine?—The one in which you want to
live, neither suffering nor inflicting humiliation.][130] Roblès had been an
early member of the *Fédération des Libéraux*, the organization that invited
Camus to Algiers for the *trêve civile* speech; he had known Camus since
1937, when the two had sympathized on their first meeting. Both were of
Spanish origin; both had lost their fathers before knowing them; both had
been raised by powerful and enigmatic mothers whom they adored. Unlike Camus, Roblès returned to Algeria after World War II to found the review *Forge* with El Boudali Safir; in their third issue, they included a poem
by a then-unknown writer named Kateb Yacine, an editorial decision that
reflected their desire to publish quality literature from all ethnic groups in
Algeria.[131] More than Audisio and Camus, Roblès maintained very close
relations with Arab and Amazigh writers; his contacts among the Muslim

intelligentsia originated in the early '30s, when he attended the École Normale de la Bouzaréah in the same class as Mouloud Feraoun. Roblès left Algeria only in 1958, after the death of his young son in a shooting accident. By that time he was already a commercially successful writer; Buñuel had made a film of his novel *Cela s'appelle l'aurore* [It's Called Dawn] (1952), and Roblès had embarked on a steady stream of novels that would taper off only a few years before his death, in 1995.

To the working-class roots he shared with Camus, Roblès added awareness of his Spanish background, which he connected closely with Arab Andalusia in a new construction of Mediterranean Algeria quite independent from the sunny idyll of French humanism. Roblès's first Mediterranean was that of a proletariat including Spanish, Arab, and Amazigh Algerians, both as opponents of capitalism and as postwar inheritors of a tradition of resistance that could legitimately act against colonial exploitation. Roblès became the first, and perhaps only, European author in Algeria to imagine a fully developed Arab or Amazigh hero and to tell a complete story from his point of view. The novel in which he does so, *Les Hauteurs de la ville* [The Heights of the City] (Prix Fémina 1948), appeared in his early series of socialist realist novels, including *L'Action* and *La Vallée du paradis* [The Valley of Paradise], both set in Algiers, and *Travail d'homme* [Man's Work], set in pre-Civil War Spain.[132] The hero of *Les Hauteurs*, Smail ben Lakhdar, is an independent and spontaneous agent of the resistance to the Vichy regime in Algeria. Almaro, a rich and cynical recruiter of Muslim workers for the Todt, the "voluntary" labor force of the German war effort, catches Smail tearing down his recruitment posters, and humiliates him. Later, in an urban repetition of the mass asphyxiations caused by colonial troops "pacifying" the countryside, Almaro illegally sequesters a group of recruits who refuse to board the ship to Germany and causes their death by suffocation in an airless room under the arcades of the Algiers waterfront. Smail knows that Almaro runs no risk of judicial condemnation and decides to kill him. His European friends in the Resistance approve his success after the fact and hide him, but he impatiently sets out for Morocco, only to be arrested before reaching the border. Though the ending implies Smail's trial and execution, the story nonetheless portrays a Muslim protagonist capable of political decisions, who fully assumes the consequences of the resulting actions.

Roblès appears to have used every detail of the novel to mark his text's distance from Camus's *L'Étranger*, the more famous literary example of an interethnic killing in Algeria. Expensive neighborhoods on the hills replace working-class quarters and the beach; Roblès's rain and dark nights replace Camus's heat and sun-bleached days. Smail is no stranger, but well integrated into several groups of Algerian and European friends and comrades-in-arms. The ideological thrust of *Les Hauteurs* makes itself felt on an entirely different level from that of *L'Étranger*. Whereas a disaffected European might kill an Arab arbitrarily, out of a strange malaise at once colonial and philosophical, an Algerian might kill a European for very good political or moral reasons. Smail, though he frightens his pacifist friends, is a model of positive engagement in a historic cause.

Roblès was not shy about drawing moral lessons from his *roman à thèse*, and attributes its composition to a political imperative: when it was written in 1946, he says, "ce récit avait le dessein de témoigner sur un aspect du désarroi qui tourmentait alors de jeunes Algériens. Il voulait également illustrer certaines aspirations, nées avec plus ou moins d'élan et de clarté, au feu des événements qui transformaient le monde. Comment, en particulier, ne pas reconnaître que, pour beaucoup de ces jeunes hommes, l'exemple de la Résistance française a été décisif?" [this narration attempted to bear witness to an aspect of the helplessness then afflicting young Algerians. It also wanted to illustrate certain aspirations, born with more or less force and clarity, in the fire of the events that were transforming the world. In particular, how could one not recognize that for many of these young men, the example of the French Resistance had been decisive?][133] Roblès may be claiming as original insights he gained only later; written in 1960, this preface inscribes the novel in a context which it predates, that of the Algerian war. The preface could hardly be clearer in assimilating the FLN with the F.F.I., and in asserting the moral equivalence between Algerian insurrection and French resistance. The text of 1960 is nevertheless not entirely a product of hindsight. Most Algerian nationalists dated the contemporary resistance to colonialism from the riots in Sétif in 1945, and Roblès addresses this early tragedy directly. In the year following the repression, during which he wrote *Les Hauteurs*, he became certain that "le brasier noyé un an plus tôt dans le sang de milliers de victimes reprendrait, plus dévorant. On tue les hommes, on ne tue pas l'idée pour laquelle ils acceptent de mourir, chacun de nous le sait." [the embers drowned a year earlier in the blood of thousands of victims would catch fire again, more fiercely. You can kill people, but you do not kill the idea for which they are willing to die: every one of us knows this.][134] Smail's act of resistance may be safely contained within a European struggle, but as a fully capable, mature Muslim political actor, his mere participation in the French Resistance counts as revolutionary. The discourse on the Muslims' sacrifices in European wars had always stressed their obedience and devotion, and never their historic initiative, precisely what Roblès emphasizes. Furthermore, the plot makes evident Smail's motives, which stem much more from desire for justice in the colony than from a wish to participate in the fight to save France from Nazism, a struggle Smail scarcely mentions.

Roblès's conceptions of participation in history evolved significantly during and after the Algerian war. His first reflection on his childhood came at the same time as Camus's in *Le Premier homme*, in a memoir published in Algiers in 1961, entitled *Jeunes saisons* [Young Seasons]; thirteen years later, he followed it with *Saison violente* [Violent Season], an autobiographical novel based on his childhood in Oran. As with Camus, the evolution of his thinking involved a change in genre, in his case from "pure" autobiography to novel. His first narration of his childhood is nostalgic, simplistic, and ahistorical; the second, disenchanted, nuanced, and politically conscious: contemplatively nostalgic. Together with *Le Premier homme*, these works suggest the necessity of analyzing the conditions under which nostalgia is produced in order to move beyond the traps colonial history laid for liberal writers.

In *Jeunes saisons*, Roblès's reflections do not reach anything like the complexity of Camus's in *Le Premier homme*, and he restricts himself to a nostalgia brought on by a sense of impending loss, a longing which Camus found impossible since for him, there was nothing left for which one could be nostalgic. Memories, says Roblès, "jaillissent surtout de chaque pierre de ce quartier sans caractère où mon enfance s'est écoulée" [spring forth particularly from every stone of this characterless neighborhood where I spent my childhood].[135] The neighborhood has changed considerably, he adds; "des figures familières nous entouraient alors qui ont disparu aujourd'hui. Où sont donc les deux guitaristes aveugles qui 'répétaient' en face de ma maison? . . . [ils] contribuaient à donner à nos rues une atmosphère andalouse qu'elles ont perdues aujourd'hui." [familiar figures surrounded us then, who have disappeared today. Where are the two blind guitarists who 'practiced' in front of my house? . . . They helped give our streets an Andalusian atmosphere they have lost today.][136] Nostalgia for lost places later served as a model for the *pied noir* memoirs that began to appear in the late 1970s, though generally in a restorative mode, and sometimes with avowedly revisionist goals. Mourning the lost country may be necessary, but unless it comes with a serious reconsideration of the politics of such nostalgia, it remains in an ideological cul-de-sac. Even Roblès, above suspicion of pro-colonialism or racism, proves incapable of analyzing ethnic relations when he has presented them in his initial nostalgic mode. Attempting to describe the relations between Arabs and Spanish in this childhood paradise, he writes: "Nous connaissions mal les Arabes. Au coeur d'un quartier essentiellement espagnol comme le nôtre, nous n'avions en classe aucun camarade musulman. Tout nous maintenait séparés d'eux, les zones d'habitation comme la différence des langues, des religions, des coutumes. Mais, contrairement aux grandes personnes, nous étions sans préjugés à leur égard." [We did not know the Arabs well. In the heart of an essentially Spanish neighborhood like ours, we had no Muslim schoolmates. Everything kept me separate from them: the zones we resided in, as well as the differences of language, religion, and customs. Unlike the grownups, however, we had no prejudices regarding them.][137] Without cynicism, post-colonial readers may doubt that this pronouncement records more than a pious wish to find in childhood a harmony that escaped the adult world. Moreover, if it aims to show peaceful coexistence with the Arabs, it does not suggest how this might have happened, nor postulate any rapprochement between the communities. Childhood memories may be ahistorical by their very nature; and to include real analysis of ethnicity and history in the city, Roblès seems to have needed to rewrite his memoir as the autobiographical novel of an adolescent hero.

Saison violente benefits from a distance on the events of the Algerian war, which a memoir published in 1961 could not enjoy. Its title alone dispenses with the kind of nostalgia in *Jeunes saisons* and introduces an idea of menace. Moreover, it refers to one particular time period, rather than to the unspecified and amorphous continuity of passing seasons alluded to in the earlier title. The text specifies the moment with a historical reference: when police suspect the narrator of assaulting an officer, they discover in searching his pockets the newspaper portrait of Sacco and Vanzetti, executed in that summer of 1927. The icon and its disguise (the young Emmanuel tells the police the two men are football stars, and gets away with it) suggest the beginnings of a political consciousness in the narrator, aware that anarchists would make poor character witnesses in right-wing Oran.[138] The protagonist's friends had indeed assaulted a Spanish police officer who had beaten an Arab street vendor whom they liked, and the protagonist himself frequents a Communist newsagent (Sarcos, not Sacco), who sells banned publications. Roblès could easily have used these details to place himself piously on the proper side of the colony's political battles, but the adult narrator foregoes piety and makes it clear that the young hero's collusion with the assault came at least partly from an instinctive tendency to side with the underdog, and from excitement at the exploit of attacking an authority figure with slingshots.[139] As for Sarcos, the narrator continues to respect him highly, but gently ironizes the hero's assumption that the newspaper vendor must know what he is talking about, simply because he sells certain magazines under the counter.[140] Neither of these qualifications undercut the book's political engagement. By honestly exploring his hero's actual motivations, Roblès begins to accumulate the details for a much closer analysis of ethnicity and history than his earlier memoirs permitted.

Roblès bases his rethinking of the political possiblities for identity on awareness of his own status as a Spanish subject in the Algerian city. He is the best-known colonial or post-colonial Algerian to do this; others thinkers tended either to valorize their naturalization into the Algerian *prépondérance française*, or, like Bertrand, to drown Spanish connections (invented, in his case) in a Latin collectivity.[141] *Saison violente* traces the very beginning of Roblès's cultural involvement with the Hispanic world, which would lead him to translate extensively from Spanish literature and travel repeatedly to Spain and Latin America.[142] In addition, it would prompt him to revive the Mediterranean consciousness, without the exclusivity of French universalism that had hobbled it in the thinking of Audisio and Camus. By beginning to understand his own subject position as Spanish and Mediterranean, but *foreign to the French*, Roblès can better comprehend his relationship with both French and Arabs. He can also work to create the sort of links with Arab and Jewish characters that Audisio nor Camus were able to portray.

Midway through *Saison violente*, the young Emmanuel's mother goes to work as a live-in maid and places her son *en pension* with Mme. Quinson, a wealthy French woman who had employed and befriended her. Mme. Quinson feels duty-bound to remind Emmanuel how lucky he is, considering his class origin, and insults him constantly with racial and social innuendo: "'On aura beau faire, tu es et tu resteras toujours un cinquante-pour-cent.' On nous appelait aussi 'caracoles' ou 'migas', du nom de nos nourritures de pauvres mais, pour méprisants qu'ils fussent ces termes m'égratignaient à peine le cuir. Au contraire, 'cinquante-pour-cent' m'atteignait au vif tant, à mes yeux, cette expression marquait la volonté de me laisser à la porte, de m'empêcher d'entrer dans le royaume." ['No matter what we do, you are and will always be a fifty percent.' They also called us 'caracoles' or 'migas' from the names of dishes of the poor, but despite the disdain in these terms, they barely scratched my skin. 'Fifty percent' on the contrary hit a raw spot, marking, in my eyes, the desire to leave me outside the door, and prevent me from entering the kingdom.][143] Emmanuel finds himself in a position analogous to that of a French-educated Arab or Amazigh faced with the impossible demand to assimilate. A European can feel this dilemma quite as strongly as an Arab; Emmanuel clearly senses the unfairness of the demand, and, while ready to forget most insults referring specifically to his ethnic background, he reacts strongly against the label that marks the futility of his efforts to become culturally French, the epithet that slams the door in his face. For Mme. Quinson, the difference between Spanish and Arabs is in any case minimal, and both languages are idioms of second-class humans.[144] The young Emmanuel studies Arabic at *lycée*, (an unusual choice), but nonetheless asserts that

j'assimilais tout, Louis XIV et Robespierre, Racine et Michelet, la Loire et la Beauce, Molière, Balzac, Hugo! Le supplice de Jeanne d'Arc me révoltait et les adieux de Fontainebleau m'embuaient les yeux de larmes. Moi, un "cinquante-pour-cent?" Moi, une moitié d'étranger? Comment était-ce concevable? Si je savais ma différence, je connaissais tout aussi bien la profondeur de ma communion. Je n'étais pas à la porte, mais à l'intérieur, non aux frontières, mais sur le territoire même de cette patrie culturelle à laquelle j'adhérais de toute mon intelligence et de toute ma sensibilité.

[I assimilated everything: Louis XIV and Robespierre, Racine and Michelet, the Loire and the Beauce, Molière, Balzac, and Hugo! The execution of Jean d'Arc revolted me and the farewell at Fontainbleau filled my eyes with tears. Me, a "fifty percent"? Me, half a foreigner? How was this conceivable? Though I knew I was different, I also knew just as well the depth of my communion. I was not at the door, but inside; not at the border, but on the very territory of this cultural homeland to which I adhered with all my intelligence and sensitivity.][145]

Emmanuel feels the contradiction inherent in the two meanings of "assimiler": he can assimilate cultural information, but members of that culture will never admit that he has assimilated himself to them. France, personified by Mme. Quinson, will at most admit that his language skills are passable for the cultural wasteland of the colony, a concession which keeps him on the border:

—Et tu es toujours premier en français?
　—Toujours, non.
　Soupir de Mme Quinson. Une vague soulève sa forte poitrine:
　—Il est vrai qu'au pays des aveugles . . .

[—And you're always first in French?
　—Not always.
　A sigh from Mme. Quinson; a wave lifted her heavy chest:
　—It's true that in the land of the blind . . .][146]

In Algeria's land of the blind, Roblès depicts Spaniards, Jews, and Arabs feeling their way to a Mediterranean acculturation that simply ignores Mme. Quinson's rejection.

The tense and complex interchanges among these groups go beyond the neighborly solidarity between the hero's mother and the Arabs who live next door, who join in pressuring the police to leave when they unfairly interrogate Emmanuel; these relationships go further than the spontaneous integration of the Jew Kalfon into the clan of boys exploring their city. Ethnic relations are both as simple and as complex as these situations. Roblès never hides the difficulties and contradictions of these temporary alliances: he describes how the police prevented Arabs from attending political meetings and how the hero himself threw a paper airplane covered with anti-Semitic slogans into the shop of his Jewish neighbor.[147] Nonetheless, the narrator feels a deep commitment to a Mediterranean cultural identity that embraces the victims of these practices, a cultural construction which could successfully integrate these contradictions and lead to their humane resolution. Oran, the city Camus blamed for its lack of history, had a layout that mapped the possibilities for such under-standing. When he and his friends go on their rowdy promenades through Oran to the beach (the *fons* of Mediterranean solidarity) ,they feel equally at home in the Spanish, Jewish, and Arab quarters; the description of these neighborhoods in the middle of Oran makes them virtually in-distinguishable. The only part of town that feels foreign to Emmanuel is the neighborhood in which his mother's abusive employers live. Social class, the least investigated of identity variables in the colony, proves more important than race in determining the novel's use of urban space.

The narrator feels that he has inherited a tradition with branches on both sides of the Mediterranean, a culture summarized in his expeditions in the city. This inheritance results from the Arab civilization of Andalu-sia rather than from French humanist interventions south of the Mediter-ranean. Describing his acquaintance with Mme. Quinson's servant Yas-mina, Emmanuel recalls attending her wedding:

> Tout l'Orient vivait dans mon sang andalou, et c'est ce qui provoqua cette joie délicate à la vue des longues robes de soie, de satin, de gaze, de dentelles, de ces gracieux pantalons bouffants, de ces boléros de velours, de ces babouches brodées, de ces bijoux, de ces écharpes, de ces coiffures coniques copiées jadis par les dames du Moyen Age. Parce que ma mère avait participé activement aux préparatifs, on avait eu la charmante idée de lui prêter une de ces parures pour qu'on pût, elle aussi, la photographier seule ou parmi les jeunes femmes qui entouraient la mariée. J'ai encore une de ces photogra-phies où ma mère, à demi-étendue sur un divan, ressemble à quelque belle Mauresque d'un somptueux palais de Damas ou de Granade.

> [All of the Orient lived in my Andalusian blood, and this was what caused this delight at the sight of the long dresses in silk, satin, gauze, and lace, and the delicate flared pants, the velour boleros, the embroidered slippers, the jewelry, the scarves, and the conical headdresses formerly copied by ladies in the Middle Ages. Because my mother had participated actively in the prepa-rations, they had the charming idea of lending her one of these outfits so they could photograph her too, alone or among the young women attending the bride. I still have one of these photographs in which my mother, half-lying on a couch, resembles some beautiful Moorish woman in a sumptuous palace of Damascus or Granada.][148]

The narrator, remembering his welcome in Arab social territory, asserts that his "Andalusian blood" predisposes him to a sensory appreciation of the luxury marking it. The staging undercuts what would otherwise be a classic piece of exoticist description: the narrator's presence is invited, and he identifies the tradition on display as part of his own, rather than as an objectified alterity. Unlike male travelers to the Maghrib who insisted upon dressing up as Arabs for studio portraits, Emmanuel's mother allows her coworkers to take the initiative to make her one of them for the duration of the party.[149] They can do so because they, and not the French, are the transmitters of a Mediterranean tradition originating with the Arabs and Imazighen of Andalusia. If anything, the French Middle Ages received a cultural inheritance from the Arabs, rather than the other way around; for Roblès, this inheritance is quite as important as the classical tradition of the humanists. Roblès's Mediterranean undoubtedly includes Ulysses as well, but the classical tradition here renders full homage to the Arabs who contributed to it in Spain. This historical reevaluation, presented as a simple and personal appreciation for hospitality, renders it at least momentarily possible for a mixed group to enjoy the sort of Mediterranean community of which Audisio and even Camus had only dreamed.

LONGEVITY AND THE MEDITERRANEAN IDEAL

The progression from Audisio to Camus to Roblès might seem to demonstrate merely that longevity and historical opportunity count for a great deal in developing a political position. Audisio, twenty years younger than writers of Robert Randau's generation, had the chance to see the shortfalls of the older writers' view of Algeria, and the time to look elsewhere and replace the ideology of Algerianism with a liberal Mediterranean of his own. Roblès outlived Camus by almost thirty-five years, a third of a century beginning with an event Camus had not foreseen, the independence of Algeria. He thus had a historical opportunity to imagine the Mediterranean community in a reconfiguration Camus could not. Before attributing everything to context and opportunity, we should nonetheless recall two facts: first, Audisio, too, lived until long after the independence of his adopted country; second, the Mediterranean community Roblès described after the Algerian war was present before independence, and Camus had seen it. Chronology alone cannot explain the development of these three authors, and the view of them in a series may be deceiving. Nonetheless, they did indeed participate in a continuum of political consensuses: Audisio constructed a Mediterranean identity based on liberal humanism which Camus revised in order to make more politically acceptable to the left, if not actually more inclusive (in practice) of the Arabs and Imazighen. Camus soon recognized that even his revised construction of Mediterranean Algeria was beholden to a view of North African history to which he could no longer subscribe; ultimately he saw that no development would be possible for French Algeria on the bases of its official historical premises.

As for Roblès, he found a way around the literary difficulties of this situation, first by completely reorienting his idea of the Mediterranean with a focus on Andalusia, and second by concentrating on a very local portion of its politics, at a narrowly defined moment in history. *Saison violente* says nothing explicit about the future of French Algeria, which both Roblès and his post-1962 readers know was short and violent. Where it explores cultural *métissage*, it does so on the level of personal relations as remembered many years later, after the events that destroyed the hopes of Audisio and Camus for an enlightened cultural solution to Algeria's problems. Roblès's Mediterranean fears no such collapse, since it is not about constructing a systematized regional nostalgia, but about interpreting childhood memories in a historical context. His Mediterranean is a deeply personal vision, which he does not propose as a rule either for his childhood Oran or for independent Algeria. Camus had already shown that the *pieds-noirs* had nothing for which to be nostalgic, at least in a restorative mode, and Roblès devotes no time to regrets for the country so many *pieds-noirs* felt they "lost" in 1962, probably because for him, an independent Algeria represented both a loss and a gain. If the advent of independent Arab nations necessarily broke Audisio's Mediterranean idyll, it may have been equally necessary for the modification of that idyll in Roblès's Oran. Nationalist consciousness, for all its ideological limitations, went hand in hand with revisions in Maghribi history and renewals in perceptions of the North African city.

NOTES

1. Garbriel Audisio, *Jeunesse de la Méditerranée* (Paris: Gallimard, 1935), 46.
2. At the Opéra on the Place Bresson in Algiers, the elder Audisio conducted the *Cantate du Centenaire* during President Doumergue's commemorative visit in May 1930.
3. Audisio's very first published work, the novel *Trois hommes et un minaret* (1926), predates *Héliotrope* by two years. It takes place in Paris and gives a comic treatment of what would later turn into virulent racial prejudices in mainland France. With it he won the Grand Prix Littéraire de l'Algérie for 1925.
4. Gabriel Audisio, *Héliotrope* (Paris: Gallimard, 1928), 203.
5. Ibid., 143–44.
6. Ibid., 28.
7. Ibid., 11–12.
8. Audisio, *Jeunesse*, 10.
9. Ibid., 47.
10. Ibid., 97.
11. Ibid., 12.
12. Gabriel Audisio, *Amour d'Alger* (Algiers: Charlot, 1938), 75.

13. Ibid., 82.

14. Jean-Jacques Deluz says that the Gouvernement Général building was the first major multistory building on the city's skyline, and also one of the most architecturally successful, due to good positioning on its site (Deluz, *L'Urbanisme et l'architecture d'Alger*, 25). G. Guiauchain, the last in a family of Algiers architects by that name, designed it.

15. Audisio, *Jeunesse*, 95.

16. Ibid.

17. Audisio, *Amour*, 15.

18. Audisio, *Jeunesse*, 12.

19. Gabriel Audisio, *Jeunesse de la Méditerranée: II, Sel de mer* (Paris: Gallimard, 1936), 103–4.

20. Peter Dunwoodie, *Writing French Algeria* (Oxford: Clarendon Press, 1998), 176.

21. Bertrand follows this itinerary in *Les Villes d'or*.

22. Audisio, *Jeunesse II*, 33, 60.

23. Ibid., 118.

24. Ibid., 117, 119.

25. Audisio, *Jeunesse II*, 214. Italics in the original.

26. No less astute a political thinker than Albert Camus endorsed this dubious argument in "Algérie 1958" (*Actuelles, III: chronique algérienne, 1939–1958* [Paris: Gallimard, 1958], 201), which I will discuss later.

27. Audisio, *Jeunesse II*, 215.

28. Ibid., 19.

29. Audisio, *Jeunesse*, 11.

30. Gabriel Audisio, "L'Algérie littéraire," in *L'Encyclopédie coloniale et maritime. Vol. 2, Algérie et Sahara*, ed. Eugène Garnier (Paris: L'Encyclopédie de l'Empire Française, 1946), 235.

31. Ibid., 236.

32. Audisio, "L'Algérie littéraire," 235. Arabic or Roman transcriptions of many Tamazight words existed, but no coherent or persistent tradition of written literature published in Tamazight exists in either alphabet.

33. Audisio, "L'Algérie littéraire," 247.

34. Ibid.

35. Ibid., 246.

36. Audisio, "L'Algérie littéraire," 236. Emphasis in original.

37. Audisio, "L'Algérie littéraire," 247.

38. Ibid., 240.

39. Ibid., 235.

40. He dates this last chance to thirty years before his 1958 publication, which places the missed opportunity some time during the preparations for the commemorations of 1930, and amidst the political formulations which would culminate in the Projet Violette, first proposed in 1930 (*Algérie méditerranée: feux vivants, 1957* [Limoges: Rougerie], 23).

41. Audisio, *Algérie méditerranée*, 26.

42. *Algérie méditerranée*, 30. Here, Audisio uses *colons* in the stricter sense: farmers of European descent, as opposed to city-dwellers.

43. Audisio, *Algérie méditerranée*, 12.

44. Ibid., 17.

45. Albert Camus, "Minotaure, ou la halte d'Oran," 1954 in *L'Été*, vol. 3, Oeuvres complètes d'Albert Camus (Paris: Gallimard, Club de l'Honnête Homme, 1983), 394.

46. For a discussion of the "liberal silence" surrounding Algeria in literature, see Alec Hargreaves, "Caught in the Middle: The liberal dilemma in the Algerian War," *Nottingham French Studies* 25, no. 2 (October 1986): 73–82.

47. All of Camus's articles in *L'Express*, including some not reproduced in *Actuelles III*, are collected in *Albert Camus éditorialiste à L'Express (mai 1955–février 1956)*, introduction and notes by Paul-F. Smets, Cahiers Albert Camus (Paris: Gallimard, 1987).

48. Conor Cruise O'Brien, *Camus* (London: Fontana, 1970), 105.

49. David Carroll, "Camus's Algeria: Birthrights, Colonial Injustice and the Fiction of a French Algerian People," *MLN* 112, no. 4 (September 1997): 521 and following.

50. Alec Hargreaves, "Caught in the Middle," 81.

51. The phrase was addressed to Camus's socialist friend Aziz Kessous in "Lettre à un Militant Algérien," published 1 October 1955. Reproduced in *Actuelles III*, 125.

52. Djeghloul made these comments in a discussion with the writer Albert Memmi, the critics Charles Poncet and Paul Thibaud, and one of the *chefs historiques* of the FLN, Hocine Ait Ahmed, reported in Maurice Robin, et al., "Remarques sur l'attitude de Camus face à la guerre d'Algérie," in *Camus et la politique: Actes du colloque de Nanterre, 5–7 juin 1985*, ed. Jeanyves Guérin (Paris: L'Harmattan, 1986), 201. For other Maghribi reactions to Camus's politics, see Wadi Bouzar, "Brêve histoire d'une déception: Camus et l'Algérie," *Revue Celfan* 4, no. 3 (May 1985): 36–40 and Nourredine Aba, "Que dire de Camus?" *Revue Celfan* 4, no. 3 (May 1985): 1–5. Emily Apter says that in the civil strife of the 1990s, Camus has represented a cosmopolitan and humanist model for Algerian intellectuals whom she qualifies as "French identified" (Emily Apter, "Out of Character: Camus's French Algerian Subjects," *MLN* 112, no. 4 [September 1997]: 499, 516). Although the violence may have led some Algerians to reconsider Camus in a more positive light, calling such people "French identified" misrepresents their background and culture.

53. Works of Roblès and Camus published by Charlot, in or out of the Méditerranéens collection, include Camus's *L'Envers et l'endroit* (1937) and *Noces* (1939), and Roblès's early novels *La vallée du paradis* (1940), *Travail d'homme* (1944), and *L'Action* (1946).

54. For the text of Camus's praise of Jean Grenier, see Roger Grenier, *Albert Camus soleil et ombre: une biographie intellectuelle* (Paris: Gallimard, 1987), 18.

55. "La Nouvelle culture méditerranéenne," *Jeune Méditerranée. Bulletin mensuel de la "Maison de la Culture" d'Alger*, no. 1 (April 1937): n.p. Camus mentions Maurras by name, without specifying which texts he has in mind. The Bibliothèque Nationale's collection of *Jeune Méditerranée*, an eight-page review, runs to two numbers, which may be the only ones published.

56. Camus, "La Nouvelle culture méditerranéenne."

57. Grenier, *Albert Camus soleil et ombre*, 33.

58. Camus, "La Nouvelle culture méditerranéenne."

59. Ibid.

60. Dunwoodie, *Writing French Algeria,* 188.

61. Camus, "La Nouvelle culture méditerranéenne."

62. Ibid.

63. Ibid.

64. O'Brien, *Camus,* 9.

65. Camus, *Actuelles III,* 202.

66. Le Corbusier, "La Nouvelle architecture," *Jeune Méditerranée. Bulletin mensuel de la "Maison de la Culture" d'Alger,* no. 1 (April 1937): n.p.

67. Michele Lamprakos, "Le Corbusier and Algiers: The Plan Obus as Colonial Urbanism, in Forms of Dominance: On the Architecture and Urbanism of the Colonial Experience, ed. Nezar Al-Sayyed (Avebury, UK: Brookfield, 1992)."

68. Both were acquitted. The Algerian militants Amar Ouzegane and Mohamed Lebjaoui have cast doubts on El Okbi's innocence; see Herbert R. Lottman, *Albert Camus: A Biography* (New York: Doubleday and Co., 1979), 197, and Grenier, *Albert Camus soleil et ombre,* 301. Camus's articles are reproduced with extensive commentary in *Fragments d'un combat 1938–1940: Alger Républicain, Le Soir Républicain,* ed. Jacqueline Lévi-Valensi and André Abbou, Cahiers Albert Camus (Paris: Gallimard, 1978).

69. Essay included in *L'Envers et l'Endroit,* 1937, Oeuvres complètes d'Albert Camus (Paris: Gallimard, Club de l'Honnête Homme, 1983). This first publication by Camus appeared with Edmond Charlot, as the second volume of the Méditerranéens collection. *L'Envers et l'endroit* remained relatively unknown in Paris, even after Camus had become a celebrity; he did not reissue it with Gallimard until 1958.

70. Camus, *L'Envers et l'Endroit,* 130.

71. Ibid., 131.

72. Ibid.

73. Albert Camus, "L'Été à Alger," 1939 in *Noces,* vol. 7, Oeuvres complètes d'Albert Camus (Paris: Gallimard, Club de l'Honnête Homme, 1983), 185–86. Translated as "Summer in Algiers," in *The Myth of Sisyphus and Other Essays,* trans. Justin O'Brien (New York: Alfred A. Knopf, 1955), 144; translation modified.

74. For evidence of this continuity, see Lucienne Favre's series of Casbah descriptions: *Tout l'inconnu de la Casbah d'Alger, Dans la Casbah,* and the later version significantly reworked, *Dans la Casbah 1937–1948.*

75. Albert Camus, "Le Désert," 1939 in *Noces,* vol. 7, Oeuvres complètes d'Albert Camus (Paris: Gallimard, Club de l'Honnête Homme, 1983), 204.

76. The one discussed here, "Minotaure, ou la halte d'Oran," was published in the Algiers review *L'Arche* in 1946, and then individually as a plaquette by Charlot in 1950.

77. Fewer than ten percent of the hundreds of nineteenth-century travel books about Algeria spend any significant time on Oran. Pauline de Noirfontaine, one of the few exceptions, devotes much of her book to describing how ugly and depressing she found the city, in *L'Algérie: un regard écrit* (Le Havre: Imp. Alph. Lemale, 1856).

78. Camus states his mistrust explicitly in a footnote to "La Nouvelle culture méditerranéenne."

79. Camus, "Minotaure, ou la halte d'Oran," 353–4/157–9. Numbers after the slash refer to "Minotaure, or The Stop in Oran," in *The Myth of Sisyphus and Other Essays*, trans. Justin O'Brien (New York: Alfred A. Knopf, 1955), 155–83.

80. Camus, "Minotaure, ou la halte d'Oran," 360/164–5.

81. Camus, "Minotaure, ou la halte d'Oran," 368–9/173–4. Translation modified.

82. Nineteenth-century exoticist painters believed that Algeria was the perfect place to find models for biblical or classical scenes. Eugène Fromentin, for example, found the Arabs appropriate models for both of the major modes of nineteenth-century academic painting: standing, they could model for history paintings, and on horseback, for genre paintings (*Un été au Sahara*, 110).

83. Camus, "Minotaure, ou la halte d'Oran," 368/174.

84. Ibid., 352/156.

85. The historian Madeleine Ribérioux considered 8 May 1945 the end of any hope for reconciliation between Arabs and French in Algeria (Arté television interview, 16 April 2000).

86. Charles Robert Ageron, *Histoire de l'Algérie contemporaine* (Paris: PUF, 1979), 94. The official commission of inquiry estimated 15,000 deaths; the U.S. consul in Algiers advanced the figure of 40–45,000. Historians after Ageron have come up with figures anywhere from 10 to 60,000. Algerian witnesses uniformly maintain that the riots started when demonstrators unfurled banners saying "Vive l'Algérie indépendante," and a policeman fired his revolver. We do not know the exact date of Camus's departure from Algeria, but only that VE Day found him in Paris; he would nonetheless have been present for the escalation of tensions that preceded the riots. Rachid Benattig details other provocations in the week before the riots in "8 mai 1945," *Algérie-Actualité*, 10–16 mai 1970.

87. Reproduced in *Actuelles III*.

88. Camus, *Actuelles III*, 106.

89. Camus, *Actuelles III*, 96–7.

90. Albert Camus, *La Peste*, 1947 (Paris: Gallimard, 1974), 13/5. Page numbers after the slash refer to *The Plague*, trans. Robin Buss (London: Penguin, 2001).

91. Camus, *La Peste*, 13/5.

92. Shoshana Felman, "Camus' *The Plague*, or a Monument to Witnessing," in *Testimony: Crises of Witnessing in Literature, Psychoanalysis and History*, Shohana Felman and Dori Laub (New York: Routledge, 1992), 102.

93. The argument which follows owes much to Felman, who develops the notion of witnessing the historically impossible in "Camus' *The Plague*, or a Monument to Witnessing," especially pages 101–14. See also Grenier, *Albert Camus soleil et ombre*, 147.

94. Camus, *La Peste*, 325/232.

95. Ibid., 98–9/65.

96. See for example his *Jeunes saisons* (1960) and *Saison violente* (1974), both set in Oran (and both analyzed below), which include several important Arab characters.

97. Camus, *La Peste*, 13/5.

98. The term *ratonnade*, meaning a violent police or army expedition against Arabs seems to date from the Algerian war. Generally, the preferred racial slur before the war seems to have been *bicots* rather than "rats" or *ratons*.

99. Camus, *La Peste*, 171/118. Camus's biographer Herbert Lottman reports that Emmanuel Roblès told Camus about a military *cordon sanitaire* imposed during a typhus epidemic he witnessed in the village of Turenne, near Tlemcen, in 1941 (Lottman, *Albert Camus: A Biography*, 241).

100. Carroll is citing Albert Memmi's *Anthologie des écrivains français du Maghreb*, 20 (Carroll, "Camus's Algeria," 548).

101. Camus, *La Peste*, 22/11–12.

102. See Said's discussion in which he encourages us to interpret Camus's novels "as interventions in the history of French efforts in Algeria, making and keeping it French" (*Culture and Imperialism* [New York: Alfred A. Knopf, 1993], 175).

103. Felman draws an analogy between the denial of the plague among the citizens of Oran and the ignorance of Hitler's plans among Jews in wartime Poland, a denial based partly on the very unimaginability of the event. Her argument applies to representation of the plague, and not of the Arabs, with whom she does not deal.

104. Camus, *La Peste*, 13/6.

105. Ibid., 332/237–8.

106. Camus, *Actuelles III*, 127.

107. Ibid., 126.

108. Ibid.

109. Carroll, "Camus's Algeria," 547, (emphasis in original). Peter Dunwoodie says further that Camus wrote as if "exploitation of the indigenous peoples could only be perpetrated by the rich" (Dunwoodie, *Writing French Algeria*, 278).

110. Camus, *Actuelles III*, 159.

111. Emmanuel Roblès, *Albert Camus et la trêve civile* (Philadelphia: Celfan Ed. Monographs, 1988). According to Roblès, Gouverneur Général Jacques Soustelle scuttled the *trêve civile* by refusing to consider a truce that would protect those he called, in his meeting with Camus, the *demi-pensionnaires* of the FLN, those whom he believed pretended loyalty by day and fought the French by night.

112. Camus, *Actuelles III*, 14.

113. Ibid., 201.

114. Camus, *Actuelles III*, 205. Edward Said has roundly criticized Camus for treating Muslim political aspirations as part of a chimerical Arab imperialism led by Nasser, in *Culture and Imperialism*, 178–79.

115. The novel, in manuscript at the time of Camus's death, was published in Cahiers Albert Camus (Paris: Gallimard, 1994); for the comments from Apter and Carroll, see Apter, "Out of Character," 512, and Carroll, "Camus's Algeria," 523.

116. Albert Camus, *Le Premier homme*, 11/3–4. Page numbers after the slash refer to *The First Man*, trans. David Hapgood (New York: Alfred A. Knopf, 1995).

117. André Aciman, "From Alexandria," *MLN* 112, no. 4 (September 1997): 695.

118. Camus, *Le Premier homme*, 20/16.

119. Ibid., 11/3.

120. Ibid., 29–30/20.

121. Raquel Scherr Salgado, "Memoir at Saint-Brieuc," *MLN* 112, no. 4 (September 1997): 587.

122. Camus, *Le Premier homme*, 79/62.

123. Ibid., 166/179.

124. Ibid., 268/226.

125. Ibid., 181/195–6.

126. Jean Pélégri, though the very opposite of a hard-liner, expresses the anguish of leaving behind the family burial plot in *Les Oliviers de la justice* (Paris: Gallimard, 1959).

127. Camus, *Le Premier homme*, 300/242.

128. Ibid., 179/150.

129. Ibid., 288/235.

130. The demand for a "truly sovereign Algeria" appeared as the journal emerged from a three-year silence in 1960; see "Nos objectifs," *L'Espoir-Algérie. Expression des Libéraux d'Algérie*, 13 May 1960. The Roblès quote appeared as the headline for the last issue of the BN collection, on 20 June 1962.

131. "Jeune poésie nord-africaine—Maurice-Robert Bataille, Louis Chaudron, Mohamed Dib, Henri-Jacques Dupuy, Yacine Kateb, Brahim Lourari, Jean Senac, Ahmed Smaili," *Forge: Cahiers littéraires*, no. 3 (April–May 1947).

132. Emmanuel Roldès, *Les Hauteurs de la ville*, 1948 (Paris: Seuil, 1960) was first published in serial form in *Le Populaire* (Paris) in 1947; Edmond Charlot brought out the first volume publication. *L'Action*, 1938 (Algiers: Charlot, 1946), Roblès's first novel, also included a well-developed Amazigh character. *La Vallée du paradis* was serialized in *Alger-Républicain* as "Place Mahon" before its publication in volume by Charlot in 1940; *Travail d'homme* appeared, again with Charlot, in 1942 and 1944. All were reprinted by Seuil in the sixties and seventies.

133. Roblès, *Les Hauteurs de la ville*, 9.

134. Ibid.

135. Emmanuel Roblès, *Jeunes saisons* (1961; Paris: Seuil, 1995), 9.

136. Ibid., 10.

137. Ibid., 31.

138. Emmanuel Roblès, *Saison violente* (Paris: Seuil, 1974), 46.

139. Elsewhere, he attributes applause for a left-wing speaker at a political meeting as much to defiance of the police outside as to leftist conviction (Roblès, *Saison violente*, 120).

140. Roblès, *Saison violente*, 69.

141. For a more complete picture, see Jean Déjeux's collection of articles on Algeria's cultural and literary exchanges with Spain, and especially Pierre Rivas, "La Quête d'identité dans l'autobiographie d'Emmanuel Roblès: Relations interéthniques et problèmes d'acculturation," in *Espagne et Algérie au XXe siècle: Contacts culturels et création littéraire*, ed. and intro. by Jean Déjeux (Paris: L'Harmattan, 1985), 161–77.

142. Roblès was an indefatigable world traveler. Beginning at sixteen with a trip to Morocco and Spain, his travel career included Germany, the Soviet Union, India, Southeast Asia, and China, all by the age of twenty. He lectured annually around the world from the sixties until he died in 1995.

143. Roblès, *Saison violente*, 82.

144. Ibid., 93.
145. Ibid., 111.
146. Ibid., 107.
147. Ibid., 119.
148. Ibid., 88.
149. Between about 1850 and 1930, most North African cities frequented by tourists had photo studios set up to cater to the rather predictable whims of these travelers. The extant photos show considerably fewer women than men disguised as *Maures* or *Arabes*, though female tourists indulged as well.

6

Kateb Yacine
and the Ruins of the Present

Several years before his death, Kateb Yacine (1929–1989) recalled the early phase of his career in Paris:

> J'ai publié dans les revues très péniblement. C'était le temps où Camus faisait la pluie et le beau temps. Les écrivains algériens n'existaient pratiquement pas, jusqu'au moment où Mohamed Dib a publié son premier livre aux Editions du Seuil. . . . Il est évident que pour les Français en général, l'Algérien idéalisé, à la limite, c'était Camus . . .
>
> Mais l'homme algérien, on ne le voyait pas. Il était pratiquement "étranger" dans toute cette littérature. Il y avait toute une école qu'on appelait l'école d'Alger, l'école de Camus qui représentait jalousement la littérature algérienne. Pour Dib, comme pour moi, comme pour les "Ben Mohamed", publier en France c'était impossible. On publiait de temps à autres des petits poèmes, pratiquement ça n'avait pas d'intérêt. Seulement, et c'est là ce qui montre la profonde liaison entre les combats politiques et les moyens d'expression, le jour où il y a eu des embuscades en Algérie, le jour où il y a eu des morts français en Algérie, où il y a eu le sang, à partir de là le public a commencé à s'intéresser à l'Algérie. Les éditeurs ont commencé à faire automatiquement la chasse aux Algériens. Dib et moi nous avons été publiés grâce à l'actualité, aux embuscades qu'il y a eu dans France-Soir tous les jours.

[I published in reviews, with great difficulty. At the time, Camus ruled the roost. Algerian writers hardly existed at all, until Mohamed Dib published his first book with Editions du Seuil. . . . Obviously, for the French in general, the idealized Algerian was ultimately Camus . . .

But you didn't see Algerians. They were practically "strangers" to all that literature. There was a whole school called "l'école d'Alger," Camus's school,

253

which jealously represented Algerian literature. For Dib, for me, and for all the "Ben Mohameds," publishing in France was impossible. From time to time, we published little poems; practically speaking, there was nothing there. However, and this is what shows the deep link between political struggles and the means of expression, the day there were ambushes in Algeria, the day there were French casualties, the day there was blood, then the public began to be interested in Algeria. Editors began to hunt automatically for Algerians. Dib and I were published thanks to current events, the ambushes that were going on every day in the pages of *France-Soir*.][1]

Kateb attributes his entry on the Paris scene, and the "arrival" of Algerian literature generally, to a violent intervention of history. In his thinking, this constituted a relation of cause and effect between political struggle and literary style, two of his lifelong commitments. Still, the relationship between Kateb's work and the history surrounding it needs clarification. After all, the first significant cluster of Francophone Algerian authors studied in the academy today, called the *génération de '52* (or '54, if the speaker wishes to emphasize the start of the war) of Mohamed Dib, Mouloud Mammeri, and Mouloud Feraoun, seems to have emerged with the gradual attainment of literary proficiency in French, concurrent with the coalescence of a sense of potential autonomy and political cohesion, rather than with the suddenness of an ambush. Furthermore, these authors published their first work before the actual outbreak of hostilities of which Kateb speaks in the interview cited.[2] Did the advent of Algerian literature in French, and Kateb's own publication, really depend on editors "hunting" Algerians, much as the French Army would do? This cause would seem better suited to explain the appearance, from 1954 on, of a variety of *témoignages* [eyewitness accounts] of the war itself, than to explain the publication of a complex and difficult novel like Kateb's *Nedjma* (1956).[3] Though one cannot deny the relevance of *Nedjma* to the immediate context of wartime events, nothing Kateb said in the interview just cited precludes the novel from responding to other imperatives beyond the need to comment specifically on contemporary events, or generally on the independence struggle. *Nedjma* comments not so much on historical events themselves, but on the way they might be retold, both within and outside the disciplines of history and archaeology.

Kateb did not limit his criticism of Camus to complaints directed more at his critical reception than at the writer himself. Embroidering on his earlier allusions to Arabs as "strangers," Kateb indicted Camus's fiction as much as his politics, in terms familiar since Conor Cruise O'Brien's denunciations.[4] He blamed Camus for putting himself, rather than Algeria or Arab and Amazigh Algerians, in the forefront of his novels; he found this a literary failing. Despite his reproach, Kateb nonetheless placed a certain hope in the political Camus and communicated it in terms that the narrator of *Le Premier homme* would have appreciated. "Mon cher compatriot," wrote Kateb in a 1957 letter to Camus,

> Exilés du même royaume nous voici comme deux frères ennemis, drapés dans l'orgueil de la possession renonçante, ayant superbement rejeté l'héritage pour n'avoir pas à le partager. Mais voici que le bel héritage devient le lieu hanté où sont assassinées jusqu'aux ombres de la Famille ou de la Tribu, selon les deux tranchants de notre Verbe pourtant unique. On crie dans les ruines de Tipasa et du Nadhor. Irons-nous ensemble apaiser le spectre de la discorde, ou bien est-il trop tard? Verrons-nous à Tipasa et au Nadhor les fossoyeurs de l'ONU déguisés en Juges, puis en Commissaires priseurs? Je n'attends pas de réponse précise et ne désire surtout pas que la publicité fasse de notre hypothétique coexistence des échos attendus dans les quotidiens. S'il devait un jour se réunir un Conseil de Famille, ce serait certainement sans nous. Mais il est (peut-être) urgent de remettre en mouvement les ondes de la Communication, avec l'air de ne pas y toucher qui caractérise les orphelins devant la mère jamais tout à fait morte.

> [Here we are exiled from the same kingdom, like two enemy brothers wrapped up in the pride of possessive renunciation, having haughtily rejected the inheritance so as not to have to share it. But now the handsome inheritance is becoming a haunted place where even the shades of the Family and the Tribe are murdered, according to the double edges of what is nonetheless our one selfsame Word. They are screaming in the ruins of Tipasa and Nadhor. Shall we go together to appease the ghost of discord, or is it too late? Shall we see in Tipasa and Nadhor the gravediggers of the UN disguised as Judges, and then as Auctioneers? I do not expect a specific response, and above all do not want publicity to make the expected noises in the press about our hypothetical coexistence. If one day a Family Council were to meet, it would certainly be without us. But it is (perhaps) urgent to set in motion the waves of Communication, while keeping the appearance of not touching them which characterizes the position of orphans before a mother, who is never quite dead.][5]

The letter underlines certain similarities in the concerns visible in Kateb's and Camus's fictions. The ideas of enemy brothers and of the shadows cast by family have uncanny echoes in both *Le Premier homme* and *Nedjma*. Camus and Kateb could both feel orphaned, both of the same torn country, and in the presence of mothers not quite "there": Catherine Camus was partially deaf, and Yasmina bel Ghazzali mentally ill. Finally, both writers have specific sites in which to reenact the primal scenes of their identification with Algeria, but the processes of Algerian history turned both sites into "haunted places." Tipasa and Nadhor become less archaeological sites than cemeteries in the carnage of the Algerian war; an equivocating international community could at best exhume bodies (or worse, dig new graves), rather than intervene productively by taking account of the history of a country invested simultaneously in Roman, Amazigh, and Arab ruins. Kateb has no hopes for outside intervention and knows that ultimately the new political leaders of his country will not include him in their deliberations. His literary production in both written and oral genres represents his oppositional contribution to the historical discourses alternately instrumentalized and ignored in the twilight and end of colonial Algeria.

The 1950s saw the beginning of a broad questioning not only of what had passed for historical fact during the colonial period, but also of the very modes of historiography applied to colonized peoples and places and monuments, whether standing or ruined. In the case of North Africa, this involved a reevaluation of one of the leading sources for the history of the region, the fourteenth-century historiographer Ibn Khaldūn (1332–1406). In the mid-nineteenth century, French scholars had "discovered" and interpreted Ibn Khaldūn as the cornerstone of their belief in the circularity of North African history and in its supposed unproductivity. One hundred years later, however, such beliefs were becoming controversial among historians; Kateb's *Nedjma* contains historical discourses that participate in the debate over how to read Ibn Khaldūn, as well as in the broader discussion of how to write a history of the Maghrib that would mesh with popular myth and collective memory, thereby allowing the colonized to become actors in it, in their own right. I will argue that *Nedjma* proposes a style, if not an actual methodology, for "reading" ruins, insisting not only on their relevance for understanding North Africa's past, but also on their productivity in creating the conditions for a politically viable Algerian present.

Before *Nedjma*, the centerpiece of his written work, and for many readers the founding text of North African Francophone literature, Kateb had published a very few extracts of what would later become the text of the novel or its "sequels," *Le Cercle des représailles* [The Circle of Reprisals] (1959) and *Le Polygone étoilé* [The Starred Polygon] (1966). In May 1945, Kateb was a boarder at the Collège de Sétif; his participation in the demonstrations there marked his entire career. Five days after the riots, police arrested and tortured him, imprisoning him for several months in a concentration camp for political prisoners. Many of those arrested with him were summarily executed.[6] His experience and its sequels figured highly in the 400-page manuscript he composed between 1948 and 1954; readers at the Editions du Seuil obliged him to cut half of it. The result was *Nedjma*, and the rest of the material underwent further rearrangement before appearing ten years later in *Le Polygone étoilé*. Kateb spoke of his publications as parts of a single work in constant gestation, always subject to recasting in other genres.[7] In the meantime, Kateb launched himself into the theater with two plays also containing episodes from the

Nedjma cycle: "Le Cercle des représailles" and "Les Ancêtres redoublent de férocité" [The Ancestors Turn Yet More Ferocious].[8] Kateb spoke of his publications as parts of a single work, constantly in gestation and always subject to complete recasting in other genres.[9] After these three volumes, he published little else in French, preferring to devote himself to theater in a mix of French and Algerian Arabic, staged on both sides of the Mediterranean with considerable success, until the Algerian authorities banned several of his plays.[10] *Nedjma* thus remains the focal point of his published oeuvre, the work in which he rethought his country's relationship to history, and the novel that reshaped its representation in fiction.

Nedjma appeared at a time of considerable formal innovation in the French novel, and several critics have shown the similarity of Kateb's techniques with those of Butor and Robbe-Grillet, even as he resists assimilation with the *nouveau roman*.[11] The editors at Seuil nonetheless felt the need to notify readers of the difficulties the novel presents, in a short text which accompanied all editions of the novel for forty years: neither a "notice" nor a *préface*, but an "Avertissement," a "warning" about the dangers of innovative Algerian writing. The text appeared unmodified in editions of the novel as late as the 1990s, and the critic Jean Déjeux has shown how the reviews of *Nedjma* repeated the phrases of the "Avertissement" with great fidelity.[12] It has also become a common reference in the academic criticism of the novel: the American pioneer of the study of North African literature in French, Eric Sellin, commented on it as early as 1971, and many critics since then have noted its condescension for the novel itself.[13] The author of the "Avertissement," Michel Chodkiewicz, a Muslim who would later direct the Éditions du Seuil, first insists upon the novel's Algerian specificity: it contained something eternally Arab and Algerian, rather than anything contingent or historical. That specificity nonetheless lay in the relationship between time and narration: the "Avertissement" draws a distinction between "European" and "Arab" thought, saying that

> Le rythme et la construction du récit, s'ils doivent quelque chose à certaines expériences romanesques occidentales,—ce que nous ne contestons pas— résultent surtout d'une attitude purement arabe de *l'homme face au temps*. La pensée européenne se meut dans une durée *linéaire*; la pensée arabe évolue dans une durée *circulaire* ou [sic] chaque détour est un *retour*, confondant l'avenir et le passé dans l'éternité de l'instant. Cette confusion des temps, que les observateurs hâtifs imputent au goût de l'équivoque, et où il faut voir d'abord le signe d'un génie de la synthèse, correspond à un trait si constant du caractère, à une orientation si naturelle de la pensée que la grammaire arabe, elle-même, en est marquée.
>
> [The narrative's rhythm and construction, if they indisputably owe something to certain Western experiments in fiction, result in chief from a purely

Arab notion of man in time. Western thought moves in *linear* duration, whereas Arab thought develops in circular duration or [sic] each turn is a return, mingling future and past in the eternity of the moment. This confusion of tenses—which a hasty observer will ascribe to a love of ambiguity and which one should see first as the sign of a genius for synthesis—corresponds to so constant a feature of the Arab character, so natural an orientation of Arab though, that Arab grammar itself is marked by it.][14]

Seuil thus claimed to deliver a truly Arab product to Parisian intellectual consumers in essentialized (if not exoticist) terms. The "warning" has trouble defining the Algerians' relationship to time, partly because it does not admit the historicity of that relationship. This idea about Arabs and their relationship to time leads European readers to the conclusion that Arabs cannot conceive of history as Europeans do: *They* do not think like *Us*. This alone seems like an odd comment, regarding an author who did not read Arabic. Before it can get any further, however, the text inadvertently undercuts its assertion of the "circularity" of Arab thought. As the critic John Erickson has pointed out, an obvious misprint undermines the text. The sentence in question reads, "la pensée arabe évolue dans une durée *circulaire* ou [sic] chaque détour est un *retour*" [Arab thought moves in a circular timeframe [in which/or] every detour is a return].[15] If we read it as printed, taking account both what it means to say and what it actually says, the text proposes two alternatives, the second of which allows the possibility of an entrance into history quite different from the relative stasis implied in the first. If the phrase "every detour is a return" could be read not as a subordinate clause but as an alternative, the sentence inadvertently suggests that the line of Kateb's thought does not have to go around in a circle, but might proliferate with curves looping back in all directions, never necessarily confining itself to a single track, let alone a circular one.

The Moroccan theorist Abdelkébir Khatibi has called *Nedjma* a "baroque" novel, justifying the remark by pointing out its anarchic profusion of images.[16] Rereading the "Avertissement," however, suggests that *Nedjma*'s baroque quality lies also in the curves, loops, and folds of its chronology. In considering exactly what a chronological fold might be, I turn to the philosopher Gilles Deleuze, who sees the fold as the defining production of the Baroque, less a static feature of decoration than an active principle of signification: "The Baroque refers not to an essence but rather to an operative function, to a trait. It endlessly produces folds. It does not invent things: there are all kinds of folds coming from the East, Greek, Roman, Romanesque, Gothic, Classical folds. . . . Yet the Baroque trait twists and turns its folds, pushing them to infinity, fold over fold, one upon the other. The Baroque fold unfurls all the way to infinity."[17] The production of folds is also a production of meaning, as blank surfaces take on contours, and with luck become readable. In their unfurling, these folds have a temporal dimension: the trait reproduces itself over time in not-quite-identical ripples across the surface, analogs of the original now impossible to isolate with certainty. What, though, has all this to do with the Maghrib and its historiography? In giving examples, Deleuze observes what he calls an "Islamic Baroque" in the clothes of women photographed in colonial-era postcards from North Africa.[18] Yet we need not assert that any such thing exists, in order to use the notion of the fold as a heuristic device for figuring the texture of history operative in *Nedjma*. In the Maghrib, the curves and waves, which define the European Baroque, seem to coincide more naturally with the arabesque than with any putative "Islamic" Baroque. In any event, they go far beyond the draperies in erotic or exotic images, toward an *infini* of historical ramifications.

A consideration of historical patterns in the Maghrib must necessarily pass via the fourteenth-century historian Ibn Khaldūn, whose *Muqaddimah*, the introduction to his *Kitab al-`Ibār* (ca. 1382), a history of the Imazighen, constitutes the first rational approach to the discipline of history.[19] Since his "rediscovery" by colonial-era orientalists, many scholars have projected their contemporary concerns onto Ibn Khaldūn, who has thus been construed as the prescient observer of a wide variety of traits ascribed to the Maghrib, from an alleged cultural atavism to a supposed penchant for Marxism, to name only two. I have no wish to make Ibn Khaldūn, in my turn, a precursor of the Deleuzian Baroque. Nonetheless, four reasons, besides his position as a theorist of history, make him important for reading Kateb. First, Kateb mentions him by name in his texts and cites him at several important junctures. Second, his observation of the cyclic rise and fall of dynasties, properly understood, fits closely with Kateb's notion of the branching curves of history's plots. Third, many North Africans have seen in Ibn Khaldūn's work the basis for an alternative vision of the region that would oppose the Arabo-Islamic cultural politics espoused by its governments; Kateb's later projects certainly included the development of the Amazigh and especially Kabyle cultural identity in a pluralist Algerian society. Finally, the years 1948–1956, in which Kateb composed and edited *Nedjma*, saw a significant revival of interest in Ibn Khaldūn, coincident with the political ferment in Algeria. We have no reason to suppose that Kateb had any particular predilection for Ibn Khaldūn: Kateb's heroes of the past were the Amazigh mytho-historical characters of Jugurtha, the king who fought the Romans, La Kahena, the queen who fought the Arabs, and more recently, Abdelkader, the Emir who fought the French. In an interview in 1972, Kateb suggests that he had only recently read all of the translated Ibn Khaldūn, so we have no reason to suppose that in the early '50s he would have known more than the extracts published in reviews.[20] My argument here addresses not an influence on or intent of the author, but rather the participation of the text in the elaboration of a historical discourse going on at the time of the novel's publication. A complete sense of *Nedjma*'s impact requires an account of its participation in the renewal of interest in Ibn Khaldūn contemporary with it.

Ibn Khaldūn had figured highly in the colonialist historiography: the historian Abdelmajid Hannoum lays out the connection between the translation of sections of the *Kitab al-`Ibār* and the *Muqaddimah* by William de Slane, and the various purposes the text served in the hands of not only the apologists, but also the strategists of the effort to colonize North Africa.[21] Slane's translation of the *Ibār*, which appeared in 1854, responded directly to the concerns of the Armée d'Afrique and formed the basis for most subsequent scholarly investigations of medieval North Africa. In the view of the colonial historian E.-F. Gautier, such investigations had to answer two questions: why had North Africa never ruled itself, and why had none of its outside rulers managed to hold it permanently? Regardless of the false premise of the first question, Gautier's *Le Passé de l'Afrique du Nord: Les siècles obscurs* (1935, reissued in 1952) made extensive use of Ibn Khaldūn's idea of cyclic dynastic patterns, in which dynasties arose in the desert, conquered the decadent city, but within four generations became decadent in their turn, and were replaced by another desert dynasty.[22] In Gautier's thinking, Ibn Khaldūn had accurately diagnosed the stasis of North Africa, condemned to spin its historical wheel in place without progressing or presenting truly new elements. History so imagined offered the non-European population no scope for significant action, nor any way forward other than in submission to French rule. Michel Chodkiewicz's "Avertissement" to *Nedjma* merely repeated this idea, which had all the credibility of received wisdom.

This point of view, however, was even then collapsing under vigorous attack by a new generation of historians, as progressive Algerians rediscovered Ibn Khaldūn, whose text, long available (in French) only in relatively scarce editions, was becoming more easily accessible as time passed. In 1952, two law professors issued a compilation in French and Arabic of highlights of Ibn Khaldūn's text for the use of students at the Université d'Alger. With greater visibility, the Moroccan-born Marxist geographer Yves Lacoste published "Les Prolégomènes d'Ibn Khaldoun" in 1953 in *Progrès*, a Communist-inspired Algerian review that also contained literary criticism and political essays; it reappeared in more developed form in the French Marxist review *La Pensée* in 1956, the year *Nedjma* appeared with Seuil. Lacoste specifically refuted earlier uses of the *Muqaddimah* that tended to characterize the North African past as uniform and static. To him, Ibn Khaldūn's most famous concept, the motor of history he called `asabiya, "group feeling," rightly constitutes more than the simple clan sentiment to which some scholars had reduced it: the term designates instead any one of a number of social or ideological structures that hold societies together and motivate conquest. Lacoste makes it clear that although Ibn Khaldūn certainly did not see historical progression as linear, neither did he view Maghribi history as spinning in place in circular revolutions. He discerned the curve of the rise and ruin of dynasties reproducing its pattern everywhere, in several directions at once; on one ruined polity might arise several new constructions, and so on ad infinitum. Similarly, the view of history advanced in *Nedjma* breaks with the circularity imposed by the "Avertissement," and escapes toward an infinite horizon, like the Baroque fold imagined by Deleuze: "this formal element [the fold] appears only with infinity, in what is incommensurable and in excess, when the variable curve supersedes the circle."[23] *Nedjma* suggests a Khaldunian conception of history by representing physical and textual space in the curves, crevices, and folds typical of Deleuze's Baroque. The Baroque topography of the novel proves fertile ground for the generation of an oppositional stance in history. With close attention to specific physical details of two cities he knew intimately, Constantine and Bône, Kateb delivers a critique of Algerian historiography and elaborates a mythology in which, through new visions of Algeria's cityscapes, he lays groundwork for reconciling the country's past with its present and future.[24]

Large portions of *Nedjma* take place in the urban landscapes of these two cities with very different historical and physical trajectories. Constantine, where the author was born in 1929, constituted the stronghold of religious reform, the Salafiya movement appearing in Algeria just after World War I (see figure 6.1). It served as base for bourgeois Islamic challenges to French authority, expressed via the Association des Oulémas, led by the Sheikh Ben Bādīs, a native of the city. More importantly for Kateb, however, Constantine's predecessor Cirta was the city of the Amazigh hero Jugurtha, leader of the resistance against the Romans. The city seems ideally situated to represent resistance; it sits on a rocky promontory, cut off from the surrounding land on three sides by the 200-meter gorges of the Rhummel; on the fourth side, a valley and hill presented major obstacles to French urbanization until the late nineteenth century.

Crowded onto its "rock," Constantine successfully fended off an initial attack that ended in disaster for the French in 1836; the next year, it surrendered (last among Algeria's major cities) only after bombardment and bloody house-to-house fighting. After the defeat, French authorities proved very reluctant to undertake the massive destruction and reconfiguration they had implemented everywhere else; they limited themselves

Figure 6.1.   Constantine, the Passarelle over the Gorge du Rhummel, and the Madrasa on the "rock" of the old city. Fonds documentaire Editions J. Gandini.

to widening a few streets and creating an esplanade on the spot where their artillery had pierced the fortifications, recalling with its name the open wound in the city's defenses: the Place de la Brèche. In addition, the colonial authorities decreed severe restrictions on real estate transactions in the city, wishing to keep Europeans out, and Arabs and Jews in. They succeeded to a considerable extent; old Constantine kept its "exotic," "traditional" look until Kateb's day, when urban deterioration, lack of capital, and administrative indifference began to cause visible degradation in the precolonial maze of narrow and twisted streets.[25] Kateb jokes that by the 1940s, the radical municipal government (which a *pied-noir* historian credits with historic preservation) refused to collect the garbage, "à titre de tradition populaire" [by way of popular tradition].[26]

While Constantine was the city the French were never able to remake, Bône was the one they liked to think they had built almost from the ground up. The Casbah was quite small, and the interest of the city for the French lay more in its port and the surrounding plain, propitious for colonization.[27] Occupation of the plain and urban construction accelerated rapidly after 1848, when the city became the port of arrival for both deportee and volunteer *colons* following the revolution. By the 1920s, an enterprising city government had built a thoroughly modern city whose residents compared its chic promenade, the Cours Bertagna, to the Champs Elysées, though comparison to the Cours Mirabeau in Aix-en-Provence might have involved less hyperbole. Industry and export funded this construction: Bône was depot and refinery to the Algerian mining industry, and its *minarets d'acier* [minarets of steel] would become emblematic for Kateb.[28] As in several other Algerian cities, Europeans (here Italians and Maltese) formed the majority of Bône's population. This demography was steadily changing everywhere, however: 1956, the year of *Nedjma*, saw for the first time Muslims outnumbering Europeans in Algiers, and the balance had by then tilted in Bône as well. The effect of demographic change appeared most clearly in the suburbs rather than in the old city centers. For the first time, most urban Arabs and Imazighen lived not in central *medinas* (still heavily overpopulated nonetheless), but in outlying *bidonvilles*. As a journalist for *Alger-Républicain*, Kateb described with a poet's sensitivity the way topographic splendor occasionally accompanied the economic misery of the slums. In an article appearing on 8 May 1952, he writes of a *bidonville* perched high above the city, "dominant le monde des buildings, des bureaux et des maisons de commerce, entre la mer, le ciel et le printemps" [overlooking the world of high-rises, offices, and trading houses, between the sun, the sky, and the spring]; on the sinister anniversary of political repression, the inhabitants of the slum can symbolically dominate the city through an effect of perspective.[29] In many Algerian cities, the Arabs and Imazighen inhabited the higher ground, a paradox until one considers that construction there was difficult or dangerous, and city services limited or nonexistent. Kateb contrasts this topographic reversal with the colonial power structure, to imply that the very terrain of the shantytowns meant they would continue to menace the Algerian political consciousness. Algerian urbanism from the forties on was largely an unsuccessful effort to curb the expansion of the slums, a task eventually made impossible by the influx of rural Algerians displaced by the war of independence. Constantine and Bône thus summarized, in Kateb's day, the past, present, and foreseeable future of the Algerian city. They also provide intricate surfaces for the propagation of the expanding folds and waves of a Khaldunian notion of history, one that shows that no regime was as stable as it believed, but that each carried the seeds of its demise in a further wave of attack by a new people with a more powerful `asabiya*.

THE STRUCTURE OF THE RUIN

Kateb's was the first novel by an Algerian of any ethnicity to adopt the "exploded text," chronological disturbances, and structural complications of twentieth-century experimental writing.[30] *Nedjma*'s structure, however, does more than bring the text into line with the preoccupations of literary critics of the mid and late twentieth century: it also contains the novel's connection between history, myth, and the physical spaces of urban topography. Though the principal events take place between about 1929 and 1954, the narration begins with a scene from 1947 and proceeds forward rapidly in a series of discontinuous jumps to the latest events, those circa 1954, before looping back to oscillate forward and back over May 1945. Individual sections narrate much earlier events: the beginnings of colonialism, or the fate of the Amazigh kingdoms of ancient North Africa. Many of Kateb's interpreters have commented on the structure, although some have discounted it as the random product of an attempt at order mandated by his editors.[31] Regardless of Kateb's intentions, the structural effects are present and interpretable. When his editors asked him to provide some order to a confused narration, Kateb divided the text into a system of chapters and sections: six chapters with either twelve or twenty-four sections, ranging in length from a single sentence to nearly ten pages. Three of the chapters (III, IV, and VI) contain double sets of sections, each numbered one to twelve; the novel thus presents a numbered nine-by-twelve grid of 108 sections altogether. In imposing this grid on a narrative which reads as if razed and rebuilt, Kateb seems at first to have employed, at the insistence of his editors, the same method as the French Army engineers imposing order on the tangled Casbahs of Algiers and Bône.

Further scrutiny, however, calls into question this characterization of Kateb's enterprise. Despite the apparently rigid precision of the numbers, the grid they form actually weighs very lightly on the baroque curves and folds of the narration; at times it is virtually invisible, not least because the size of the units varies so. Furthermore, the grid produces a considerably more subtle effect than simply imposing order and providing landmarks. The structure uses two chiasms in the section numbering to formalize connections between key events in history and the plot, on the one hand, and essential descriptions of Constantine and Bône, on the other. The most important event for the novel's mythic content, Nedjma's sequestration in Nadhor by her ancestor Keblout's clan, is narrated in sections IVa: 5–6, leading into the structural midpoint of the text. Sections IVa: 8–9, leading out of that center, narrate Rachid's arrival in and description of Constantine, positioned as the mirror image of the sequestration scene. The other major piece of urban description, Lakhdar's arrival in Bône in II: 10 (22 sections from the beginning of the novel) falls into a second chiasm, pairing it with the most important historical event of the plot, the riots in Sétif in VIa: 2 (22 sections before the end). The ancient city and the myth of the decimated Kebloutis form the central chiasm; the modern city and the irruption of history into the plot form another, around it. From the point of view of Nedjma herself, her adolescence and freedom in Bône is paired with the impossibility of political liberties for Algerians; her confinement in Nadhor, with the potential for resistance among the ruins in Constantine.

Constantine and Bône, however, do not admit such easy categorization. The conservative Constantine is also the site of one of the most erotically charged encounters with Nedjma's sexuality; the modern Bône is also the site in which the characters wander, disoriented, after the events of May 1945. Lakhdar's arrival in Bône occasions the first real grappling with the problems of history and space in the novel. He arrives by train, shortly after his liberation from prison, where police tortured him for his participation in the riots. A typically Katebian description reports his impressions from the moving train; the text stresses the historical disjunction between a politically active Algerian and the

> terne avenir de la ville décomposée en îles architecturales, en oubliettes de cristal, en minarets d'acier repliés au coeur des navires, en wagonnets chargés de phosphates et d'engrais, en vitrines royales reflétant les costumes irréalisables de quelque siècle futur, en squares sévères dont semblent absents les hommes, les faiseurs de route et de trains, entrevus de très loin dans la tranquille rapidité du convoi, derrière les moteurs maîtres de la route augmentant leur vitesse d'un poids humain sinistrement abdiqué, à la merci d'une rencontre machinale avec la mort, flèches ronflantes se succédant au flanc du convoi, suggérant l'une après l'autre un horaire de plus en plus serré, rapprochant pour le voyageur du rail l'heure de la ville exigeante et nue qui laisse tout mouvement se briser en elle comme à ses pieds s'amadoue la mer, complique ses noeuds de voies jusqu'au débarcadère, où aboutit parallèlement toute la convergence des rails

> [somber future of the city decomposing in architectural islands, in oubliettes of crystal, minarets of steel screwed into the heart of ships, in trucks loaded with phosphates and fertilizer, in regal shop windows reflecting the unrealizable costumes of some century to come, in severe squares where human beings, makers of roads and trains, seem to be missing, glimpsed in the distance from the train's calm speed, glimpsed too behind the wheels of cars, masters of the road, adding to their speed the human weight ominously abdicated, at the mercy of a mechanical encounter with death, humming arrows following each other alongside the train, suggesting in series an ever-tighter schedule, bringing closer to the passenger the moment of the naked, demanding city which lets every movement break up within it as the sea fawns at its feet, tightens its knots of rails as far as the platform where all tracks . . . converge and end][32]

Bône sits at the terminus of the network, where the curves and knots of track converge and end: hardly encouraging for a character like Lakhdar, already disoriented by his near miss in a concentration camp terminus.

The city imposes a terminal itinerary on its inhabitants, in addition to a timetable leading to a mechanized and dehumanizing existence. Its empty squares and industrial landscape suggest human absence, abdication, and abandonment. A character like Lakhdar, who had consciously tried to break step with the colonial order, has no chance here: Bône, the city of colonial modernity, offers no future to such a person. Its glittering architecture breaks into incoherent blocks, offering only "oubliettes" to those coming out of historical trauma. The future is somber, and the goods displayed for sale are impossible fantasies. In any case, they were not displayed for the likes of Lakhdar. The impatience of the colonized with the unrealizable promises of commercial display may lead quickly to an "ever tighter schedule"; the colonial city's time is running out.

Lakhdar nonetheless takes his time in Bône, where he has relatives: among them, Nedjma herself, an adopted cousin whom he has never met. Before reaching the Villa Nedjma, however, Lakhdar wanders in Bône for seven months unnarrated in the novel's exploded chronology. He has literally lost his way after the riots:

> Plus d'un passant s'exaspère, croit buter sur la fixité de ces prunelles de veau évadé, et donne du coude au vagabond sans réaction, qui ne se rend vraisemblablement pas compte qu'il tourne en rond; il a de nouveau l'horloge de la gare à sa gauche, mais on le devine sollicité par la montée de la Place d'Armes, à la façon dont sa démarche dévie et s'alourdit, tandis que le fumet des brochettes retient sa respiration; il s'arrête devant la montée; son orientation se confirme en cette halte pensive, et il se remet en marche, avec un masque de patient fuyant sur un tranchant de lame quelque passé d'enchantement et de cruauté, savane de chloroforme poussant sur un jeune corps insensiblement attaqué.

> [more than one pedestrian turns back in a fury after colliding with the fixity of those calflike pupils, elbowing the unreacting wanderer who evidently doesn't realize he's walking in circles; again the station clock is on his left, but you can tell he is attracted by the slope of the Place d'Armes from the way his gait swerves and retards, while the smell of the roasting food makes him catch his breath; he stops in front of the slope; his direction is decided by this pensive halt, and he starts walking again, his face the mask of a patient fleeing down a scalpel from some past of witchcraft and cruelty, a prairie of chloroform growing upon a young body imperceptibly attacked.][33]

This passage could serve as a commentary on the disorienting effect of grid urbanism on subjects used to less rectilinear cities. The text makes it clear, however, that the confusion does not arise from the contrast between "traditional" and "modern" organizations of space or apprehensions of time, or from Lakhdar's incapacity to read the terrain. Lakhdar in fact shows a surrealist sensitivity to urban detail. The critic Hédi Abdel-

Jaouad has analyzed the parallel between *Nedjma* and *Nadja*; details like the smell of brochettes grilling and the walker's constantly deviating itinerary suggest Breton and Aragon's mode of promenade, the urban walk as an unconscious quest for palpable traces of history.[34] Surrealist metaphor ends the passage, with the "patient fleeing down a scalpel" and the "prairie of chloroform," with which the city anesthetizes the walker, disorienting him as he flees from past cruelty in an urban wilderness.

While precolonial history remains present only *en filigrane*, the passage invokes colonial confrontation in two details: the Place d'Armes and the train station clock, artifacts of two different moments of French construction in Algeria. The Place d'Armes represents the style of intervention that later French colonial urbanists would disavow: the razing of a large number of houses in the very center of the old city to make a rectilinear plaza with dimensions calculated for reviewing troops. Algiers had one as well, constructed in the phase of initial occupation in the mid-1830s, but quickly renamed "Place Royale" and later "Place du Gouvernement." Bône's version of this military focal point kept its name, and thereby the memory of conquest, but this did not stop the colonized from putting it to their own uses. In Kateb's description, brochette vendors have reoccupied the site conceived for the French army, using the tactics of reterritorialization that enabled the colonized subjects to take back portions of the rebuilt city, even those with names that appeared to exclude them most blatantly. A later phase of urban intervention produced the Bône train station (see figure 6.2): the French President Doumergue laid its cornerstone on his centennial visit in 1930.[35]

The "sacerdotal eye" of its clock has fascinated *Nedjma*'s critics, who have generally seen in it the representation of the European conception of time, dominating the colonized and imposing an unchallengeable substitution for mythic or circular time.[36] Even if architecture once again figures the basic terms of colonial confrontation, it nonetheless complicates them immediately: the station clock in Bône sits not in a simple tower or architrave, but on an art-deco imitation of a minaret. Lakhdar's wanderings between the chic Cours Bertagna and the port center not on an unmediated symbol of European chronological oppression, but on a hybrid product of colonial history.[37] This kind of neo-Moorish design that added "Islamic" details to virtually any public building was not a product of mainland France alone, but of the interactions between Algerians and French which made up colonial history and culture. Kateb shows Lakhdar prey to a disorientation more historical than chronological: at stake here is not "un Arabe face au temps," as the "Avertissement" would have it, but "an Algerian in history," as expressed in the landmarks of Bône. Lakhdar takes some time to discover how to move in the space dominated by such landmarks, brutally reordered by the events of May 1945. Kateb,

Figure 6.2.   Bône (Annaba), the train station. Fonds documentaire Editions J. Gandini.

like many colonized subjects, reterritorializes the language of spatial fiction and the day-to-day uses of space in the colonial order. In doing so, he challenges the view of history concretized in the urban landscape.

In the meantime, other characters in *Nedjma* arrive in Bône and Constantine, where they face analogous problems. Rachid's arrival in Constantine uses a very different urban landscape to get at similar issues of colonial history. He does not have Lakhdar's problem on arrival: having spent most of his life in Constantine, he already knows his way. His difficulty lies less in finding his way spatially than in situating himself historically in the maze of references visible in the city and its ruins. These ruins are familiar to him from the landscape of his memory, which occasionally overlaps the topography of the city's history. The street in which he was born and spent his childhood contains traces of the French artillery assault of 1837, covered with a garden gone wild, but still apparent to those who know to look. Rachid's own house, which "faisait frontière entre le ghetto et la ville ancienne" ["made a frontier between the ghetto and the old city"], evokes the city's conquest,

maison par maison par le sommet du Koudia (aujourd'hui la prison civile où les vaincus purgent leur peine sous d'autres formes pour un forfait bien plus ancien que celui dont on les dit coupables, de même que leur banc d'infamie repose en réalité sur un silence de poudrière abandonnée) qu'occupait la batterie de siège, pulvérisant les nids de résistance l'un après l'autre; puis, par la place de la Brèche à partir de laquelle allait être bâtie la ville moderne, enfin par la porte du marché, l'entrée de Lamoricière en personne, la hâche d'une main et le sabre de l'autre. . . . 'Pas loin de sept heures', pensait Rachid. . . . L'heure à laquelle se montra le chef des Français, dans les décombres qu'un siècle n'a pas suffi à déblayer.

[house by house, to the height of the Koudia (today the civil prison where the conquered work off their sentences in other forms, for a crime much older than the one they were said to be guilty of, just as their bench of infamy actually rests on the silence of an abandoned powder magazine) which the besieging battery occupied, pulverizing the resistance nests one after the other; then, through the Place de la Brèche, where the modern city was to be built, and finally through the market gate, the entrance of Lamoricière himself, an axe in one hand, a saber in the other. . . . 'Near seven,' Rachid thought. . . . The hour when the French leader appeared in the ruins a century hasn't been enough to clear away.][38]

Everything in Constantine dates back further than it first appears. The rubble still visible in odd corners comes not only from recent urban decay, but also from Damrémont's cannonade; the crimes of prisoners in the city jail go back a century at least; the prison itself is literally a historical powder-house. The city still preserves the memory, down to the hour, of the French takeover now figured in its urban fabric by the Place de la Brèche built where days of bombardment breached the city wall. This pattern of conquest, partial destruction, and stagnation seems to have an equivalence in the narration of Rachid's fate: history apparently holds him hostage. He had participated in political agitation (with a movement inspired by Ben Bādīs in the *madrasa*, the Islamic school he attended); however, he abandoned politics well before 1945.[39] On his return to the city, he wanders its twisting streets for a while among these landmarks, but gradually confines himself to a *fondouk*, a traditional hotel (in this case inhabited by hashish smokers). At the end of the novel's chronology, he remains immobilized there, telling his stories of Nedjma's sequestration and his friends' misfortunes. Kateb includes a note to explain that Constantine was known as *qusantina ad-dahma*, "Constantine the crushing."[40] The novel seems at first to have sacrificed Rachid, crushed by the stagnated and oppressing history of Constantine.

The positioning of the narrative eye, however, suggests less of a retreat from history than Rachid's progressive shutting-in would lead readers to expect. The balcony of Rachid's *fondouk* provides a fine aerial perspective over the gorges and countryside surrounding Constantine, and this wide-open space serves as the locus of narration of Rachid's stories. The site over which he has such a good view is itself historically invested in ways that ultimately prove liberating:

> Elevée graduellement vers le promontoire abrupt qui surplombe la contrée des Hauts Plateaux couverts de forêts, au sol et au sous-sol en émoi depuis les prospections romaines et les convois de blé acheminés par les Gênois pour finir impayés dans les silos du Directoire, Constantine était implantée dans son site monumental . . . à chaque détour, chaque escapade, chaque maléfice de la brusque, la persistante ville—Écrasante de près comme de loin—Constantine aux camouflages tenaces, tantôt crevasse de fleuve en pénitence, tantôt gratte-ciel solitaire au casque noir soulevé vers l'abîme: rocher surpris par l'invasion de fer, d'asphalte, de béton, de spectres aux liens tendus jusqu'aux cimes du silence, encerclé entre les quatre ponts et les deux gares, sillonné par l'énorme ascenseur entre le gouffre et la piscine, as-sailli à la lisière de la forêt, battu en brèche . . . où la terre tremble et se présente le conquérant et s'éternise la résistance: Lamoricière succédant aux Turcs après les dix ans de siège, et les représailles du 8 mai, dix ans après Benbadis et le Congrès Musulman, et Rachid enfin, dix ans après la révoca-tion puis l'assassinat de son père.

> [Rising gently toward the steep promontory that overhangs the wooded re-gion of the High Plateau, its earth in turmoil since the Roman prospectors and the Genoese wheat caravans that rotted, unpaid for, in the Directory si-los, Constantine was planted on its monumental site . . . at each loop and curve, each escapade, each trick of the sudden persistent city—"crushing" close up as far away—Constantine with its stubborn camouflages, now the crevice of a hidden river, now a solitary skyscraper with its black helmet raised toward the abyss: a rock surprised by the invasion of iron, asphalt and concrete, specters linked to the peaks of silence, encircled by four bridges and two railroad stations, furrowed by the huge elevator between the gulf and the pool, assailed at the forest's edge, forced open . . . where the ground shudders and the conqueror appears and the resistance endures: Lamoricière succeeding the Turks after ten years' siege, and the reprisals of May 8, ten years after Benbadis and the Moslem Congress, and Rachid finally, ten years after his father's recall and murder.][41]

The city's site contains references to a history of colonization far longer than the 110 years of French presence. Romans and Turks left their traces, and the ground itself records the origin of the dispute over a debt that eventually provided a pretext for the French invasion in 1830: the wheat for which the Directory had not paid. The history thus evoked is a violent one, a series of defeats culminating in the murder of Rachid's father, prob-ably by Si Mokhtar, Rachid's mentor. These events do not amount to a glorious or monumental past, or even to a coherent one: the city is subject to tremors and convulsions and always on the verge of decadence. Nonetheless, Constantine in the novel continues to survive; though the conquerors break through the walls, the resistors dig in their heels. In its curious topography, Constantine provides the beginnings of spatial and historical reinterpretation. The viewer cannot easily grasp the city from any single perspective; its "loops and curves," "escapades," and "stubborn camouflage" mark its resistance to both penetration and all-encompassing views. Moreover, its striking orography suggests a Baroque surface folded onto itself. The elevator down the side of one of the cliffs appears to move in a furrow rather than a tower; the tallest buildings raise their roofs toward the depths, rather than the sky. If the layout and facades of a city register the movements of its history on horizontal and vertical screens, here those surfaces appear bent or folded: horizontal and vertical are inverted, and the screens become baroque films of ripples and folds, on which an inscribed line almost automatically becomes a series of curves and detours. The city thus resists the projection of a linear history and invites the sort of reading to which the "Avertissement" unwittingly alludes, an interpretation of history in which "each turn is a return." These "returns" do not lead back to an endlessly reiterated beginning, as in the colonial misreading of Ibn Khaldūn's cycles. They form instead a devious and circuitous progression.

This progression wends its way among the descriptions of ruins that cover the novel's landscape in layers. Ruins constitute a major feature of the novel's two cities and form the connection between them; they are also Kateb's raw material for extrapolating myth from history. Rachid describes his native city in an extended poetic musing, focusing on the role of ruins in the urban scene: "La Providence avait voulu que les deux villes de ma passion aient leurs ruines près d'elles, dans le même crépuscule d'été, à si peu de distance de Carthage; nulle part n'existent deux villes pareilles, soeurs de splendeur et de désolation qui virent saccager Carthage et ma Salammbô disparaître, entre Constantine [. . .] et Bône." ["Providence had willed it that the two cities of my passion should have their ruins nearby, in the same summer twilight, so near Carthage; nowhere are there two such cities, sisters in splendor and desolation, that saw Carthage sacked and my Salammbô disappear, between Constantine . . . and Bône."][42] Rachid's version of Flaubert's *Salammbô* is of course Nedjma, the object of the pursuit of all four protagonists. Salammbô's replacement enables Kateb to reinvest Flaubert's classicized Carthage with Amazigh signifiers. For him, Carthage is a corner of the triangle formed with the ancient Amazigh cities of Hippone (Bône) and Cirta (Constantine), which outlasted it. These cities have their ruins nearby, keeping the past close to hand.

Uncovering the archaeological vestiges of a glorious past is a common move in Algerian historiography, and proved very powerful in the hands of colonial historians, who started from the premise of a justified French presence. Reading Kateb and Ibn Khaldūn together, however, suggests some other possibilities for interpreting ruins. These two strongholds of the Numidian kingdom that united much of North Africa before the Roman colonization are far from intact, and their ruins do not engender an unproblematic model for Algerian history. The fact of their near destruction, more than their existence itself, gives them their evocative power. The nostalgia of Kateb's characters does not spur them to restore, but only to contemplate. Rachid specifically contrasts the Amazigh ruins of Cirta with the better preserved Roman ruins of Lambèse, the ancient *colonia* on which Napoléon III built a penitentiary for political prisoners. Speaking of his native Constantine, Rachid insists

> Pas les restes des Romains. Pas ce genre de ruine où l'âme des multitudes n'a eu que le temps de se morfondre, en gravant leur adieu dans le roc, mais les ruines en filigrane de tous les temps, celles que baigne le sang dans nos veines, celles que nous portons en secret sans jamais trouver le lieu ni l'instant qui conviendrait pour les voir: les inestimables décombres du present. . . . J'ai habité tour à tour les deux sites, le rocher puis la plaine où Cirta et Hippone connurent la grossesse puis le déclin dont les cités et les femmes portent le deuil sempiternel, en leur cruelle longévité de villes-mères; les architectes n'y ont rien à faire, et les vagabonds n'ont pas le courage d'y chercher refuge plus d'une nuit; ainsi la gloire et la déchéance auront fondé l'éternité des ruines sur les bonds des villes nouvelles.

> [Not the remains of the Romans. Not that kind of ruins, where the soul of the multitudes has only time to waste away, engraving their farewell in the rock, but the ruins watermarked from all time, the ruins steeped in the blood of our veins, the ruins we carry in secret, without ever finding the place or the time suitable for seeing them: the inestimable ruins of the present. . . . I have lived in both places, the rock, then the plain where Cirta and Hippone knew greatness and afterwards the decline for which the citadels and the women wear their sempiternal mourning, in their cruel longevity of mother-cities; the architects have nothing to do there, and the vagabonds have not the courage to seek refuge longer than a single night; thus glory and defeat have founded the eternity of ruins upon the growth of new cities.][43]

Figures of ruins generally oppose notions of permanence, but despite Rachid's elegiac tone, he neither laments past glory nor condemns all present and future constructions (physical or political) to dust. For him, ruins are not part of the past, but of the present; rather than leaving stable traces ("engraving their farewell in the rock") they appear "en filigrane de tous les temps," watermarked into the surface of paper or cloth, a surface subject to rippling, folding, or distortion. These "ruins of the present" are paradoxically constructed on top of cities which otherwise appeared new. To the practiced eye, they form a baroque overlay rather than a classical base for new construction; Kateb imagines that Algerian history has somehow folded back over itself to place the ruins on top of the new. This represents perhaps the ultimate reversal of the favorite restorative move of the proponents of Latin Africa, who imagined their cities springing from the Roman ruins sprinkled across Algeria. By inverting their positions, Kateb suggests the absurdity of restorative nostalgia, but also the unrelenting presence of the past.

In addition to their ambiguous placement, ruins offer at best an unclear symbolism; they may prove virtually unreadable. At several points, neither protagonists nor narrator seem to know how to name them, uncertain if they are looking at the ruins of Cirta, or of some city with an older name.[44] Cirta and Hippone may not actually have represented the earliest origins of North African civilization; Rachid feels, furthermore, that the two cities pull him in opposite directions, just as their modern replacements leave him torn between closure and coherence on the one hand, and openness and modernity on the other. Nedjma herself appears trapped between the two cities after her sequestration, endlessly travelling the road from one to the other in a closed carriage, unable to arrive in either one. Even Kateb's rejection of the myth of Arab and Islamic unity (problematic in Algeria) does not lead to a less conflicted construction of the past. Certainly the ruins are "Numidian" and therefore Amazigh rather than Arab, but the Amazigh-identified past remains just as difficult to build upon as the glorified Arab conquest. Even as he connects the ruined cities to a "mother-city," to Salammbô, or to Nedjma herself, Kateb suggests that while a new nation might find it natural or necessary to build on these symbols, there are dangers inherent in basing a new national identity on such slippery signifiers. Nedjma's sequestration in the clan stronghold of Nadhor shows the danger, for women, in basing Algerian national identity on an overdetermined symbol of femininity.[45] The same danger may lie in imagery that confines the female inhabitants of these "mother-cities" to "sempiternal mourning."

The pitfalls of the city as symbol are of two sorts: first, the apparent ease with which a city's structure may be violated, and second, the rapidity with which it may become unresponsive and sclerotic, literally clogged with ruins. First, identifying the city as female can lead too easily to perceiving the colonial "penetration" as the rape of an urban structure. This seems especially true in Bône, where the city was so heavy-handedly rebuilt with money derived from resource extraction: *Nedjma*'s protagonists see the city physically mauled by the European industrial complex, and their country's riches visibly flowing out of its port. The novel, however, does not present colonized cities or subjects passively taking abuse; the narrators know from looking closely at the city's structure that it results from an active, if unequal, exchange between colonized and colonizer. The violation model by itself is too simple to account for the presence of ruins in Algeria's colonial past, or the construction of the monuments of its present. The second difficulty, that of urban sclerosis or stagnation, becomes yet more serious. In Rachid's city, "les architectes n'ont rien a y faire" ["the architects have nothing to do there"], since he is very suspicious of grand projects and their symbolism: "Les grands chantiers qu'on se proposait de mettre en marche avaient toujours passionné les habitants comme un rêve exotique, digne de l'ère nucléaire, et que la plupart attendaient pour fonder un foyer ou acheter une chemise . . . quelques immeubles gigantesques, quelques usines anarchiques, et le chômage persistant dans le plus riche des trois départements, dans la ville même 'où de Gaulle vint m'accorder la citoyenneté . . .'" ["The great work-sites that were supposed to be opened had always excited the inhabitants like an exotic dream, worthy of the nuclear age, and which most of them were waiting for in order to start a family or buy a shirt. . . . A few gigantic apartments, a few anarchic factories, and the persistent unemployment in the richest of the three departments, in the very city 'where de Gaulle came to grant me citizenship . . .'"].[46] The hope of progress expressed in ruinous projects (on sites themselves soon indistinguishable from ruins) leads only to stasis, as the inhabitants constantly push back their own projects, and the novel pushes forward its own circuitous motion.

Politics, too, suffer from such constructions imposed from above: Constantine, where de Gaulle proclaimed the political rights of the Muslims in 1944, did not escape the repression of the following year. Later, the four protagonists work on the site of a new project, incomprehensible, probably pointless, and frequently postponed: "Y en a qui sont morts sans être sûrs d'avoir vraiment travaillé. . . . A supposer que le projet soit réel, qui sait si le marché couvert ne se transformera pas en commissariat de police?" ["Some died without ever being sure they really worked on something . . . supposing the project is a real one, who knows if the market won't be turned into a police station?"][47] The worker speaking here expresses a perfectly reasonable concern, given the police crackdown in May 1945. The Gouvernement Général's banner projects of the late forties and early fifties were the *cités* of suburban Algiers, where market squares soon became heavily patrolled zones of confrontation.[48] Again, in a scene in the last work of the *Nedjma* cycle, *Le Polygone étoilé*, situated ambiguously either during the war or after independence, Kateb describes a concentration camp of laborers working on a project which the authorities declare vital to national prestige. It is neither described nor completed; even if it were, the *note d'urbanisme* [whiff of urbanism] it would bring to the region would benefit only the foreign experts in charge and the retired military men who would monopolize it.[49] The narrator insists on the impossibility of couching a national identity in a design:

"Chaque fois les plans sont bouleversés" [Every time the plans are up-set].[50] Grand building projects symbolizing Algerian identity or under-taken in the name of national pride lead to the strangulation of the living city actually inhabited by ordinary citizens. Such projects, furthermore, prove irrelevant for national identification when history and identity re-main as shifting and polyvalent as Rachid's "inestimable ruins of the present."

Despite these difficulties, ruins maintain a connection with the mythic elements of *Nedjma*, and an ideological overinvestment in the mother-city may be a necessary danger in a novel where the fathers are decadent or absent. Ruins and ancestors derive their power for Kateb not from their symbolism as vestiges of past grandeur, but from the very fact of their de-struction. All the major characters descend from such a ruined ancestor: the mythologized Keblout. He appears in two incarnations, seven hun-dred years apart: the clan's ultimate ancestor, an Amazighized member of the invading Beni Hillal tribe in the twelfth century, and the leader based in Nadhor at the time of the French invasion. Kateb explains that the sec-ond Keblout mysteriously disappeared and his sons died at the hands of the French, who co-opted, dissipated, and divided the generation inter-vening between them and the fathers of the four protagonists. Only one of the four branches remains in Nadhor, in steady decline despite its re-sistance to penetration from outside. The other branches are represented by the dissolute fathers of the four protagonists and Nedjma; their deca-dence causes confusion of the paternal blood lines. Nedjma's paternity is uncertain, and Si Mokhtar, her most likely father, fails to prevent her mar-riage to a man who may be his son (and therefore, at two removes of un-certainty, her half-brother). Si Mokhtar himself exemplifies the ruined and yet mythically powerful progenitors. An unbeliever and fast liver, he nonetheless claims a genuine authority on Islam, and heads the Algerian delegation of pilgrims to Mecca; thoroughly imbued with the culture of French spa towns and the Riviera, he nonetheless serves as the repository of the Keblout clan's history.[51] His power stems from his decadence, ruin, and resurgence; much like the city of Constantine, the mythic elements of his persona provide material for historical recovery. After Si Mokhtar's generation of the diaspora dies out, the Nadhor Kebloutis are all that re-main. Left with their collapsing mosque, their rituals of sacrifice, and their emblematic vultures (yet another symbol of collapse and decomposition), they represent the "ruins of the present" of the clan. With the biological fathers thus eliminated, the ruins of the clan and the myth of Constantine, the mother-city *battue en brèche* but surviving by ruse, engender a type of history based not on the restoration of male-line inheritance, but on de-tours and dodges among the ruins.

HISTORY VANDALIZED

Nedjma remains the book of the collapse of colonialism, since its chronology conveniently ends in 1954, the year the Algerian war broke out. The fictional cycle continues, however, to include events explicitly set during the war itself in the play *Le Cercle des représailles* (1959), and finally in a world ambiguously situated as colonial or post-colonial in *Le Polygone étoilé* (1966). Published at the height of the war, the play portrays the most arresting urban spectacle of the conflict, the Battle of Algiers two years before. Lakhdar and Mustapha, the most politically active characters of *Nedjma*, reappear as A.L.N. operatives; Nedjma herself has joined the struggle with them. In doing so, she transforms herself from mythic object into historical agent. Her reappearance after the sequestration and her speaking role after her silence in the novel prove that confinement is not the necessary end point for a woman embodying the conflict between love and revolution, myth and history. She survives the play, free, as she will again in *Le Polygone étoilé*; her days of fruitless shuttling between Constantine and Bône are over.

The play's twisted chronology presents Lakhdar's death in the first scene, and then circles around several times to lead up to it once again in the end. All of this takes place in the living ruin of the Casbah of Algiers, overpopulated, ruinous, and overrun with General Massu's infamous paratroopers. The play opens "after the fact," as the demonstration and fusillade fatally wounding Lakhdar has already taken place. The stage directions specify "Casba, au-delà des ruines romaines. Au bout de la rue, un marchand accroupi devant sa charrette vide. Impasse débouchant sur la rue en angle droit. Monceau de cadavres débordant sur le pan de mur. Des bras et des têtes s'agitent désespérément. Des blessés viennent mourir dans la rue." [the Casbah, beyond the Roman ruins. At the end of the street, a merchant crouching in front of his empty cart. A cul-de-sac giving onto the street at a right angle. A heap of corpses overflowing onto a section of wall. Heads and arms moving desperately. Wounded people coming to die in the street.][52] Kateb goes well "beyond" the Roman ruins almost absent in Algiers, visible mostly to colonial historians wishing to justify the regime with an ancient precedent. Here, we see more bodies than ruins: the crumbling wall emerges from a pile not of rocks, but of corpses, and the ruined buildings have their analog in ruined flesh. The itinerant merchant with nothing to sell is silent witness to the destruction; the real witness to this holocaust is the street itself, personified by the wounded Lakhdar: "Ici est la rue des Vandales. C'est une rue d'Alger ou de Constantine, de Sétif ou de Guelma, de Tunis ou de Casablanca. Ah! l'espace manque pour montrer dans toutes ses perspectives la rue des mendiants et des éclopés, pour entendre les appels des vierges somnambules, suivre des cercueils d'enfants, et recevoir dans la musique des maisons closes le bref murmure des agitateurs. Ici je suis né, ici je rampe encore pour apprendre à me tenir debout, avec la même blessure ombilicale qu'il n'est plus temps de recoudre; et je retourne à la sanglante source, à notre mère incorruptible." [This is the Rue des Vandales. It is a street of Algiers or Constantine, Sétif or Guelma, Tunis or Casablanca. There is no space to show all the perspectives on this street of beggars and the lame, to hear the calls of sleepwalking virgins, to follow the coffins of children, to pick up over the music of the whorehouses the brief murmurings of the agitators. Here I was born, and here I am still crawling in order to learn to stand upright, with the same umbilical wound that it is too late to stitch up. And I am returning to the bloody source, to our incorruptible mother.][53] Lakhdar refuses to embark on the exotic inventory de rigueur for a street description in the old city of Algiers: there is no longer any space for touristic details. Local color tended to go together with "picturesque" misery in clichéd Casbah descriptions by French Algerian writers, but here, the misery is no longer anything but shameful. The battle of Algiers staged in *Le Cercle des représailles* destroys the picturesque by refuting the supposed historical stagnation that it needed in order to function.

Of all the "picturesque" streets in which that battle took place, Kateb chooses the Rue des Vandales, and his version of the war revalorizes urban vandalism both historical and literal. The street's name evokes one of the shortest-lived, least productive, and least appreciated foreign empires in Algeria, and suggests a parallel with that other short and unappreciated foreign domination just then being overthrown after 130 years, a brief interval in the many centuries of North African history. In their enthusiasm for using the urban toponymy to commemorate their colonizing predecessors, the municipal authorities had ignored the reputation of the Vandals and memorialized them in the same way they had the Phoenicians and Romans. Kateb uses the destructive resonances of the Vandals, ravagers as well as builders of empire, to interrupt the succession of memorialized foreign dominations that supposedly constituted Algerian history. He turns the Vandals against the French, and also against the conception of colonial history that had led to their odd commemoration in Algiers. Lakhdar, the corpses, the street, and the whole Casbah were victims of Massu's vandalism, but they also become Vandals themselves, the *déclassés* of history (scavengers and cripples, prostitutes and plotters), who will ravage the French city. Far from the showcase boulevards, one street becomes emblematic of urban North Africa as a whole; and one historical episode portrays invaders, resistors, and destroyers of empire.

In a life cycle reaching from birth to death, Lakhdar rejoins the city, his "incorruptible mother" despite (or perhaps because of) its accumulation of undesirables. He comes to identify himself with the street's crowd, and his body with its structure. He has already spoken of the "umbilical" connection he feels with the street's "bloody source," and when he returns to name it once more, he insists on its corporality: "Ici est la rue des Vandales, des fantômes, des militants, de la marmaille circoncise et de nouvelles mariées; ici est notre rue. Pour la première fois je la sens palpiter comme la seule artère en crue où je puisse rendre l'âme sans la perdre. Je ne suis plus un corps, mais je suis une rue. C'est un canon qu'il faut désormais pour m'abattre. Si le canon m'abat je serai encore là, lueur d'astre glorifiant les ruines, et nulle fusée n'atteindra plus mon foyer. . . . Ici est la rue de Nedjma mon étoile, la seule artère où je veux rendre l'âme. C'est une rue toujours crépusculaire, dont les maisons perdent leur blancheur comme du sang, avec une violence d'atomes au bord de l'explosion." [This is the street of the Vandals, the phantoms, the militants, the freshly circumsized brats, and the new brides; this is our street. For the first time I feel it palpitating like the only artery in flood in which I can give up the ghost without losing my soul. I am no longer a body, but a street. From now on it will take a cannon to knock me down. If the cannon knocks me down, I will still be here, with starlight glorifying the ruins, and no missile will ever again hit my home. . . . This is the street of Nedjma, my star, the only street in which I want to die. It is always a twilight street, in which the houses lose their whiteness like blood, with the violence of atoms on the verge of an explosion.] The street becomes an artery with a human pulse, and Lakhdar becomes a body with a street's structure. He and the Rue des Vandales together possess the simultaneous strength and resilience of ruins: knocking them down with cannon will do no further harm: they are *already* ruined, like the cities that owe their strength to having "connu trop de sièges . . . [et qui] ne sauraient être surprises ni vaincues" ["besieged too often . . . [and that] can never be surprised, nor vanquished"].[55] Destroying a Katebian ruin is impossible, since it consists only in traces that evoke memory; if destroyed, the traces of what once occupied the site will leave traces of their own. We see here the resilience of the contemplative nostalgic project. Similarly, Lakhdar's death is a fading away, paralleled by the draining of the famous "whiteness" which had given Algiers its defining epithet. In this twilight of the colony, the mother-city reappears as Nedjma herself ("star" in Arabic). On her intervention Lakhdar can replace himself in the urban fabric: "Je me retrouve dans notre ville. Elle reprend forme. Je remue encore mes membres brisés, et la rue des Vandales prend fin à mes yeux. . . . Je sors enfin de cette Mort tenace et de la ville morte où me voici enseveli." [I find myself in our city. It is taking shape again. I am still moving my broken limbs, and the Rue des Vandales is coming to an end in my sight. . . . I am finally leaving that tenacious Death and the dead city where I am buried.][56] Kateb is constructing a spatial fiction, fully immersed in an ideological myth of the founding of a nation, yet with processes of signification rooted in the physical existence of historical traces.

The last work of the *Nedjma* cycle, *Le Polygone étoilé*, emphasizes that the rebirth of the city can never be a definitive act, but instead demands repeated exhumations and reconsiderations of the previous city's ruins. Published in 1966, several years into the socialist military regime that wished to make Algeria a leader of the formerly colonized world, the text casts the country in a dubious historical moment, difficult to situate before or after independence. Its refrain, "Et chaque fois les plans sont bouleversées" [and every time, the plans are upset] casts serious doubt on the possibility of permanent constructions on top of "les ruines de tous les temps qui caractérisent l'Algérie" [the ruins of every period which characterize Algeria], as he had described them seven years earlier in another play, "Les ancêtres redoublent de férocité."[57] Kateb finds on the contrary that "notre statut, de mémoire d'Algérien, fut toujours provisoire, et chaque fois qu'on le définit, il devient un peu plus vague" [for as long as Algerians can remember, our status has always been provisional, and every time we define it, it becomes a little vaguer]; Camus's ideas on the incompleteness of Algerian memory find their extension here.[58] All constructions based on the ruins embodying memory will of necessity be provisional and incomplete.

Kateb ironizes the official discourse of "Five-Year Plans" administered by foreign experts and a government more concerned with personal advantage than national development. The period of chaotic growth in Algerian cities after the war amply proved the incoherence of such plans, and for Kateb, their inadequacy had cultural and literary consequences: "Chacun a son plan. Et chaque fois, les plans sont bouleversés. D'ailleurs, notre cité pourrait bien être originale à ce prix: être édifiée sans plan, ce qui impose, soit dit en passant, un surcroit de méthode, un adieu déchirant aux fantômes de la tribu. Ne sont-ils pas en partie responsables de leur survivance? Bien qu'irréels, ne sont-ils pas les sombres fondateurs des forteresses complexes et médiévales? C'est une absurdité bien établie, ils ont une certaine tendance à transgresser leurs propres plans." [Everyone has his plan. And every time, the plans are upset. For that matter, our city could well be original at this price: being built without a plan, which demands, let it be said in passing, a greater method, and a wrenching farewell to the ghosts of the tribe. Are they not partially responsible for their survival? However unreal they are, are they not also the somber founders of complex medieval fortresses? It's a well-known absurdity that they have a certain tendency to transgress their own plans.][59] The lack of an urban plan implies an abdication of responsibility by the ancestors: their myth is henceforth inadequate, and the situation demands a wrenching farewell to the "ghosts of the tribe," who in any case violate their own blueprints for the future.

If they wish to build a city in which they can move in historically consequential ways, Kateb urges his fellow Algerians not to rely on the self-perpetuating elite that inherited power from the *chefs historiques* of the FLN, and to do more than administer five-year plans of dubious relevance. He suggests instead a positive interpretation of a phrase of Ibn Khaldūn, cited from an unnamed secondary source: "Tout ce qui est arabe est voué à la ruine" [Everything Arab is headed for ruin], says the observer of the rise and fall of dynasties.[60] For Kateb, the phrase holds as much promise as menace: the *Nedjma* cycle establishes the productivity of ruins, as well as their destabilizing influence. Ibn Khaldūn knew that ruins were never an end point in North African history, and this issue lay at the center of the debate regarding his work in the 1950s. The baroque folds and complexities of his account of the historical process allowed ruins to overlay living cities, as much as cities could be built on ruins. For him, and for Kateb, ruins are waypoints through which new historical developments pass as they set out along their curving paths. As such, they are ideal grounds for reterritorialization. In Algeria, the reterritorialization of the colonized in the colonial city took place via a process of recreating or reimagining ruins and overlaying them like a transparency on top of the French (re)constructions. Any historiography of the Maghrib must take into account this circuitous process. Kateb's work, as it participates in contemporary debates over the construction of postcolonial history, implies learning to use such overlays to build a provisional historical account on shifting ground, as a means of finding one's way among the ruins of the present.

NOTES

1. Olivier Corpet, Albert Dichy, and Mireille Djaider, eds., *Kateb Yacine, éclats de mémoire* (Paris: IMEC, 1994), 60. Kateb's phrase, "faire la chasse aux Algériens," clearly recalls the phrase then in informal use by the French army in Algeria to describe their raids.

2. Jean Déjeux attributes the phrase *génération de 1954*, which he says explains little, to the Algerian poet Henri Kréa (*Littérature maghrébine de langue française: Introduction générale et Auteurs* [1973; Sherbrooke: Naaman, 1978], 26).

3. Henry Alleg's banned account of surviving torture at the hands of the paratroopers in Algiers, *La Question* (Paris: Maspéro, 1957) [*The Question* (New York: Braziller, 1958)] is only one of the most famous of the participant accounts favorable to indepence; other participant or journalistic accounts, often more sympathetic to the French army, appeared in considerable number.

4. See the interview cited in Corpet, Dichy, and Djaider, *Kateb Yacine, éclats de mémoire*, 61; O'Brien develops a very similar argument in *Camus*. Kateb died in 1989, before the rediscovery of *Le Premier homme*.

5. Corpet, Dichy, and Djaider, *Kateb Yacine, éclats de mémoire*, 33. The editors do not specify the date, beyond the year; nor do they note whether Camus responded.

6. Yacine Kateb, *Soliloques* (1946; Paris: La Découverte, 1991), preface. The phrase *camp de concentration* is Kateb's.

7. Yacine Kateb, *L'Oeuvre en fragments*, ed. and intro. Jacqueline Arnaud (Paris: Sindbad, 1986), 14.

8. Both appeared in *Le Cercle des représailles* (Paris: Seuil, 1959), but only the title selection was performed. Jean-Marie Sarrau directed two performances of it in Brussels in November 1958, in which Douta Seck, one of the preeminent West African Francophone actors of his generation, played the Coryphée.

9. Kateb, *L'Oeuvre en fragments*, 14.

10. A selection of these plays, reproduced from sketchy manuscripts and sound recordings, appeared in *Boucherie de l'espérance*, ed. Zebeida Chergui (Paris: Seuil, 1999).

11. See Marc Gontard's *Nedjma de Kateb Yacine: Essai sur la structure formelle du roman*, which, of all the contemporary critiques, goes the furthest toward an analysis of *Nedjma* in its similarities to the *nouveau roman*, and also his "A propos de la séquence du Nadhor," where Gontard defends himself against critics who wish to see Kateb as more "poetic" and particularly Maghribi than an association with the *nouveaux romanciers* would imply. Gontard suggests that this view tends to valorize the author in essentialist terms. As for Kateb himself, he did not appreciate that "on a voulu me 'foutre' dans le nouveau roman, on a essayé de spéculer sur mon nom" (Corpet, Dichy, and Djaider, *Kateb Yacine, éclats de mémoire*, 60).

12. Jean Déjeux, "Réception critique de *Nedjma* en 1956–57," in *Actualité de Kateb Yacine*, ed. Charles Bonn (Paris: L'Harmattan, 1993), 113.

13. Sellin in turn cites Mohamed Salah-Dembri, who had written acidly about it in an Algerian review in 1967 (Eric Sellin, "Algerian Poetry: Poetic Values, Mohammed Dib and Kateb Yacine," *Journal of the New African Literature and the Arts*, no. 9–10 [1971]: 60). Déjeux credits the Moroccan critic and poet Mohamed Aziz Lahbabi as the sole exception among the reviewers of the day to reject the premises of the "Avertissement," in "Notes sur la culture arabo-musulmane," *Confluent* 14, (July 1957) (Déjeux, "Réception critique," 114).

14. Yacine Kateb, *Nedjma* (1956), 6/ix, translation modified to reflect typographic error; emphases in original. Further citations of *Nedjma* will give page numbers in the 1996 edition, and, after the slash mark, in the English version: *Nedjma*, 1961, trans. Richard Howard, introd. Bernard Aresu (Charlottesville, VA: Caraf Books, University of Virginia Press, 1991).

15. This is not the sentence Erickson discusses, since he situates the misprint in the sentence following the one in which it actually occurs; the *où* in the sentence he cites in fact carries the correct accent in all editions. He points out that the misprint persisted for many years in subsequent printings of the novel ("Kateb Yacine's *Nedjma*: A Dialogue of Difference," *Sub-Stance*, no. 69 [1992]: 30). The preface has disappeared altogether in editions since the mid-1990s.

16. Abdelkébir Khatibi, *Le Roman maghrébin* (Paris: François Maspero, 1968), 106.

17. Gilles Deleuze, *The Fold: Leibniz and the Baroque*, trans. Tom Conley (Minneapolis: University of Minnnesota Press, 1993), 5. I am not the first to consider *Nedjma* in the light of Deleuze and Guattari's work: Bernard Aresu evokes rhizomatic structures in Kateb's poetics in *Counterhergemoic Discourse from the Maghreb: The Poetics of Kateb's Fiction* (Tubingen: Narr, 1993), 75.

18. His mention of the *Baroque islamique* comes in a discussion of the photographer and psychiatrist Clérambault, whose preferred photographic subjects were veiled women (Deleuze, *The Fold: Leibniz and the Baroque*, 38).

19. The *Kitab al-`Ibār* is often translated as *A History of the Berbers*. The text of the introduction is available English as *The Muqaddimah: An Introduction to History*. Trans. Franz Rosenthal (New York: Pantheon Books, Bollingen Series, 1958).

20. Yacine Kateb, *Parce que c'est une femme* (Paris: Des femmes, 2004), 41.

21. Abdelmajid Hannoum, "Translation and the Colonial Imaginary: Ibn Khaldūn Orientalist," *History and Theory* 42 (February 2003): 61–2.

22. Though Ibn Khaldūn called these dynasties "Arabs," meaning that they were originally nomads, most were Imazighen. Colonial-era readers did not always understand that "Arabs," for Ibn Khaldūn, were not the people so designated by the French, that is, speakers of dialectal Arabic who considered themselves more arabized than their Tamazight-speaking neighbors.

23. Gilles Deleuze, *Le Pli: Leibniz et le baroque* (Paris: Editions de Minuit, 1988), 53. Page 38 in the English edition.

24. For a sampling of Kateb criticism focused on "space" generally, see the articles in *Actualité de Kateb Yacine* (ed., Charles Bonn [Paris: L'Harmatton, 1933]), as well as Elizabeth Pease's "L'Espace, la mère, l'impasse: *Nedjma* de Kateb Yacine," and Jacqueline Arnaud's "Les villes mythiques et le mythe de Nedjma dans le roman de Kateb Yacine"; Charles Bonn comments on the prevalence of interest in space in *Problématiques spatiales du roman algérien*, 33. Jacqueline Arnaud suggests a chronology for Nedjma in *Recherches sur la littérature maghrébine de langue française*, 671.

25. Bernard Payand deals with this deterioration in *La Médina de Constantine: De la ville traditionnelle au centre de l'agglomération contemporaine* (Poitiers: Centre interuniversitaire d'études méditerranéennes, 1989).

26. Kateb *Nedjma*, 154/204. The historian is Michèle Biesse-Eichelbrenner, in *Constantine: la conquête et le temps des pionniers* (1985), 42.

27. The essential reference in English on the city of Bône is also a first-rate work on the French implantation in Algeria: David Prochaska's *Making Algeria French* (Cambridge, UK: Cambridge University Press, 1990).

28. Kateb *Nedjma*, 69/92.

29. Yacine Kateb, Mohammed Dib, and Pierre Laffont, "Le Chômage, cette plaie," *Alger Républicain*, 8 May 1952.

30. Khatibi noted as early as 1968 that Kateb's complexities meshed with the interests of French intellectuals of the day, in *Le Roman maghrébin* (Paris: François Maspero, 1968), 101. See also the last section of Marc Gontard's *Nedjma de Kateb Yacine* (Paris: L'Harmattan, 1985), where the author compares Kateb to Robbe-Grillet, Faulkner, and Dos Passos.

31. Eric Sellin and Kristine Aurbakken suggest geometric and arachnean explanations, respectively, while Jean Déjeux protests that Kateb's lack of intentions regarding the structure should be taken as definitive (Eric Sellin, "The Algerian Novel of French Expression," *The International Fiction Review* 1, no. 1 [1974]: 43–44; Kristine Aurbakken, *L'Étoile d'araignée: une lecture de Nedjma de Kateb Yacine* [Paris: Publisud], 207; Déjeux, "Réception critique," 101).

32. Kateb *Nedjma*, 64/92–3, translation modified.

33. Kateb *Nedjma*, 68/97–8.

34. See Hédi Abdel-Jaouad's "Kateb Yacine's Modernity: Rewriting Surrealism," *Sub-Stance*, no. 69 (1992): 11–29.

35. The founding ceremony itself provided a staged and selective aperçu of Bône's history as, according to the newspaper account, Doumergue listened to a recitation of the city's capture "avec une attention émue" ("Le Voyage du Président de la République en Algérie," *L'Afrique du Nord illustrée*, 17 May 1930, 7).

36. Charles Bonn, *Problématiques spatiales*, 22–23, and *Kateb Yacine: Nedjma* (Paris: PUF, 1990), 51.

37. Hubert Cataldo reproduces a photograph of the station in his memoir of the colonial town, *Bône 1832–1962 et Hippone la Royale*, 2 vols. (Montpellier: Africa Nostra, 1986), n.p. Kateb mentions its unique distinguishing feature in *Nedjma*, 174/246.

38. Kateb *Nedjma*, 145–6/204–5.

39. Alek Baylee Toumi and others have stressed Kateb's secularism, communism, and activism in the Amazigh cultural movement, traits that make unlikely any sympathy with the movement of an Arabizing bourgeois like Ben Bādīs, whose political goals seemed considerably less radical by the 1950s (Alek Baylee Toumi, *Maghreb divers: Langue française, langues parlées, littératures et représentations des Maghrébins, à partir d'Albert Memmi et de Kateb Yacine* [New York: Peter Lang, 2002], 40, 48–9). Whatever Kateb's own convictions, however, he clearly links his character to this movement (Kateb *Nedjma*, 148–9/208).

40. Kateb *Nedjma*, 142; does not appear in the English version. Many cities in the Arabic-speaking world have epithets: "Marrakesh the Red," "Meccah the Venerated," "Algiers the White," etc.

41. Kateb *Nedjma*, 143–4/200–02, translation modified.

42. Kateb *Nedjma*, 172/243–4, translation modified.

43. Kateb *Nedjma*, 164–5/232–3, translation modified.

44. Kateb *Nedjma*, 173/246.

45. This is Winifred Woodhull's argument in "Rereading *Nedjma*: Feminist Scholarship and North African Women," *Sub-Stance*, no. 69 (1992): 49–63.

46. Kateb, *Nedjma*, 153/205.

47. Ibid., 47–8/51.

48. "Alger, ville-pilote de l'Afrique du Nord," *Alger-Revue*, May 1955, documents the official promotion of the Diar es-Saada, Diar es-Shems, and Diar al-Mahçoul projects, while articles in *Chantiers Nord-Africains*, a monthly magazine devoted to public works, provide a more technical view. Zeineb Çelik gives these projects extensive analysis in *Urban Forms and Colonial Confrontations* (Berkeley: University of California Press, 1997), although she does not distinguish between projects actually built and those that existed only as plans.

49. Yacine Kateb, *Le Polygone étoilé* (Paris: Seuil, 1966), 11, 101.

50. Ibid., 10.

51. Among spa towns, Si Mokhtar knows Vichy best; it was in fact a favorite destination between the world wars for rich Franco-Algerians and the Muslim elite that imitated them. Kateb leaves to the reader's imagination the ironic possibilities of his character's frequenting Pétain's future capital.

52. Kateb, *Le Cercle des représailles*, 17.

53. Ibid.

54. Ibid., 18.

55. Kateb, *Nedjma*, 174/231.

56. Kateb, *Le Cercle des représailles*, 27.

57. The phrase occurs in a stage direction at the beginning of "Les ancêtres redoublent de férocité" (Kateb, *Le Cercle des représailles*, 125).

58. Kateb, *Le Polygone étoilé*, 133.

59. Kateb, *Le Polygone étoilé*, 11. For a consideration of several monumental projects of post-colonial utopianism, see Nnamdi Elleh's *Architecture and Power in Africa* (Westport, CT: Praeger, 2002).

60. This seems to be a paraphrase of one of several such pronouncements in Ibn Khaldūn; cp. his Title 25, "Places that succumb to the Arabs are quickly ruined" *Muqaddima*, I: 302. Kateb is citing without attribution several pages of a secondary work (*Le Polygone étoilé* 81). I have not found these exact words in any source of the period on Ibn Khaldūn.

7

Mohammed in the Métro: Remembering 17 October 1961 and the Novels of Rachid Boudjedra

The French win at the World Cup in 1998 came as an opportune relief for the country that had spent the preceding year recalling some of the most unpleasant moments of its history. The rise of the Front National had reappeared on television screens when a young FN tough received twenty years in prison for pushing a man of Moroccan origin into the Seine and watching him drown.[1] This, however, seemed like juvenile court compared to the trial of Maurice Papon for crimes against humanity committed while a Vichy bureaucrat in 1942 and '44. Also, as if the recollection of collaboration were not embarrassment enough, the beginning of Papon's trial in October 1997 unexpectedly brought to public attention another set of accusations against him: what part did he play in the "forgotten" massacre of Algerians in Paris in 1961? On 17 October of that year, near the end of the Algerian war of independence, the Parisian police repressed a peaceful demonstration of Algerians organized by the FLN (Front de Libération Nationale) and likely murdered between two hundred and three hundred demonstrators. Victims both living and dead were thrown into the Seine, in numbers we will never know, while others were cornered and shot in the streets, shot or beaten to death in the courtyard of the Préfecture de Police, or simply clubbed as they emerged from the Métro for the demonstration. The massacre, almost but not quite unreported at the time, had been forgotten, asserted the press in 1997.

France's football victory clearly provided relief from racial, ethnic, and religious tension as a variety of opportunists spoke of "la France beur, blanc, black," making slang of the minorities while leaving to the ethnic majority the supposed neutrality of standard French. The step from a dubious assertion of amnesia about 1961 in the press to actual forgetting among the public proved easy, as the triumph of 1998 took over. The crowds of French supporters of the footballer Zinédine Zidane had manifestly forgotten their insecurities of the previous months over their historic entanglements with Algerians. In front of the Cinéma Rex on the Boulevards, where in October 1961 police shot an unknown number of unarmed Algerians, a car raced by honking victory in the summer night of 1998, with a man perched on the passenger's window sill, holding a meter-long Algerian flag. The French cheered from the sidewalks, leaving me to wonder if it were out of relief, and if I should ever see such a thing again.

More importantly for us here, however, the moment also allowed at least a temporary pause in the flood of purportedly new information and the continuing agony of remembering the allegedly forgotten. Yet the Papon trial brought out very little new data about either the deportation of Jews in Bordeaux or the massacre of Muslims in Paris. Contemporary war-crimes trials do not usually reveal the previously unknown, but they do provide a theatrical venue for accrediting the known-but-ignored. For the French courts, the defendant's entire background before and after the events of the accusation constitutes admissible evidence regarding his character, and so even though Papon stood accused only of assisting in the deportation of Jews, he had to face the presentation of evidence regarding his responsibility for the killing of Muslims as well. Although the many commentators on the trial expressed their surprise during that week of October 1997 at the information about the Paris massacre brought before the court by the historian Jean-Luc Einaudi, none of it broke new ground. The massacre may have seemed not to figure in the French collective memory, but surely hundreds (if not thousands) of eyewitnesses retained personal memories of it. We know in fact that many did, because since the mid-eighties, a growing set of books from major French publishers had appeared containing such evidence, clearly directed at popular audiences.[2] Could too much information have the same effect as too little?

In response to the spate of public remembering apparently triggered by the evocation of the massacre in the Papon trial, the Minister of Culture Catherine Trautmann announced the opening of archives related to the event, which would otherwise have been sealed for many years longer. (The prospect of indefinite closure was very real, given that the massacre had been the object of ongoing, active cover-up until as recently as 1996.)[3] For thirty-five years, the official count had recorded all of three deaths; at his trial, Papon himself admitted to a total of fifteen or twenty. The press, supposedly having lacked historical documentation that actually had been available for more than ten years, published a flurry of interviews, a remarkable number of which turned out to feature perpetrators rather than victims.[4] These personal memories of those involved in the massacre joined those of the aging handful who had survived Papon's deportations, and reached flood stage in a crest of painful testimony and remembering. Faced with growing demand for details on the part of journalists and a public suddenly aware of what it had forgotten, the government stalled on opening the archives in order first to publish its own report, the first ever publicly released, which in May 1998 revised the number of dead to seven.[5] The story did not immediately disappear from the press: the *rebondissements*, as French journalists like to say, persisted for months and then years, eventually prolonged by Papon himself when he sued the historian Jean-Luc Einaudi for defamation in January 1999, only to have his case thrown out of court.[6] All these dates suggest a special intensity in the connections between events and memories bridging a thirty-five- to forty-year gap between the early 1960s and the late 1990s up to the present. Such a special relationship may indeed exist, as it becomes politically possible, following the Papon trial and public remembering of Vichy, to undertake similar work on the Algerian war. Furthermore, the archival resources for doing so may be opening, if slowly: the forty-year prohibition on releasing many government documents expired in 2002, for papers dating to 1962. Of course, public figures concerned with these documents will yet have many recourses to prevent their coming to light: notably the sixty-year rule applicable to papers that touch on "sensitive" affairs of state. Even so, scholars now have at least the legal possibility for research in the Archives Nationales covering the totality of the war.[7]

Any number of reasons thus point to a particular awareness or presence since 1997 of the events of 1961–1962 and their aftermath. Yet the emphasis the French press placed on the *revival* of memory after a long period of amnesia seems rather peculiar. The rhetoric of 1997–1998 obscured the persistence throughout the forty-year interval of memories of events concerning Algerians in Paris. It also suggested that nothing occurred to swell this history of violence between the end of the war in 1962 and the rise of FN-sanctioned hooliganism in the 1990s. Yet several factors indicate the continued presence of memories of violence toward Algerians in the '70s and '80s, memories both of events that took place during the war, and of others during the years of Algerian immigration that followed, under reputedly peaceful conditions. The Algerian government began in 1968 to commemorate the event with a holiday: 17 October became the "Journée nationale de l'émigration."[8] However, these commemorations had more to do with recuperating the efforts of the Algerians in France as part of the government's monolithic master-narrative of continuous and unanimous national struggle, than with any real attempt to integrate emigrants' memories on their own terms. Historian Joshua Cole points out that "nobody, including the official veteran's [sic] group, the Organisation

national des moujahidine (ONM), had ever bothered to undertake a sys-
tematic collection of first-hand accounts of police violence"; Ali Haroun's
La Septième wilaya: La Guerre du FLN en France, 1954–1962, published by
Seuil in 1986, was only just then making available a substantial history of
these events to a quasi-scholarly audience.[9] A survey of the titles of over
300 histories of the war published in Algeria and throughout the Arab
world, in both Arabic and French, finds no hint of coverage of the events
in Paris, before the appearance in Paris of the stream of works I referred
to earlier. Given the difficulties of maintaining congruence between collective memories of Algerians on both sides of the Mediterranean, it is far
from certain that even the publication of official histories commemorating
October 1961 in either language would have done much to solidify recollections among immigrants and their descendants in France.

It is true that several novels published in the last ten years may lead us
to suspect a resurgence of the collective memory of 1961 among the immigrant community. Yet we must take care to avoid anachronism: the
publication of novels like Leila Sebbar's *La Seine était rouge* (1999), or Paul
Smaïl's *Vivre me tue* (1997) may say more about the moment of their publication than about the period they describe; in addition, by revealing his
origins as ethnic French, Smaïl has further complicated the reception of
his work. As Anne Donadey has pointed out, several works in the same
vein by Magribis had also appeared in the period of France's painful rediscovery of the history of Vichy: Nacer Kettane's *Le Sourire de Brahim*
(1985) and Tassadit Imache's *Une Fille sans histoire* (1989). Finally, and
most compelling for us here, persistent readers of Algerian literature will
remember another novel that appeared more than twenty years before the
Bordeaux trial, Rachid Boudjedra's *Le Vainqueur de coupe* [The Trophy
Winner] (1981), that has as much to say about historical amnesia as the
subsequent literary treatments of the events. In it, the narrator refers to a
Prefect of Police "au nom qui rappelle le bruit d'un klaxon" [with the
name that recalls the sound of a klaxon]; over the *pan-pon* of the riot-
police sirens, we hear the name of the *Préfet* Papon.[10] Someone remembered, even then.

In this chapter I will examine here two complex narratives by Rachid
Boudjedra, published in the putative years of forgetting in the 1970s and
1980s: *Topographie idéale pour une agression caractérisée* [Ideal Topography
for an Aggravated Assault] (1975) and *Le Vainqueur de coupe*.[11] Though the
plots of both novels stage failed investigations, each embarks on a more
substantial rewriting of the history of the struggle for decolonization than
any government commission has yet accomplished. I will explore the connections they establish between memory and history, and between movement and topography. Although we may notice a number of parallels between events in each novel and those of October 1961, I am less interested

in the novels' somewhat shaky mimesis of history than in its suggestions for how to produce and use it. These novels suggest that memory and an appreciation of history are together necessary to move successfully in the city. When they manage to learn this skill, Boudjedra's characters become successful users and reinventors of what the historian Pierre Nora has called *lieux de mémoire* [realms of memory], the places of intersection between collective reconstruction and recollection. I share the appreciation of Nora and his colleagues in the *Lieux de mémoire* project for particular places as nexuses or commonplaces for cultural meanings to collect over relatively long periods of time, in accumulations that large groups can apprehend. However, I will argue that the process immigrants to France go through in developing their own *lieux de mémoire* differs notably from those of the ethnic French people with whom Nora and his colleagues principally concern themselves. Today, France is attempting simultaneously to manage memories of its recent history and to come up with new ways of integrating immigrants (especially from the Maghrib) into the very society that is only now recollecting parts of its sometimes abysmal treatment of them. Discovering what might constitute *lieux de mémoire* for North African immigrants and their descendants, and imagining how they might function both for them and for post-colonial France as a whole, is therefore vital to understanding the multiethnic society that now stands as a simple fact of life in the *Hexagone*. It is also central to the contemporary extension of this book's argument about the uses of urban description in projects of restorative and contemplative nostalgia.

Rachid Boudjedra (1941–), who came of age during the 1954–1962 war, carries to the metropole the post-colonial Algerian struggle for a fuller perception of their history that would allow them to act effectively in it. He advances a reinterpretation of the Parisian topography as the historically necessary complement to the new vision of urban Algeria that developed during the war of independence, notably in Kateb Yacine's recreations of Bône and Constantine in *Nedjma* (1956). From his earliest novels, topography was never indifferent to Boudjedra; in his first two, *La Répudiation* (1969) and *L'Insolation* (1972), the protagonists have suffered disorientation and dissociation similar to that of Kateb's character Lakhdar arriving in Bône after the trauma of 8 May 1945. Boudjedra's first two novels trace the protagonists' dissolution after assaults on their psyches more personally directed than that suffered by the victims of the French repression of 1945. The first recounts the repudiation of the narrator's mother and the dislocation of his family, while the second narrates the violent end of an illicit love affair and the protagonist's internment in a psychiatric ward. In later works, Boudjedra moves from individual to collective dislocation, in a move that correlates well with his turn to more explicitly historical subjects. Through a much more specific thematization of time and topography than in these early novels, he suggests ways of working though the traumas caused by the assaults of tendentious stories about the past.

EMIGRATION AND AMNESIA:
TOWARD A POST-COLONIAL *LIEU DE MÉMOIRE*

The unnamed *émigrant* who is the protagonist of Boudjedra's aptly named *Topographie idéale pour une agression caractérisée* spends the entire novel, one long day, lost in the Paris Métro. Those familiar with the Métro know that if one gets lost in it, it cannot be for want of a map, since several varieties of map appear prominently on walls throughout the system. As for the emigrant, however, the map and every other textual marker in the Métro system is useless, as he cannot read Roman characters. In a manner reminiscent of the *nouveau roman*, the narrator repeatedly describes this map in details so minute that they become incomprehensible, and the description, virtually nonreferential. For him, the map has no link with his surroundings; the nonreferential description mirrors his experience of the image, since he cannot fathom the relationship between the map and the space it represents. For readers, who share some of his bewilderment, it suggests a link between the description of the protagonist's physical space and the mapping of his processes of memory.[12]

Specifically, the map descriptions create two crucial associations: first, between topography and memory, and second, between disorientation and amnesia. They do so in a way that Pierre Nora's characterization of the conditions leading to the constitution of *lieux de mémoire* cannot fully explain. Nora stresses the "curiosité pour les lieux ou se cristallise et se réfugie la mémoire" ["curiosity about the places in which memory is crystallized"] that he finds in French culture in the twentieth century, during which "la conscience de la rupture avec le passé se confond avec le sentiment d'une mémoire déchirée; mais où le déchirement réveille encore assez de mémoire pour que puisse se poser le problème de son incarnation" ["a sense of rupture with the past is inextricably bound up with a sense that a rift has occurred in memory. But that rift has stirred memory sufficiently to raise the question of its embodiment"].[13] Nora suggests, however, that this rift has not yet occurred in France's former colonies. He rehearses the idea common to colonial historiography everywhere, that history in the colonized world began quite recently, if indeed it has begun at all: he speaks of societies "réveillées par le viol colonial de leur sommeil ethnologique" ["awakened from their ethnological slumbers by colonial violation"] and of "toutes les ethnies, groupes, familles, à fort capital mémoriel et à faible capital historique" ["all the ethnicities, groups, and families that until recently had amassed abundant reserves of memory but little in the way of history"].[14] Nora apparently finds history in short supply in such places, but independence-era debates among European and Muslim Algerians over how to interpret or even recreate history demonstrate that there was always plenty of it to deal with. It seems unlikely that the citizens of former colonies and their descendants in France would construct their *lieux de mémoire* in the same ways as the French, for whom the notion of *terroir* and *patrie* inform such constructions in ways almost certainly closed to a post-colonial subject, let alone to an emigrant. How then do *lieux de mémoire* function for them? The emigrant's fate in the Métro will suggest some answers.

Disorientation, amnesia, and ignorance of the Parisian topography lead to the protagonist's bloody end, beaten to death by a gang, at the very moment he miraculously emerges from the Métro at the station he set out to reach. Despite his vain attempts at reading the maps described in the novel, and the extreme difficulty he has understanding the directions given him by well-meaning Parisians, the protagonist comes remarkably close to his destination (a cousin's apartment at the Porte de Clichy). Nonetheless, the narrative never lets him arrive; his designation in the text, *l'émigrant*, itself seems to obviate any possibility of ever arriving anywhere. Interpreting his wanderings, it seems tempting to follow the example of the police officer in charge of investigating his murder, since the officer conceives of his job as reconstructing the protagonist's itinerary from fragments of witnesses' accounts. The officer admonishes his assistant: "un conseil: lisez attentivement la carte du métro—c'est là que la lumière peut jaillir!" [a piece of advice: read the Métro map carefully—that's where light might shine on this case!][15] However, he proclaims his lack of sympathy with the victim too often for his investigation to be credible, let alone for it to guide our reading of a fragmented narration of the crime. In fact, the police investigation fails completely, since it focuses solely on retracing the emigrant's physical movements in the Métro. The officer is as obsessed with these details as the narrator with the Métro map, and he actually never takes any steps whatever to identify the aggressors. Apart from the tidiness of the affairs of his precinct, only his future ability to defend himself to investigators or historians concerns him. His interest in the details will ultimately prove irrelevant, even obstructive, to the intersection of history and memory that underpins the novel.

The officer's injunction to study the map notwithstanding, we might wonder how any light could come from reading the prose description of it, a nightmarishly complicated presentation of a network that seems to fascinate the narrator.[16] Even readers familiar with Paris transports would not be able to find their way using Boudjedra's description of a Métro map, despite its two pages of excruciatingly precise abstraction: "lignes noires, rouges, jaunes, bleues, vertes, rouges à nouveau mais cette fois hachurées de noir, puis bleues mais hachurées de rouge, puis vertes et hachurée de blanc avec des ronds vides à l'intérieur et des ronds avec un centre noir, puis des numéros qu'il savait lire (10, 12, 7, 1, 2, 5, 13, etc.), puis des noms, les uns écrits en caractères plus gras que d'autres mais l'ensemble dessiné avec des lettres comme à l'envers" [black lines, red lines, yellow ones, blue ones, green ones, red ones again, but this time with black dashes, then black but with red dashes then green and white dashes with circles empty inside and circles filled in with black, and then numbers he could read (10, 12, 7, 1, 2, 5, 13, etc.), then names, some written in bolder characters than others but the whole thing drawn with letters as if it were backwards].[17] In a description so divorced from its referent, the details become illegible, further obstacles to comprehension. Our experience as readers of these repeated descriptions parallels that of the protagonist: the details render it impossible to interpret in a way that would lead to understanding how to move in the space it represents. The protagonist suffers an additional handicapped imposed by the counterintuitive left-to-right writing, an orientation that the lettering imparts to the map as a whole. Having a map does him no good, since he cannot translate a schematic, two-dimensional, left-to-right representation into three full dimensions of potential movement. Among other things, *Topographie idéale* is an extended commentary on the inability to interpret signs and a reflection on the conditions of their legibility.[18]

The emigrant feels assaulted by the left-to-right lettering he cannot read, victimized by signs that do not tell him anything, and even more, by people who assume they do or should.[19] His disorientation goes far beyond a simple inability to read French, however, and must be figured as one of memory, in which hostile topography prevents the emigrant from absorbing and assuming his own experiences. Here, he is looking, for the first of many times, at the plan of the Métro:

Habitué aux contrées difficiles [. . .] Il n'avait quand même pas compris grand-chose au plan qu'on lui avait indiqué du doigt.
Où les lignes zigzaguent à travers des méandres donnant à la mémoire des envies de se délester d'un trop-plein d'impressions vécues depuis deux ou trois jours et se superposant les unes au-dessus des autres à la manière de ces lignes noires, rouges, jaunes [. . .] à moins qu'il ne s'agisse avec une ligne en bleu et blanc dont le tracé plus gras fait un méandre comme un bras de mer coupant le plan en deux zones égales ou peut-être pas tout à fait égales la partie du bas certainement plus petite que celle du haut, ne sachant pas quel est le nord du sud et quel est l'est de l'ouest avec, autour de l'enchevêtrement des lignes, un tracé en pointillé comme s'il s'agissait de quelque frontière honteuse ébauchée en hâte, un peu en catimini, au cours d'une nuit très pluvieuse, pour mettre ceux qui sont au-delà du tracé devant le fait accompli.

[Used to difficult country . . . he had nonetheless not understood much of the plan they had pointed out to him.

Where the lines zigzagged through meanders that made his memory want to lighten itself of an overload of impressions experienced over the last two or three days, which superimposed themselves one on top of the other like those lines in black, red, yellow . . . unless it were actually with a blue and white line whose wider path made a curve like an arm of the sea dividing the plan into two zones of equal surface area or perhaps not quite equal, since the bottom part was certainly smaller than the top, not knowing north from south and east from west, and around the tangle of lines, a dotted line as if it were some shameful border hurriedly and stealthily sketched out in the course of a very rainy night, to place those who were on the other side of the line before a fait accompli.][20]

Despite his ability to read rough country in his native mountains, the emigrant cannot make out the only natural land form of Paris represented on the map, the river. Had he been able to, he would have discovered that cardinal directions have little reality or use in the city: comprehension of Parisian topography, even above ground, depends on experience and landmarks, not a compass rose. More significantly, this passage provides its own reply to the endlessly punned "dis-Orient-ation" recorded by European visitors lost in the labyrinths of Arab cities.[21] The emigrant lost in Paris finds the alleged Cartesian simplicity of French networks and their diagrams (to say nothing of French syntax) just as disorienting, and literally cannot distinguish the map's orient from its occident. For him, the tangle of zigzagging lines on the plan, indecipherably superimposed, does not represent terrain or paths at all, but rather the memories of his long journey from his village to Algiers and Paris. It tells him only about past trials and says nothing about future possibilities.

The protagonist does know that the object he stares at is a map, yet its evocations for him are radically different from those of the habituated. To experienced users, the Métro plan serves as a reminder of names, directions, and connections between lines in a system with which they are already familiar, and in which they already have memories of previous trips to guide them. As the anthropologist Marc Augé points out in *Un Ethnologue dans le métro* (1986), "C'est bien un privilège parisien que de pouvoir utiliser le plan du métro comme un aide-mémoire, un déclencheur de souvenirs" [it is indeed a Parisian privilege to be able to use the Métro map as an aide-mémoire, a trigger for memories].[22] The emigrant, however, has no Parisian memories to trigger. Instead of helping him sort out his confused memories, seeing the Métro's complexity represented graphically makes him want simply to rid himself of them, as if their confusion were entangling him in a disordered internal topography. The map itself hints at the geographic exclusion that has historically prevented the likes of him from becoming Parisians in Augé's sense. It imposes an inter-diction in the dotted line of the fare zone limit around central Paris, the judgment-without-appeal that places so many Parisians of North African descent outside the city, in truly "difficult country" from which one can-not reach the center on a standard ticket. Kept perpetually outside, the protagonist never manages to become an *im*migrant anywhere; he is al-ways the *e*migrant, the one who has left his old place, but never arrived in a new one.

For the emigrant, disorientation begins at home. The narrator suggests no earlier stage of rooted plenitude for him in his village and treats with venomous satire the older villagers who could have given him life-saving advice before he set out. The novel demonstrates a failure in the process of transmission of a collective memory that would have helped keep the protagonist out of trouble. The mistrust the emigrant feels in the Métro stems originally not from incomprehensible signs, but from his dealings with the only people who could have helped him in his own language, de-spite his illiteracy: the "laskars" of his village, a handful of older men, for-mer emigrants and veterans of campaigns in the metropole, during the war of independence.[23] These men are too busy shoring up a shaky posi-tion of authority based on their war stories and pension checks to help any future migrants, whom they would rather let fail. The protagonist re-members a conversation with one of them, who gave him "aucun indice susceptible de l'aider, non parce qu'il pouvait prétexter l'oubli ou l'ef-facement de souvenir, mais parce qu'il pensait que c'était absolument in-utile" [no clue capable of helping him, not because he could plead forget-fulness or the effacement of memory, but because he thought it was totally useless].[24] The laskars are convinced that the endless formalities de-manded of departing Algerians will stop him in Algiers, and they do not warn him of any possible dangers, should he succeed in crossing the Mediterranean. Boudjedra commented in an interview in the Moroccan journal *Lamalif* that he wanted to alert young Algerians of the "trap" of emigration, since he felt that those who had already crossed the border were passing on insufficient warnings.[25]

The novel demonstrates that the collective memory of the Algerian im-migrant community did indeed contain vital survival knowledge, and that the laskars could have been excellent conduits of this memory, had they chosen. No one would have been better suited to transmit the sur-vival knowledge in the Algerian immigrant collective memory than the laskars. They are strangers neither to borders, nor to the Métro; during the war, they participated actively in organizing the FLN in France: "[ils] avaient alors appris, par coeur, tous les itinéraires du métro et en con-naissaient tous les recoins, toutes les issues, toutes les lignes, toutes les stations, tous les escaliers mécaniques, tous les portillons, tous les méan-

dres et toutes les courbes, puisqu'ils y donnaient leurs rendez-vous clan-
destins, déposaient, dans ses corbeilles à papier, des armes et des tracts
que d'autres venaient, discrètement, récupérer" [they had then learned by
heart all the itineraries of the Métro and knew all the corners, all the exits,
all the lines, all the stations, all the escalators, all the gates, all the meanders and curves because they arranged their secret rendezvous there, and
dropped off weapons and leaflets in the trash cans, which others came
discreetly to collect].[26] The laskars were experts in their day, carrying in
their heads the map of the Métro which the protagonist could not assimilate without the benefits of time, historical imperative, and, not least,
their help. The Métro was indeed a dangerous place, as any of the crowd
of Algerians clubbed at the exit of the Concorde station in October 1961
could attest. However, at other times, those with the right sort of spatial
memory mastered the public space and learned to move in it at will and
undetected. In doing so, the laskars survived the war and helped bring
about their country's autonomy. The emigrant, by contrast, overwhelmed
and dominated by the same space, cannot move on his own other than at
random; ultimately, he will not survive the undeclared war on Algerian
immigrants. For him, arriving in 1973, all the useful weapons have already been removed by his predecessors from their caches in the Métro,
and he will find nothing with which to defend himself from the gang of
attackers. His only response to what little the laskars left for him is "Ils auraient dû me prévenir" [they should have warned me], repeated a propos
of everything from train noises to provocative posters.[27] The moment of
historic heroism is over, as the laskars know; now it is a question of simple survival for the emigrant and his fellows.

The historical memory of the laskars has furthermore become heavily
mythologized, ludicrously inadequate to guide a would-be citizen of the
modern world. In their capacity as political commissars to the village
known as Le Piton, they make ineffective and outdated attempts to in-
doctrinate their fellow villagers with newsreels, the only previous visual
culture the emigrant possesses before setting foot in the Métro. The villagers are

> fascinés . . . par les bandes d'actualité d'antan où les personnages ont con-
> stamment la bougeotte et où les chefs d'Etat offrent des crises d'épilepsie à
> des publics friands de discours-fleuves dont les habitants du Piton sont
> privés parce que l'appareil de projection 16 mm n'est pas doté de parlant;
> sursautant, tressautant, ataxiques, épileptiques, les personnages des bandes
> d'actualité (les films de fiction étant exclus parce que les gens de la boutique
> voulaient à travers l'actualité, même trop ancienne et historiquement
> dépassée, donner des leçons de haute politique, sûrs qu'ils étaient de la
> répétition mécanique des faits historiques) avaient cette même inconsistance
> de l'image gigotante et renversée du train, plaquée sur la paroi du tunnel de

la ligne no. 1 (Chateau-de-Vincennes-Pont-de-Neuilly) avec en plus cette grêle saccadée, foisonnante de striures et de hachures grésillantes comme si elles allaient crever l'écran de carton-pâte passé à la chaux, et caractéristique des vieux films que les laskars passaient et repassaient, à l'appui de leurs théories fallacieuses.

[fascinated . . . by old-time newsreels where the characters are always jumpy and where heads of state display their seizures to audiences eager for their endless speeches of which the inhabitants of Le Piton were deprived because the 16 millimeter projector had no speaker; the jumping, twitchy, epileptic characters of the newsreels (fictional films were excluded because the people from the store wanted to teach lessons of advanced politics with the films, even if they were too old and historically outdated, since they could be sure of the mechanical repetition of historical facts) had the same lack of solidity as the jumpy, backward image of the train against the wall of the tunnel of line no. 1 (Chateau-de-Vincennes-to-Pont-de-Neuilly) with, in addition, the jerky static, full of striations and hachures crackling as if to break the screen of whitewashed paste-board, and typical of the old films the laskars played and replayed in support of their fallacious theories.][28]

Their fallacies, for example, Ataturk was a true revolutionary because he made the Turks wear hats, constitute the only historical or ideological background dispensed by the heroes-turned-Party-hacks who constitute the local backbone of the RCV, the "République Communiste Verdoyante."[29] The people may be fascinated, but left without the words, like the emigrant in the Métro passages, they can scarcely sort through the series of fleeting and jumpy images to arrive at any coherent historical vision. The lessons of nationalist or socialist politics which the laskars wish to promulgate by simple repetition of disjointed historical images are no more comprehensible than the flickering and fuzzy image of the train on the tunnel wall, and as inconsistent as that image, viewed from the train itself. Curiously, the laskars' version of history makes no connection between their own participation in it and the grand lessons they wish to impart: they never mention their activities in the Revolution. Only such a connection between global histories and personal memories could have helped the emigrant link his own experiences to those of his predecessors, giving him both concrete information and a means of coping with the space which assails him.

Our memories are both triggered by and constitutive of the real spaces in which we move. For this reason, the emigrant, lacking coherent connections, is bound to project his own confusions on the underground topography, thus complicating an already hostile environment. In short, the representations of the Métro begin to reflect the confused conditions of the emigrant's psyche, with its lines "enchevêtrées les unes dans les autres, s'arrêtant arbitrairement là où l'on s'y attend le moins, se coupant au mépris de toutes les lois géométriques, se chevauchant, se ramifiant, se dédoublant, se recroquevillant un peu à la façon de la mémoire toujours leste à partir mais aussi leste à revenir se lover sinusoidalement au creux des choses, des objets, des impressions, formant, elles aussi, un lacis parcourant en tous sens les méandres du temps" [tangled up in one another, stopping arbitrarily where one least expected it, cutting each other off, disregarding all the laws of geometry, overlapping, branching, doubling, curling up a little like memory, always eager to take off but also eager to come back and coil up sinusoidally in the hollows of things, objects, and impressions, which themselves form a network which runs out in all directions through the meanders of time].[30] The Métro, at first, seems to qualify as one of Nora's *lieux de mémoire*. Travelling in it, the anthropologist Augé argues, reflects a will to remember, and the train system itself is the object of a ritual which overdetermines both the history it is supposed to represent and the memories associated with it.[31]

The Métro has a history of its own, and despite the desire of some of its users to invest it with a fixed set of memories, it remains alive, as *lieux de mémoire* do, through its aptitude for historical metamorphosis:

> Autant de stations, autant de situations ou de personnages reconnus, retenus, magnifiés: la rame se faufile dans notre histoire à vitesse accélérée; inlassable, elle fait la navette sans désemparer et dans les deux sens, entre les grands hommes, les hauts lieux et les grands moments, passant sans tergiverser de Gambetta à Louise Michel, de la Bastille à l'Etoile ou de Stalingrad à Campo-Formio et inversement. Prendre le métro, ce serait donc en quelque sorte célébrer le culte des ancêtres.

> [So many stations, so many situations or characters recognized, remembered, magnified: the train threads its way through our history at an accelerated pace. It shuttles untiringly in both directions without stopping, among great men, important places and great moments, passing without equivocation from Gambetta to Louise Michel, from the Bastille to the Etoile, or from Stalingrad to Campo Formio and back. To take the train could therefore be to engage in some way in ancestor-worship.][32]

The train has the potential, *for a Parisian*, to function like a successful version of the jerky and sped-up newsreels shown at Le Piton, as French history flickers past from station to station. However, it does not function in anything like the fertile and multifarious ways of the *lieux de mémoire* in Nora's collection, which operate by connecting memory (ostensibly unmediated, particular, or personal) with history (constructed, distanced, and often claiming to be national or universal). The village steeples of a French childhood vacation, for example, may be linked both to a tradition of historiography around country churches and to the perennial idea of a nation united by cultural Catholicism; one's own familiar town hall takes its place in a series of public buildings all over the country that are the physical elaboration of the Republic. The Métro, however, is a different case altogether. Despite the suggestive names, Augé allows that even for a Parisian, "bien des noms de stations ne disent rien à ceux qui les lisent ou les entendent, et ceux à qui ils disent quelque chose ne pensent pas nécessairement à la chose quand ils prononcent le nom. Si culte il y a pourrait-on alors objecter, c'est un culte mort." [many station names mean nothing to those who read or hear them, and those to whom they mean something do not necessarily think of that thing when they say the name. If there is a religion involved, one might then object, it is a dead religion.][33] In fact, the Métro represents a very problematic *lieu de mémoire* because even when individual travelers perceive that they share certain historical references or fragments of the past, the experience is rarely collective. Moreover, it certainly cannot work as a *lieu de mémoire* for Boudjedra's emigrant, who has no link to the elements of French history evoked in the names on the map, and in any case cannot so much as read them. For a traveler like the emigrant, who repeats the name "BA-STILL-E" as set of meaningless phonemes, this "religion" is a closed, secretive cult.[34] For him, the Métro represents not a *place* of memory but at best a *process* of memory, when the outline of the train flickering along the tunnel wall calls to mind the similarly disjointed images familiar to the emigrant from the laskars' weekly newsreel showings. This is quite different from acting as a point of intersection for personal memories and national history. Furthermore, in the instances where we see the Métro's memory process at work, the memories evoked prove incomplete, incoherent, or insignificant. Nora asserts that the media's metaphorical substitution of a "pellicule éphémère de l'actualité" ["an ephemeral newsreel"] for any genuine and intimate memory has resulted in a "prodigieusement dilaté" ["prodigiously dilated"] historical consciousness.[35] Just the opposite seems true in the case of the emigrant, for whom newsreels *literally* substitute for memory: the result is historical constriction.

The narrator goes so far as to invent a word for this, *paramnésie*, suggesting a process of forgetting as much as remembering:

Et lui se demandant s'il n'avait pas déjà vécu cette situation hallucinante, mélangeant la topographie de l'espace et celle de la mémoire, les confondant même et les malaxant à travers une chose bizarre que le voyeur s'empresse d'appeler pompeusement: paramnésie, mais qui échappe au voyageur à moitié assommé, épongé et paniqué par l'odeur de la femelle imprégnant son corps, ses vêtements, sa valise et même l'atmosphère de la caverne dans laquelle il se démène toujours se demandant s'il n'a pas déjà vécu cette.

[He asked himself if he had not already lived through this striking situation, combing the topography of space with that of memory, even confusing the two and mixing them through a strange phenomenon which the voyeur loses no time in pompously calling "paramanesia," but which escapes the traveler who is half knocked out, wiped out, and panicked by the female smell impregnating his body, his clothes, his suitcase, and even the cave-like atmosphere in which he was still struggling, asking himself if he had not already lived through this.][36]

Several critics have analyzed the emigrant's troubled response to the advertisements covering the Métro walls, and have suggested ways in which the sexual menace or mystery these posters convey counteracts the extreme kindness of "Céline/Aline," the only woman in the book who takes the trouble to accompany the emigrant on part of his trip, and whose half-remembered name ironically evokes one of France's most famous literary racists.[37] As these critics have pointed out, women and their images play a very significant role in both orienting and disorienting the protagonist. The "female smell" seems to be a mix of odors sensed psychosomatically from posters with figures of women suggestively selling nylons and tampons; the smell serves as metonymy for the marketing and consumerism in the Métro and as metaphor for the disorientation felt there. The cave-like atmosphere, the tunnel, and the odor evoke a traumatic birth, the ultimate experience of which no memory, in the traditional sense, subsists. The advertisements help suppress even the memory of whether the emigrant has been in a place before, a piece of information at the very base of any process of orientation. The repetition of the posters confuses him by making one turn in a corridor seem very like another. The topographic confusion of the Métro does more than reflect the emigrant's internal confusion; it also spawns further memory troubles of its own, evidenced by a sentence which breaks off in the French with a demonstrative demonstrating nothing, since the protagonist cannot even name what he might (or might not) have experienced already.

In this context, the irruption of historical events, in the form of contemporary newspaper articles on violence against Algerians, reproduced in double columns in the text, can only be fatal for the protagonist. In 1975, the year of publication of Boudjedra's novel, the spate of racist attacks of September 1973 remained a very recent memory, all the fresher since it had led to the decision of the ruling *Conseil de la Révolution* in Algiers to suspend emigration to France. Further attacks had kept the issue alive and in the public eye, as they have done to this day. Despite French declarations of their own amnesia, such events have become part of both the memory and the history of Franco-Algerian relations. The police officer in charge of the investigation of the emigrant's murder knows how fresh and easily exhumed such memories are: "je n'aime pas trop les affaires classées un jour ou l'autre elles vous sautent au visage changement de politique mauvaise conscience ou manie stupide on exige que le dossier soit exhumé . . . parfois même il suffit qu'un ministre aille faire du tourisme par là-bas pour que l'affaire devienne tout à coup sérieuse à ce moment-là c'est moi le responsable" [I don't much care for closed cases, some day or other they blow up in your face; change of policy, bad conscience, or stupid fad, they order the file dug up again. . . . Sometimes it's enough for a minister to go play tourist over there for the case to become serious all of a sudden and then I'm the one responsible].[38] The officer knows that interpretation of the event depends on the climate of international relations and public opinion, the larger forces to which his actions must respond. His sole worry, in fact, is that amnesia may prove all too fleeting.

Nothing in the several narrations of the murder suggest that the emigrant had the slightest knowledge of any such issues, let alone of the racism with which he was contending. He cannot imagine his sudden addition to the list of victims that historians would reconstitute from newspaper articles, such as the one the narrator cites that gives the names of a dozen of them. By the time the attack occurs, it is too late for any such realization. As his aggressors beat him,

> Ainsi s'ouvrait, à même sa mémoire ensanglantée, figée dans une crispation douleureuse, des brèches colmatées par les derniers souvenirs dont le rythme endiablé rappelait les bandes d'actualité projetées par les quatre compagnons, chaque dimanche après-midi et dont l'accélération, le grésillement, les striures et autres hachures faisaient rire les enfants impitoyablement chassés par les organisateurs de ces colloques hautement cinématographiques, allergiques à toute forme de chahut; et sécrétant—les souvenirs—leur propre substance peinte de toutes les couleurs des panneaux publicitaires et tournant autour de la signification plus ou moins cachée de toutes les images et de tous les thèmes vantant les oranges, les soutiens-gorges, les plats cuisinés, les paysages exotiques, les yoghourts, les rouges à lèvres.

> [Thus, in his bloodied memory, clenched in a painful cramp, there opened breaches plugged with the last recollections whose frenzied rhythm recalled the newsreels played by the four laskars every Sunday afternoon, and whose acceleration, crackling, striations, and other hachure marks made the children laugh who were relentlessly chased away by the organizers of these highly cinematographic seminars, allergic to any kind of ruckus; and secreting—the recollections—their own substance painted in all the colors of the billboards and revolving around the more or less hidden meaning of all the images and themes singing the praises of oranges, bras, pre-cooked foods, exotic landscapes, yogurts, and lipsticks].[39]

The text figures the protagonist's death as the death of memory, in which his recollections bleed out in a pool of commercial images based on consumption of women's bodies and exotic countries, images that have replaced any other topographic or memorial landmark in the Métro. The emigrant cannot fathom their "hidden meaning" any more than he could understand the historical significance of the laskars' newsreels; as he dies, his memory takes on the consistency of that jerky film footage, another failed connection to historical consciousness.

Toward the end of *Topographie idéale*, the emigrant, still lost, wanders about Saint-Lazare station hoping to be recognized by some acquaintance of the laskars, who might give him yet another set of directions. The narrator supplies the question such an acquaintance would certainly ask about his old friends now back in their village: were they not tortured in the raids of 1956, or drowned in the Seine or beaten to death in the riots of 1961?[40] Though their imagined questions focus on moments when the Algerian community in Paris was victimized in ways beyond contemporary comprehension, they demonstrate a high consciousness of the history that community both made and survived. The text lets us guess at what would constitute effective *lieux de mémoire* for an Algerian in Paris. The sites chosen would differ from those valorized by the French: perhaps the Concorde Métro stop and the bridges, where bodies suddenly rendered historical objects suffered and disappeared forever, or the river banks downstream where the Seine, refusing to become the Lethe, washed some of them up. Or perhaps the Préfecture de Police in the Cité, where an unknown number were murdered, a building all the spookier for looming in the minds of today's immigrants as the place where an arbitrary administration delivers or withholds residency permits. The real difference between this set of *lieux de mémoire* and that of the dominant culture, however, would lie in their mode of operation. Instead of serving as nexuses for ritual and textual commemoration, they would serve as places for oral narration, for the exchange of news about survivors and victims, and for the transmission of streetwise lore to help the newly arrived. Like the traditional *lieux de mémoire*, these places would help resist amnesia. However, what Nora characterizes as the "sensation" in contemporary French culture of losing history is for the emigrant more than a sensation. It is a very real process of amnesia, beginning long before he left his village. Despite the hints at how migrant memory might be revived in oral culture, the chance meeting at Saint-Lazare never happens, and the emigrant never hears the questions of his elders. Just as he did throughout his day of switching trains, he misses the connection. He never discovers the history that he himself can neither make nor survive, but only be swallowed by, as a mute piece of physical evidence to an unpunished crime.

THE HOME FIELD ADVANTAGE

Appropriately, the title of *Topographie idéale pour une agression caractérisée* obscures the protagonist, wholly insignificant in the face of the over-whelming and malevolent topography. The title of *Le Vainqueur de coupe*, by contrast, focuses on the novel's hero, who will discover how to tri-umph over the terrain and to use it for his own ends: the assassination of an opponent to the Algerian nationalist cause. In this way he arrives at an apotheosis as a historical actor, successfully revolting against those who had tried to contain him spatially, in shantytown suburbs and immigrant dormitories, and historically, in the stasis of colonized peoples never al-lowed to act on their own account in the grand history of world powers.

Le Vainqueur de coupe presents the history of the actual assassination of a former vice president of the Assemblée Algérienne, the "Bachagha" Mo-hammed Chekkal, at the end of the final match of the Coupe de France de football, which he attended with French President René Coty on 26 May 1957. In Boudjedra's fiction, Chekkal's assassin, Mohammed ben Sadok, aka Staline, is head of a Parisian brigade of the "Organisation" (never more precisely named), that is pursuing a campaign of attacks against colonial targets in Paris, and canvassing the city to collect money from immigrant workers to support the fighters in Algeria. The plot of the assassination, in-vestigation, and trial is as simple as that of *Topographie idéale*, and its end-ing seems much more heavily predetermined. In *Topographie idéale*, readers can guess the protagonist's fate only after the officer in charge of the in-vestigation begins speaking of him in the past tense, but in *Le Vainqueur*, Boudjedra needs no such device since anyone aware of the fate of captured assassins during the Algerian war should be able to guess the outcome. Contrary to all expectations, however, the protagonist escapes the guillo-tine and returns to a free Algeria, amnestied at Independence after serving only a few years of his life sentence. Sadok thus escapes the fate that the history of decolonization would seem to render inevitable. He manages this through his own knowledge of that history and of its place in the larger history of the Arabo-Muslim world. The text's descriptions of urban details, otherwise difficult to account for, evoke both of these histories ex-plicitly. Michel de Certeau's extension of the military theory of tactics and strategy seems useful here, and I will consider it more fully further on. By first mastering the tactics of movement in an essentially hostile urban ter-rain, Sadok learns how to move in a historically consequential way. He can then accede to the level of strategy, ordering his space and history about him, from a point of view of his own choosing.[41]

A detour of the nonlinear narration lets us know in advance that we need no longer fear the hero's doom; we learn the trial verdict in the mid-dle of the novel. Boudjedra gives this merciful relief to the reader long before the protagonist, and in further twists of the timeline, we see Sadok's return to Algeria before witnessing his assassination of Chekkal. Readers observe the whole, including major digressions, flashbacks to Sadok's childhood in the eastern Algerian port city of Bône, and an extensive prison correspondence with his mother, through a narrative screen made up of transcriptions of the repetitive and jargon-filled radio commentary on the football match at which the assassination occurred. These transcriptions of the match itself, set apart at the beginning of each chapter, serve several purposes in shaping interpretation, not least of which is to heighten the suspense. Also, they reveal the presence of two Algerians on the winning team, giving the commentators the opportunity to display a remarkable set of stereotypes. By casting the Algerians on the field as unthreatening and likable, the commentary distances them from their threatening cohorts, condemned without explicit mention. The comments serve the public a red herring, masking the actions of the only Algerian in the stadium of real interest to the narration, who is in fact extremely dangerous. Finally, the events of the match provide the text with temporal order, in chapters titled with the updated score ("Toulouse 1-Angers 0," "Toulouse 2-Angers 0," "Half-Time," etc.). As in *Topographie idéale*, the chapter titles (numbers of Métro lines) pursue a linear course, while the narration wanders all over the map. From one novel to the other, spatial organization gives way to a temporal or historical order, insofar as the changing score marks the passage of time and the movement of players on the field.

The football commentary connected with the repeated scores provides a level of detail which Sadok and the reader must read against, in order to understand the importance of the plot. Boudjedra once again provides the figure of an officer of the law, this time the public prosecutor, as an example for the reader not to imitate. Just as the officer in *Topographie idéale* bungled the investigation by insisting on knowing the exact itinerary of the murder victim (a detail almost irrelevant to the crime), the prosecutor here derails his inquiry by repeatedly demanding to know at exactly what instant of the game Sadok pulled the trigger. Sadok himself points out the futility of the question by asking the prosecutor if the exact hour and minute the blade falls matters to the person being guillotined. Details can become small enough to obscure understanding, when the search for precision places the event in the wrong context altogether. It matters not at all whether Sadok fired at the 89th or 91st minute of the match (the narration relates both, and gives readers no way to decide which is correct), since the game is simply the wrong context in which to view the act. As Sadok discovers, it matters far more when he acted in relation both to the chain of events of the Algerian revolution and to the larger narrative of his discovery of Islamic history.

These discoveries will take both time and movement, in Paris in the main narration and in Bône in the flashbacks. Sadok himself realizes afterward that he scarcely looked at the match he attended; everything we learn about it comes from the radio commentary, rather than from the hero, entirely mute on the subject.[42] The narration thickens, and the protagonist's perspective sharpens, when he reminisces about the neighborhoods where he grew up in Bône, or describes his wanderings in Strasbourg where he first settled in France, or his movements in Paris where he successfully arranges a coup of admittedly debatable significance in the history of Algerian resistance, but which nonetheless allows him to enter history as an autonomous agent. From the beginning, the narrator emphasizes the importance for the terrorist of perfecting an urban savoir-faire, exactly the knowledge that the protagonist of *Topographie idéale* so badly lacked. This second Mohammed in the Métro, the master-terrorist, is "le seul à en connaître les impasses, les culs-de-sac, les butoirs et les murs verglacés par la sueur d'une humanité en perpétuelle transhumance et en inlassable nomadisation parce que prise d'une bougeotte irrépressible; alors que lui, gris et blafard . . . les papiers en règle, il déambule calmement parce qu'il sait comment faire pour que, le moment venu, il sache retrouver le centre d'un tel déploiement fastidieux" [the only one who knew the dead ends, the cul-de-sacs, the buffers, and the walls glazed with the sweat of a human mass in constant migration and tireless nomadism, seized with irrepressible fidgeting; while he, gray and pale . . . with his papers in order, walked calmly because he knew what to do so that, when the time came, he could find the center of this tedious layout].[43] Sadok masters the space around him, moving with the calm of someone who has the documents to convince the police of whatever identity he claims, and who knows exactly what itinerary will put him at the right place at the right time. This represents a high degree of what Certeau calls tactical mastery, a sort of gamesmanship taking place in the "space of the other": "Aussi doit-elle [la tactique] jouer avec le terrain qui lui est imposé tel que l'organise la loi d'une force étrangère. Elle fait du coup par coup. Elle profite des 'occasions' et en depend. . . . Il lui est possible d'être là où on ne l'attend pas. Elle ruse." ["Thus [tactics] must play on and with a terrain imposed on it and organized by the law of a foreign power. . . . It operates in isolated actions, blow by blow. It takes advantage of 'opportunities' and depends on them. . . . It can be where it is least expected. It is a guileful ruse."][44] Sadok seems even to have reached a higher level of skill in that he is prepared for mishap and does not seem to depend on circumstances alone to provide him with opportunities. In a network like the Métro, there is no absolute center, but rather many relative centers, points of intersection between lines, lines and streets, lines and people. In making events happen around him, Sadok seems able to constitute for himself the nexuses he needs, at will. He knows how to concentrate or loosen the network about him, how to avoid the impasses and culs-de-sacs fatal to a man wanted by the police.

In contrast to him, the Parisians appear as a silent, undistinguished crowd, in a situation remarkably similar to the stereotypical situation of the colonized Algerians, whom colonial historiography saw largely as no-mads, raiders, or migrants, whose unstable movements kept from achiev-ing the status of historical actors. The Parisians' movements resemble those of a herd, repetitive, blind, aimless, and above all without initiative: despite theories of mass psychology reaching back to Le Bon, the crowd does not make history here. The city attempts to impose norms of move-ment on its inhabitants, wholly cowed by the "gigantisme des construc-tions" [hugeness of the buildings], but the terrorist succeeds in his ma-neuvers to escape this control.[45] Arriving in Paris, Sadok

> marchait très vite, lui qui ne savait que flâner, comme pris déjà par le mimétisme consistant à faire de lui une sorte d'automate bien réglé, graissé, mis au point selon les normes universelles de ces cités interminables, telle-ment vite qu'il en suait malgé le froid qui le tenaillait fermement aux flancs [. . .] se disant: "Ce n'est pas avec ça qu'ils vont m'avoir. . . . Certainement pas. Ils ne me jetteront pas dans le fleuve qui traverse la ville et au-dessus duquel on a jeté des ponts en métal des ponts en fer et des ponts en bois et des arches en béton, parce que j'agirai le premier. . . . Il faudra que je prenne contact avec l'Organisation, et je ne veux surtout pas qu'on me demande des palabres. . . . Je veux agir, passer à l'action.

> [who had only known how to stroll, walked very fast, as if already prey to the mimicry that consists of making of him a sort of well-regulated, oiled au-tomaton, perfected according to the universal standards of these endless housing projects, so fast that he sweated from it in spite of the cold gnawing him around the sides [. . .] saying to himself: "they won't get me this way. . . . Certainly not. They won't throw me in the river which crosses the city and over which they have thrown bridges of metal and bridges of steel and bridges of wood and arches of concrete, because I will act first. . . . I'll have to contact the Organization, and above all I don't want them to ask me for talk. . . . I want to act, to move into action.][46]

Evoking the now-infamous housing projects under construction during the war, the hero senses and rejects the city's desire to crush him with standardized and interminable apartment blocks. An Algerian can hardly be a Parisian *flâneur*, at home in every neighborhood and self-confident enough to walk at his leisure. Twentieth-century Paris imposes a rapid, al-most furtive gait on its inhabitants, and especially on the immigrants tol-erated in many neighborhoods only if visibly on business. Even as Sadok concedes to this imposition of a pace, which after all does not prevent him from later becoming an effective undercover agent, he refuses to allow his body to become a docile and subservient part of Paris's urban tissue. The passage suggests a link between his body and the bridges across the Seine (the use of the verb *jeter* with both body and bridges, and the otherwise odd enumeration of construction materials); the reader half expects to hear of "bridges of flesh." As the hero knows, the *quais* and bridges of Paris were dangerous places for Algerians at the time, with drownings one of the common ends of the *ratonnades* or raids against immigrants. Instead of becoming history's victim, he seeks a call to action.

Following the hero in one of his promenades just after arriving in Paris, we find him

> renvoy[é] du côté du fleuve, à arpenter ses quais et ses ponts, à découvrir la ville dans ce qu'elle a de plus raffiné, à saisir l'envol tissuré, tendu, vergeturé, de la superstructure urbaine organisée comme un filet de veines et de lumières qui circulent à l'intérieur de ses limites irrévocables . . . une fois traversé le pont Saint-Michel, il tombe sur les parvis impériaux et pontificaux de Notre-Dame et vite, franchit un autre pont pour regarder, accoudé à une balustrade moyenâgeuse, les deux tours de la Conciergerie où des rois et des reines ont attendu qu'on vienne leur couper la tête. Baguenaudant aussi et déambulant dans une civilisation qu'il avait jusque là méprisée, il se met à aimer la ville un petit peu.

> [sent back down by the river, walking its banks and bridges, discovering what is most refined about the city, grasping the tight, textured, stretch-marked surface of the urban superstructure organized like a net of veins and lights circulating inside its irrevocable limits . . . once he had crossed the Pont Saint-Michel, he quickly crossed another bridge in order to gaze, while leaning on a medieval balustrade, at the two towers of the Conciergerie where kings and queens waited for them to come cut off their heads. Loafing and strolling amidst a civilization that he had scorned up to then, he began to like the city a little.][47]

What does he find to like in the city that represents a culture he had previously disdained? What about it is "most refined" for him? Like Breton's Nadja, Sadok senses the tension in an urban fabric that shows marks of strain (*vergeturé*) of historical pressures and processes. Just around the corner from the place Dauphine, where Nadja had her first revelations of the violently haunted history that underlies the monuments and streets of Paris, Sadok discovers in Notre-Dame a spectacular symbol of past authority, and in the Conciergerie a place where history on the grandest scale could overtake its individual actors. Given the power of these symbols, he affirms that he would never have become a militant had he remained at home, and he makes contact with the Organisation immediately after this out-of-the-ordinary tourist promenade. Opportunities for action and escape from regimentation thus lie hidden even under the repetitive itineraries of the masses. Echoing the contemporary historian Arlette Farge's description of the archives, we might characterize the narrator's representation of Paris as a *lieu pour l'histoire*, a place where history becomes present and possible.[48] The urban layout forms an archive of revolutionary acts, each with historical consequences. Unlike the landmark events of French revolutions, often cited by their dates or months alone (e.g., the 18th of Brumaire, the September massacres), the revolutionary activities in *Le Vainqueur* stand in memory as locations: the bomb at the Palace, the arson at 23 Rue Tilsit, the cache of weapons with a high-class prostitute in the Avenue des Marronniers. The presence of these landmarks in the same urban network as the medieval stone, Notre-Dame, and the Conciergerie presents every possibility for active historical participation.

As in *Topographie idéale*, this participation depends on the opportunities afforded (or lacking) in the place, but also on the hero's capacity to integrate personal memories into the weave of history. Mohammed Sadok, aka Staline, was born in Bône in 1931, one year after the centenary of French occupation, the year the historian Charles-Robert Ageron qualifies as the last moment one could still believe everything was going well in the colony. Sadok's birth coincides with the first cracks in the facade of colonial optimism. For him, Bône has always had something constricting and suffocating about it, along with a certain falseness in its monuments that he can at first barely articulate. It was certainly one of the most strikingly polarized Algerian cities, between the Europeans' center and the Muslims' periphery; with Oran and Algiers, its demographics showed a pervasiveness of the European presence far less visible elsewhere. The downright architectural weirdness of many of the colonial-era constructions lends an unreal quality to the protagonist's memories of the city,

> comme une carte postale imprimée sur sa peau, coupée en deux par la Seybouse. Rive gauche. Rive droite. Les Français d'un côté. Les Arabes de l'autre. Cours Bertania avec platanes luminescents et jeunes filles hâlées par le soleil des plages se tenant par la main, montant et remontant l'immense allée à la recherche du fiancé idéal, et au bout l'église ridicule, sertie d'enluminures d'un autre âge et la gare, de style saharien alors que le pont accable de ses câbles et de sa câblure l'espace taraudé à vif, sorties tout droit (la gare et l'église) d'un rêve colonial brumeux, à l'odeur d'absinthe et de jujube, en dehors du temps et de l'histoire avec, dominant le tout, la cathédrale Saint-Augustin et la vierge en stuc qui bénit la ville lorsque le sirocco souffle et que sur l'autre rive s'embrasent les bidonvilles.

> [like a postcard printed on his skin, cut in two by the Seybouse river. Left bank. Right bank. French on one side. Arabs on the other. The Cours Bertania with luminous plane trees and young girls bronzed by the sun of the beaches, going hand in hand up and down the immense promenade

searching for the ideal fiancé, and the ridiculous church at the end, ornamented with decorations of another era, and the train station in
the Saharan style while the bridge with its cables and its span overwhelmed
the space cut to the quick, the station and the church straight out of a hazy
colonial dream smelling of absinthe and lozenges, outside time and history,
with, overlooking it all, the Cathédrale Saint-Augustin and the plaster virgin
who blesses the city when the sirocco blows and the shantytowns burn on
the other bank.][49]

Bône at first seems like a topographic double of Paris on the other side of
the Mediterranean, a postcard city laid out on two complementary banks.
However, the Seybouse divides more than it unites, acting as the city's
ethnic barrier, even if it carries no bodies of drowned demonstrators. Seg-
regation keeps the Arabs in the narrow space assigned to them, while the
Europeans, eager to demonstrate their mastery over the space they ap-
propriated, show a ridicule much more apparent here than in Algiers. The
fake Gothic church at the top of a promenade itself most comparable to
the very un-Gothic Cours Mirabeau in Aix, the "Saharan"-style mosque
details on a train station by the Mediterranean, even the plaster statuary
of Bône's Sacré Coeur, the Cathédrale de Saint-Augustin, all testify to confusion and ineptitude in the city's extremely rapid Europeanization (see
figures 7.1 and 7.2).

Figure 7.1.   Bône (Annaba), the Cours Bertagna. Fonds documentaire Editions J. Gandini.

Figure 7.2. Bône (Annaba), inland end of the Cours Bertagna: the cathedral, with the courts building and prison just to the left. Fonds documentaire Editions J. Gandini.

Taken together, these buildings represent (at least to Sadok) not so much the city's history, as a mistily focused dream situated outside history, a dream of colonial stasis exempt from historical development. Sadok's description emphasizes the qualities of the city that make it unlikely to encourage any real participation in history. Elsewhere he evokes the confusion of styles and periods presented in the cathedral and its "décor douteux en carton-pâte où se mêlent tant de styles abracadabrants où chaque immigrant doit retrouver une part de l'église de son village sarde ou andalou ou sicilien ou grec, méridional en tout cas" [dubious pasteboard decor with so many crazy styles combined, in which each immigrant must be able to find part of the church of his village, whether Sardinian, Andalusian, Sicilian, Greek, or at any rate southern].[50] This conglomeration brought together to manufacture memory (in Nora's words, a "lien vécu au présent éternel" [bond tying us to the eternal present]), functions as such only for those who came from Europe.[51] Even they must settle for pastiche, despite their domination of the city's culture, since the colonial decor of Bône is conceived not for those who make history, but for those who consume it in provincial backwaters. In any case, this architectural pastiche offers scant features for the Muslims' consumption.

In this context, the hero's memories cannot grow via an integration with the history of his city, erased, or of the Algerian people, no less obscured. Only in Paris does he begin, little by little, to understand and reconnect bits of his past. The medal he remembers his mother hanging around the neck of her cow was in fact his father's military decoration, awarded posthumously for bravery in the Ardennes. The deceased uncle he remembers reading Communist tracts, and, drunk, singing the *Internationale* and shouting "Vive Staline!" (hence Sadok's *nom de guerre*) was in fact killed in the *maquis*. These connections between personal memories and world history underlie political engagement in the novel. The hero must add up "le bilan de son passé, de son présent et de son avenir, pour savoir et comprendre—non le sens de cette révolution à laquelle il a appartenu dès le début—mais celui de ce vertige, de ce tourbillon et de cette tourmente qui engloutissent tous ses mouvements, ses moindres gestes et jusqu'à ses rêves embrumés et embués par le cristal de l'histoire et de la mémoire qu'il a de sa ville natale" [the sum of his past, present, and future, in order to know and understand the meaning—not of the revolution which he supported from the beginning—but of this vertigo, whirlwind, and torment that swallowed up all his movements, his slightest gestures, and even his hazy dreams misted with the crystals of history and the memory he possessed of his hometown].[52] In ordering his memories and attaching them to historical events, he succeeds in finding his own place among them. His vertigo comes from the sensation of looking at his city from a height, a perspective he reconstructs from an intimate knowledge of Bône's topography, and that allows him a comprehensive view from a distance appropriate for reflection.

The move from memory to history thus implies a change of perspective, from street-level to bird's-eye, and of movement, from tactical to strategic. Certeau alludes to the limits of tactical movement, which does not have "le moyen de se tenir en elle-même, à distance, dans une position de retrait, de prévision et de rassemblement de soi: elle est mouvement 'à l'intérieur du champ de vision de l'ennemi'" ["the means to *keep to itself*, at a distance, in a position of withdrawal, foresight, and self-collection: it is a maneuver 'within the enemy's field of vision'"].[53] This describes nicely Sadok's initial situation in Paris; even if his ruses frequently allow him to escape surveillance momentarily, he remains there inside the field of vision of the colonial power and lacks the perspective to predict his opponent's next move.[54] Paradoxically, in the best ruse of his life, he accedes to the level of strategy while in prison, the classic space of surveillance and punishment. While the tactician exercises mastery by movement, the strategist exercises "une maîtrise des lieux par la vue. La partition de l'espace permet une pratique panoptique à partir d'un lieu d'où le regard transforme les forces étrangères en objets qu'on peut observer et mesurer, contrôler donc et 'inclure' dans sa vision" ["a mastery of places through sight. The division of space makes possible a *panoptic practice* preceeding from a place whence the eye can tranform foreign forces into objects that can be observed and measured, and thus contol and 'include' them within its scope of vision"].[55] Sadok manages this with his gaze from on high, including the entire city from a single point of view based on experience on the ground. Since physical movement is not necessary to the privileged strategic observer, his incarceration in the panopticon of the Fresnes prison does not prevent him from occupying the center of a historical panopticon of his own. In his cell, he dreams of soaring over the shanty-towns, in a birds-eye escape from prison; he develops the capacity to fill the historical and architectural voids of the colonized city. Before arriving in France, he had made a long circuit through the Middle East, "à la recherche des hauts lieux de l'architecture musulmane" [looking for the prime sites of Muslim architecture]; he can now reconstitute them to supplement Bône, mentally strolling "entre Tunis et Fès, Damas et Le Caire, [où] il avait suivi à la trace ce qui avait jalonné son enfance et qui avait complètement disparu de son paysage natal" [between Tunis and Fez, Damascus and Cairo, where he had traced what had marked out his childhood and which had completely disappeared from his native land-scape].[56] By associative memory, he restores to Bône a heritage of Arabo-Islamic history that the European Algerians disregarded in their view of the place as an entirely modern metropolis that owed everything to their constructions. Once he has transformed his personal geography by placing Bône next to Damascus and Cairo (despite its lack of monumental mosques), he can reinterpret his *paysage natal*.[57]

He immediately sees the limits imposed by the ideology which ordered that landscape and works to escape its hold, just as he worked to profit from the possibilities for escape in the urban fabric of Paris. As he reads the letters from his mother back in Bône, the prize city of the *colons* appears to him as

une surface polie et étale se déployant humide dans une perspective habilement truquée, comme si elle était un décor de cinéma en carton-pâte, mais trop courte, trop anarchique et pas assez horizontale pour faire l'effet d'une vraie ville, gardant cet aspect de pacotille qu'il lui avait connu . . . comme dans les mauvais films d'auteurs du cinéma coloniale de l'époque et des autres réalisateurs étrangers qui avaient fait de la ville et de sa région toute entière un simple décor permanent et douteux et avaient poussé le cynisme jusqu'à transformer le pays tout entier en studio naturel de mauvais cinéma exotique.

[a polished surface like slack water spreading out wetly in a cleverly faked perspective, as if it were a paper-maché cinema backdrop, but too short, too anarchic, and not horizontal enough to have the effect of a real city, keeping

the shoddy look he had known it to have . . . like in bad films by the colonial
filmmakers of the time, and by other directors who had simply made the city
and its entire region into a dubious and permanent backdrop, and had cyni-
cally gone so far as to transform the entire country into a natural studio for
bad exotic cinema.][58]

The local news recounted by his mother (stories of the savagery of anti-
FLN repression in the city) has the power to expose the colonial dream as
bad cinema and to reduce the pretty European city of Bône to a low-
budget movie set. The illusion no longer satisfies or convinces. We see the
back of the set and realize that the perspectives (both historic and architectural) that it tried to impose were faked: too much was crammed into
a perspective too short. Furthermore, Sadok has now seen the French
cities containing the originals of some of the monuments imitated in Bône,
notably Strasbourg cathedral and Notre-Dame, which inevitably make his
native city's flamboyant church look like a cheap copy at reduced scale in
a studio back lot. Having thus demystified the architecture and topography of his childhood, Sadok can trace a new time line in his history.

The list of major dates in Algeria's resistance to the French recurs a
number of times in the novel as a leitmotif of the protagonist's political
engagement. Marked by these dates, the new historical pilot chart will
permit the Algerian people to set out

> courant à travers les géographies laissées et léguées par les ancêtres qui
> avaient tracé un chemin vers les avenues larges de l'avenir, marquant de
> dates ineffaçables les portulans de la résistance à l'ennemi: 1830, 1849, 1871,
> 1881, 1911, 1945, 1954 . . . inscrits dans la genèse de sa préhistoire, sachant que
> les legs et les testaments étaient insuffisants et que, face à la force en-
> vahissante, il fallait se débrouiller et récrire l'histoire, sans hypnose ni talis-
> mans, sans signes cabalistiques ni rituels de sang, mais en faisant le plus pro-
> prement possible une guerre qui lui était imposée.

> [running across the geographies left and bequeathed by the ancestors who
> had traced a path toward the broad avenues of the future, marking the Por-
> tulan charts of resistance to the enemy with ineffaceable dates: 1830, 1849,
> 1871, 1881, 1911, 1945, 1954 . . . inscribed in the genesis of its prehistory,
> knowing that the legacies and testaments were insufficient and that, facing
> the invading force, they would have to get by somehow and rewrite history,
> without hypnosis or talismans or cabalistic signs or blood rituals, but by
> waging as cleanly as possible a war imposed on them.][59]

These dates mark the prehistory of the resistance movement, that is, the
necessary precondition for having a history, let alone rewriting it. Boudjedra rejects the fallacies and traps of an ancestral legacy, emphasizing the
inadequacy of this collective inheritance that must be reinterpreted in order to become usable. Unfortunately, events would disappoint anyone

hoping for a "clean" war in Algeria. The text leaves the reader to suspect that Algeria is attempting to plot its course on an outdated map like a Portulan, an old and highly figurative chart, more beautiful than useful for contemporary navigation. Boudjedra's hope seems to lie in a return to the level of tactics. Although Sadok's appreciation of history viewed from above seemed necessary to give him the power once enjoyed exclusively by the colonialists, the rewriting of history must occur on the very ground he soared above. It will be an act of *débrouillardise*, in the double sense of the word: the idiomatic, the supremely tactical game of making the most of one's opportunities, and the literal, the dissipation of the foggy colonial dream.

To return, finally to connect this rewriting with remembering, the "fog" of the colonial dream may be more than the (not quite) benign screen that lets popular culture dream pleasantly about the colonial idylls represented in, for example, the reprinted exoticist tourist posters from the 1930s, available for purchase in every city in France. In fact this fog recalls the sinister shroud obscuring horrifying truths thematized in Alain Resnais's documentary on Hitler's death camps, *Nuit et Brouillard* (1955). The French press was not entirely wrong in saying that the massacre of October 1961 was obscured in the collective memory, not least by the deaths of (ethnic French) demonstrators at the Charonne Métro station a few months later in 1962. We might nonetheless recall two vital facts. First, many events and memories did indeed pierce the thirty-five supposedly foggy years; and many people, perhaps more than the press imagined, had never forgotten, and indeed could not forget. Second, the citizens of France who consider themselves part of the dominant culture of Republican universalism are not alone in nourishing the French collective memory, or in selecting and maintaining *lieux de mémoir*. Nor have they been for many years now. They (and we) have a vested interest, not only in discovering one another's realms of memory, but also in allowing them the space to function.

NOTES

1. The crime took place on 1 May 1995. Whatever inspired the man and his two accomplices to act, the antiracist associations that declared themselves *parties civiles* in the case blamed the FN rally earlier that afternoon, though the prosecutor did not emphasize this.

2. These books included Michel Levine's *Les Ratonnades d'Octobre: un meurtre collectif à Paris en 1961* (Paris: Editions Ramsay, 1985), Jean-Luc Einaudi's *La Bataille de Paris* (Paris: Seuil, 1991), and Paulette Péju's *Ratonnades à Paris, précédé de Les harkis à Paris* (Paris: La Découverte), which the government censored, and did not

appear until 2000. For brief accounts of the events and their evocation of them in the courtroom in Bordeaux, see the Paris papers of 12 and 13 October 1997, or in English, Charles Masters, "Papon 'ordered secret Paris massacre of 1961'," *Sunday Times* (London), 12 October 1997. Joshua Cole has written the best secondary work on the historiography of the event, "Remembering the Battle of Paris: 17 October 1961 in French and Algerian Memory," *French Politics, Culture, and Society* 21, no. 3 (Fall 2003): 21–50; see also Jim House and Neil MacMaster's "*Une journée portée disparue*: The Paris Massacre of 1961 and Memory," in *Crisis and Renewal in France, 1918–1962*, ed. Kenneth Mouré and Martin S. Alexander (New York: Berghan Books, 2002), 267–90.

3. "As recently as October last year, on the 35th anniversary of the massacre, copies of the Algerian daily *Liberté* which examined Papon's role in the slaughter were confiscated by customs officers at Lyons airport. The interior minister who ordered the seizure was Jean-Louis Debré, the son of the former prime minister" (Masters, "Papon"). Michel Debré was prime minister in 1961.

4. See for example Darius Sanai, "'It was like unleashing a pack of rabid dogs'," *The European*, 23 October 1997, 14ff, an interview with a former Paris policeman. The issue of *L'Express* of 17 October 1997 contained an interview with another policeman; *Libération* published several as well.

5. This document, the *rapport Mandelkern*, was in fact intended as a survey of materials in the archives of the Préfecture likely to be of interest to historians investigating the massacre, and to stop unauthorized leaks, such as the one in *Libération*, mentioned below ("Une enquête est ouverte: Archives du 17 octobre 1961," *Sud Ouest* (Bordeaux), 23 October 1997). Nonetheless, the Mandelkern report advanced its own count of victims. Complaining about the delays in opening the archives, Einaudi says "Sept mois après les déclarations de Catherine Trautmann, faites au moment même où je témoignais . . . je n'ai toujours pu consulter aucune archive" (Jean-Luc Einaudi, "Octobre 1961: pour la vérité, enfin," *Le Monde*, 20 May 1998). However, another historian, David Assouline, was able to obtain an extract from documents of the Paris courts (*parquet de Paris*), and in an article in *Libération* of 22 October 1997, wrote that at least seventy people had died.

6. Jean-Luc Einaudi, "Monsieur Papon ne me fera pas taire," *Le Monde*, 2 February 1999. In the meantime, another government report based on police archives, and released by the Ministère de l'Intérieur on 4 May 1998, had said that "dozens" had probably died ("Tale of 1961 Massacre of Algerians in Paris," *New York Times*, 5 May 1998, 16). Finally, in May 1999, Lionel Jospin's office annouced that independent historians would indeed be allowed to look through the archives ("France to Open Files on Algerians Killed in '61," *New York Times*, 5 May 1999, 13). The persistence of news on the topic suggests at the very least a certain sluggishness in the administrations concerned, if not actual obstruction by officials below cabinet level.

7. There is in fact no shortage of well-documented histories treating the Algerian war and the memories it left, beginning with the substantial output of Benjamin Stora, particularly his *Histoire de la guerre d'Algérie, 1954–1962* (Paris: La Découverte, 1993); *La France en guerre d'Algerie: novembre 1954-juillet 1962. Collection des publications de la BDI* (Nanterre: Edition Bibliothèque de documentation inter-

nationale contemporaine, 1992); and *La Gangrène et l'oubli: la mémoire de la guerre d'Algérie*.

8. Cole, "Remembering the Battle of Paris," 31.

9. Ibid.

10. Rachid Boudjedra, *Le Vainqueur de coupe* (Paris: Denoel, 1981), 234.

11. Other literary treatments of the Parisian topography by Algerians or French writers of Algerian descent include Mourad Bourboune's *Le Muezzin* (Paris: Christian Bourgeois, 1968) and Mounsi's *La Cendre des villes*, 1993 (Paris: Editions de l'aube, 2003). Paul Smaïl's *Vivre me tue* [*Smile*, 1999] features a family traumatized by the memory of the narrator's uncle, murdered by the police in October 1961.

12. The critic Karen Holter begins to make a similar point in "Topographie idéale pour un texte maghrébin ou: la lecture du réseau métropolitain de Rachid Boudjedra," *Revue romane* 29, no. 1 (1994): 85. Holter's is the best work on this novel since the poet Hédi Bouraoui published a remarkable review the year after the novel's appearance, cited in the bibliography.

13. Pierre Nora, "Entre Mémoire et Histoire: La problématique des lieux," in *Les Lieux de Mémoire: I, La République*, ed. Pierre Nora (Paris: Gallimard, 1984), xvii/1. Page numbers appearing after the slash refer to "General Introduction: Between Memory and History," in *Realms of Memory: Rethinking the French Past*, ed. Pierre Nora and Lawrence Kritzman (New York: Columbia University Press, 1996), 1–20.

14. Pierre Nora, "Entre Mémoire et Histoire," xviii/2.

15. Rachid Boudjedra, *Topographie idéale pour une agression caractérisée* (Paris: Denoel, 1975), 27.

16. Armelle Crouzières-Ingenthron, "Le labyrinthe de symboles: intratextualité chez Rachid Boudjedra," *Francographies*, no. 2 (1995): 148. In an interview with Crouzières-Ingenthron in the *Journal of Maghrebi Studies* 1, no. 2 (Fall 1993), Boudjedra declares his fascination with the labyrinthine and declares his preference for the term *écriture en réseau* over *écriture en abyme*. When the *réseau* in fact functions as a classic *mise en abyme*, the change of term may reflect only a very slight nuance.

17. Boudjedra, *Topographie*, 18.

18. Holter, "Topographie idéale pour un texte maghrébin," 88.

19. Boudjedra, *Topographie*, 9.

20. Boudjedra, *Topographie*, 18–19. The second ellipsis elides the portion of the map description cited earlier.

21. The critic Richard Terdiman uses the construction in the title of his chapter on Flaubert in Egypt in *Discourse/Counter-Discourse* (Ithaca, NY: Cornell University Press, 1985); others have taken it up elsewhere. The pun does not seem to have been much in use among the nineteenth-century authors like Nerval or Fromentin, themselves clearly "dis-Oriented" in their exotic travel narratives.

22. Marc Augé, *Un ethnologue dans le métro* (Paris: Hachette, 1986), 8.

23. Regardless of the bilingual resonance with "rascals," the name given these old men seems to be the Arabic *al-àskarī*, pl. `*asākir*, soldier. Anglophone readers may be more familiar with the Urdu-derived "lascar," an East Indian sailor or artilleryman.

24. Boudjedra, *Topographie*, 23.

25. Selim Jay, "Rachid Boujedraa répond," *Lamalif,* no. 78 (March 1976): 46.

26. Boudjedra, *Topographie,* 202.

27. Ibid., 49.

28. Ibid., 90.

29. Ibid., 96.

30. Ibid., 137.

31. Pierre Nora, "Entre Mémoire et Histoire," xxxv.

32. Augé, *Un Ethnologue dans le métro,* 33.

33. Augé, *Un Ethnologue dans le métro,* 34.

34. Ibid., 45.

35. Pierre Nora, "Entre Mémoire et Histoire," xviii/2.

36. Boudjedra, *Topographie,* 138.

37. Holter, "Topographie idéale pour un texte maghrébin," 96; Crouzières-Ingenthron, "Le labyrinthe de symboles," 155.

38. Boudjedra, *Topographie,* 27.

39. Ibid., 156–57.

40. Ibid., 202.

41. Michele de Certeau, *L'Invention du quotidien,* ed., Luce Girard (Paris: Gallimard, 1990) 80–101/57–68. Page numbers after the slash refer to the translation: *The Practice of Everyday Life.*

42. Boudjedra, *Vainqueur,* 117.

43. Ibid., 18.

44. Certeau, *L'Invention du quotidien,* 60–1/37.

45. Boudjedra, *Vainqueur,* 123–24.

46. Ibid., 125–26.

47. Ibid., 136.

48. Arlette Farge, *Des lieux pour l'histoire* (Paris: Seuil, 1997).

49. Boudjedra, *Vainqueur,* 47.

50. Ibid., 60.

51. Pierre Nora, "Entre Mémoire et Histoire," xix/3.

52. Boudjedra, *Vainqueur,* 59.

53. Certeau, *L'Invention du quotidien,* 60/37.

54. Boudjedra, *Vainqueur,* 165–66.

55. Certeau, *L'Invention du quotidien,* 60/36.

56. Boudjedra, *Vainqueur,* 166.

57. Ibid., 60.

58. Ibid., 246–47.

59. Boudjedra, *Vainqueur,* 152–53. The dates: 1830, conquest of Algiers; 1849, surrender of Abd-el-Kader; 1871, revolt of El-Mokrani in Kabylia; 1881, last Kabyle revolt of the century; 1911, unrest in Tlemcen when a group of Muslims refused to perform their military service and emigrated to Syria; 1945, riots of 8 May and their bloody repression; 1954, beginning of the war of independence.

Conclusion

"Rien n'aura eu lieu que le lieu."
[Nothing will have taken place but the place.]

—Stéphane Mallarmé, *Un Coup de dès jamais n'abolira le hazard*

What does it mean to say that an event "took place"? The expression associates happening (the condition of existence for an event) with location: an event needs a physical location in order to live, and its occurrence is the act in which it takes possession of a spot on the globe or in the human imagination. In doing so, the event would seem to make a claim on posterity by becoming intimately associated with the place it has "taken." Some, of course, do so more successfully or tenaciously than others, changing the way we think about the places in question, or even altering the places themselves. Furthermore, places stay with us when other traces of an event have disappeared and seem to offer temptingly tangible remnants of a past often difficult to apprehend in any other way. Official commemorations may favor certain places over others, but those that lack official sanction nonetheless retain multifarious links to the events which "took place" there, the historical moments that "took the place" and made it into a site of history. A dozen everyday examples illustrate this process in Paris. At one of the entrances to the Charonne Métro stop, a plaque marks the spot where eight ethnic French people died in 1962, in a riot-police charge during a demonstration against the Organisation Armée Secrète, the pro-Algérie française terrorist group. Like most commemorative plaques, it appears as a blur to most people who pass it. The official inscription of the event into the Parisian landscape may count for little, but the place did not require that to retain its significance. The event continues to take the place and use it to distill a moment of history which otherwise exists only diffusely in memories and texts. Another example: on 17 October 2001, the mayor of Paris Bertrand Delanoë presided over the unveiling of a plaque on the Pont Saint-Michel, marking the spot where the police had thrown Maghribi immigrants into the river forty years before, comfortably far enough in the past that such a ceremony was even possible. Yet it had been less than six years since another man of Maghribi origin had lost his life in a frighteningly similar way, frighteningly close by.[1] Walking along the banks of the Seine with the knowledge of these events, one is tempted to say that nothing took place there, but the place. As stages for commemoration, or more often, as simple sites of past events, the very concreteness of places gives observers the illusion of a solid frame in which to situate history. Yet nothing is as slippery as a place invested by multiple and sometimes contradictory histories.

In cases where several histories have "taken (a) place" in the same spot, signification itself is multiplied, as new events and their commemorations overlay old ones. In the months following independence, streets and squares throughout Algeria received the names of the heroes of national revolution; Ben M'hidi Larbi, Zighout Youcef, and Didouche Mourad replaced the Michelets, Pasteurs, and Républiques previously honored. The process did not take place overnight, leaving many place-names untouched for years, and its gradual progress produced some odd juxtapositions: on one map from the late sixties, the boulevard of the assassinated French president Sadi Carnot persisted alongside that of the tortured Algerian leader Ben M'hidi Larbi. Monuments, too, underwent radical change. The Place du Gouvernement, known at various times as the Place d'Armes, the Place Louis-Philippe, and the Place de la République, had been called the Place du Cheval in popular speech, after the equestrian statue of the Duc d'Orleans erected there in the late 1840s. Shortly after independence, the eponymous horse was taken down and shipped to France, where it stands in the city of Nemours, bearing silent witness to the fate of monuments that have outlived their causes. Though the square received a new name, Sahat Al-Shuhadā', "Square of the Martyrs," a significant number of Algerians continued for several decades to refer to it in the old way, despite the lack of any visible horse. While some monuments were sent packing with the departing *pieds-noirs*, others disappeared in stranger ways. The government of 1930 had taken advantage of the official celebrations to inaugurate a Monument aux Morts on an esplanade just below the then-new Gouvernement Général building. The imposing sculpture featured a group of soldiers, including one in Algerian dress, carrying a fallen comrade. After independence, the new occupants of the Gouvernement Général decreed the construction of a monument to the martyrs of the revolution for the site. The designer of the truly monu-mental sculpture that took the place of the old did not call for the removal of its predecessor, but simply had the plinth for his own monument con-structed around it. The Monument aux Morts from the 1914–1918 war, later updated to include those of 1939–1945, thus disappeared, walled into the base of the new monument to the dead of the struggle for inde-pendence. The colonial past is never far below the surface in Algeria. However, this does not mean that it constitutes the place's only past, or even the most determinant; many other episodes of Algerian history ex-ert significant influence over its current cultural productions.

This book has examined only a few of them and considered what the colony and post-colony made of them in literature. I have argued that the discussion surrounding the country's past advanced most notably through portraits of its cities and the physical traces in them of historical events. From Louis Bertrand to Randau and the Algerianists, to the writ-ers of Centenary propaganda, and from Audisio, Camus, and the École d'Alger to Kateb and Boudjedra, history has remained a privileged con-cern of Algerian literature. No doubt this follows generally from the im-portance of collective memory in identity formation. In the colony, how-ever, as I have shown, consciousness of the historicity of urban places was the subject of continuous discussion, invention, and reenvisioning. I at-tribute this in large part to the anxieties that Alain Calmes pointed to in his characterization of the colonial condition as "une précarité qui s'éternise" [an eternal precarity], that colonizers felt the need to address by finding ways to emphasize their permanence.[2]

Louis Bertrand began by simply discarding major elements of the Maghribi past that could not justify the French presence, and just before 1900 presented French Algeria with a bad idea whose time had come: Latin Africa, the answer to a colonialist's prayer. In inventing the idea that would keep him in print and justify the colonial exploit for several decades, Bertrand also showed how a project of restorative nostalgia could place regionalist literature in the service of national renewal, be-yond anything Maurice Barrès had imagined when he proclaimed the sanctity of *la terre et les morts*. The next novelist to lead the colony's effort at literary self-identification, Robert Randau, seemed to abandon Bertrand's concept of the colony's past, though he did not shift the focus of his efforts from attempts to create an awareness of Algerian colonial identity in history. Ostensibly dispensing with nostalgia for an ancient past, Randau nonetheless retained the affect, changing only the object it valorized: no longer descendants of Roman colonizers, his heroes are the inheritors of "Berberized" *colon* pioneers. Although Randau's followers declared nothing Algerian alien to them, they did little to move represen-tation of the Muslims beyond alibis for colonial violence against them.

Just as importantly, Algerianism also constituted an attack on the Parisian literary establishment, proclaiming its own attachment to pro-colonial verisimilitude in defiance of the prescription of metropolitan taste. All this, they thought, would advance the interests of the colony, their prime declared motivation for writing.

In chapter three I argued that Europeans writing in the genre of the *roman indigène* took the same position of possessors of insider knowledge about the Muslims in order to legitimate their stories as quasi-scientific documents and themselves as experts. They deployed a host of prefaces, notes, and semischolarly references to back up their assertions of personal knowledge of the supposedly timeless manners and customs of their subjects. Far from supporting the myth of easy assimilation of the Kabyles, they actually tended to undercut the idea that assimilation of any Muslim could ever succeed. As if in answer, a number of Muslim authors wrote novels portraying the hazards of assimilation, though with far more ambiguity, making their messages difficult to pin down. Among them, moreover, we see the first examples in the colony of a nostalgia other than restorative, in *Ahmed Ben Mostapha, goumier* and *El Euldj, captif des barbaresques*. Ben Cherif and Chukri both evoke previous periods as models for their present, not in order to rebuild a lost paradise, but as inspiration for political stances in their own periods. Without suggesting any possibility of return to the glorious Muslim past, both remind their readers that Algeria was not always a colony, and that the cards of the assimilation game were not always so stacked against the colonized. In so doing, they introduce the possibility of political evolution, which reality in the colony would soon disavow.

The political evolution that did not happen remains one of the most notable features, from today's perspective, of the centenary of French Algeria in 1930. Ageron and others have called it a missed opportunity, seemingly agreeing with writers like Audisio, Camus, and Roblès who would all have, at varying degrees, the sense that their calls for political reform and cultural openness were too little, too late.[3] The whole climate of 1930 in Algeria appears submerged in a wave of restorative nostalgia to an extent that may seem surprising given the emphasis in public discourse on the modernity and dynamism of France's Algerian provinces. Yet the colonial administration's gesture in creating replicas of the regiments of 1830 and marching them through Algiers demonstrates the extent to which the supposedly forward-looking vision of Algeria that the administration attempted to popularize in fact bathed in restorative nostalgia. It seems inevitable that such commemorations would fail to satisfy those who advocated a more all-encompassing vision of the country, let alone those who demanded political reforms. Restorative nostalgia, unlike its contemplative cousin, must inevitably select its objects rather narrowly, since it actually proposes recreating them.

Audisio, Camus, and Roblès all saw the necessity of abandoning restorative nostalgia, whether for Latin Africa or anything else, as I showed in chapter five. Audisio and Camus argued explicitly against narrow restorative projects, as their concept of Mediterranean man included all the civilizations around the sea. The work of creating a Mediterranean culture in colonial Algeria, however, represented a challenge far too large for the relatively few authors who proposed it, especially since neither Audisio nor Camus offered any real vision for the inclusion of non-European cultural productions on their own terms. Under these circumstances, Camus especially had to face the failure of the Franco-Algerian historical model, based on the premise that each colonist represented in some sense a "first man" on his territory. Yet (or perhaps for this reason), Camus managed to produce a powerful literature of the failure of memory: though he allows his hero to indulge in nostalgia, the narrator remains painfully aware that this can only be longing for a history and a memory that would make nostalgia for anything else possible. His friend and contemporary Emmanuel Roblès also complicated his perspective on his childhood in the interval between his two literary reworkings of it. He speaks of the real if ephemeral solidarity possible among the working class of all ethnicities, without suggesting that it meant an end to prejudice. By reaching out to the heritage of Muslim Spain, one that he claims as his own despite (but also because of) his ethnic background, he opens the possibility for a truly inclusive and productive Mediterranean culture. Of course, by then, he could no longer postulate cultural domination within it.

In the last two chapters of this book, I discussed the ways in which Kateb Yacine and Rachid Boudjedra evoke urban topographies to produce new views of the Algerian past and to open new possibilities for their political present. Kateb's narrative contains a critique of the banal, dehumanizing, and controlling urban design imposed on colonial Bône by the French, but it concerns itself much more with discovering ways for the colonized to navigate successfully in the new space. It also insists on the value of ruins, in a nostalgic manner far different from that of Bertrand and his followers. In Kateb's contemplative nostalgia, it is more the fact of the ruin's persistence as a ruin, than its evidence of anything once whole, that gives it its potential for use in the cultural construction of the new Algeria. Boudjedra for his part demonstrates how the would-be restorative nostalgia of former independence fighters fails the test of protecting and advancing a post-colonial migrant. He also indicts the pro-colonial nostalgia evidenced in both the architecture of Bône and the image that the colonial past now projects in France. His narrator declares old maps inadequate and attempts to chart new, politically effective ways of moving and living in urban space.

If places change despite our expectations of constancy, literature that valorizes, commemorates, or reconfigures places proves even slipperier. Writing about the Casbah of Algiers today cannot have the same meaning as during or after the battle of 1957, or during the ideological struggles of 1930. Study of such writing demands close attention to the way history and literature interact to change the place in question. In both Algeria and France, the dialogue of literary and historical discourses focused on the city reflects urban change, but also participates in it. This study demonstrates the interconnections of fiction and nonliterary genres in reworking our understanding of a place and its history.

In addition, it shows the continued relationship between Paris and Algiers, which goes far beyond the struggles over cultural influence, "westernization," and *intégrisme*. The recent literary and cinematic celebrations of *pied-noir* nostalgia in France, and the revalorization by several public figures of their Algerian roots, are the very visible facets of this influence.[4] However, life in the French urban topography is perhaps more significantly marked by the cultural inventions and consumption of hundreds of thousands of immigrants and their descendants, who play a growing role in defining the shape of the French city today. Colonies and capitals, former colonies and their former metropoles: all remain bound together in a literature that, as many critics have pointed out, is often produced in France, for French audiences. Rather than taking this as evidence for the alienation of Francophone authors, this study draws attention to the ways cultural, historical, and physical interconnections complicate notions of "authenticity" defined as attachment to a given place. The Algerian authors most visibly attached to place are also those who most thoroughly undermine the idea of constancy, either in the places they valorize or in their relationships to them. Those relationships evolved in response to historical and physical change, and to understand them, we must concentrate on discursive practices in and out of literature, at the most local level. Neither the city nor its literature is ever still.

This study has several consequences for our thinking about the difficult literary-critical notion of postcoloniality. The global reach of a concept originating in the study of the later days of British rule in India has alarmed many critics, who have warned of the dangers of imposing postcoloniality as a unitary and leveling view of the cultures of societies ruled in diverse ways, and for relatively brief periods, from Europe. If any more proof were needed, this book has shown that no such systemwide view can account for the disparate realities observed within even one colony, let alone the divergences between areas ruled under different terms by the colonizing power. In Morocco, for example, Hubert Lyautey and the other creators of the French protectorate valorized less the Roman occupation than several of the Arab and Amazigh dynasties that they saw as the apogee of Moroccan history. Any study of Morocco analogous to this one of Algeria would thus follow a significantly different development of imperial nostalgia.

This book has also demonstrated the possibility of analyzing works generally viewed through the postcolonial lens without resorting to some of the clichés of postcolonial theory (e.g., mimicry and hybridity), and yet still keeping sight of the political context. Leaving aside these tired notions turns out not to impoverish our understanding of the cultural politics of literature outside of Europe. On the contrary, it allows us to avoid the leveling clichés that these notions, once intended as an escape from essentialist thought, have come to be. I hope that this book provides an example of the evidence-based testing of theoretical perspectives that our ideological commitments make us too ready to wish into truth. Careful examination of evidence is not necessarily or even generally the work of reactionaries. Nor should we allow it to be the province of ostensibly apolitical scholarship (only ostensibly, since nothing is as political as proclaiming oneself apolitical). I have tried to exercise critical judgment without fear that my conclusions (about the political compromises of early Arab and Amazigh writers, for instance) could be seized upon to discredit people who deserve respect. The benefits of clearer sight outweigh this risk.

NOTES

1. I refer to the crime mentioned in the opening paragraph of chapter 7.

2. Alain Calmes, *Le Roman colonial en Algérie avant 1914* (Paris: L'Harmattan, 1984), 13.

3. Charles-Robert Ageron, *Histoire de l'Algérie contemporaine: de l'insurrection de 1871 au déclenchement de la guerre de libération (1954)* (Paris: PUF, 1979), 410–11.

4. Consider the foundation in the mideighties in Montpellier of the significantly named "Association Africa Nostra," publishing *pied-noir* memoirs, or the conjunction in the spring of 2000 of the release of the film *Là-bas, mon pays* and the televised reminiscences of the Algerian Jewish actor Roger Hanin, whose last name is a homonym for an Arabic word for "longing" or "nostalgia."

Bibliography

I. PRIMARY SOURCES

A. Archives d'Outre-Mer, Aix-en-Provence

Gouvernement Général de l'Algérie: Series GGA 1-N, 2-N, 3-G, 64-S, 8-X, 12-X.
Fonds du Département d'Alger: Series F-2, 10-I.
Fonds ministériels: F-80.
Fonds iconographiques: 2-FI, 4-FI, 9-FI.
"Procès-verbal de la 35e séance du Conseil Supérieur du Centenaire." Gouvernement Général de l'Algérie, GGA Carton 8-X-8.
"Procès-verbal de la réunion du Conseil Supérieur du Centenaire du 11 octobre 1930." Gouvernement Général de l'Algérie, GGA Carton 8-X-8.
"Procès-verbal de la réunion du Conseil Supérieur du Centenaire du 29 mai 1929." Gouvernement Général de l'Algérie, GGA Carton 8-X-8.

B. Periodicals Surveyed

Apart from the major Algiers dailies, most of these publications were extremely sporadic, and their collections are often incomplete at the Bibliothèque Nationale. Dates indicate the period examined.
Afrique: Bulletin de critique et d'idées. Algiers. 1924–1939.
L'Afrique du Nord illustrée. Algiers. 1929–1931.
Annales africaines. Ain-Taya. 1928–1932.
Chantiers nord-africains. Algiers. 1929–1930.
Demain: Le Travailleur. Algiers. 1929–1930.
La Dépêche Algérienne. Algiers. 1929–1930; 1938–1940.
L'Écho d'Alger. Algiers. 1930.

El Hack: Le Petit Egyptien. Oran. 1911.
L'Évolution nord-africaine. Algiers. 1929–1931.
La Kahena: Bulletin des écrivains de l'Afrique du Nord. Tunis. 1930–1939.
Notre rive: Grand magazine de l'Afrique du Nord. Algiers. 1927–1929.
La Presse libre. Algiers. 1928–1932.
La Revue algérienne littéraire et artistique. Ain Taya. 1935–1936.
La Revue de l'Afrique du Nord. Algiers. 1921–1922.
Terre d'Afrique illustrée. Algiers. 1928–1932.
La Voix des humbles. Oran/Constantine/Algiers. 1925–1931.
La Voix indigène. [*Al-Sawt al-ahli*.] Constantine. 1929–1931.
Journal des colonies: Organe de politique coloniale. Marseille. 1928–1930.
Revue des deux mondes. 1925–1932.

C. Newspaper Articles

(Bracketed titles reflect the topics of untitled articles, or first lines.)

Ait-Kaci. "La Représentation des indigènes au Parlement." *La Voix des humbles* 74 (May 1929).
"Après le Centenaire." *La Voix indigène*, 5 June 1930.
"Au coeur de la colonisation française." *Terre d'Afrique illustrée*, no. 143 (June 1930).
"Le Cahier du Centenaire." *La Voix indigène*, 1 May 1930.
"Le Centenaire: revendications politiques." *La Voix indigène*, 21 November 1929.
Charles-Collomb. "[Editorial]." *L'Evolution nord-africaine*, 1 January 1930.
"Défilé des troupes de l'Armée d'Afrique." *Dépêche algérienne*, 19 April 1930.
"'Esclave en Alger' par Henriette Celarié." *Dépêche algérienne*, 10 January 1930.
"Etienne Dinet." *La Presse libre*, 6 January 1930.
"Les grandes fêtes de l'union Franco-Musulmane à Sidi-Ferruch." *l'Afrique du Nord illustrée*, 21 June 1930.
Hadj Cadi. "De la naturalisation." *La Voix indigène*, 24 October 1929.
Kateb, Yacine, Mohammed Dib, and Pierre Laffont. "Le Chômage, cette plaie." *Alger Républicain*, 8 May 1952.
Labiod. "À propos du Centenaire." *La Voix indigène*, 6 February 1930.
———. "Désillusion et espérance." *La Voix indigène*, 10 July 1930.
"[Le Musée des beaux arts et les bidonvilles]." *La Presse libre*, 18 June 1930.
Mélia, Jean. "L'Humiliante platitude." *La Presse libre*, 2 February 1930.
———. "L'Oeuvre néfaste: la plus dangereuse erreur du Commissariat Général du Centenaire." *La Presse libre*, 4 March 1930.
———. "Une lettre de M. Jean Mélia à M. André Tardieu. L'oeuvre néfaste du Commissariat général du Centenaire de l'Algérie." *La Presse libre*, 11 January 1930, 1.
"Nos objectifs." *L'Espoir-Algérie. Expression des Libéraux d'Algérie*, 13 May 1960.
"[Note de la rédaction]." *La Presse libre*, 30 April 1930.
"Une opinion discutable sur un Général factieux et déserteur." *Annales africaines* 42, no. 2 (15 January 1930): 17.
"Le rapprochement est-il sincère ou factice?" *Annales nord-africaines*, 1 June 1930.
Recouly, Raymond. "La France et l'Algérie: un glorieux centenaire." *Annales Africaines*, 15 October 1929.

"[Réponse du Commissariat du Centenaire à Jean Mélia]." *La Presse libre*, 17 January 1930, 1.

Spielmann, Victor. "En marge du Centenaire." *Demain*, 31 May 1930.

———. "Le Wagon Présidentiel." *Demain*, 3 June 1930.

"Le Voyage du Président de la République en Algérie." *L'Afrique du Nord illustrée*, 17 May 1930.

D. Books and Journal Articles

Abbas, Ferhat. *Le Jeune Algérien: de la colonie vers la province.* Algiers-Paris: La Jeune Parque, 1931.

Akoun, Charles. "Nécessité des méthodes algérianistes." *Afrique*, no. 51 (June 1929).

"Alger, ville-pilote de l'Afrique du Nord." *Alger-Revue*, May 1955.

Audisio, Gabriel. *Algérie méditerranée: feux vivants*, 1957. Limoges: Rougerie, 1958.

———. *Amour d'Alger*. Algiers: Charlot, 1938.

———. *Héliotrope*. Paris: Gallimard, 1928.

———. *Jeunesse de la Méditerranée*. Paris: Gallimard, 1935.

———. *Jeunesse de la Méditerranée: II, Sel de mer*. Paris: Gallimard, 1936.

———. "L'Algérie littéraire." In *L'Encyclopédie coloniale et maritime*. Vol. 2, *Algérie et Sahara*. Edited by Eugène Garnier, 235–47. Paris: L'Encyclopédie de l'Empire Française, 1946.

———. "À Propos d'une concurrence touristique." *Terre d'Afrique illustrée* 139 (January 1930): 12.

Azan, Gen. Paul. "Le Centenaire de 1830." "Le Centenaire de l'Algérie." Special issue, *Revue des vivants*. (1929).

Baamer, Sliman ben Ibrahim. *Khadra, danseuse Ouled Nail.* Illustrated by Etienne Dinet. Paris: H. Piazza, 1926.

Barrès, Maurice. *Les Déracinés.* 1897. Paris: Robert Laffont, 1994.

———. *L'Appel au soldat.* 1900. Paris: Robert Laffont, 1994.

———. *Leurs figures.* 1902. Paris: Robert Laffont, 1994.

———. *Scènes et doctrines du nationalisme.* 1902. Paris: Éditions du Trident, 1987.

———. *La Terre et les morts (sur quelles réalités fonder la conscience française).* Paris: Ligue de la Patrie Française, 1899.

Ben Cherif, A. *Ahmed ben Mostapha, goumier.* Paris: Payot, 1920.

Berbrugger, Louis Adrien. *Algérie historique, pittoresque et monumentale. Recueil de vues, monuments, cérémonies, costumes . . . des habitants de l'Algérie.* 3 vols. Paris: J. Delahaye, 1843.

Bertrand, Louis. *Alger.* Paris: Sorlot, 1938.

———. *La Cina.* Paris: Ollendorff, 1901.

———. *D'Alger la romantique à Fès la mysterieuse.* Paris: Éditions des Portiques, 1930.

———. *Un destin: Sur les routes du Sud.* Paris: Arthème Fayard, 1936.

———. *Discours prononcés dans la séance publique tenue par l'Académie française pour la réception de M. Louis Bertrand, le jeudi 25 novembre 1926.* Paris: Firmin-Didot, 1926.

———. *Hitler*. Paris: Fayard, 1936.

———. *Les Nuits d'Alger*. Paris: Flammarion, 1929.

———. *Pépète le bien-aimé*. Paris: Ollendorff, 1904.

———. *Le Roman de la conquête*. Paris: Arthème Fayard, 1930.

———. *Le Sang des races*. Paris: Ollendorff, 1899.

———. *Le Sens de l'ennemi*. Paris: A. Fayard, 1917.

———. *Les Villes d'or. Algérie et Tunisie romaines*. Paris: Arthème Fayard, 1921.

Boudjedra, Rachid. *Topographie idéale pour une agression caractérisée*. Paris: Denoel, 1975.

———. *Le Vainqueur de coupe*. Paris: Denoel, 1981.

Bourboune, Mourad. *Le Muezzin*. Paris: Christian Bourgeois, 1968.

Camus, Albert. *Actuelles, III: chronique algérienne, 1939–1958*. Paris: Gallimard, 1958.

———. *Albert Camus éditorialiste à L'Express (mai 1955-février 1956)*. Introduction and notes by Paul-F. Smets. Cahiers Albert Camus. Paris: Gallimard, 1987.

———. "Le Désert." 1939 in *Noces*, vol. 7. Oeuvres complètes d'Albert Camus. Paris: Gallimard, Club de l'Honnête Homme, 1983.

———. *The First Man*. Translated by David Hapgood. New York: Alfred A. Knopf, 1995.

———. *Fragments d'un combat 1938–1940: Alger Républicain, Le Soir Républicain*. Edited by Jacqueline Lévi-Valensi and André Abbou. Cahiers Albert Camus. Paris: Gallimard, 1978.

———. *L'Envers et l'Endroit*. 1937. *Oeuvres complètes d'Albert Camus*. Paris: Gallimard, Club de l'Honnête Homme, 1983.

———. "L'Été à Alger." 1939 in *Noces*, vol. 7. *Oeuvres complètes d'Albert Camus*. Paris: Gallimard, Club de l'Honnête Homme, 1983.

———. "Minotaure, ou la halte d'Oran." 1954 in *L'Été*, vol. 3. *Oeuvres complètes d'Albert Camus*. Paris: Gallimard, Club de l'Honnête Homme, 1983.

———. "Minotaure, or The Stop in Oran." In *The Myth of Sisyphus and Other Essays*. Translated by Justin O'Brien, 155–83. New York: Alfred A. Knopf, 1955.

———. "La Nouvelle culture méditerranéenne." *Jeune Méditerranée. Bulletin mensuel de la "Maison de la Culture" d'Alger*, no. 1 (April 1937): n.p.

———. *La Peste*. 1947. Paris: Gallimard, 1974.

———. *The Plague*. Translated by Robin Buss. London: Penguin, 2001.

———. *Le Premier homme*. Cahiers Albert Camus. Paris: Gallimard, 1994.

———. "Summer in Algiers." In *The Myth of Sisyphus and Other Essays*. Translated by Justin O'Brien, 139–54. New York: Alfred A. Knopf, 1955.

Célarié, Henriette. *Esclave en Alger*. Paris: Hachette, 1930.

Charles-Brun, Jean. *Les Littératures provinciales, avec une esquisse de géographie littéraire de la France, par M. P. de Beaurepaire-Froment*. Paris: Bloud, 1907.

Charles-Collomb. *Vérités nord-africaines*. Algiers: Deltrieux et Joyeux, 1932.

Charmetant. *Les Peuplades kabyles et les tribus nomades du Sahara*. Montreal, 1875.

Chollier, Antoine. *Alger et sa région*. Grenoble: B. Arthaud, 1929.

———. *Drusilla, dame d'Alger*. Algiers: Soubiron, 1930.

Chukri, Khodja. *El Euldj, captif des barbaresques*. Paris: Editions de la Revue des Indépendants, 1929.

Le Corbusier. "La Nouvelle architecture." *Jeune Méditerranée. Bulletin mensuel de la "Maison de la Culture" d'Alger*, no. 1 (April 1937): n.p.

Cotereau, M. J. "Les Architectures méditerranéennes du passé." *Chantiers nord-africains*, February–May 1930.

———. "La Maison mauresque." *Chantiers Nord-Africains*, June 1930.

Courtin, Charles. *La Brousse qui mangea l'homme: images de la vie africaine*. Paris: Éditions de France, 1929.

Daudet, Alphonse. *Aventures prodigieuses de Tartarin de Tarascon*. Paris: E. Dentu, 1872.

Daumas, Eugène. *La Grande Kabylie, études historiques*. Paris, 1844.

———. *Moeurs et coutumes de l'Algérie: Tell—Kabylie—Sahara*. 1853. Paris: L. Hachette, 1858.

Duchêne, Ferdinand. *Au pas lent des caravanes*. 1922. Paris: Albin-Michel, 1931.

———. *Au pied des monts éternels: roman berbère*. Paris: Albin-Michel, 1925.

———. *Les Barbaresques: l'aventure de Sidi Flouss*. Paris: Albin-Michel, 1929.

———. *Le Berger d'Akfadou, roman kabyle*. Paris: Albin-Michel, 1928.

———. *La Rek'ba, histoire d'une vendetta kabyle*. Paris: Albin-Michel, 1927.

———. *Thamil'la*. Paris: Albin-Michel, 1923.

Dugas, Père Joseph. *La Kabylie et le peuple kabyle*. Paris, 1877.

Favre, Lucienne. *Dans la Casbah 1937–1948*. Paris: Ed. Colette d'Halloin, 1949.

———. *Dans la Casbah*. Paris: Grasset, 1937.

———. *Tout l'inconnu de la Casbah d'Alger*. Algiers: Baconnier, 1933.

Fournier, Édouard. *Paris démoli: mosaique de ruines*. 1853. With a preface by Théophile Gautier. Paris: E. Dentu, 1855.

Géniaux, Charles. *Le Choc des races*. Paris: Arthème Fayard, 1923.

———. *Sous les figuiers de Kabylie: Scènes de la vie berbère*. Paris: Flammarion, 1917.

Gsell, Stéphane. *Histoire ancienne de l'Afrique du Nord*. Paris: Hachette, 1913.

Guimet, Émile. *Arabes et Kabyles: pasteurs et agriculteurs*. Lyon, 1873.

Guy, Robert. *L'Architecture moderne de style arabe*. Paris: Librairie de la construction moderne, n.d.

Hanoteau, Gen. Adolphe, and A. Letourneux. *La Kabylie et les coutumes kabyles*. Paris, 1872–73.

Hardy, Georges. "Préface." In *Méditerranée nouvelle: Extraits des pricipaux écrivains contemporains de Tunisie, Algérie, Maroc*, ed. Camille Bégue. Tunis: La Kahena, 1937.

Ibn al-Hachemi, Emir Khaled. *La Situation des Musulmans d'Algérie: Conférences faites à Paris les 12 et 19 juillet 1924*. 1924. Algiers: Editions du Trait d'Union, Victor Spielmann, 1930.

Ibn Khaldūn. *The Muqaddimah: An Introduction to History*. Translated by Franz Rosenthal. New York: Pantheon Books, Bollingen Series, 1958.

Imache, Tassadit. *Une Fille sans histoire*. Paris: Calmann-Lévy, 1989.

"Jeune poésie nord-africaine—Maurice-Robert Bataille, Louis Chaudron, Mohamed Dib, Henri-Jacques Dupuy, Yacine Kateb, Brahim Lourari, Jean Senac, Ahmed Smaili." *Forge: Cahiers littéraires*, no. 3 (April–May 1947).

Kateb, Yacine. *Boucherie de l'espérance*. Ed. Zebeida Chergui. Paris: Seuil, 1999.

———. "C'est africain qu'il faut se dire." Interview by Tassadit Yacine. In *Le Poète comme un boxeur*. Paris: Seuil, 1994.

———. *Le Cercle des représailles*. Paris: Seuil, 1959.

———. *L'Oeuvre en fragments*. Ed. and intro. Jacqueline Arnaud. Paris: Sindbad, 1986.

———. *Nedjma*. 1961. Translated by Richard Howard, with an introduction by Bernard Aresu. Charlottesville, VA: Caraf Books, University of Virginia Press, 1991.

———. *Nedjma*. 1956. Paris: Seuil, 1996.

———. *Parce que c'est une femme*. Paris: Des femmes, 2004.

———. *Le Polygone étoilé*. Paris: Seuil, 1966.

———. *Soliloques*. 1946. Paris: La Découverte, 1991.

Kettane, Nacer. *Le Sourire de Brahim*. Paris: Denoel, 1985.

Klein, Henri. *Feuillets d'El-Djezair*. Algiers: Fontana, 1910.

———. *Feuillets d'El-Djezair*. Algiers: L. Chaix, 1937.

Lebel, Roland. *Histoire de la littérature coloniale en France*. Paris: Larose, 1931.

Leblond, Marius-Ary, ed. *Anthologie coloniale, morceaux choisis d'écrivains français*. Paris: Peyronnet, 1929.

Lecoq, Louis. "[L'Immigration]." *Afrique*, no. 2 (May 1924).

———. "[Notice sur *La brousse qui mangea l'homme*]." *Afrique*, no. 55 (January 1930).

Lespes, René. *Alger: étude de géographie et d'histoire urbaine*. Paris: Felix Alcan, 1930.

Leune, Jean. *Le Miracle algérien*. Paris: Berger-Levrault, 1930.

Livre d'or du Centenaire de l'Algérie française. Son histoire. L'oeuvre française d'un siècle. Les manifestations du Centenaire. 1830–1930. Algiers: Fontana, 1931.

Martino, Pierre. "La littérature algérienne." In *Histoire et historiens de l'Algérie*. Collection du Centenaire, 331–48. Paris: Félix Alcan, 1931.

Masqueray, Emile. *Formation des cités chez les populations sédentaires de l'Algérie*. 1886. With an introduction by Fanny Colonna. Aix-en-Provence: Edisud, 1983.

———. *Souvenirs et visions d'Afrique*. Paris: E. Dentu, 1894.

———. *Voyage dans l'Aurès: études historiques*. Paris, n.d.

Mélia, Jean. *Le Centenaire de la conquête de l'Algérie et les réformes indigènes*. Paris: Ligue française en faveur des indigènes musulmans d'Algérie, 1929.

Mille, Pierre. "Préface." In *Philoxène ou de la littérature coloniale*, Eugène Pujarniscle. Paris: Firmin-Didot, 1931.

Morand, Marcel. "Le Statut de la femme kabyle et la réforme des coutumes berbères." *Revue des études islamiques* 1 (1927): 47–94.

Mounsi, Mohand. *La Cendre des villes*. 1993. Paris: Éditions de l'aube, 2003.

Murat, Henri. "Cent années d'urbanisme et de construction." *La Presse libre*, 7 January 1930.

Noirfontaine, Pauline de. *L'Algérie: un regard écrit*. Le Havre: Imp. Alph. Lemale, 1856.

Notre Afrique, anthologie des conteurs algériens. With a preface by Louis Bertrand. Paris: Éditions du Monde Moderne, 1925.

Ould Cheikh, Mohammed. *Myriem dans les palmes*. Oran: Éditions Plaza, 1936.

Palais des Beaux-Arts de la Ville de Paris. *Exposition du Centenaire de la Conquête de l'Algérie, 1830–1930*. With a preface by Camille Gronkowski. Paris: Impr. de Fraiser-Soye, 1930.

Pélégri, Jean. *Les Oliviers de la justice*. Paris: Gallimard, 1959.

Poirel, Léopold-Victor. *Mémoire sur les travaux à la mer, comprenant l'historique des ouvrages exécutés au port d'Alger, et l'exposé complet et détaillé d'un système de fondation à la mer au moyen de blocs de béton.* Paris: Carilian-Goeury et V. Dalmont, 1841.

Pomier, Jean. "Àgir." In *A cause d'Alger.* Toulouse: Édouard Privat, 1966.

——. "Algériennement." *Afrique*, no. 1 (April 1924).

——. "Attitudes devant l'Islam: celle d'Etienne Dinet." *Afrique*, no. 56 (February 1930).

——. "Chez les poètes." *Afrique*, no. 55 (January 1930).

——. "[Notice sur Stephan]." *Afrique*, no. 61 (July–August 1930).

——. "Le Prix Littéraire Algérien et la politique du prix." *Afrique*, no. 3 (June 1924).

——. "Robert Randau, son art, sa pensée." *Afrique*, no. 52 (July 1929).

——. "[Sur la mort de Musette]." *Afrique*, no. 62 (September–October 1930).

Pujarniscle, Eugène. *Philoxène ou de la littérature coloniale.* Paris: Firmin-Didot, 1931.

Randau, Robert. *Cassard le Berbère.* 1922. Algiers: Jules Carbonel, 1926.

——. *Les Colons.* 1907. Paris: Albin-Michel, 1926.

——. *Les Colons: roman de la patrie algérienne.* Paris: E. Sansot, 1907.

——. "Inactualité d'André Gide." *Afrique*, no. 195 (June 1944): 14–16.

——. "La Littérature coloniale, hier et aujourd'hui." *Revue des deux mondes*, 15 July 1929, 416–34.

——. *Le Professur Martin, petit bourgeois d'Alger.* Illustrated by Brouty. Algiers: Baconnier, 1936.

——. *Sur le pavé d'Alger.* Illustrated by Hans Kleiss. Algiers: F. Fontana, 1937.

Rasteil, Maxime. *À l'aube de l'Algérie française: le calvaire des colons de 48.* Paris: Eugène Figuière, 1931.

Robert, Claude-Maurice. "Un livre impie." *Afrique*, no. 58 (April 1930).

Roblès, Emmanuel. *Albert Camus et la trêve civile.* Philadelphia: Celfan Ed. Monographs, 1988.

——. *Les Hauteurs de la ville.* 1948. Paris: Seuil, 1960.

——. *Jeunes saisons.* 1961. Paris: Seuil, 1995.

——. *L'Action.* 1938. Algiers: Charlot, 1946.

——. *Saison violente.* Paris: Seuil, 1974.

Rousseau, Jean-Jacques. *Dictionnaire de musique.* 1768. Genève: Éditions Minkoff, 1998.

Sabatier, Camille. *Étude sociologique sur les Kabyles.* Comptes rendus de l'Association française pour l'avancement des sciences, 1881.

Sautayra, and Eugène Cherbonneau. *Droit musulman du statut personnel et des successions.* Paris: Maisonneuve et Cie., 1873–74.

Sebbar, Leila. *La Seine était rouge.* Paris: Éditions Thierry Magnier, 1999.

Spielmann, Victor. *En Algérie: le centenaire au point de vue indigène.* Algiers: Éditions du Trait-d'Union, 1930.

Smaïl, Paul. *Vivre me tue.* Paris: Éditions Balland, 1997.

Surdon, Georges, and Léon Bercher, eds. *Recueil de textes de Sociologie et de Droit public musulman contenus dans les "Prolégomènes" d'Ibn Khaldoûn.* Bibliothèque de l'Institut d'Études Supérieures Islamique d'Alger. Algiers: Imprimerie officielle, 1951.

Trenga, Docteur Victor. *Berberopolis, tableaux de la vie nord-africaine en l'an quarante de la République berbère. Préface posthume d'Eugène Fromentin.* Algiers: Impr. de Rives-Lemoine-Romeu, 1922.

Violette, Maurice. *L'Algérie vivra-t-elle?* Paris: Félix Alcan, 1931.

Weiss, René. *Le Centenaire de l'Algérie française (1830–1930).* Paris: Imprimerie nationale, 1930.

Zaccone, Pierre, ed. *Les Rues de Paris, ou Paris chez soi, Paris ancien et nouveau . . . avec tous les changements exécutés ou projetés récemment. . . . Terminé par une Revue générale du nouveau Paris.* Paris: P. Boizard, 1859.

II. SECONDARY SOURCES

Aba, Nourredine. "Que dire de Camus?" *Revue Celfan* 4, no. 3 (May 1985): 1–5.

Abdel-Jaouad, Hédi. "Kateb Yacine's Modernity: Rewriting Surrealism." *SubStance*, no. 69 (1992): 11–29.

Abu-Lughod, Janet. *Rabat: Urban Apartheid in Morocco.* Princeton: Princeton University Press, 1980.

Achour, Christiane, and Simone Rezzoug. "Brisure dans une cohérence discursive: l'autochtone dans les textes coloniaux de 1930 en Algérie." In *Des années trente: groupes et ruptures.* Edited by Anne Roche and Christian Tarting. Paris: Éditions du CNRS, 1984.

Aciman, André. "From Alexandria." *MLN* 112, no. 4 (September 1997): 683–97.

Ageron, Charles-Robert. *France coloniale ou parti colonial?* Paris: PUF, 1978.

———. *Histoire de l'Algérie contemporaine: de l'insurrection de 1871 au déclenchement de la guerre de libération (1954).* Paris: PUF, 1979.

———. "L'Exposition coloniale de 1931: Mythe républicain ou mythe impérial?" In *Les Lieux de Mémoire: I, La République.* Pierre Nora, 561–91. Paris: Gallimard, 1984.

Akhtar, Salman. "'Someday' and 'If Only' Fantasies." In *The Subject and the Self: Lacan and American Psychoanalysis.* Edited by Judith Feher Gurewich and Michel Tort, 203–33. Northvale, NJ: Jason Aronson Inc., 1996.

AlSayyad, Nezar. "Colonialism and National Identity." In *Forms of Dominance: On the Architecture and Urbanism of the Colonial Experience.* Edited by Nezar Al-Sayyad, 183–210. Avebury, UK: Brookfield, 1992.

———. "The Islamic City as a Colonial Enterprise." In *Forms of Dominance: On the Architecture and Urbanism of the Colonial Experience.* Edited by Nezar Al-Sayyad, 27–43. Avebury, UK: Brookfield, 1992.

Apter, Emily. "Out of Character: Camus's French Algerian Subjects." *MLN* 112, no. 4 (September 1997): 497–516.

Aresu, Bernard. *Counterhergemoic Discourse from the Maghreb: The Poetics of Kateb's Fiction.* Tubingen: Narr, 1993.

Arnaud, Jacqueline. *Recherches sur la littérature maghrébine de langue française: le cas de Kateb Yacine.* Université de Paris III, 1978.

———. "Les villes mythiques et le mythe de Nedjma dans le roman de Kateb Yacine." In *Journée Kateb Yacine: Actes du colloque organisé par le Départment de*

Français, Université de Tunis I (5 mai 1984). Tunis: Faculté des Lettres de la Manouba, 1990.

Augé, Marc. *Un ethnologue dans le métro*. Paris: Hachette, 1986.

Aurbakken, Kristine. *L'Étoile d'araignée: une lecture de Nedjma de Kateb Yacine*. Paris: Publisud, 1986.

Barrière, Louis-Augustin. "Le Puzzle de la citoyenneté en Algérie." *Plein droit*, no. 29–30 (November 1995).

Batcho, Krystine Irene. "Nostalgia: A Psychological Perspective." *Perceptual and Motor Skills* 80 (1995): 131–43.

Benaita, Farouk. *Alger: agrégat ou cité: l'intégration citadine de 1919–1979*. Algiers: SNED, 1980.

Benattig, Rachid. "8 mai 1945." *Algérie-Actualité*, 10–16 May 1970.

Berque, Jacques. *Le Maghreb entre deux guerres*. Paris: Seuil, 1962.

Béguin, François. *Arabisances: décor architectural et tracé urbain en Afrique du Nord 1830–1950*. Paris: Dunod/Bordas, 1983.

Biesse-Eichelbrenner, Michèle. *Constantine: la conquête et le temps des pionniers*, 1985.

Bolzinger, André. "Jalons pour une histoire de la nostalgie." *Bulletin de psychologie* 42, no. 389 (January–April 1989): 310–21.

Bonn, Charles. *Kateb Yacine: Nedjma*. Paris: PUF, 1990.

———. *Problématiques spatiales du roman algérien*. Algiers: ENAL, 1986.

Bouraoui, Hédi. "Le Récit tentaculaire du nouveau roman engagé: 'Topographie' de Rachid Boudjedra." *Afrique littéraire et artistique*, no. 39 (1976): 24–32.

Bouzar, Wadi. "Brève histoire d'une déception: Camus et l'Algérie." *Revue Celfan* 4, no. 3 (May 1985): 36–40.

Boym, Svetlana. *The Future of Nostalgia*. New York: Basic Books, 2001.

Buisine, Alain, Norbert Dodille, and Claude Duchet, eds. *L'Exotisme*. Saint-Denis-de-la-Réunion: Université de la Réunion, 1988.

Calmes, Alain. *Le Roman colonial en Algérie avant 1914*. Paris: L'Harmattan, 1984.

Carroll, David. "Camus's Algeria: Birthrights, Colonial Injustice and the Fiction of a French Algerian People." *MLN* 112, no. 4 (September 1997): 517–49.

Cataldo, Hubert. *Bône 1832–1962 et Hippone la Royale*. 2 vols. Montpellier: Africa Nostra, 1986.

Certeau, Michel de. *L'Invention du quotidien. 1. Arts de faire*. 1980. Edited by Luce Girard. Paris: Gallimard, 1990.

———. *The Practice of Everyday Life*. Translated by Steve F. Rendall. Berkeley: University of California Press, 1984.

Cole, Joshua. "Remembering the Battle of Paris: 17 October 1961 in French and Algerian Memory." *French Politics, Culture, and Society* 21, no. 3 (Fall 2003): 21–50.

Cooper, Frederick. *On the African Waterfront: Urban Disorder and the Transformation of Work in Colonial Mombasa*. New Haven: Yale University Press, 1987.

Corpet, Olivier, Albert Dichy, and Mireille Djaider, eds. *Kateb Yacine, éclats de mémoire*. Paris: IMEC, 1994.

Courcelles, Dominique de, ed. *Littérature et exotisme: XVI–XVIIIe siècle*. Paris: École des chartes, 1997.

Crouzières-Ingenthron, Armelle. "Interview with Rachid Boudjedra." *Journal of Maghrebi Studies* 1, no. 2 (Fall 1993).

———. "Le Labyrinthe de symboles: intratextualité chez Rachid Boudjedra." *Francographies*, no. 2 (1995): 147–59.

Çelik, Zeynep. *Displaying the Orient: Architecture of Islam at Nineteenth-Century World's Fairs*. Berkeley: University of California Press, 1992.

———. *Urban Forms and Colonial Confrontations: Algiers under French Rule*. Berkeley: University of California Press, 1997.

Deleuze, Gilles. *The Fold: Leibniz and the Baroque*. Translated by Tom Conley. Minneapolis: University of Minnnesota Press, 1993.

———. *Le Pli: Leibniz et le baroque*. Paris: Éditions de Minuit, 1988.

Deluz, Jean-Jacques. *L'Urbanisme et l'architecture d'Alger: Aperçu critique*. Alger: Pierre Mardaga/Office des Publications Universitaires, 1988.

Déjeux, Jean. Introduction *Espagne et Algérie au XXe siècle: Contacts culturels et création littéraire*. Edited by Jean Déjeux. Paris: L'Harmattan, 1985.

———. *Littérature maghrébine de langue française: Introduction générale et Auteurs*. 1973. Sherbrooke: Naaman, 1978.

———. *Maghreb littératures de langue française*. Paris: Arcantère, 1993.

———. "Réception critique de *Nedjma* en 1956–57." In *Actualité de Kateb Yacine*. Edited by Charles Bonn, 109–26. Paris: L'Harmattan, 1993.

———. *Situation de la littérature maghébine de langue française: approche historique, approche critique, bibliographie méthodique des oeuvres maghrébines de fiction 1920–1978*. Algiers: Office des Publications Universitaires, 1982.

Dirlik, Arif. "The Postcolonial Aura: Third World criticism in the age of global capitalism." In *Contemporary Postcolonial Theory: A reader*. Edited by Padmini Mongia, 294–320. London: Arnold, 1996.

Djeghloul, Abdelkader. *Éléments d'histoire culturelle algérienne*. Algiers: ENAL, 1984.

Djiait, Hichem. *Al-Kufa, naissance de la ville islamique*. Paris: Maisonneuve et Larose, 1986.

Doane, J., and D. Hodges. *Nostalgia and Sexual Difference: The Resistance to Contemporary Feminism*. New York: Methuen, 1987.

Donadey, Anne. "Anamnesis and National Reconciliation: Re-membering October 17, 1961." In *Immigrant Narratives in Contemporary France*, edited by Susan Ireland and Patrice Proulx, 47–56. Westport, CT: Greenwood Press, 2001.

Dugas, Guy. "Les Algérianistes et Gide." *Bulletin des Amis d'André Gide* 22, no. 102 (April 1994): 287–311.

———. "André Gide en Algérie: Les écrivains d'Algérie face à la morale gidienne." *Bulletin des Amis d'André Gide* 22, no. 102 (April 1994): 249–68.

Dunwoodie, Peter. *Francophone Writing in Transition: Algeria 1900–1945*. Bern: Peter Lang, 2005.

———. *Writing French Algeria*. Oxford: Clarendon Press, 1998.

Einaudi, Jean-Luc. *La Bataille de Paris*. Paris: Seuil, 1991.

———. "Monsieur Papon ne me fera pas taire." *Le Monde*, 2 February 1999.

———. "Octobre 1961: pour la vérité, enfin." *Le Monde*, 20 May 1998.

Elleh, Nnamdi. *Architecture and Power in Africa*. Westport, CT: Praeger, 2002.

"Une enquête est ouverte: Archives du 17 octobre 1961." *Sud Ouest (Bordeaux)*, 23 October 1997.

Erickson, John D. "Kateb Yacine's *Nedjma*: A Dialogue of Difference." *Sub-Stance*, no. 69 (1992): 30–45.

Farge, Arlette. *Des lieux pour l'histoire*. Paris: Seuil, 1997.

Felman, Shoshana. "Camus' *The Plague*, or a Monument to Witnessing." In *Testimony: Crises of Witnessing in Literature, Psychoanalysis and History*, by Shohana Felman and Dori Laub, 93–119. New York: Routledge, 1992.

Forsdick, Charles, and David Murphy. "Introduction: The Case for Francophone Postcolonial Studies." In *Francophone Postcolonial Studies: A Critical Introduction*. Edited by Charles Forsdick and David Murphy, 1–14. London: Arnold, 2003.

"France to Open Files on Algerians Killed in '61." *New York Times*, 5 May 1999, 13.

Gautier, Emile-Félix. *Le Passé de l'Afrique du Nord: les siècles obscurs*. Petite bibliothèque Payot. Paris: Payot, 1964.

Geesey, Patricia. "Collective Autobiography: Algerian Women and History in Assia Djebar's *L'amour, la fantasia*." Dalhousie French Studies 35 (Summer 1996): 153–67.

Gontard, Marc. *Nedjma de Kateb Yacine: Essai sur la structure formelle du roman*. Paris: L'Harmattan, 1985.

———. "A propos de la séquence du Nadhor." In *Actualité de Kateb Yacine*. Edited by Charles Bonn, 133–44. Paris: L'Harmattan, 1993.

Graebner, Seth. "'Unknown and Unloved': The Politics of French Ignorance in Algeria, 1860–1930." In *Identity, Memory, and Nostalgia: Algeria 1800–2000*. Patricia Lorcin. Syracuse, NY: Syracuse University Press, 2005, 49–62.

Greene, G. "Feminist Fiction and the Uses of Memory." *Signs: Journal of Women in Culture and Society* 16, no. 2 (1991): 290–321.

Grenier, Roger. *Albert Camus soleil et ombre: une biographie intellectuelle*. Paris: Gallimard, 1987.

Hamadeh, Shirine. "Creating the Traditional City: A French Project." In *Forms of Dominance: On the Architecture and Urbanism of the Colonial Experience*. Edited by Nezar AlSayyad, 241–59. Avebury, UK: Brookfield, 1992.

Hannoum, Abdelmajid. "Translation and the Colonial Imaginary: Ibn Khaldūn Orientalist." *History and Theory* 42 (February 2003): 61–81.

Hargreaves, Alec G., ed. *Memory, Empire, and Postcolonialism: Legacies of French Colonialism*. Lanham, MD: Lexington Books, 2005.

Hargreaves, Alec G., and Mark McKinney. "Introduction: The Post-colonial Problematic in Contemporary France." In *Post-Colonial Cultures in France*. Edited by Alec G. Hargreaves and Mark McKinney, 3–25. London: Routledge, 1997.

Hargreaves, Alec. "Caught in the Middle: The Liberal Dilemma in the Algerian War." *Nottingham French Studies* 25, no. 2 (October 1986): 73–82.

Haroun, Ali. *La Septième wilaya: La Guerre du FLN en France*, 1954–1962. Paris: Seuil, 1986.

Hodeir, Catherine. *L'Exposition coloniale: 1931*. Paris: Éd. Complexe, 1991.

Holter, Karin. "Topographie idéale pour un texte maghrébin ou: la lecture du réseau métropolitain de Rachid Boudjedra." *Revue romane* 29, no. 1 (1994): 83–101.

Horne, Alistair. *A Savage War of Peace: Algeria 1954–1962*. 1977. London: Papermac, 1996.

House, Jim, and Neil MacMaster. "*Une journée portée disparue*: The Paris Massacre of 1961 and Memory." In *Crisis and Renewal in France, 1918–1962*. Edited by Kenneth Mouré and Martin S. Alexander, 267–90. New York: Berghan Books, 2002.

El Houssi, Majid. "Louis Bertrand et le mythe de la colonisation." *Awal: Cahiers d'études berbères*, no. 16 (1997).

Ihaddaden, Zahir. "L'Histoire de la presse 'indigène' en Algérie, des origines jusqu'en 1930." Thèse de doctorat du 3eme cycle. Université de Paris II, n.d.

Ireland, Susan. "Rewriting the story in Tassadit Imache's *Une Fille sans histoire*." *Women in French Studies*, no. 3 (Fall 1995): 112–22.

Irving, Robert Grant. *Indian Summer—Lutyens, Baker, and Imperial Delhi*. New Haven: Yale University Press, 1981.

Jay, Selim. "Rachid Boujedraa répond." *Lamalif*, no. 78 (March 1976): 45–46.

Kelly, Debra. *Autobiography and Independence: Selfhood and Creativity in North African Postcolonial Writing in French*. Liverpool: Liverpool University Press, 2005.

Khatibi, Abdelkébir. *Le Roman maghrébin*. Paris: François Maspero, 1968.

King, Anthony D. *Colonial Urban Development: Culture, Social Power, and Environment*. London: Routledge, 1976.

Kleiner, J. "On Nostalgia." *Bulletin of the Philadelphia Association for Psychoanalysis* 20 (1970): 11–30.

Laachir, Karima. "The Interplay between History/Memory/Space in Tassadit Imache's *Presque un frère* and *Le Dromedaire de Bonaparte*." *Modern and Contemporary France* 13, no. 4 (November 2005): 449–64.

Lacoste, Yves. "La Grande oeuvre d'Ibn Khaldoun." *La Pensée*, no. 69 (October 1956): 10–33.

———. "Les Prolégomènes d'Ibn Khaldoun." *Progrès* 1, no. 2 (April–May 1953): 28–39.

Lacoste-Dujardin, Camille. "Génèse et évolution d'une représentation géopolitique: l'imagerie kabyle à travers la production bibliographique de 1840 à 1891." In *Connaissances du Maghreb: Sciences sociales et colonisation*. Edited by Jean-Claude Vatin. Paris: CNRS, 1984.

Lamprakos, Michele. "Le Corbusier and Algiers: The Plan Obus as Colonial Urbanism." In *Forms of Dominance: On the Architecture and Urbanism of the Colonial Experience*. Nezar AlSayyad, 183–210. Avebury, UK: Brookfield, 1992.

Lanasri, Ahmed. *La Littérature algérienne de l'entre-deux-guerres: génèse et fonctionnement*. Paris: Publisud, 1995.

Levine, Michel. *Les Ratonnades d'Octobre: un meurtre collectif à Paris en 1961*. Paris: Editions Ramsay, 1985.

Lombard, Denys, ed. *Rêver l'Asie: exotisme et littérature coloniale aux Indes, en Indochine et en Insulinde*. Paris: Editions de l'EHESS, 1993.

Loomba, Ania. "Overworlding the 'Third World'." In *Colonial Discourse and Post-Colonial Theory: A Reader*. Edited by Patrick Williams and Laura Chrisman, 305–23. Hemel Hempstead, UK: Harvester Wheatsheaf, 1993.

Lorcin, Patricia M. E. *Imperial Identities: Stereotyping, prejudice and race in colonial Algeria*. London: I. B. Tauris, 1995.

———. "Rome and France in Africa: Recovering Colonial Algeria's Latin Past." *French Historical Studies* 25, no. 2 (Spring 2002): 295–329.

Lotfi, Martine Astier. *Littérature et colonialisme: L'expansion coloniale vue dans la littérature romanesque française, 1871–1914*. Paris: Mouton, 1971.

Lottman, Herbert R. *Albert Camus: A Biography*. New York: Doubleday and Co., 1979.

Masters, Charles. "Papon 'ordered secret Paris massacre of 1961'." *Sunday Times* (London), 12 October 1997.

McConnell, Daphne. "Family, History, and Cultural Identity in the Beur Novel." In *Maghrebian Mosaic: A Literature in Transition*. Edited by Mildred Mortimer, 253–68. Boulder, CO: Lynn Reinner, 2000.

McDermott, Sinead. "Future-perfect: Gender, Nostalgia, and the Not Yet Presented in Marilynne Robinson's *Housekeeping*." *Journal of Gender Studies* 13, no. 3 (November 2004): 259–70.

Milligan, Melinda J. "Displacement and Identity Discontinuity: The Role of Nostalgia in Establishing New Identity Categories." *Symbolic Interaction* 26, no. 3 (Summer 2003): 381–403.

Morton, Patricia A. *Hybrid Modernities: Architecture and Representation at the 1931 Colonial Exposition*, Paris. Cambridge, MA: MIT Press, 2003.

Nora, Pierre, ed. *Les Lieux de mémoire*. Paris: Gallimard, 1984.

———. "Entre Mémoire et Histoire: La problématique des lieux." In *Les Lieux de Mémoire: I, La République*. Edited by Pierre Nora, xvii–xlii. Paris: Gallimard, 1984.

———. "General Introduction: Between Memory and History." In *Realms of Memory: Rethinking the French Past*. Edited by Pierre Nora and Lawrence Kritzman, 1–20. New York: Columbia University Press, 1996.

O'Brien, Conor Cruise. *Camus*. London: Fontana, 1970.

Oulebsir, Nadia. "Discours patrimonial et création architecturalé: le Comité du Vieil-Alger." In *Alger: Une ville et ses discours*. Najet Khadda and Paul Siblot, 131–54. Montpellier: Praxiling, 1996.

Pageaux, Daniel-Henri. "Le Mirage latin de Louis Bertrand." In *Espagne et Algérie au XXe siècle: Contacts culturels et création littéraire*. Edited by Jean Déjeux. Paris: L'Harmattan, 1985.

Payand, Bernard. *La Médina de Constantine: De la ville traditionnelle au centre de l'agglomération contemporaine*. Poitiers: Centre interuniversitaire d'études méditerranéennes, 1989.

Pease, Elizabeth Scali. "L'Espace, la mère, l'impasse: *Nedjma* de Kateb Yacine." *Francofonia: Studi e Ricerche sulle Letterature di Lingua Francese* 14, no. 26 (Spring 1994): 87–101.

Péju, Paulette. *Ratonnades à Paris, précédé de Les harkis à Paris*. Paris: La Découverte, 2000.

Planche, Jean-Louis. "Charles Courtin, romancier de l'affrontement colonial." *Revue de l'Occident Musulman et de la Méditerranée*, no. 37 (1985): 37–46.

Prochaska, David. "History as Literature, Literature as History: Cagayous of Algiers." *American Historical Review* 101, no. 3 (Fall 1996): 670–711.

———. *Making Algeria French: Colonialism in Bône, 1870–1920*. Cambridge, UK: Cambridge University Press, 1990.

Rabinow, Paul. *French Modern: Norms and Forms of the Social Environment*. Cambridge, MA: MIT Press, 1989.

Ricord, Maurice. *Louis Bertrand l'Africain*. Paris: Fayard, 1947.

Rivas, Pierre. "La Quête d'identité dans l'autobiographie d'Emmanuel Roblès: Relations interéthniques et problèmes d'acculturation." In *Espagne et Algérie au XXe siècle: Contacts culturels et création littéraire*. Edited by Jean Déjeux, 161–77. Paris: L'Harmattan, 1985.

Roberts, Hugh. *The Battlefield of Algeria 1988–2002: Studies in a Broken Polity*. London: Verso, 2003.

Robin, Maurice, Hocine Ait Ahmed, Albert Memmi, Paul Thibaud, and Charles Poncet. "Remarques sur l'attitude de Camus face à la guerre d'Algérie." In *Camus et la politique: Actes du colloque de Nanterre, 5–7 juin 1985*. Edited by Jeanyves Guérin, 185–202. Paris: L'Harmattan, 1986.

Roussel, Eric. "Préface." In *Maurice Barrès: Romans et voyages*. Edited by Vital Rambaud. Paris: Robert Laffont, 1994.

Said, Edward. *Culture and Imperialism*. New York: Alfred A. Knopf, 1993.

Salgado, Raquel Scherr. "Memoir at Saint-Brieuc." *MLN* 112, no. 4 (September 1997): 576–94.

Sanai, Darius. "'It was like unleashing a pack of rabid dogs'." *The European*, 23 October 1997, 14ff.

Sedikides, Constantine, Tim Wildschut, and Denise Baden. "Nostalgia: Conceptual Issues and Existential Functions." In *Handbook of Experimental Existential Psychology*. Edited by Jeff Greenberg, Sander L. Koole, and Tom Pyszczynski, 200–214. New York: Guilford Press, 2004.

Sellin, Eric. "The Algerian Novel of French Expression." *The International Fiction Review* 1, no. 1 (1974): 38–47.

———. "Algerian Poetry: Poetic Values, Mohammed Dib and Kateb Yacine." *Journal of the New African Literature and the Arts*, no. 9–10 (1971): 44–67.

Serrano, Richard. *Against the Postcolonial: 'Francophone' Writers at the Ends of French Empire*. Lanham, MD: Lexington Books, 2005.

Siblot, Paul, ed. *Vie culturelle à Alger*, 1900–1950. Montpellier: Praxiling, Université de Montpellier III, 1996.

Sternhell, Zeev. *Maurice Barrès et le nationalisme français*. Paris: Presses de la Fondation Nationale Scientifique, 1972.

Stora, Benjamin. *La France en guerre d'Algerie: novembre 1954-juillet 1962. Collection des publications de la BDI*. Nanterre: Édition Bibliothèque de documentation internationale contemporaine, 1992.

———. *La Gangrène et l'oubli: la mémoire de la guerre d'Algérie*. Paris: La Découverte, 1991.

———. *Histoire de l'Algérie coloniale (1830–1954)*. Paris: La Découverte, 1991.

———. *Histoire de la guerre d'Algérie, 1954–1962*. Paris: La Découverte, 1993.

Suleiman, Susan Rubin. *Authoritarian Fictions: The Ideological Novel as a Literary Genre*. New York: Columbia University Press, 1983.

"Tale of 1961 Massacre of Algerians in Paris." *New York Times*, 5 May 1998, 16.

Terdiman, Richard. *Discourse/Counter-Discourse: Theory and Practice of Symbolic Resistance in Nineteenth-Century France*. Ithaca, NY: Cornell University Press, 1985.

Thiesse, Anne-Marie. *Ils apprenaient la France: L'exaltation des régions dans le discours patriotique*. Paris: Éditions de la Maison des sciences de l'homme, 1997.

Toumi, Alek Baylee. *Maghreb divers: Langue française, langues parlées, littératures et représentations des Maghrébins, à partir d'Albert Memmi et de Kateb Yacine*. New York: Peter Lang, 2002.

Vale, Lawrence. *Architecture, Power, and National Identity*. New Haven: Yale University Press, 1992.

Von Henneberg, Krystyna. "Imperial Uncertainties: Architectural Syncretism and Improvisation in Fascist Colonial Libya." *Journal of Contemporary History* 31, no. 2 (April 1996): 373–95.

Woodhull, Winifred. "Rereading *Nedjma*: Feminist Scholarship and North African Women." *Sub-Stance*, no. 69 (1992): 49–63.

Wright, Gwendolyn. *The Politics of Design in French Colonial Urbanism*. Chicago: University of Chicago Press, 1991.

Index